ORIGINALISM, FEDERALISM, AND THE AMERICAN CONSTITUTIONAL ENTERPRISE

ORIGINALISM, FEDERALISM, AND THE AMERICAN CONSTITUTIONAL ENTERPRISE

A HISTORICAL INQUIRY

Edward A. Purcell Jr.

Yale University Press
New Haven & London

Set in Galliard and Copperplate types by The Composing Room of
Michigan, Inc.
Printed in the United States of America.

Library of Congress Cataloging-in-Publication Data

Purcell, Edward A.
    Originalism, federalism, and the American constitutional
enterprise : a historical inquiry / Edward A. Purcell, Jr.
        p.   cm.
    Includes bibliographical references and index.
    ISBN 978-0-300-12203-9 (cloth : alk. paper)   1. Federal
government—United States.   2. Constitutional history—United
States.   3. United States—Politics and government.   I. Title.
    JK325.P87 2007
    320.473′049—dc22

                                            2007012352

A catalogue record for this book is available from the British
Library.

The paper in this book meets the guidelines for permanence and
durability of the Committee on Production Guidelines for Book
Longevity of the Council on Library Resources.

10 9 8 7 6 5 4 3 2 1

CONTENTS

PART III. CONCLUSION

ACKNOWLEDGMENTS

This book could not have been completed without the assistance and support of a great many people and institutions. It is gratifying to acknowledge their contributions and to express my deep appreciation for their help.

I am indebted to my colleagues at New York Law School for both their personal friendship and intellectual inspiration, and I thank them, as well as the members of the faculty colloquium at the University of Pennsylvania Law School and the Legal History Colloquium at New York University Law School, for their helpful comments on early drafts. Special thanks also go to Richard B. Bernstein, Robert Blecker, Stephen J. Ellmann, Barry Friedman, Helen Hershkoff, Alfred S. Konefsky, William P. LaPiana, Jethro K. Lieberman, Richard A. Matasar, Frank Munger Jr., William E. Nelson, Terri Jennings Peretti, Sadiq Reza, David S. Schoenbrod, Richard K. Sherwin, Catherine Struve, and Harry H. Wellington. In addition, I express my deep appreciation for the repeated readings and unusually insightful suggestions that my late colleague, Denise C. Morgan, so generously provided. I also thank my patient and understanding secretaries, Robin Dingle and Sondy Ortiz, and acknowledge the invaluable help given by a series of superb research assistants: Lauren Borrone, Natasha Carroll-Ferrary, Catherine Hughes Corwin, Adam Hahn, John Michael Harkey, Lisa Ornest, Susanna Roif, Sharon Sorkin, Christina Trapani, Melissa Wagner, and Scott Woller.

Particular thanks are also due to the staff and administration of New

York Law School. The library and its staff made heroic efforts in tracking down obscure sources and providing me with all the research materials I requested, and in particular I thank Professor Joyce Saltalamachia, Joseph Marino, and Michael McCarthy for their persistent and reliable efforts on my behalf. The school's administration, especially Deans Richard A. Matasar, Jethro K. Lieberman, and Steven J. Ellmann, provided steady support and encouragement over the years.

Similarly, Yale University Press provided generous and thoughtful editorial supervision and secured readers whose astute comments aided substantially in improving the manuscript and sharpening its argument. In particular, I thank Clyde Spillenger and Robert Justin Lipkin for helpful reviews, and Michael O'Malley, Alex Larson, Ann-Marie Imbornoni, and Jessie Dolch for their encouragement and careful shepherding of the manuscript through its various stages. Slightly modified versions of Chapters 8 and 9 originally appeared in Volume 50 of the *New York Law School Law Review* as part of a symposium sponsored by the Federal Courts Section of the Association of American Law Schools, and I thank the *Review* for permission to reprint that material here.

Above all, my deepest thanks go to my wife, Professor Rachel Vorspan, and my children, Daniel and Jessica, for their continued love, support, and encouragement. They make everything possible and worthwhile.

INTRODUCTION

THE INQUIRY

1

AMERICAN CONSTITUTIONAL FEDERALISM AS A NORMATIVE PROBLEM

As the twenty-first century began, two major and related developments seemed to be reshaping American constitutional law. One was the frequent invocation of theories of "originalism," claims that the Constitution should be interpreted in light of the "original" meaning it held for those who drafted and ratified it.[1] The other was a "federalism revival," an intensifying effort to employ constitutional provisions to limit the powers of the national government and protect the sovereignty of the states. The two developments, moreover, seemed mutually supportive. The "original" relationship between nation and states—in contrast to the evolving series of relationships that developed over the subsequent centuries—had seen the national government exercising less extensive powers and the states holding sway over larger areas of American life. Thus, it was hardly surprising in the early twenty-first century that reinvigorated commitments to "originalism" and "federalism" might flourish in tandem.

Further, the growing popularity of originalism and federalism crossed political and ideological lines. Libertarians, economic "conservatives," and some other elements of the post-Reagan Republican coalition aggressively advanced both.[2] Justice Antonin Scalia, for example, repeatedly stressed the importance of preserving state sovereign immunity[3] and proclaimed that all constitutional decisions should be based on "the original meaning of the text."[4] At the same time, many liberals, progressives, and moderates began climbing aboard the double-teamed bandwagon. In 1999 President Bill Clinton issued an executive order that identified nine

"Fundamental Federalism Principles" and directed federal officials to follow them in carefully scrutinizing actions that might cause "substantial direct effects on the States." He did so, the president announced, "to guarantee the division of governmental responsibilities between the national government and the States that was intended by the Framers of the Constitution."[5]

In spite of such frequent invocations, both originalism and federalism raised the same fundamental and deeply troublesome question of constitutional law. To what extent was either capable of providing clear and authoritative constitutional norms? Could either, in truth, provide specific and determinative directions in resolving contested constitutional questions?

In helping to revive both originalism and federalism, the Rehnquist Court illustrated the extent to which the two ostensible norms provided uncertain and ambiguous directions. In the years after 1992 five of its justices began frequently to invoke "the essential principles of federalism" and the "original understanding of the Constitution" held by the "founding generation."[6] When they did so, the Court immediately split, fragmenting badly in a train of important and potentially far-reaching decisions. Repeatedly, the other four justices dissented, often in sweeping and sometimes defiant terms.[7] Indeed, after protesting a series of decisions that limited the power of Congress and expanded the sovereign immunity of the states, the four boldly announced their "continuing dissent" from the "aggressive" new federalism jurisprudence that made the Court "the champion of States' rights."[8] The dissenters, however, did not invariably agree among themselves and on occasion broke ranks on federalism issues.[9] Far more striking and revealing, however, was the fact that the five justices in the "originalist" and "pro-federalism" majority also divided among themselves and did so with increasing frequency.[10] In *Idaho v. Coeur d'Alene Tribe of Idaho*, for example, two of the five explained and applied their view of the "basic principles of federalism,"[11] while the other three wrote separately to reject the analysis of the first two as "flawed in several respects."[12] Similarly, dealing with the scope of national power in another case, one of five chided the other four for not adopting "a standard more consistent with the original understanding."[13] Indeed, in one recent decision four of the Rehnquist Court's five "pro-federalism" justices voted to assert national authority and thereby limit state power, while the fifth joined the four so-called nationalist justices in limiting national authority and expanding state power.[14]

Such swings, divisions, and inconsistencies were hardly unprecedented. Over the decades, Americans had disagreed continuously and often passionately about the nature of their federal system. Their disagreements had begun at the Constitution's birth, moreover, and they were almost invariably rooted in conflicting visions of its "original" meaning.

It was true that when the Constitution was ratified, some of its provisions carried relatively clear and accepted meanings. There was no dispute that the new charter established a central government with three distinct branches and ordained that each would have certain characteristics and powers, nor was there any dispute that it also limited those national branches in various ways. Equally, there was no dispute that the Constitution confirmed the existence of the states and made them constituent elements of the new central government, and there was no dispute that it also limited the powers of those states and made federal law "supreme." The widespread acceptance of that basic institutional structure—supported by a broad cultural consensus among the nation's elite, long experience with the practice of representative government among the people, and the immense prestige of the man elected to serve as the nation's first president— enabled the new central government to organize itself and begin operations. That bare initial achievement, James Madison believed, was by itself "a miracle."[15]

At the same time, however, disagreements about the powers of those levels and branches and about their proper working relationships erupted immediately, and the earliest and most explosive raged over the disputed line between state and national authority. Over the course of the following centuries those controversies seldom flagged. Given that history of congenital disputation, the current revival of originalism and federalism provokes two paramount and related questions.[16] One goes to the Constitution itself: What, in fact, was the "original" nature of the federal structure it established? The other goes to the persisting disagreement about the way that federal structure was to function: Why did Americans fight over its proper operation so immediately, so continuously, so broadly, and so fiercely?

This inquiry seeks, and proposes, answers to those two questions. On the first, it concludes that the "original" federal structure was marked by four inherent characteristics. It was doubly blurred, fractionated, instrumental, and contingent. The claim is not that those four characteristics were parts of any original "meaning" or "understanding" but, rather, that they were built-in characteristics of the constitutional structure and that they existed independent of any intentions or understandings of the founders. On the second question, the inquiry concludes that those four characteristics made the original federal structure intrinsically elastic, dynamic, and underdetermined. Those qualities made constitutional disagreements about federalism inevitable, and they made most of those disagreements—insofar as Americans sought to settle them by reference to some "original" constitutional meaning or understanding—inherently unresolvable. Hence, immediate, continuous, broad, and fierce disputation.

The inquiry argues, then, that any claim that the "original" nature of American federalism can serve as a specifically directive norm—such as Chief Justice William Rehnquist's invocation of "the Framers' carefully crafted balance of power between the States and the National Government"[17]—is simply mistaken. No such "true" or "correct" balance ever existed.[18] Equally important, the inquiry also argues that, even had there been some true "original" balance, the constitutional structure the founders established was inherently incapable of maintaining it. To understand American federalism, in other words, one must consider far more than constitutional text, structural relationships, and "originalist" sources; one must also understand federalism's inherent elasticity and dynamism.

Stated so briefly, those conclusions require three points of immediate clarification. First, it is essential to distinguish between the federal "structure" and the working processes, or evolving "systems," of American federalism. The Constitution's federal structure—the existence of diverse levels and branches of government with distinctive institutional characteristics and powers—was both evident and uncontested. The way that structure was to function in practice—how the levels and branches would operate, how far their powers would reach, and how they would interact with one another—was not. The doubly blurred, fractionated, instrumental, and contingent nature of the constitutional structure, then, had its paramount effect not on the federal structure itself but on the structure's operations, on the working processes of what came to be called the federal system. Second, the inquiry's conclusions are not based on any theory or assumption about the general "indeterminacy" of law or language. To the contrary, the inquiry assumes that words, rules, concepts, and principles may convey meanings that are fairly determinable either generally or in specific contexts. Its conclusions, then, are based not on general theories of language or meaning but on empirical evidence from the nation's history. Third, those conclusions do not purport to apply necessarily to other areas of constitutional law. The inquiry's focus is narrow and specific. It concentrates on only one aspect of the U.S. Constitution—its federal structure and its resulting federal system of government—and attempts to answer only questions about that particular constitutional issue.

Specifically, then, the inquiry suggests that the Constitution neither gave the federal structure any single proper shape as an operating system of government nor mandated any particular and timeless balance among its components. It suggests, rather, that the Constitution established a structure that accepted certain types of change as natural and desirable. It concludes, then, that there was no "original" intention, understanding, or meaning that prescribed either a single and true federal system or a single and true set of relationships among the structure's constituent parts; further, it concludes that, even had such a "true" system existed in some "original" intent or understanding, the governmental structure the founders established could not have preserved it unchanged over time.

Further, the inquiry suggests that the workings of the federal structure cannot be understood without examining the separation of powers at the national level. Although federalism and separation of powers were different concepts embodied in different institutional arrangements and subject to different sets of incentives and limitations, they were nonetheless inextricably intertwined in their operations.[19] Both constitutional law and national politics were shaped by their continuous, shifting, and varied interactions. The idea of American federalism as a simple binary division between "the nation" and "the states," then, is an artificial abstraction unrelated to the actual history and operations of the nation's constitutional system.

The separation of powers vastly multiplied the complexities and uncertainties of American constitutional federalism for two readily apparent reasons. First, the existence of three separate national branches meant that the central government would sometimes be riven by internal conflicts and consequently unable to articulate and enforce consistent and unified "national" policies. The attitude of the three national branches toward the states and the federal structure would vary and often conflict, sometimes sharply and profoundly. Second, the constitutional provisions specifying the powers of the national branches were, like the provisions dividing state and national powers, imprecise and incomplete. The claim that the Constitution established an "assigned balance of responsibility and power among the three [national] branches,"[20] in other words, is as mistaken as the claim that the Constitution established a "carefully crafted balance" between states and nation. Thus, the inquiry argues, institutional divisions and constitutional ambiguities in the separation of national powers radically compounded the divisions and ambiguities that were inherent in the relationship between nation and states.

The inquiry argues that the Constitution did create a governmental structure with an essential and unalterable core, but it suggests that the core lay not in any "assigned" or "carefully crafted" balance but rather in a dynamic combination of three interrelated elements that allow a range of acceptable permutations. The first element was the principle of divided but interconnected and potentially "checking" powers. The second was the institutional specification of that principle along two crosscutting and internally divided dimensions, multiple individual units on the state level and separated powers on the national level. The third was the moral and political ideal that the principle of divided powers and its institutional embodiment were designed to serve, that of a free, just, and self-governing society.[21]

Further, the inquiry suggests that ideas and attitudes about the federal structure and its "original" form have invariably been shaped not simply by the Constitution and accepted "originalist" sources but also by the personal views of the individuals who held those ideas and attitudes. It does not deny that many individuals believed passionately in their various conceptions of the federal structure or that many also believed sincerely that their conceptions were mandated by the Constitution itself. The inquiry argues only that their conceptions could not, in fact, have come solely from those authoritative sources. The inquiry suggests, rather, that those who held such beliefs were either unable or unwilling to recognize the ways in which their personal values, interests, and assumptions shaped the particular meanings they attributed to the federal structure.[22] The inquiry counsels, consequently, that all specific prescriptions allegedly derived from either the federal structure or "originalist" ideas about that structure must be evaluated not just in terms of formal constitutional arguments but also in light of the particular values and interests of those who advance them and, most important, in light of the practical implications and social consequences that the prescriptions would likely entail if accepted.

Many scholars, of course, have recognized that personal views shape interpretations of the Constitution.[23] The inquiry extends that insight in two ways. First, it suggests that, with respect to American constitutional federalism, such subjectivism is inherent and unavoidable. The Constitution does not establish any single and true balance in the federal structure, and the structure itself is, in any event, too elastic, dynamic, and underdetermined to sustain any such unchanging balance. Thus, specific normative interpretations of federalism must necessarily be rooted in the personal values and interests of their advocates. Second, and consequently, the inquiry suggests that sound constitutional reasoning on federalism issues must move beyond invocations of general "principles" and "original" meanings and ground itself on specific, pragmatic, and empirically based analyses of the operations of the federal structure and the likely practical consequences involved in accepting any particular interpretation of its nature and limits. Focusing on such careful pragmatic analyses, it argues, would help cabin the inherent, if often ignored or denied, subjectivism involved in deciding federalism issues. It would force interpreters to recognize and account more fully for the interests, purposes, assumptions, and values that shape their views, and it would help channel decision making along lines more likely to achieve the substantive goals of the nation's constitutional enterprise.[24]

Finally, the inquiry suggests that the federal structure is best understood not as a freestanding institutional construct, or as a simple embodiment of an "original" architectural blueprint, but as an integral part of the collective constitutional enterprise of the American people, the concerted intergenerational effort to realize and sustain the ideal of a free, just, and self-governing society. The continuing legitimacy of the nation's constitutional government, after all, derives not from any original social contract capable of binding later generations and providing them with specific directions. Rather, it derives from other, and far more compelling, sources: the continuing popular judgment that the Constitution embodies both political and moral wisdom and the inspiring but sobering fact that we—the current people of the United States—are the inheritors and beneficiaries of the work of successive generations that created, defended, and interpreted the Constitution in their collective efforts to secure the "Blessings of Liberty" for themselves and their posterity, that is, for us and for our own posterity.[25]

In reaching and explaining its conclusions, the inquiry proceeds in three parts. The first, comprising Chapters 2 through 5, examines the four intrinsic characteristics of the "original" federal structure. The second, comprising Chapters 6 through 9, explores some of the consequential dynamics that resulted from those original characteristics. Finally, the third part, Chapter 10, reflects on the more general significance of the inquiry's analysis and conclusions.

In Part I, Chapter 2 considers the structure's intrinsically doubly blurred nature, the fact that the Constitution divided power between national and state governments in a manner that was both ambivalent and ambiguous. The division was ambivalent because the Constitution gave the two levels of government overlapping powers and responsibilities in conducting republican government and protecting republican values. It thereby ensured that they would exist in tension and that, on disputed issues, both could claim to stand for the nation's highest moral and political principles. The division was ambiguous because the Constitution failed to identify the boundaries between the two levels with clarity and completeness, thereby ensuring that each would frequently have grounds to dispute the other's authority. From the beginning, then, the two levels were placed in tension with neither their realms nor their relationships adequately prescribed.

Chapter 3 explores the structure's fractionated nature. The Constitution did not create a simple binary structure but rather one that was many-sided and multi-linked. It divided the national side into three parts, and for good measure bifurcated one of those three parts into two differently constituted and differently empowered halves. Similarly, the Constitution embraced an even more fragmented division on the state side, encompassing many separate entities, providing for their steady multiplication over time, and allowing each to subdivide into as many local governing units as it chose. Thus, the Constitution created a structure that loosely and flexibly linked three separate and quite different national branches—one of which was itself divided internally—with an expanding multitude of diverse and often conflicting state and local government units. It was a complexly fractionated structure that proved inherently dynamic, generating over time a virtually infinite number of varied and shifting geographical and institutional alliances, all of which crosscut the Constitution's formal binary divide between "national" and "state" governments. That fractionated structure gave birth to a kaleidoscopic interstate politics that further blurred the boundaries of authority in the federal structure by pressing new and shifting meanings onto its doubly blurred constitutional lines and by preventing either "the states" or "the nation" from acting consistently and cohesively as unified entities to maintain any timeless division between their powers.

Chapter 4 examines the intrinsically instrumentalist nature of the federal structure. The founders assumed that ambition and self-interest drove "factions" to exploit government and that mere "parchment" lines would be insufficient to block factional aggrandizements. Only purposive human actions could check other purposive human actions. Consequently, they designed the federal structure as an instrument to control factions by dividing power among diverse levels and branches capable of "checking" one another's abuses and aggrandizements. Providing the framework, components, and incentives for such purposive and responsive actions, then, the federal structure was inherently an instrument of human goals and ambitions. Its doubly blurred lines, however, did not adequately specify the conditions under which one level or branch was properly to "check" another, and it consequently allowed factions ample leeway in justifying their efforts to exploit the power of whichever governmental components they happened to influence or control. "Checking," then, quickly proved to be but one of many possible forms of response open to the structure's components. Others included acquiescing, deflecting, adapting, facilitating, exploiting, and extending. That wide range of possible responses compounded the structure's inherent elasticity and dynamism; and, as those who controlled its various components acted and responded in diverse ways, they created shifting sets of institutional interrelationships that altered the powers of the various levels and branches and, in the process, reshaped the operations of the federal structure.

Chapter 5 considers the structure's contingent nature, the fact that its lines of division were dependent on constitutional provisions that incorporated numerous principles of change. The chapter identifies the ways in which the Constitution mandated some changes, authorized others, and invited yet more. Thus, as the nation and its surrounding world environment evolved, some changes were compelled by constitutional mandates, others flowed from constitutionally authorized choices, and still others resulted from the new significance that changes in the world environment gave to many constitutional provisions. As those varied changes occurred, new matrices of pressures, conditions, and assumptions remolded the federal structure. Whether the Constitution's provisions mandated, authorized, or merely invited change, they combined to make the federal structure inherently malleable and adaptive.

Those four characteristics, the section concludes, explain the dynamic and underdetermined nature of American federalism. They created a governing structure that was marked by far too many ambiguities and elasticities to define any single and "correct" balance between states and nation. It was a structure composed of far too many dynamic and interconnecting parts, all of which were themselves both mutable and manipulable, to sustain any particular and timeless balance.

Part II considers some of the specific consequences that those four characteristics brought to the federal structure and the nation's constitutional enterprise. Chapter 6 examines the volatile and pragmatic interstate politics that grew out of the structure's fractionated nature. Although political organizations and interests worked within the Constitution's binary division, they also exploited it ruthlessly and methodically. As ever-expanding numbers and varieties of interests clashed in their efforts to exploit the different levels and branches of government, they generated ever-multiplying and ever-shifting sets of interstate alliances and counteralliances that continuously stretched and reshaped the doubly blurred lines between "national" and "state" authority. Their practices nourished ideas, interests, coalitions, expectations, and interconnections that overflowed the Constitution's binary categorization and forged a kaleidoscopic interstate politics whose pressures repeatedly remolded the workings of the federal structure and shifted its lines of operative authority.

Chapter 7 focuses on the federal structure's institutional components themselves, especially its three national branches. The chapter examines the ways in which the structure's intrinsic characteristics enabled and encouraged those institutions to reshape themselves as they adapted to changes in the world around them, including changes that were occurring in the other levels and branches of government. Exercising broad and often undefined powers, and enjoying substantial discretion over their own internal structure and operations, the national branches expanded their distinctive powers in divergent and sometimes conflicting ways, while each evolved into a distinctive and complex set of interlocking—and quite imperfectly integrated—bureaucracies. Over the years they repeatedly reshaped their actions and readjusted their relationships, and their efforts—sometimes separately and sometimes in combination—altered the operations of the individual branches and stretched the boundaries of their powers. Indeed, in the early twenty-first century not one of the federal branches remained the same in size, operation, organization, significance, or scope of authority as it had been in the nineteenth century or even much of the twentieth century, let alone as it had been "originally" in 1789.

Chapter 8 examines one of the Constitution's paramount ambiguities, its failure to specify a mechanism for enforcing divisions between national and state power. It explores the varied theories that the founding generation launched, the intensifying disputes that only a Civil War could begin to resolve, and the subsequent debates that increasingly focused on whether the U.S. Supreme Court could and should enforce the constitutional division between state and national power. Questions about the Court's proper role, like many other questions about the federal structure, went unresolved by the founders. The resulting uncertainties led to an unending train of disputes that could be settled by neither the language of the Constitution nor the "original" views of the founders but only by the politics, ideologies, and practicalities of their respective times.

Chapter 9 moves to a broader level and considers some of the ways in which general ideas about the federal structure and the Constitution changed over the centuries. It focuses, in particular, on changes in ideas about the "values" and "nature" of federalism itself, and it suggests that constitutional commentators have consistently been unable to transcend the uncertainties and dynamics that were rooted in the federal structure's four inherent characteristics. The chapter concludes that normative theories founded on interpretations of the "values" and "nature" of federalism reflected rather than resolved those uncertainties and dynamics and that, as those underlying ideas and assumptions evolved, both the understanding and operation of the federal structure evolved as well.

Finally, Part III, Chapter 10, attempts to synthesize the lessons to be drawn from a recognition of the elastic, dynamic, and underdetermined nature of the federal structure. It offers no specific normative theory of federalism and suggests that the Constitution neither mandates nor requires any such specific theory. It closes not in resignation or despair, however, but in hope and commitment. If the inquiry's conclusions are sound, the chapter suggests, it does not mean that the nation's constitutional enterprise lacks either understandable norms or, in at least some of its provisions, relatively clear and guiding rules and principles. It means only that the Constitution itself, with or without the aid of "originalist" sources, could not and did not provide specifically directive norms capable of resolving the contested issues of federalism that divided Americans after 1787. It also means that they cannot do so in the future. That ever-present and ineluctable burden, the inquiry concludes, rests on each succeeding generation of Americans, the very posterity on whose behalf the founders—and, of course, the succeeding generations who broadened the concept of national citizenship to include those originally excluded—sought to act.

PART

I

STRUCTURAL INTRINSICS

2

FEDERALISM AS DOUBLY BLURRED

The federal structure was marked by imprecise and uncertain lines of authority for two quite different reasons. First, the Constitution gave the structure's two distinct levels of government overlapping powers and charged each with safeguarding the same vague and contested values against the other's depredations. Second, the provisions establishing the authority and responsibility of the two levels were incomplete and imprecise, and they failed to identify any clear and comprehensive line between them. American federalism, in other words, was doubly blurred because it was both ambivalent and ambiguous.

Ambivalence

The Constitution created a structure that placed two counter-poised levels of government in inherent tension by giving them overlapping powers, jurisdictions, and responsibilities. It provided that the two levels could legislate over the same people in the same territory and, to a large extent, over the same subjects. "The government of the Union, like that of each State, must be able to address itself immediately to the hopes and fears of individuals," Alexander Hamilton wrote, and it must "possess all the means, and have a right to resort to all the methods, of executing the powers with which it is intrusted, that are possessed and exercised by the governments of the particular States."[1] Thus, in contrast to the Articles of Confederation, the Constitution was designed to "extend the authority of the Union to the persons of the citizens."[2] Over large areas of American life, the central and state governments were to exercise "concurrent" jurisdiction.[3] The states would retain "all the rights of sovereignty" except those "*exclusively* delegated to the United States," Hamilton explained. Consequently, the two levels would exercise overlapping authority in a wide range of areas, even "where the exercise of a concurrent jurisdiction might be productive of occasional interferences in the *policy* of any branch of administration."[4]

Further entwining the two levels, and immeasurably heightening the tension between them, were the common—but imprecise and contested—values that both were intended to protect. The Constitution designed each level to check the other in protecting the nation's fundamental values—liberty, property, and republican government.[5] The two levels would "be the means of keeping each other in their proper places," Madison declared, and their "mutual relations" would thereby preserve "the genius of republican liberty."[6] The "important idea" animating "both the general government, as well as the particular state governments," Gilbert Livingston explained to the New York ratifying convention, was "that they conjointly are the guardians of the rights of the whole American family."[7] The nature and content of those rights, however, were subjects of intense and wide-ranging debate. In spite of their shared commitments to certain generalities, the founders divided sharply when they considered "what liberty was, who deserved it, how much of it was desirable, how it was to be obtained, how it was secured." In law, for example, neither "liberty" nor "property" was a simple concept, for "each was a complex and subtle combination of many rights, powers, and duties, distributed among individuals, society, and the state."[8] Thus, by dividing responsibility for protecting values that were themselves complex, imprecise, and disputed, the Constitution's federal structure ensured that fundamental controversies would continually arise and that, when they did, both national and state governments would be able to see themselves as the true protectors of the people and their most fundamental rights. When the Civil War finally came, both the Union and Confederate sides proclaimed passionately that they were fighting for "liberty."

The founders, moreover, infused yet more uncertainty into the federal structure with their new theory of "popular sovereignty."[9] One of the principal flaws of the Articles of Confederation, Hamilton argued, was that it had "no better foundation than the consent of the several [state] legislatures," a fact that spawned the idea that those legislatures could withdraw their state's commitment to the central government whenever they chose. The "foundations of our national government," he continued, should rest on something "deeper" than the mere "delegated authority" of state legislatures. That deeper foundation should be "the solid basis of THE CONSENT OF THE PEOPLE," the "pure, original fountain of all legitimate authority."[10] Madison sounded the same principle. The "ultimate authority" in a republican government "resides in the people alone," he declared, for "the people are the only legitimate fountain of power."[11]

Two elements of that novel theory of popular sovereignty combined to place a profound uncertainty at the heart of the federal structure. First, the theory removed sovereignty from all the levels and branches of government. "The Federal and State governments," Madison explained, "are in fact but different agents and trustees of the people, constituted with different powers, and designed for different purposes."[12] Thus, "a constitution established by the people" was "unalterable by the government."[13] Because "sovereignty resides in the people,"[14] James Wilson agreed, both state and national governments were merely agents and trustees. Neither held any "inherent" sovereignty that raised it above the other. "When the principle is once settled that *the people* are the source of authority," Wilson reasoned, "the consequence is, that they may take from the subordinate governments powers with which they have hitherto trusted them, and place those powers in the general government."[15] Thus, the founders' theory of popular sovereignty meant that the Constitution did not compromise the "sovereignty" of the states, for the states themselves were not inherently "sovereign."[16] Second, the theory of popular sovereignty bound "the people," once they had ratified the Constitution, to honor its procedures and to forego the right to govern directly. The new fundamental law authorized them to act only through their representatives or through the formal procedures of a burdensome amendment process.[17] Thus, by denying sovereignty to any institution of government and by further denying "the people" the right to govern directly, the founders diffused the concept of "sovereignty" and, as a practical matter, made it virtually impossible to locate.[18]

The process the founders established for ratifying the Constitution—requiring an up-or-down vote by specially elected conventions in each state—compounded the uncertainty about the nature and locus of sovereignty.[19] Beyond considerations of expedience, there was no clear reason why the "sovereign people" could or should be prohibited from offering amendments to the proposed new charter. The convention nonetheless decided that "the people," whose consent was necessary to give the Constitution its authority and legitimacy, should not be allowed to amend it. Further, the process of ratifying by states created a fundamental question: what exactly was the role of the states, as states, in the ratification process? Were they a convenience or a necessity? And, if a "necessity," why?[20] The founders' answers left the matter clouded. "Each State, in ratifying the Constitution, is considered as a sovereign body, independent of all others," Madison wrote, but their power to ratify was "derived from the supreme authority in each State,—the authority of the people themselves."[21] With respect to ratification, then, the states were on the one hand "sovereign" but on the other hand only "considered" so for the purpose of exercising a delegated power. Ratification, Madison summarized aptly, "will not be a *national,* but a *federal* act."[22] Indeed, it surely was a "federal" act, but its "federal" character meant only that it would be a "mixed" act, incapable of definition as either exclusively "national" or exclusively "state." Thus, the ratification process was, like the Constitution itself, "a composition of both."[23] What the term "federal" meant more generally or more precisely remained unanswered.

The protean ambivalence of the founders' work would spur unending disputes. Was the "United States of America" the creation of "We the People" or the "sovereign states"? Was the Constitution an indissoluble charter or a voidable compact? Did the nation suffer a "Civil War" or a "War between the States"? Was the very name, the "United States of America," singular or plural? While over the centuries untold numbers of individuals offered purportedly definitive answers to those questions, no such answers existed in the Constitution or in the collective intention or understanding of the founders. To the contrary, the Constitution created something novel and pragmatic, and at the time of its ratification the founders shared no common understanding of its "true" nature nor any clear vision of how it would operate or where its numerous and imprecise lines of authority would run.

It was no surprise, then, that the term "federal" was consistently used in inconsistent and confusing ways.[24] Even in the 1770s "the concept of federalism had not yet been developed as a constitutional doctrine or, at best, was only vaguely understood in America," John Phillip Reid explained. Moreover, when ideas of "federalism" did begin to surface, they were not understood in terms of either geographical lines or "concurrent" jurisdictions. Early discussions, Reid concluded, "illustrate the imprecision of eighteenth-century constitutional law."[25] As late as 1786 Madison used the term "federal" to refer to the government that existed under the Articles of Confederation,[26] while Hamilton conversely identified "federal measures" with the new Constitution.[27] Surely, the latter was right when he told the Constitutional Convention that the word covered a wide variety of governmental forms and that "[g]reat latitude therefore must be given to the signification of the term."[28]

During the ratification process, the Constitution's supporters quickly appropriated the term in an effort to portray their relatively centralizing views as relatively noncentralizing, while their opponents proclaimed themselves true "federalists" but were nonetheless stuck with the negative label of "Anti-Federalists."[29] During the Philadelphia Convention Rufus King had scornfully dismissed the Articles of Confederation as establishing "a mere federal government of states," but during the ratification battle he quickly embraced the name of "Federalist" for himself and the Constitution's other supporters.[30] On the opposing side, an Anti-Federalist pamphleteer sought to recapture the label by adopting the name "Federal Farmer" and describing the "Federalists" as "pretended federalists" and their adversaries as "honest federalists." Revealingly, however, the "Federal Farmer" described the differences between the two sides by using the term "federal" in conflicting ways.[31] From the Constitution's very birth, then, the term and its cognates were used both inconsistently and tactically, serving as pliable labels that all parties sought to turn to advantage.

While usage continued to evolve, over the course of more than two centuries the term remained ambiguous, changing, and contested.[32] By the 1820s, for example, the collapse of the Federalist Party had made the labels

"Federalist" and "Federalism" terms of derision used to tar opponents of the triumphant Republican-Democratic Party.[33] Perhaps most striking, by the twentieth century the term "federal" was commonly used to convey two radically different meanings. On one hand, it referred to the nation's decentralized governmental structure; on the other, it referred to the centralized national government itself. From the nation's beginning the term "federal" stood equivocally as the Janus of American constitutional law.

Replying to states' rights attacks on his decision in *McCulloch v. Maryland*, Chief Justice John Marshall identified the inherently ambivalent nature of the federal structure. In examining national powers, he explained, "it is not allowable to assume as a postulate that the interests of the people are necessarily on the side of the state which contests that power, or that the cause of liberty must be promoted by deciding the question against the government of the union."[34] His reasoning was rooted in his recognition of the ambivalent nature of the federal structure. "In fact, the government of the union, as well as those of the states, is created by the people," and they "are as much interested, their liberty is as deeply concerned, in preventing encroachments on that [central] government, in arresting the hands which would tear from it the powers they have conferred upon it, as in restraining it within its constitutional limits."[35]

Thus, "federalism" did not mean simply that the rights and powers of the states must be recognized and enforced, for it meant equally that the rights and powers of the national government must also be recognized and enforced. Indeed, if anything was clear from the history of the founding, it was that the Constitution was intended to unify the nation and create an "energetic" central government that would be powerful enough to overcome the weakness and disruption caused by thirteen varied, unstable, and sometimes conflicting states.[36] "The mutability of the laws of the States is found to be a serious evil," Madison wrote Thomas Jefferson in 1787. "The injustice of them has been so frequent and so flagrant as to alarm the most stedfast [*sic*] friends of Republicanism."[37] Thus, he feared, the Constitution's beneficent operation was "much more likely to be disturbed" by "the vicissitudes and uncertainties which characterize the State administrations"[38] than by the powers conferred on the new national government.[39] Hamilton concurred. "[T]he danger which most threatens our political welfare," he insisted, "is that the State governments will finally sap the foundations of the Union."[40] Marshall, who helped lead the ratification fight in the Virginia convention, put the point bluntly. "I partook largely of the suffering and the feelings of the [Revolutionary] army," he explained, and his subsequent "entrance into the state legislature opened to my view the causes which had been chiefly instrumental in augmenting those sufferings." The pettiness and jealousies that marked "the general tendency of state politics" meant "that no safe and permanent remedy could be found but in a more efficient and better organized general government."[41] The Federalists "were much more troubled over the irresponsibility and small-mindedness of the state legislatures in the years immediately following the Revolution than they were over the deficiencies of the Articles of Confederation," Stanley Elkins and Eric McKitrick concluded. "What most offended them were such short-sighted actions as paper money laws, debtor relief laws, local tariffs, tax postponements, and a tendency to beat down court reforms and similar undertakings intended for the larger public benefit."[42] "Federalism," then, was not the founders' goal, but the potentially lethal problem they sought to overcome.[43]

Thus, to say that an issue raised "federalism concerns," as judges and scholars often did, could not mean that an issue required special sensitivity to the states as opposed to the central government.[44] Such "concerns" pointed not in one but in two different directions, and together they could do little more than highlight one problematic aspect of some constitutional questions.[45] Indeed, citing "federalism concerns" to tilt a constitutional question against national authority was like invoking "metal concerns" to justify calling a coin toss "tails."

Along the same lines, the so-called values of federalism that judges and commentators often invoked to limit national power were, like the term "federalism" itself, equally ambivalent. The reason was obvious. The true values of American federalism included not only the values associated with decentralization but, equally, the values associated with centralization: unity, harmony, consistency, and coordination. In theory, and sometimes in practice, decentralization fostered economic efficiency, underwrote diversity, encouraged citizen participation, allowed narrow solutions for local problems, and safeguarded liberty by checking tyrannical national majorities.[46] Also in theory, and sometimes in practice, centralization fostered economic efficiency, created desirable uniform standards, underwrote national prosperity and security, allowed comprehensive solutions to interstate and international problems, and safeguarded liberty by checking tyrannical local majorities. Both sets of values and goals, not just one, constituted the true values of American federalism.

Thus, those "values" could not identify proper lines and limits for a working federal system in general or in the abstract. Only detailed analysis of individual issues in specific contexts could establish how constitutional federalism might best be construed to achieve the full advantages of both centralization and decentralization. Before ascending the high bench, then-professor Antonin Scalia highlighted "this duality of meaning in the word 'federalism.'" The label, he concluded, was "a stick that can be used to beat either dog."[47]

Ambiguity

Federalism was also blurred for a second reason, because the relevant constitutional provisions were imprecise and incomplete. In spite of repeated references to "the principles of federalism," no one was able to compile an authoritative list or, more to the point, obtain official agreement on their specification.[48] One political scientist identified thirty-four types of federalism, while another bested him by ten, counting forty-four.[49] Over the years the ambiguous nature of American federalism inspired a variety of descriptive labels—including "coercive," "competitive," "cooperative," "co-optive," "creative," "dual," "false," "fiscal," "franchise," "functional," "judicial," "lip-service," "market-preserving," "neurotic," and "permissive" as well as colorful metaphors invoking "fences" (picket and bamboo) and "cakes" (layer, marble, birthday, and fruit)—offered to explain its nature. Similarly, it also inspired a seemingly unending stream of variously hyped, if unimaginatively titled, "new" federalisms. Aaron Wildavsky, a passionate defender of decentralization, reported a study that counted 267 separate characterizations of the term, a result that led him to conclude unhappily that "federalism is so far out of control that we do not know what to call it."[50]

The root of the problem lay in the fact that the founders had to be both practical and imaginative. The former compelled them to compromise, the latter to innovate. Gouverneur Morris told the convention's delegates in disgust that their behavior made him "suppose that we were assembled to truck and bargain for our particular states,"[51] while Hamilton dismissed the position of the small states on representation as a simple "contest for power, not for liberty."[52] Acknowledging that the "convention had been much divided in opinion," Caleb Strong of Massachusetts sounded the premise that drove its work. "If no accommodation takes place," he told the delegates, "the Union itself must soon be dissolved."[53] In dealing with the "intricate and perplexed" question of national power, John Jay explained during the ratification debates, the drafters were compelled to "reconcile the different views and interests of the different states, and the clashing opinions of their members." The final document was "the result of accommodation" and "mutual concessions."[54] Indeed, the convention's letter transmitting the Constitution to the Confederation Congress made that exact point: "[T]he Constitution, which we now present, is the result of a spirit of amity, and of that mutual deference and concession which the peculiarity of our political situation rendered indispensable."[55]

Benjamin Franklin described the convention's work in more colorful terms. "The players of our game are so many, their ideas so different, their prejudices so strong and various, and their particular interests independent of the general, seeming so opposite," he explained, that the delegates were compelled to resort to compromise and avoidance. "[N]ot a move can be made that is not contested; the numerous objections confound the understanding; [and] the wisest must agree to some unreasonable things, that reasonable ones of more consequence may be obtained." The Constitution's final draft was as much the result of accident and circumstance as of reason and deliberation. Thus, "chance has its share in many of the determinations," he concluded, "so that the play is more like *tric-trac* with a box of dice."[56]

Madison agreed. The Constitution's final form "shows that the convention must have been compelled to sacrifice theoretical propriety to the force of extraneous considerations." Many disagreements among the delegates "could be terminated only by compromise."[57] It was "not pretended that every insertion or omission in the Constitution is the effect of systematic attention," he admitted in 1791. "This is not the character of any human work, particularly the work of a body of men."[58] Indeed, as Lance Banning has shown, Madison's own thinking about the proper structure of the Union and the nature of its new Constitution evolved throughout the 1780s, shifted during the convention itself, changed again as he wrote his *Federalist* essays, and continued to evolve thereafter.[59]

Confirming the founders' own sense of their experience, a comprehensive study of voting patterns at the convention showed that over its four-month course the delegates formed themselves into at least five different majority coalitions as they struggled to resolve the various issues they faced. Debate over "general principles" identified certain broad themes, the study concluded, but practical considerations usually carried the day. The "diverse political, economic, and geographic interests" of the delegates for the most part "determine[d] the modifications, adjustments, and allowances that principled consistency must make to political expedience."[60] That tough and complicated bargaining stamped the Constitution with the hallmarks of compromise: ambiguity, incompletion, and avoidance.

The founders, moreover, recognized and even gloried in the innovative nature of the Constitution they created. "The novelty of the undertaking immediately strikes us," Madison declared in the *Federalist*.[61] In the Virginia ratifying convention he was more sweeping. The Constitution established a government "in a manner unprecedented; we cannot find one express example in the experience of the world," he proclaimed. "It stands by itself."[62] More aggressively, Hamilton transformed the Constitution's novelty into a point of national pride. The American people "have not suffered a blind veneration for antiquity," he boasted, but used their "own good sense" and "the lessons of their own experience" to develop "numerous innovations" in government. Pursuing their "new and more noble course," they made "a revolution which has no parallel in the annals of human society" and created "governments which have no model on the face of the globe."[63]

The founders' principal compromise and novelty lay in establishing one "extended" national government while preserving thirteen "independent" states, but as they pursued that goal they quickly came to realize the impossibility of dividing power between nation and states in a clear and definitive manner. That impossibility became apparent when the Philadelphia Convention considered giving Congress a veto over state laws. Almost immediately the delegates recognized that they could identify no line adequate to the task. John Dickinson told the convention that he "deemed it impossible to draw a line between cases proper & improper" for exercising such a national veto, while James Wilson declared that the effort to identify such a boundary was "impracticable."[64] "[W]hen we come near the line" between national and state power, he confessed, "it cannot be found."[65] Madison supported the proposal because he considered it simply "impossible" to define such a "line of jurisprudence" as a general or abstract matter.[66] Hence, he reasoned, it was essential to provide for an institution that could authoritatively make such determinations as specific issues arose in specific contexts. Indeed, Madison argued, such a veto "must extend to all cases" where Congress chose to act because any parchment line "[would] only be a fresh source of contention between the two authorities."[67] George Mason ultimately refused to sign the Constitution because he concluded that no satisfactory structure could be framed "by drawing a line between the general and state governments."[68]

The meanings of the various provisions incorporated in the final document, moreover, were frequently unclear and disputed.[69] The Contract Clause, for example, which prohibited the states from enacting any "Law impairing the Obligation of Contracts,"[70] seemed a major victory for those who feared the prodebtor policies of the state legislatures. Exactly what the clause meant and how far it reached, however, were entirely unsettled. The framers adopted it belatedly and with little discussion, and the ratification debates demonstrated "a diversity of opinions about the meaning and prospective impact of the clause."[71] In Madison's view it fell "short of the mark" and was simply "not sufficient."[72] After its passage, moreover, the states continued for a quarter of a century to enact and enforce bankruptcy and debtor-stay laws, and as late as 1814 ten of the original thirteen states retained such laws on their books. While the Marshall Court eventually gave the clause a relatively clear and broad meaning, its rulings were the products not of any "original" understanding of the Constitution but of the transforming culture and politics of the early republic.[73] "Almost no one cared about the contract clause either at the Constitutional Convention or during the ratification controversy," Leonard W. Levy explained, and its meaning remained unsettled until "Marshall's transforming interpretation" in *Fletcher v. Peck*,[74] which "disdained original intent."[75]

While the Constitution's resulting ambiguities and lacunae were numerous, three seemed particularly arresting and demonstrated the document's materially incomplete nature. One was the simple fact that it nowhere used the words "national," "federal," or "sovereignty." The Constitution, in other words, failed to take an explicit stand on some of the most divisive federalism issues that the framers and ratifiers debated. As Rufus King told the delegates in Philadelphia, the terms "national" and "federal" had been "often used & applied in the discussion inaccurately and delusively."[76] Although the drafters addressed many issues, they refused to attempt to define, or even use, three key terms that might have clarified the nature of the new government and helped identify a line between national and state authority. Second, the Constitution made no provision for, or mention of, political parties. The framers hoped that such organizations would not arise, but parties nonetheless began to coalesce during George Washington's presidency. By the election of 1800 they were acting cohesively to select individuals for office and control national policy, creating an elaborate practice of government that operated wholly outside the assumptions and structures of the Constitution. Third, the Constitution did not authorize, or even mention, judicial review. The absence was particularly surprising because the practice was widely discussed during the 1780s. As it became increasingly accepted during the following decade and officially embraced by the Supreme Court in the next,[77] judicial review gradually evolved into an awesome constitutional power. It remained, nonetheless, one for which the Constitution itself made no express provision and about which the founders held diverse, incomplete, and changing views.

During the ratification debates, in fact, the Anti-Federalists repeatedly charged that the Constitution was ambiguous.[78] Its powers were "loosely given" and would be "interpreted with great latitude," Edmund Randolph insisted,[79] while "Cato" charged that its "latitudinal powers" were "vague and inexplicit" and would prove "unbounded."[80] Elbridge Gerry warned that "some of the powers of the [federal] legislature are ambiguous, and others indefinite and dangerous";[81] the pamphleteer "Agrippa" charged that the Constitution created "an undefined system";[82] and George Clinton declared "that inexplicitness seems to pervade this whole political fabric."[83] The Necessary and Proper Clause would allow members of Congress to "extend their powers as far as they shall think proper," Mason contended,[84] while another pamphleteer charged that the clause authorized "*undefined, unbounded and immense power*."[85] The "Federal Farmer" chimed in. The Constitution conferred "vast undefined powers," and it was "almost impossible to have a just conception of these powers, or of the extent and number of the laws which may be deemed necessary and proper to carry them into effect." Strictly worded amendments were essential to establish "fixed known boundaries," for otherwise "the state governments must be annihilated."[86] "Brutus," perhaps the most able of the Anti-Federalist writers, insisted that "most of the articles" in the Constitution "which convey powers of any considerable importance, are conceived in general and indefinite terms, which are either equivocal, ambiguous, or which require long definitions to unfold the extent of their meaning." Such ambiguous provisions, he insisted, "may receive a construction to justify the passing of almost any law."[87]

Most historians agreed that the Anti-Federalist claim was well founded.[88] In spite of Federalist assurances, Herbert J. Storing concluded, the Anti-Federalists had "good reason" for their skepticism. It was "doubtful" that "a clear line could now be drawn between the general concerns of the Union and the particular concerns of the states."[89] Jack Rakove reached the same conclusion. "Far from simplifying the concept of federalism," he wrote, "this course of debate led the framers to compound its nuances and uncertainties."[90] Even Justice Joseph Story, who revered the Constitution and wrote one of the first systematic treatises on its meaning, readily acknowledged the same truth. "Frame constitutions of government with what wisdom and foresight we may," he admitted in 1821, "they must be imperfect, and leave something to discretion, and much to public virtue."[91]

More telling, the Federalists largely conceded the point.[92] The convention itself formally acknowledged as much in its letter transmitting the Constitution to the Confederation Congress. "It is at all times difficult to draw with precision the line between those rights which must be surrendered [by the states], and those which may be reserved," it explained. Indeed, it highlighted the problem by adding that "on the present occasion this difficulty was encreased [*sic*] by a difference among the several States as to their situation, extent, habits, and particular interests."[93]

Many Federalists sought simply to confess and avoid the problem. The charge of ambiguity "may be brought against every human composition, and necessarily arises from the imperfection of language," Oliver Ellsworth acknowledged. Declaring that even "the most perspicuous and precise writers are in a degree chargeable" with such ambiguities, he sought to dismiss the indictment by stressing that it "was an excellency of this Constitution that it is expressed with brevity and in the plain common language of mankind."[94] Roger Sherman, who had told the convention "that it would be difficult to draw the line between the powers of the Genl. Legislatures, and those to be left with the States,"[95] candidly acknowledged the charge of ambiguity and similarly sought to avoid it. He insisted that the "sole question" before the ratifying conventions was whether the structure of Congress would allow the people to control its actions. "Decide this," he proclaimed, "and then all the questions about their power may be dismissed for the amusement of those politicians whose business it is to catch flies."[96] Even Hamilton gave ground. "If mankind were to resolve to agree in no institution of government, until every part of it had been adjusted to the most exact standard of perfection," he pleaded, "society would soon become a general scene of anarchy, and the world a desert."[97]

Wilson showed both candor and wisdom in acknowledging the problem. "But it is not pretended that the line is drawn with mathematical precision," he admitted; "the inaccuracy of language must, to a certain degree, prevent the accomplishment of such a desire." Applying the Constitution's principle of divided powers to "particular cases" would, therefore, "be accompanied with much difficulty" and require "great discretionary latitude of construction." On "a subject so peculiarly delicate as this," he counseled, "much prudence, much candor, much moderation, and much liberality should be exercised and displayed both by the federal government and by the governments of the several states."[98] That was surely sound advice, but equally surely it was a forthright admission that the founders had drawn no "line" that clearly divided national from state power.

Madison, too, admitted that the document failed to demarcate the federal-state boundary.[99] Indeed, he flatly acknowledged the "impossibility of dividing powers of legislation, in such a manner, as to be free from different constructions by different interests, or even from ambiguity in the judgment of the impartial."[100] Most pointedly, he explained at painstaking length exactly why the "task of marking the proper line of partition between the authority of the general and that of the State governments" was not merely "arduous" but beyond human capacity. Three factors made such a goal unattainable: first, the inherent "obscurity" and "complexity" that marked all "the institutions of man"; second, "the imperfections of the human faculties" themselves; and third, the "cloudy medium" of language whose "unavoidable inaccuracy" compounded as the "complexity and novelty" of its subject increased. "The convention, in delineating the boundary between the federal and State jurisdictions," he concluded, "must have experienced the full effect of them all." Those inherent sources of "vague and incorrect" thinking inevitably produced a Constitution with "a certain degree of obscurity."[101]

The Tenth Amendment, added shortly after ratification in 1791, confirmed the Constitution's inherent ambiguity on the federalism issue. The state ratifying conventions proposed a number of amendments to strengthen the states and restrict congressional powers, especially over such subjects as taxes, commerce, and the military. Although Madison supported their recommendations in order "to complete the Federalists' ratification victory," Herbert J. Storing explained, he accepted "none of the amendments regarded by the opponents to the Constitution as fundamental."[102] Thus, the Tenth Amendment, which affirmed the principle that the central government held only delegated powers, was artfully framed. Its original draft provided that "powers not *expressly* delegated to the United States" remained with the states or the people. Madison, however, insisted that "it was impossible to confine a government to the exercise of express powers" and that "there must necessarily be admitted powers by implication." Congress responded by eliminating the word "expressly," seeming thereby to sanction the principle of implied powers. In that final form, Madison announced, the amendment was "superfluous" and "unnecessary."[103] The point was not that eliminating the word "expressly" proved anything about the exact scope of delegated or implied national powers but, rather, that the First Congress purposely chose to preserve in the Tenth Amendment the crucial ambiguities that were already inherent in the original Constitution.[104]

It was particularly illuminating, though hardly surprising, that views about the Constitution's ambiguous qualities began to shift as soon as the new government formed.[105] During the ratification debates the Federalists had argued that the central government's powers were few and enumerated, but after ratification many of them began to adopt more expansive views. Although Hamilton had defended a theory of "implied" powers during the ratification debates,[106] he had also denied that the controversial Necessary and Proper Clause—"the source of much virulent invective and petulant declamation"—added anything of substance to national powers.[107] After ratification, however, when he proposed establishing a Bank of the United States, he boldly reinterpreted the idea of "delegated" powers to include not just "express" powers but also secondary "implied" powers and even tertiary "resulting" powers. More important, he argued that the Necessary and Proper Clause meant that the national government possessed "plenary & sovereign authority" to make any "necessary" law and, crucially, that "necessary" meant "no more than *needful, requisite, incidental, useful, or conducive to.*"[108] Thus, in his later view, the clause conveyed the most far-reaching powers imaginable.

A nascent postratification Federalist Party rallied around Hamilton's program and the constitutional approach he offered to support it. Rufus King, who had initially defended the Constitution on the ground that national powers were "explicitly defined both as to quantity and the manner of their exercise," quickly embraced both Hamilton's proposed bank and his expansive interpretation of national powers.[109] Fisher Ames, another ardent Federalist, did the same, defending Hamilton's theory by cleverly turning the charge of ambiguity back against the bank's opponents. The principle of "implied power" was not "a new doctrine," Ames maintained, but one "often" cited and which "we can scarcely proceed without." It was those who rejected such a settled doctrine, he charged, who created confusion by proposing "obscure" new rules that failed to "mark out the limits of the power which they will leave to use."[110]

First Washington, then Congress, and finally the Supreme Court accepted Hamilton's bank and the expansive constitutional theory that justified it. Seeking to implement the national commercial policies they favored, the Federalists "generally treated constitutional argument as a species of political reasoning continuous with the specifically political and policy considerations of statesmanship," H. Jefferson Powell noted. "The Federal courts in the first decade of the nineteenth century, dominated by Federalist judges, usually shared this approach."[111] Indeed, in 1819 when the Court upheld the constitutionality of the second Bank of the United States and endorsed Hamilton's theory, it did so by emphasizing that the Constitution's provisions were both open-ended and general. Any effort to specify "an accurate detail of all the subdivisions of which its great powers will admit," Marshall wrote in *McCulloch v. Maryland,* would require "the prolixity of a legal code, and could scarcely be embraced by the human mind." Instead, he explained, the founders understood that the very "nature" of the Constitution required "that only its great outlines should be marked, its important objects designated" while "minor ingredients" were left to "be deduced from the nature of the objects themselves." Thus, he argued, "the framers of the American constitution" intended to create a document that was both flexible and far-reaching, and their intent was to be inferred from both "the nature of the instrument" and the general language they used.[112]

Equally illuminating, and equally unsurprising, those who opposed Hamilton's program—including many who had previously criticized the Constitution for granting the central government "unbounded" and "undefined" powers—began suddenly to insist that the document's language was both precise and sharply restrictive. When he led the Anti-Federalists in the Virginia ratifying convention, Patrick Henry denounced the powers the Constitution conferred on the new central government as vast and unlimited; but when he condemned Hamilton's plan for federal assumption of state debts in 1790, he portrayed those grants of national power as narrow and well defined.[113] Qualifying his own earlier views about implied powers,[114] Madison, too, rejected Hamilton's more sweeping theory. "If implications, thus remote and thus multiplied, can be linked together," he objected, "a chain may be formed that will reach every object of legislation, every object within the whole compass of political economy."[115] Jefferson similarly opposed the bank and warned that ignoring the "boundaries thus specifically drawn around the powers of Congress" would make the authority of the central government "boundless" and "no longer susceptible of any definition."[116]

Into the early nineteenth century those who opposed what they saw as an expanding central government echoed those claims and insisted that the Constitution's limits on national power were sharp and definite. One of the hallmarks of the emerging jurisprudence of the Jeffersonian Republicans was a rigid textualism that conceived of constitutional construction as a technical lawyerly practice that demonstrated the clear and highly restrictive limits that shackled national power.[117] The Constitution drew a "grand boundary" that identified "obvious limits between the federal and state jurisdictions,"[118] St. George Tucker insisted,[119] while John Taylor of Caroline maintained that the Constitution established "a definite and permanent division of power."[120] Attacking *McCulloch* in 1819, Spencer Roane relied heavily on the Tenth Amendment to confirm the proposition that the Constitution imposed manifest and rigid limits on national powers. "It is not easy," he announced with bold certainty and bolder misstatement, "to devise stronger terms to effect that object than those used in that amendment."[121]

Thus, as the new government took its first infant steps, the views of many of the founders began quickly to shift and realign. Most striking were changes in their views about the Constitution's relative clarity or ambiguity. During the ratification debates those who supported a strong central government claimed that the Constitution granted only defined and limited powers, while those who defended state authority charged that it conferred vague and unbounded powers. After ratification, the former began to claim that the Constitution granted the central government broad and elastic powers, while the latter quickly countered that it conferred only narrow and well-defined powers. As the two sides exchanged their premises and rhetoric, their calculated adaptations launched a practice of strategic constitutional interpretation that subsequent generations would habitually and avidly emulate. The spontaneous and instantaneous appearance of that serviceable practice, as much as anything the founders said or did, signaled the true "original" nature of American federalism.

Considering the Constitution as a truly historical document, then, its gaps and ambiguities were understandable, as were the conflicting and shifting views of those who debated its ratification and application.[122] It was incomplete and ambiguous for easily understandable and wholly unavoidable reasons: born of conflict, compromise, invention, and expedience, it was a product of art and finesse.[123] A delegate to the North Carolina ratifying convention put the matter clearly. There was "real difficulty in conciliating a number of jarring interests, arising from the incidental but unalterable difference in the states in point of territory, situation, climate, and rivalship in commerce." Consequently, it "was not easy to reconcile such a multiplicity of discordant and clashing interests." Those conflicts explained the incomplete and ambiguous nature of the convention's final product. "Mutual concessions," the North Carolinian recognized, "were necessary to come to any concurrence."[124] Neither Hamilton nor Madison was satisfied with that final product,[125] and even during the ratification debates the two disagreed on a number of issues, including the scope of power granted to the new national government.[126] "[T]he founders disagreed among themselves about how to design institutions so as to achieve or approach unanimity," Robert A. Burt concluded insightfully, "and they did not resolve but rather implicitly embedded this disagreement in the constitutional scheme."[127]

It was only to be expected, then, that the nation's first decade under the Constitution would witness the reemergence of most of the significant conflicts that the convention had muffled or avoided. In "the 1790s the newness of the Constitution, the widespread sense of its fragility, and the bitter antagonism between the contending groups in American society," James Roger Sharp explained, "prevented that document from providing limits to the political debate and serving as the consensual touchstone for the nation." As early as 1792 large numbers of Americans "agreed that there was a great disparity between how the new government was supposed to have worked and how it was actually working."[128] Indeed, by 1792 Madison and Hamilton were not merely at loggerheads but at one another's throats. The former drafted a series of public attacks charging the latter's economic program with being elitist, plutocratic, anti-republican, and "a perversion of the natural order of things," while the latter accused the former of advancing views that were "subversive of the principles of good government and dangerous to the union, peace, and happiness of the Country."[129] R. Kent Newmyer aptly summarized the decade's experience: "Translating the words of the Constitution into practice, it would appear, was an act of creativity hardly less impressive or disputatious than framing the document in the first place." Translating the new government from parchment to practice, "rather than quieting disagreements over the Constitution, only escalated the debate."[130]

Matters deteriorated badly, and the new nation's politics quickly turned "peculiarly violent." The "ferocity and passion of political attitudes" and the "brutality of both expression and behavior," concluded one historian, grew from the fact that "the political battles of the 1790s were grounded upon a complete distrust of the motives and integrity, the honesty and intentions of one's political opponents."[131] By 1796, when Federalist congressman Frederick Muhlenberg cast the deciding vote in support of Jay's Treaty, anger drove his outraged Republican brother-in-law to stab him. Two years later, when Federalist congressman Roger Griswold and Republican congressman Matthew Lyon argued on the floor of the House, they exchanged insults, then spat at one another, and finally attacked with canes. Muhlenberg's earlier stabbing had incited no further violence, but the Griswold-Lyon battle ignited a congressional tinderbox, goading infuriated Federalists and Republicans into a series of fights on and off the chamber's floor for the rest of the day.[132]

There was, finally, yet another reason for both the Constitution's ambiguities and the founders' uncertainties. The nation drafted and ratified its new Constitution while in the midst of a revolutionary cultural, economic, and political transformation. The very "vocabulary of political discourse was, during the eighteenth century, in a state of flux," Forrest McDonald explained, and at the Constitutional Convention the "delegates had different understandings" of many of the most basic terms they used, including such fundamental concepts as "liberty," "property," "society," and "rights."[133] The imprecise and shifting vocabulary that was available to them not only limited their ability to convey precise meanings but also limited their ability to capture in the provisions of the Constitution those points on which they did agree. Further, the "Revolution did not just eliminate monarchy and create republics," Gordon S. Wood explained; "it actually reconstituted what Americans meant by public or state power and brought about an entirely new kind of popular politics and a new kind of democratic officeholder."[134] Such intellectual and political tumult inevitably left ideas about government unsettled and plastic. "[A]s crucial as the idea of federalism was to the Federalists in explaining the operation of their new system," Wood continued, "it seems clear that few of them actually conceived of it in full before the Constitution was written and debated."[135] During the decade following ratification the actions of the founders compelled only one conclusion about their "intentions," "understandings," or "meanings" concerning the federal structure: they were vague, varied, uncertain, mutable, incomplete, and conflicting.

Thus, the Constitution was, in Cass Sunstein's term, "incompletely theorized," and unavoidably so. It established certain principles and institutions, but it failed to provide any specific "series of steps" to connect those principles and institutions to "concrete conclusions" about the structure's boundaries and operations. That ambiguity, moreover, was essential to the Constitution's drafting and ratification, for it meant that its supporters "need not agree on what it entails in particular cases."[136] Whatever else they understood, the founders knew they had no choice but to leave those challenges to the future. "Federalism was a possible, not a certain, solution," Bernard Bailyn noted; "its essence was not automatic harmony but an uncertain tension which statecraft alone could maintain."[137]

3

FEDERALISM AS FRACTIONATED

The formal division of power between nation and states was but one component of the nation's constitutional structure. Four major fault lines crosscut the binary division between central and state governments, generating fissures and tensions that fractionated the structure's operations. The "federal republic," Madison explained, would be founded on a society "broken into so many parts, interests, and classes of citizens, that the rights of the individuals, or of the minority, will be in little danger."[1] His conclusion did not always hold, but his premise surely did. Those "many parts, interests, and classes" generated continuous pressures along the structure's four fault lines, preventing both the states and the central government from consistently upholding an unchanging division of authority between them, making the structure's operations inherently dynamic, and continually reshaping its doubly blurred boundaries.

The National Level: Separation of Powers

First, and most obvious, the Constitution created a second structural axis, that of "separation of powers." Rather than creating a simple "federal republic," the founders also divided national powers among three distinct branches. Like the division of powers between states and nation, the separation of national powers was designed to preserve liberty, property, and republicanism by preventing "factions" from gaining control of the national government and abusing its powers. "In the compound republic of America, the power surrendered by the people is first divided between two distinct governments, and then the portion allotted to each subdivided among distinct and separate departments," Madison wrote. "Hence a double security arises to the rights of the people."[2]

The same theory further inspired the founders to subdivide what they regarded as the most powerful national branch, the legislature, into two distinct parts. The House of Representatives would constitute the truly "popular" branch, while the Senate would serve as a more elite, state-oriented body. A "senate, as a second branch of the legislative assembly, distinct from, and dividing the power with, a first, must be in all cases a salutary check on the government," Madison explained. "It doubles the security to the people, by requiring the concurrence of two distinct bodies in schemes of usurpation or perfidy."[3] The power to check corruption and abuse, Hamilton declared in the New York State ratifying convention, was "the peculiar excellence of a division of the legislature."[4]

Separating powers at the national level multiplied the complexities that would plague the federal structure. First, and immediately apparent, dividing the national government into "three great provinces" compounded the structure's fundamental ambivalence. For, in providing its "double security," the Constitution imposed on each of the national branches the same conflicting duty that it imposed on the states: the duty to protect "the people" and their rights from the potential depredations of the other levels and branches of government. Thus, the Constitution created the systemic likelihood that the three national branches would, like the states, pursue their own agendas, come into conflict with one another, and understand—or at least be able to justify—whatever actions they took as efforts to protect the people and their rights.

Second, separating national powers multiplied the structure's complexities because the framers failed to attain any more precision in specifying the distinctive powers of the national branches than they achieved in allocating powers between state and central governments.[5] Their failure was understandable, for the distinctions between the powers of the three branches were inherently murky and the founders understood their natures differently. The authors of the *Federalist,* for example, held contrasting views of the "judicial Power." While Madison announced that the judiciary, like the other branches, "should have a will of its own,"[6] Hamilton insisted that the judiciary had "neither FORCE nor WILL, but merely judgment."[7] Not surprisingly, then, the first federal judges had vague and diverse ideas about their role, and they "neither understood nor desired a strict divide either between themselves and the other branches or between law and politics."[8] Further, colonial practices varied widely, and the three branches performed somewhat different functions in different states. In Massachusetts and some other colonies the legislature played a critical "judicial" role, serving as the highest court of appeal, a role the legislatures maintained through ratification and into the early republic.[9] Similarly, in many colonies the power to adjudicate monetary claims against the government—a power that later generations would come to consider "judicial"—also rested in the legislature.[10] Evidencing the uncertain nature of the lines between the new national branches, the First Congress placed power to adjudicate such claims in neither the judicial nor the legislative branch but in the federal Treasury Department, an agency it located in the executive branch but made partly responsible to the legislature.[11] Along the same lines, the Second Congress gave the federal judiciary a role in military decision making, providing that in emergencies when Congress was not in session the executive could federalize state militias only if a federal judge certified that the civil authorities in an area were inadequate to maintain public order.[12]

Thus, confusion and uncertainty about the proper lines between the branches was apparent. "Experience has instructed us," Madison acknowledged, "that no skill in the science of government has yet been able to discriminate and define, with sufficient certainty, its three great provinces— the legislative, executive, and judiciary."[13] To Jefferson, he confessed that "the boundaries between the Executive, Legislative, and Judiciary powers, though in general so strongly marked in themselves, consist in many instances of mere shades of difference."[14] The problem was particularly acute, Madison believed, with respect to Congress. Compared with the powers of the executive and judiciary, the legislature's "constitutional powers" were "more extensive, and less susceptible of precise limits."[15] In 1787 the idea of separation of powers, Martin Flaherty wrote, was but one unformed element in a "complex, messy, and at times contradictory ferment in constitutional thinking."[16] The founders, Gerhard Casper concluded similarly, were "not doctrinaire" on separation-of-powers issues "because there was no clear doctrine."[17]

Third, the three national branches themselves were neither simple nor monolithic. The Constitution divided the legislature into two different parts, and Congress immediately established a system of lower courts in the judicial branch and began creating a variety of governmental offices and departments within both the executive and legislative branches.[18] Over the years those component institutions would multiply and increasingly fragment the national branches. They would generate varieties of diverse and sometimes conflicting institutional interests and incentives and make it ever more difficult for the formal branch "heads"—Congress, the president, and the Supreme Court—to exercise close and effective control over their growing power and ever wider ranging activities.[19] The idea of a national "branch" would itself become a kind of constitutional abstraction, a concept related only uncertainly and imperfectly to the mass of de facto institutional components that constituted the overall government of the United States.

The kinds of problems that such a complex and imprecisely defined structure would generate surfaced quickly. Only two years after the seminal debate over Hamilton's bank, the issue of implied powers arose again, this time in the context of separation of powers. In 1793 war broke out between England and France, raising "the kind of constitutional question that no one seems to have anticipated in 1787: Which branch of the government, President or Congress, has authority to make a declaration of American neutrality in a foreign war?"[20] The founders quickly fell to disagreement, and Washington seized the initiative by issuing a presidential Neutrality Proclamation that ignored the Franco-American treaty of 1778, declared the United States formally neutral, and, as a practical matter, aided the English cause.

The action enraged the emerging and passionately pro-French Jeffersonian Republicans, and the pro-English Hamilton, writing as "Pacificus," came forward to defend Washington's action on the basis of a sweeping theory of implied power. The "vesting" clause of Article II conferred "the executive Power," Hamilton maintained, and that power was a "comprehensive grant" whose scope was limited only by express restrictions in the

Constitution itself. Insofar as the legislature had any role in foreign affairs, its powers should "be construed strictly—and ought to be extended no further than is essential to their execution." To cap his sweeping interpretation of executive power, Hamilton added a striking new claim in opaque but unnerving words. While the legislature held the power to declare war, he declared, "the Executive in the exercise of its constitutional powers, may establish an antecedent state of things which ought to weigh in the legislative decisions."[21] Deeply agitated, Jefferson exhorted Madison to reply—"For God's sake, my dear Sir, take up your pen."[22] Responding as "Helvidius," Madison condemned Hamilton's views as "vicious in theory," "dangerous in practice," and conducive to "tyranny." They "strike at the vitals of [the] constitution." If accepted, Hamilton's principles would undermine not only the legislative branch but the judiciary as well, throwing the Constitution's plan for separated national powers into "absolute hotchpot" and "a general scramble." Then, even "the most penetrating jurist," Madison declared, "would be unable to scan the extent of constructive prerogative."[23] Washington's proclamation stood, however, and the controversy gave the founding generation yet another glimpse of the ambiguities and lacunae in the structure of divided powers they had erected.

To further complicate separation-of-powers issues, the Constitution not only left the nature of the three powers inadequately defined but also allocated them among the three branches in intermixed and blended forms. The executive was given a limited veto over acts of the legislature, for example, and the approval of the Senate was required for executive actions in making treaties and appointing national officials.[24] While Anti-Federalists warned that such "blended" powers violated Montesquieu's "political maxim" that required complete separation, the Constitution's supporters argued that intermixed powers were necessary to enable the three branches to hold one another in check. "[U]nless these departments be so far connected and blended as to give to each a constitutional control over the others," Madison explained, "the degree of separation which the maxim requires, as essential to a free government, can never in practice be duly maintained."[25] The idea of "blending" national powers was astute, but it compounded the problem of unclear lines of authority by purposely structuring those powers to overlap and conflict. John Quincy Adams—

who served in both the Senate and the House, won election as president, and declined appointment to the Supreme Court—had the keenest familiarity with the early workings of the federal branches. Their blended powers, he concluded, "melt so imperceptibly into each other that no human eye can discern the exact boundary line between them."[26]

Adams's comment was apt. Indeed, as Washington's Neutrality Proclamation spotlighted ambiguities in the way the Constitution granted powers to the national branches, the pitched battle over Jay's Treaty in 1795–96 exposed ambiguities in the way it blended those powers.[27] While the president negotiated the treaty and the Senate ratified it, funds were necessary to implement some of its provisions. Hence, though the Constitution gave the House no express role in treaty making, its spending provisions nonetheless made supportive action by the House essential.[28] When Washington requested funds but refused to present the actual treaty, opposition forces in the House demanded that the president furnish it with all instructions, correspondence, and other materials relating to the treaty. Washington refused, denying that the House had any proper role in the treaty-making process and warning that compliance with its request would constitute a "dangerous precedent." After two months of bitter wrangling, Washington's still considerable prestige and the shrewd tactics of the treaty's supporters combined to erode the opposition's majority, and the House finally approved the necessary funds.[29] The episode, however, highlighted and left wholly unresolved major constitutional questions involving the existence and scope of executive privilege as well as the extent to which the House's expressly granted power over revenue measures should properly give it a voice in "executive" and "senatorial" functions. The Constitution, which purposely blended the powers of the three branches to create its system of checks and balances, provided no clear answers to such questions.

Similarly, ambiguities in the way the Constitution separated and blended national powers also revealed themselves in the office of vice president.[30] During the nation's first decade many of the founders considered the office—whose only constitutional duty was to preside over the Senate—as part of the legislative, not the executive, branch.[31] John Adams, the nation's first vice president, regularly presided over the Senate, helped shape its agenda, participated in debates, lobbied for votes, and ruled on key procedural issues.[32] Jefferson, who followed Adams in the office, shared his predecessor's view. "I consider my office as constitutionally confined to legislative functions," he declared, and accordingly "I could not take any part whatever in executive consultations."[33] In spite of those original attitudes and practices, the Senate increasingly came to view the vice president as an intruder, and by the early nineteenth century its developing system of rules and party leadership began to confine the office to a peripheral and largely symbolic role. By midcentury, practice identified it with the executive branch.[34] That result, subsequently sanctioned by history and tradition, was hardly prescribed by the Constitution and contradicted the understanding of many of the founders.

Perhaps more striking, if less well known, even Hamilton—the indefatigable proponent of national power—recognized the uncertainties that marked the relationship among the three branches when they faced questions involving the power of the states. Although he stood as the preeminent spokesman for a strong national judiciary and defended the principle of federal judicial review, his reaction to the passage of the Virginia and Kentucky Resolutions in 1798 was particularly revealing.[35] The resolutions condemned the Federalist-sponsored Alien and Sedition Acts and declared that the states held ultimate authority to interpret the Constitution. Responding anxiously to their challenge, Hamilton sought recourse not in the national judiciary but in the national legislature. He urged the appointment of a special congressional committee to "make a report exhibiting with great luminousness and particularity the reasons which support the constitutionality and expediency of those laws." The report, he continued, "should conclude with a declaration that there is no cause for a Repeal of the laws."[36]

The salient point was not that Hamilton either changed his mind or acted inconsistently but rather that, a decade after ratification, even the staunchest proponent of both national power and a strong federal judiciary recognized the institutional complexities and tactical options that separation of powers added to questions of federal-state relations. The powers of the three federal branches were different, and their scope was unsettled. As matters of both law and practice, what each branch could or should seek to accomplish in trying to control the states was highly uncertain.

Equally important, after the escalating political rancor of the 1790s, it no longer seemed certain, or perhaps even likely, that the three national branches would act in concert when dealing with the states. To the contrary, with the obviously critical election of 1800 looming, it seemed more probable that they would adopt inconsistent or conflicting positions. Indeed, they quickly did. When the Jeffersonian Republicans gained control of both the executive and legislative branches, they not only showed increased deference to the states but also quickly turned against the Federalist-dominated national judiciary. They repealed the Federalist Judiciary Act of 1801, cutting the jurisdiction of the national courts and abolishing the new judgeships it created, and then threatened the remaining Federalists on the bench with impeachment, successfully removing a district judge and coming close to removing Supreme Court Justice Samuel Chase.[37]

Thus, separation of powers fragmented the national side of the federalism equation and drastically compounded the complexities inherent in the Constitution's structure. The three national branches could easily split over issues involving state power, with one or more asserting national authority and one or more upholding state authority or taking some neutral or intermediate position. Moreover, the fact that members of the national branches were selected at different times and under different principles increased the likelihood that they would view specific federalism issues differently.[38] Members of the Senate, chosen by state legislatures, seemed particularly likely to represent the interests of their states,[39] for example, while the federal judiciary, appointed rather than elected and guaranteed institutional independence, seemed more likely to stand aloof from those interests. Critically, however, neither the Senate nor the judiciary invariably played those anticipated roles, and the branches of the central government frequently divided among themselves in varying combinations when they addressed issues of state and national power.[40] Indeed, the great foundational "federalism" decisions of the Marshall Court—*Martin v. Hunter's Lessee*,[41] *Cohens v. Virginia*,[42] *Gibbons v. Ogden*,[43] and *Osborn v. Bank of the United States*[44]—were as much about allocating powers among the three federal branches as they were about drawing lines between state and national power.

Separation-of-powers ideas, then, stood ready to complicate almost any issue of state and federal power. In the late twentieth century, for example, they were used to challenge federal administrative and spending measures that delegated power to state and local officials who administered cooperative federal-state programs. After the 1960s such programs became increasingly complex, usually imposing national conditions and standards but allowing states substantial leeway in determining how to apply their requirements. By using state and local agencies to implement federal law, the statutes delegated considerable authority and discretion.[45] Thus, some came to argue, such programs implicated the powers and responsibilities of the president by contravening the "vesting" clause and constraining his ability to "take Care that the Laws be faithfully executed."[46] Although the Supreme Court essentially ignored that concern for a century, in 1997 the five "profederalism" justices on the Rehnquist Court suddenly seized on it as a crucial constitutional problem. Writing for a majority in *Printz v. United States,* Justice Scalia declared that a federal gun-control statute assigning enforcement duties to local police officials intruded not only into state matters but also into national executive authority. "[T]he power of the President would be subject to reduction," he explained, "if Congress could act as effectively without the President as with him, by simply requiring state officers to execute its laws."[47] The statute, the Court held, violated the principles of both federalism and separation of powers.

Printz illustrated one type of potential interaction between separation-of-powers and federalism doctrines.[48] Justice Scalia's opinion gave voice to the idea of the "unitary executive," the Hamiltonian claim that the Constitution conferred on the president all of the executive power of the national government and required that the president be able to direct, and if necessary remove, all officials involved in enforcing federal law.[49] The idea was revived and expanded during the 1980s when the Reagan administration repeatedly challenged the constitutionality of independent federal agencies and special prosecutors operating beyond the president's control.[50] Those who opposed the extensive national programs that the federal government had sponsored since the New Deal came to see the idea's potential as a constitutional device to undermine and reduce the reach of national power in a broad range of regulatory and welfare-related areas. If the executive was "unitary," and the Constitution required direct presidential control over all agents enforcing or administering federal law, then much of the modern national administrative state that had developed since the late nineteenth century was arguably unconstitutional.[51] The idea of the "unitary executive," in other words, rooted in separation-of-powers ideas, could readily be turned to reach major "federalism" issues and used to curtail the powers of the national government.[52]

Those and similar problems repeatedly confounded the Supreme Court, which, for more than two hundred years, failed to do more than sketch generally plausible but nonetheless rubbery lines between the national branches.[53] Sometimes the Court employed formalistic reasoning—claiming to rely on "essential" characteristics of the branches[54]—and sometimes it employed a "pragmatic, flexible view"[55] of their relationships. Sometimes it found that separation of powers compelled the judiciary to defer to the other branches, and sometimes it found that the doctrine required the judiciary to overturn the actions of those other branches.[56] Usually the Court split over such issues, often badly.[57] The "Constitution's central mechanism of separation of powers," it confessed in 1992, "depends largely upon common understandings of what activities are appropriate to legislatures, to executives, and to courts."[58] A standard based on the "common understanding" of what was "appropriate" was hardly precise, nor was it a standard that the Constitution itself clarified. It was, in fact, a highly pragmatic and flexible standard, one that suited the complexities of the federal structure but failed to provide any specific direction for resolving its many uncertainties.

The State Level: Multiplicity and Fragmentation

Though the Constitution gave the states a prominent place in the new central government as both independent political units and constituent elements, it also recognized that they were diverse entities with conflicting interests and internal divisions. States could be free or slave, large or small, commercial or agricultural, claiming or lacking western lands, and nestled safely away from or bordered by foreign threats. Their conflicts and jealousies provided one of the principal spurs that drove the founders to press for a new and stronger central government. "[I]f not restrained by a national control," Hamilton warned, the states' shortsighted policies would multiply into "serious sources of animosity and discord" that could lead to the Union's dissolution.[59]

The Constitution itself encouraged further diversity by providing for the admission of new states and, hence, for the steady multiplication of novel and conflicting interests among them.[60] The "immediate object of the federal Constitution" was not only to unite the original thirteen colonies, Madison explained, but "to add to them such other States as may arise in their own bosoms, or in their neighborhoods."[61] Indeed, in July 1787, as the Constitution was being drafted, the Confederation Congress passed the Northwest Ordinance, organizing the nation's northern territories and providing for their admission as future states equal in status to the existing states.[62] Like the national side of the "compound republic," then, the state side was also divided internally. Compared with the divisions of the former, however, those of the latter were far more numerous and far more varied.

On the state side, conflicts operated on three distinct levels. On one, states sought to protect politically dominant interests and joined other states in coalitions to advance those interests and oppose the conflicting interests of rival state alliances. Most of the significant disputes the new nation faced, the founders knew, "pitted different clusters of states against one another on the basis of well-defined interests."[63] On a second level, states were split internally by a variety of lesser or more localized interests—rooted in such factors as religion, geography, ethnicity, and economic basis—that fragmented their internal populations and divided their interior regions, generating in the process intrastate conflicts that frequently reached fierce proportions.[64] From the nation's earliest days substate governmental units and the localized interests they represented pushed themselves into interstate and national politics, cooperating and competing with combinations of local governmental units and interests in other states. The House of Representatives came to serve as the prime institutional forum within the national government for the assertion of such specific and more localized intrastate interests, a role that was strengthened after 1842 when Congress made the use of geographically defined districts mandatory in House elections.[65] On a third level, perhaps the most common and volatile, the units and interests that competed on the first two levels combined in infinite varieties of diverse and shifting coalitions, with states often divided internally and opposed by some of their own substate elements and interests, which allied themselves on particular issues with other states and substate elements and interests in other states.

The federal structure, then, consisted of far more than the simple binary relationship between two monolithic constitutional categories, "the states" on one side and a "central government" on the other. It encompassed, instead, the far more varied, unstable, and multidimensional relationships that existed between three separate and often conflicting national branches—one of which was itself internally divided—and three crosscutting levels of interstate politics: that between and among states and coalitions of states ("state-level" interstate politics), that between and among substate elements and coalitions of substate elements drawn from different states ("substate-level" interstate politics), and that between and among coalitions that included both states and substate elements and in which intrastate divisions placed states and some of their own substate elements on opposite sides of the same issue ("mixed-level" interstate politics).[66] Regularly and avidly those states and their substate elements and interests sought the ear and usually the pocket of the national government, and they frequently found it necessary to distinguish sharply among the three federal branches, praising the wisdom and legitimacy—or denouncing the intrusions and usurpations—of one or more as changing situations and calculations required. Thus, the "compound" of Madison's republic was infinitely complex, and its dynamic never one of simple one-on-one balancing. Incorporating a diverse, unstable, and multiplying potpourri of institutions and interests, it was multifaceted and kaleidoscopic: tripartite on one side; fragmented and multitudinous on the other; and inherently volatile in the ways its innumerable components and subcomponents linked their interests, checked their rivals, shifted their alliances, and justified their varied and countless demands in terms of the Constitution's doubly blurred lines of authority.

The multileveled conflicts that marked the nation's interstate politics provided the empirical inspiration for the founders' theory of "the extended republic."[67] While Madison famously extolled the advantages of those diverse interests in the Tenth *Federalist*, however, he also warned against their potential dangers in the Thirty-Seventh. The "variety of interests" in the states "may have a salutary influence" on government, he acknowledged, "yet every one must be sensible of the contrary influence." Because each of the states was "divided into different districts, and its citizens into different classes," they were driven by "contending interests" to adopt "interfering pretensions" and form varieties of self-serving "combinations." As the large and small states had done at Philadelphia, Madison explained, those "contending interests" would "marshal themselves in opposition to each other on various points."[68] Thus, the paramount goal of the "extended republic" was to prevent state and substate interstate politics from forging "a coalition of a majority of the whole society" that would operate "on any other principles than those of justice and the general good."[69]

Recognizing the volatility of the various levels of interstate politics, then, the founders designed the Constitution to limit and control their effects. To deal with the state level, it adopted provisions to protect the territorial and governmental integrity of the states,[70] limit their ability to enter into formal agreements with one another,[71] prevent a variety of possible depredations and discriminations between and among them,[72] provide a neutral judicial forum to decide controversies between them,[73] bar them from keeping troops and ships of war during peacetime,[74] and prohibit them from actually going to war.[75] To deal with substate levels, the Constitution guaranteed to each state "a Republican Form of Government,"[76] authorized federal assistance to quell "domestic violence,"[77] provided that state Electors could report divided votes in presidential elections,[78] allowed senators to vote individually rather than by state,[79] and enabled Congress to counter entrenched local minorities by overriding state legislatures in establishing the "Times, Places and Manner" for electing members of the House.[80] Further, to protect citizens of one state against discrimination by other states, it provided that "Citizens of each State shall be entitled to all Privileges and Immunities of Citizens in the several States,"[81] and it granted the federal courts jurisdiction to hear suits between citizens of different states and between states and citizens of other states.[82]

During the ratification debates, both Madison and Hamilton argued that the states had no reason to fear the proposed new central government because, if it ever attempted to transgress their rights, the states would immediately unite and quickly defeat the effort. "But ambitious encroach-

ments of the federal government, on the authority of the State governments, would not excite the opposition of a single State, or of a few States
only," Madison predicted. "They would be signals of general alarm" that
would prompt a united response from all. "Every [state] government
would espouse the common cause."[83] Hamilton advanced the same claim.
"[I]n all questions that affect the general liberty and prosperity," he argued, the states would "stand ready to sound the alarm when necessary"
because they would "have the same interest."[84]

As a general matter, when live controversies arose, such a united response and consequent binary stand-off was precisely what did not happen. From the 1790s to the Civil War, for example, individual states occa-
sionally challenged and sometimes defied the authority of the Supreme
Court. At varying times and on varying issues Pennsylvania, Georgia, Virginia, Kentucky, South Carolina, Ohio, New York, Wisconsin, and Massachusetts advanced "states' rights" arguments in efforts to avoid the
Court's mandate. In such confrontations, the Court sometimes tempo-
rized, especially when it lacked the support of the national executive. At no
point, however, did the states act generally and in unison to defy the
Court's rulings; nor, with a single exception (the adoption of the Eleventh
Amendment in 1798), did they combine to amend the Constitution and
limit the scope of federal power.[85]

Indeed, if truth be told, it seems questionable whether Madison and
Hamilton ever held much faith in their claim that the states would commonly unite against intrusive actions by the national government. After
all, the contention seemed to fit awkwardly with their argument for an
"extended" republic—that a central government was necessary to control
the diverse factions that too easily came to dominate small states and oppress local minorities.[86] If one accepted that premise about the role of factions, there seemed little reason to believe that the states would normally
share a common view about the nature and consequences of proposed national actions. The premise, in other words, made it seem highly unlikely
either that the states, as individual entities, would be united internally in
opposing actions of the central government or that, taken collectively, the
states would be under the control of factions with the exact same interest
in those national actions.

In any event, the theory that diversity and conflict would mark the actions of the states in the "extended" republic proved closer to the truth—and far more salient in understanding the dynamics of the federal structure—than the "same interest" theory.[87] As the new nation got under way, states and substate elements competed among themselves for a variety of advantages, including a burgeoning range of benefits available from one or more of the three national branches. When they received the sought-after benefits, they tended to support the national branch or branches that favored them. Similarly, when the costs and burdens of national actions fell on others, they tended to stand aloof from the disputes that resulted. As a matter of the nation's ordinary politics, then, what the states in most cases lacked in dealing with the new central government was precisely a sense that they shared a "common cause" or "the same interest."

Thus, the ever more numerous states and their ever more numerous and varied internal factions interacted with a central government divided into three distinct and often opposed branches, and together they created a constitutional dynamic that was anything but binary. Complex, volatile, and multileveled, it was a highly fractionated system whose kaleidoscopic shiftings of interests and alliances kept the operations of the federal system flexible. The structure's kaleidoscopic politics prevented both "the central government" and "the states" from acting consistently as monolithic forces to maintain a clear and definitive line between their respective spheres of authority, and its operations over time repeatedly infused new meanings and interpretations into the Constitution's doubly blurred federalism provisions.

4

FEDERALISM AS INSTRUMENTAL

The oldest and most enduring method of referring to the Constitution, Michael Kammen wrote, was "simply as an 'instrument.'"[1] If the Constitution was an instrument, a writing empowered to accomplish certain legal ends, so too was the federal structure it established. It has been widely recognized, perhaps almost universally acknowledged, that Americans consistently used federalism as a manipulable device to advance their interests. Even its strongest defenders admitted as much. "It is common knowledge on Capitol Hill that federalism or states' rights are nonstarters as objections to legislation," explained Marci Hamilton, a strong defender of decentralized government. "Members spout federalism rhetoric to block legislation they oppose for other reasons, but it is never a dispositive consideration."[2]

Less widely recognized, or perhaps accepted, is the additional fact that the federal structure was designed to be an instrument. Justice Clarence Thomas made the point clearly. "[F]ederalism, per se, is not an evil or a good," he declared, "it is just a construct, just as the separation of powers is a construct—they are both means that serve certain ends."[3] American federalism is instrumental, in other words, not merely in practice but in essence.[4]

James Wilson put the matter succinctly in the Pennsylvania ratifying convention when he acknowledged the "great discretionary latitude" that would be necessary in determining the scope of national and state powers: "The states should resign to the national government that part, and that part only, of their political liberty, which, placed in that government, will produce more good to the whole than if it had remained in the several states."[5] That criterion heralded the structure's inherently instrumental nature and suggested that the ultimate line of division between the central government and the states was necessarily an uncertain matter subject to shifting conditions and practical judgments as to what, in fact, brought "more good to the whole."

Checks and Balances

The Constitution's federal structure, Madison explained, was designed to serve as an instrument in five related but distinct ways. First, it was instrumental by its very nature. All government structures, that is, were instrumental because all were potential tools for factions seeking to turn public power to private gain.[6] The factions that "tainted our public administrations" were omnipresent and irrepressible, Madison concluded, for their "latent causes" were "sown in the nature of man; and we see them everywhere."[7] Indeed, "the *causes* of faction cannot be removed."[8] Thus, because factions would always exist and strive to exploit the agencies of government, the federal structure would inevitably be an instrument.

Second, the federal structure was instrumental because it was a calculated device designed to help control the deleterious effects of those factions. Madison's theory of the "extended" republic made that exact point. Small states were at high risk because they contained few "distinct parties and interests" and thus were susceptible to a "smaller number of individuals" who could effectively "concert and execute their plans of oppression."[9] In contrast, larger states promised to protect liberty and republican government because they encompassed "a greater variety of parties and interests," and their greater diversity made it less likely that any single faction could gain control of their governments.[10] Thus, by enabling many smaller states to join into one "extended" republic, the federal structure served as an instrument to help check the evil consequences of faction by multiplying the number of conflicting groups and interests in the political mix. Their greater number and diversity would increase the likelihood that they would hold one another in check and that none could dominate the government.

Third, the federal structure was an instrument designed to counter governmental oppression by dividing power among multiple governing units and thereby increasing the likelihood that abuse by any one such unit would be checked by some other unit.[11] "[B]y so contriving the interior structure of the government," Madison argued, the "several constituent parts may, by their mutual relations, be the means of keeping each other in their proper places."[12] Madison developed the idea in a brilliant series of essays that blended federalism with separation of powers and integrated both into his theory of factions. First, separation of powers in the central government would, like the division of power between states and nation, create a set of institutionalized checks on government action.[13] Such checks were essential because "power is of an encroaching nature" and "ought to be effectually restrained from passing the limits assigned to it."[14] Together, the two structural divisions created a "double security" for "the rights of the people."[15] Second, integrating that idea into his theory of factions, Madison maintained that the "double security" required a structure that would give "to those who administer each department the necessary constitutional means and personal motives to resist encroachments of the other." Human beings were not "angels" but self-seekers, and government officials consequently would too often follow their own personal ambitions and interests. Accordingly, it was necessary to connect "the constitutional rights of the place" with the "interest of the man" who held the place. When the government was properly structured, then, "the private interest of every individual may be a sentinel over the public rights."[16] Thus, like separation of powers, federalism was an instrument for controlling governmental power by dividing it and harnessing individual interest and ambition to the service of republican ends.

Fourth, federalism was an instrument that would enable the sovereign people themselves to protect their rights by giving them an opportunity to choose, when necessary, among competing levels and branches of government. "The federal and State governments are in fact but different agents and trustees of the people," Madison declared, and the "ultimate authority" to make decisions properly "resides in the people alone." By dividing power and using the levels and branches to check one another, the Constitution sought to ensure that government would ultimately "depend on the sentiments and sanction of their common constituents." If the national government did not earn "the confidence of the people," its "schemes of usurpation will be easily defeated by the State governments, who will be supported by the people."[17] Hamilton agreed. In disputes between the state and national governments, he maintained, the people "by throwing themselves into either scale" would determine which side would prevail. "If their rights are invaded by either, they can make use of the other as the instrument of redress."[18] Thus, federalism was also an instrument of "the people" in their sovereign capacity, a tool that would enable them, if and when necessary, to intervene actively to secure their rights and liberties by blocking the abusive actions of one governmental unit with the checking powers that existed in another.

Finally, federalism was an instrument for securing the nation's common good. The "aim of every political constitution," Madison explained, was first "to obtain for rulers men who possess most wisdom to discern, and most virtue to pursue, the common good of the society" and then "to take the most effectual precautions for keeping them virtuous whilst they continue to hold the public trust."[19] The structure of the "compound" republic would accomplish both those goals. Its larger population would produce more individuals who were truly "fit" for office; the wider availability of "fit" candidates would make elections "more likely to centre in men who possess the most attractive merit and the most diffusive and established characters"; and the larger electorate would make it "more difficult for unworthy candidates to practise with success the vicious arts by which elections are too often carried."[20] Similarly, the compound republic's structure of divided power and its multitude of conflicting interests would check, or at least severely limit, the ability of officeholders to pursue their own private interests, either "keeping them virtuous" or blocking their selfish inclinations and turning them reluctantly to the service of the public good.[21]

Federalism, then, was in its very nature an "instrument." It was premised on the assumption that individuals were diverse, self-interested, and faction-prone and that they would persistently be tempted to use the levels and branches of government for their advantage. "Remorse and shame are but too feeble restraints on interested individuals," Madison insisted,[22] and even carefully chosen words and phrases were only "parchment barriers" that could not stand consistently "against the encroaching spirit of power."[23] The remedy was to divide and counterpoise governmental powers in ways that led individual and factional interests to block and counteract one another. The "great security against a gradual concentration of the several powers in the same department, consists in giving to those who administer each department the necessary constitutional means and personal motives to resist encroachments of the others," Madison concluded. "Ambition must be made to counteract ambition."[24] In allocating governmental powers, Hamilton maintained, "the best security for the fidelity of mankind is to make their interest coincide with their duty."[25]

While the structure was designed to harness those pressures, however, it could hardly cabin them rigidly or completely. First, in attempting to use the institutions of American government, the ambitious and self-interested would commonly seek to stretch the powers of the institutions they controlled, and even the most virtuous and well-intended would find themselves unable to define the exact reaches of the powers that belonged to the various levels and branches. The structure's doubly blurred boundaries would usually allow the former to find some basis on which to justify their actions, while it would confound the latter with genuine problems of uncertainty.[26] Second, while the idea of making officeholders' "interests coincide with their duty" was clever, it was also unreliable. The "interests" of both individuals and factions arose from sources external to political institutions, and those driving outside sources would press relentlessly against the confining limits of governmental duty. Further, most individuals—especially in the larger legislative branch and the multiplying and expanding departments of the executive—would have but little personal stake in the "proper" duties of their branches, while the lure of constitutionally defensible but interest-serving accommodations within, without, and across the branches would constantly generate temptations. Regardless of governmental architecture, in other words, personal interests could not be made to "coincide" automatically or inevitably with institutional duties. Third, though designed to enable its components to "check" and "balance" one another, the federal structure could not determine—nor the Constitution prescribe—the specific nature of the proper responsive actions that the different levels and branches should take on any given issue. As each of the structure's components exercised discretion in performing its role, so each enjoyed discretion in determining in what ways and to what extent it would respond to the actions of the other components. Each component, in fact, had discretion to determine whether it would, or should, seek to "check" and "balance"—that is, block or counter—another component or whether some other type of response— acquiescing, deflecting, modifying, supporting, or compounding—might, in any particular circumstance, constitute a more useful or desirable course of action.[27] For the operations of the federal structure, in other words, "checking" and "balancing" turned out to be radically underinclusive options, idealized functions that proved to be only subcategories of a far more general category, that of the discretionary and loosely cabined—and therefore faction-prone—institutional response.

With the almost immediate appearance of political parties, common control of two or more branches of the national government often counseled against "checking" and urged, instead, cooperation and facilitation, varieties of responses rendered easy to justify by the Constitution's doubly blurred lines dividing state and national powers. Indeed, neutralizing the system of checks and balances became one of the key—if often unacknowledged—functions of political parties. Federalist control of the three branches of the national government in the 1790s encouraged expansive exercises of national powers, as did similar multibranch party control in the hands of the Jeffersonian Republicans, the Republican Party during and after the Civil War, the Democratic Party in the 1930s and again in the 1960s, and the Republican Party at the beginning of the twenty-first century.[28] Thus, at varying times and under varying conditions, the self-interest that the founders feared combined with the nation's changing politics to deflect or negate the "checking" function and to inspire, instead, cooperative and facilitating interactions among the three national branches. Frequently, those supportive actions realigned and stretched the powers of the structure's components; and those changes, in turn, radiated out and generated an unpredictable variety of responsive counterpressures, adaptations, and innovations by the structure's other components. Over time, that continuous dynamic of factional and institutional interaction reshaped the powers and practices of those interconnected components and remolded the operations of the working federal system.[29]

Getting It Done

As the new system of government began to creak into motion, the founders immediately divided over the scope and use of its powers. As Washington's secretary of the treasury, Hamilton moved methodically to strengthen the central government, while Jefferson and Madison quickly grew dubious and then opposed. As disagreements accumulated and sharpened, the Virginians rallied an opposition, forged an alliance between the middle and southern states, and carried the election of 1800 for Jefferson.[30] The early-born battles of the 1790s helped establish the nation's new political system, setting patterns that persisted into the twenty-first century and demonstrating that the federal structure was not simply an instrument, but an instrument in its essence.

On a relatively high level, Madison's career illustrated the point. Understanding that the Constitution established no clear and complete division between federal and state power, he sought to tack wisely between commitments to nation and states as issues and circumstances dictated.[31] During the ratification debate he accepted the need for implied powers,[32] but during the battle over the Bank of the United States he rejected Hamilton's broad interpretation of the doctrine.[33] When he thought national power was being egregiously abused by the adoption of the Alien and Sedition Acts, he swung toward a "states' rights" position in the late 1790s. Subsequently, when the expiration of Hamilton's bank and the War of 1812 brought financial chaos to the young republic, he accepted a broader version of implied powers and, as president in 1816, signed the bill that established the second Bank of the United States.[34] Similarly, although he supported the rights of the states, when South Carolina claimed authority to nullify federal law, Madison supported Andrew Jackson's strong nationalist position, rejecting the theory of nullification and insisting that established constitutional procedures provided the only remedies available to disaffected states.[35] Over the course of his career, Madison was prepared, as he had informed George Washington in 1787, to accept "any middle ground" that would "support a due supremacy of the national authority" while leaving local authorities in control "wherever they can be subordinately useful."[36] He understood that the location of that "middle ground" was necessarily changing and that only wisdom and judgment enabled people to place it properly at any given time and on any given issue. He understood, too, that in the end the location of that "middle ground" depended on what was truly "useful," an instrumentalist standard par excellence but hardly a precise or predetermined one.

While the nation's subsequent history was complex and varied, its experience revealed three distinctive traits that marked the operations of the federal structure, all of which illustrated its intrinsically instrumental nature. The first was the flexibility and opportunism that parties, groups, interests, states, and regions demonstrated in selecting and applying its "principles." Those who embraced one side of the nation-state divide at some times and on some issues found themselves at other times and on other issues embracing the opposite side.[37] It took little more than a decade, for example, for the nation's first two political parties to reverse their original positions. Opposing the bill to fund Jefferson's Louisiana Purchase, Federalists in Congress abandoned their Hamiltonian roots and denied that the Constitution gave the national government authority to acquire "foreign" territories. Countering their rival's about-face with one of their own, Republicans defended Jefferson's Embargo Act by invoking Hamilton's argument that the Constitution granted the national government broad and implied powers.[38]

Almost a century ago Arthur Schlesinger Sr. identified the classic macropattern. In the 1790s Jefferson and Madison formulated what became the antinationalist doctrine of "states' rights" on behalf of the southern states, but in 1814 Hamilton's old Federalist Party seized the doctrine after losing control of the central government and retaining power only in New England. Then, in succession, South Carolina's nullifiers revived it in the late 1820s; northern antislavery forces turned it to use in the 1840s; and southern secessionists reclaimed it during the following decade.[39] The repeated shifts demonstrated the fundamental truth that Madison had adumbrated: federalism was naturally and intrinsically an instrument of faction.

Such diachronic inconsistencies, moreover, were commonly matched by synchronic ones. Parties, groups, interests, states, and regions took inconsistent positions on different federalism issues at the same time. Jefferson was a classic example. He held aloft the banners of both strict construction and states' rights throughout his presidency, but he also used the powers of his office to wage an undeclared war with Tripoli, arrange the controversial Louisiana Purchase, and persuade Congress to adopt the dubious and ill-fated Embargo Act, which shut off most of the nation's international trade as a response to the war between England and France. Even more striking and cynical, when the Connecticut state courts refused to take action against his Federalist critics, Jefferson acquiesced in, if he did not encourage, the use of the national courts to prosecute them under a controverted federal criminal common-law jurisdiction—a jurisdiction that Jefferson himself condemned both publicly and privately as illegitimate and unconstitutional.[40]

Similar examples abound. Justice Stephen J. Field passionately defended the authority of the states but acknowledged that he and the Court had repeatedly invoked a "federal common law" on those occasions when they found it desirable "to control a conflicting law of a State."[41] Justice David J. Brewer invoked the principles of federalism in denying national lawmaking power to the Congress he distrusted, but he abandoned those principles when he wished to confirm the same national lawmaking power in the federal judiciary he admired.[42] Justice Felix Frankfurter deferred to the states and fought incorporation of the Bill of Rights under the Fourteenth Amendment, but he readily agreed to subject the states to the command of an incorporated Establishment Clause when issues of religion came before the Court.[43] The five "profederalism" justices on the Rehnquist Court set aside the results of state proceedings and asserted national judicial power to decide the presidential election of 2000.[44]

Strikingly obvious was the behavior of the South. Antebellum southern constitutionalists embraced the doctrine of "state sovereignty," but in the 1850s they nonetheless maintained that the Constitution made slavery a national institution and gave the U.S. government the power—and the duty—to protect it in every state and territory across the land.[45] Then, with secession, the South jettisoned its commitment to states' rights and immediately erected for itself a powerful central government. The "all-encompassing economic and social controls of the Confederacy were in fact so extensive," Richard Franklin Bensel noted, "that they call into question standard interpretations of southern opposition to the expansion of federal power in both the antebellum and post-Reconstruction periods." It was not any general principles of federalism that explained the South's frequent opposition to centralized power before and after the war, he concluded, but its fear of "the anticipated deleterious impact of the northern industrial program on the plantation South."[46] The opinions of southern state judges throughout the nineteenth century confirmed that conclusion. On issues of slavery and race they remained rigid and consistent, while on other questions involving federalism they "shifted depending on the political universe" and "varied depending on the political and social context."[47]

Similarly, ideas about the companion doctrine of separation of powers were also refashioned regularly as political contexts changed and the branch affinities of partisans shifted. In the twentieth century, for example, a series of activist presidential reformers—Theodore and Franklin Roosevelt, Woodrow Wilson, Harry S Truman, John F. Kennedy, and Lyndon Johnson—led progressives and liberals to herald the desirability of a strong and energetic executive. After the election of Richard M. Nixon, however, those groups began to warn against a dangerous "imperial presidency" and to call for serious restrictions on the powers of the office. Moving in the opposite direction, after 1968 conservatives—who had previously warned ominously against the abuses of executive power—showed a rapidly declining concern about its dangers as they came to dominate the office. Indeed, comfortably in power during the 1980s they embraced the attitude that progressives and liberals had recently abandoned and developed theories to support the concept of an exceptionally powerful "unitary" executive. The same pattern of politically inspired reversal was equally evident in attitudes toward the federal judiciary. Progressives and liberals attacked the national courts for half a century before the New Deal but began defending them passionately after they embraced liberal values in the years after 1937. Conversely, conservatives praised the national courts lavishly over the course of the same half-century but began to denounce them fiercely after the "Roosevelt Revolution." By the 1980s the wheel was turning once again. As Republicans came to dominate the federal judiciary and reorient its jurisprudence, they again grew content with the uses of national judicial power, while liberals and progressives turned sharply critical and began praising the virtues of "judicial restraint."[48] Finally, although attitudes toward Congress were, like Congress itself, more complex and conflicted, both liberals and conservatives tailored their views as their political fortunes in the national branches fluctuated. From 1969 to 1994, for example, liberals tended to praise Congress because they needed it to check Republican presidents,[49] while Republicans took the opposite tack. In 1988, for example, Congressman Newt Gingrich charged that the nation faced danger not from an "imperial presidency"—the executive branch then resting securely in the hands of Republican Ronald Reagan—but rather from "an imperial Congress reigned over by an imperial Speaker," that is, a Congress dominated at the time by Democrats.[50]

The structure's second distinctive historical trait was its responsiveness to attitudes about race.[51] Slavery haunted the debates at the Philadelphia Convention,[52] influenced the Constitution's structure and determined many of its provisions,[53] and—as Schlesinger's classic account of the "states' rights" doctrine demonstrated—largely determined ideas about federal-state relations during the nation's first eight decades. The pervasive impact of race, however, hardly ended with the abolition of slavery. Indeed, racial attitudes continued to shape both general ideas about the federal structure and major decisions of the Supreme Court determining national and state powers.[54] After Congress prohibited racial discrimination in public facilities in the Civil Rights Act of 1875, for example, Justice Joseph P. Bradley privately declared that it "can never be endured that the white shall be compelled to lodge and eat and sit with the negro."[55] Seven years later he wrote the Court's opinion in the *Civil Rights Cases* that invalidated the statute.[56] Woodrow Wilson, a distinguished and progressive scholar, was equally infuriated by national efforts to supervise congressional elections in the South. Such actions, he charged, imposed "subordination" on the states, "impair[ed] the self-respect of state officials," created "hateful privileges," and gave vent to "the very ugliest side of federal supremacy."[57] Coming from a man who prided himself on his professionalism as an objective political scientist, such extreme and emotional language seemed explicable only in the context of his intensely held views about "southern rights," that is, his belief that southern whites had the "right" to disenfranchise and segregate their black co-citizens. Indeed, after his election to the presidency in 1912, Wilson instituted formal racial segregation in some departments of the national government.[58]

Similarly, during the 1930s and 1940s white southerners continued to use ideas of federalism and local control to preserve their region's system of racial segregation and oppression. In Congress, for example, they repeatedly limited the reach of major national reform legislation—Social Security, the National Labor Relations Act, the Fair Labor Standards Act, and the G.I. Bill of rights—to preserve the "southern way of life." They minimized the benefits that the new programs conferred on blacks and ensured that their administration would conform to "local values," that is, that local officials would be allowed to operate the programs in racially discriminatory ways.[59]

The long struggle over race that followed *Brown v. Board of Education*[60] illustrated the same truth. Condemning *Brown* for "creating chaos and confusion," ninety-six southern members of Congress issued a "manifesto" indicting the Supreme Court for violating "the reserved rights of the States and the people."[61] It was race, however, not "principles of federalism," that fired their anger and shaped their views.[62] Responding to *Brown,* for example, James Jackson Kilpatrick condemned the "deification of the Federal government," deplored "the corruption of a constitutional Union," and invoked the theories of John C. Calhoun in an effort to revive ideas of interposition and nullification. Kilpatrick, however, had the virtue of candor, for he refused to mask the implacable racism that determined his views about federalism. Deploying every derogatory racial stereotype available, he proclaimed the overriding need to prevent "widespread racial amalgamation and a debasement of the society as a whole."[63] State sovereignty, Kilpatrick maintained, was the essential instrument for achieving those goals. No one captured the fundamental truth about federalism, the South, and race more directly than the liberal southerner Charles L. Black Jr. "The South fought to keep slavery, and lost. Then it tried the Black Codes, and lost," he explained. "Then it looked around for something else and found segregation."[64] Racism was the engine; federalism merely the device.

Indeed, *Brown* demonstrated the power of race to shape concerns and assumptions at the highest levels of constitutional thinking, for it spurred lawyers and judges to reconsider fundamental issues about the Supreme Court's role and authority. For much of the nation's history, especially after the Civil War, constitutional thinkers commonly and the well-to-do classes almost uniformly had defended the Court with what might be called a "counter-majoritarian boast." As Hamilton had originally phrased it, an important part of the Court's role was to protect "the minor party in the community" from the "ill humors" of "a majority."[65] After *Brown*, however, that minority-protective role became newly suspect to many Americans who insisted that the Court's desegregation rulings were inconsistent with the principle of majority rule, a principle they put forward with a new ardor as the fundamental and seemingly unqualified principle of American democracy. On that principle, judicial review appeared a dangerous and "deviant institution in the American democracy," and even the Court's defenders came to see its decisions as posing a vastly perplexing "counter-majoritarian difficulty."[66] It seems fair to say that the history of American federalism could not possibly be understood without recognizing the omnipresent and compelling racial considerations that pervasively shaped its course.[67]

The structure's third distinctive historical trait was the sheer plasticity of its doubly blurred nature, the ease with which its principles and provisions could be adapted to the diverse and conflicting purposes that animated the nation's shifting politics over the centuries. It was a common and frequently repeated idea, for example, that the Constitution divided federal and state authority into two separate "spheres." The states, Madison had written in the Thirty-Ninth *Federalist,* were "no more subject, within their respective spheres, to the general authority, than the general authority is subject to them, within its own sphere."[68] That idea, however, like other elements of American federalism, was highly malleable. In their efforts to limit congressional power, for example, the Rehnquist Court's five "profederalism" justices used it to expand state immunity from national authority. The constitutional structure of separate federal and state "spheres," they maintained, "preserves the sovereign status of the States" and, consequently, barred Congress from using its Article I powers to subject the states to private suits for damages. Not surprisingly, the Court's four dissenters had little trouble turning the sphere idea to support the opposite conclusion. "The point is that matters subject to federal law are within the federal sphere," they pointed out, "and so the States are subject to the general authority where such matters are concerned."[69]

Those conflicting interpretations of the "separate spheres" idea illustrated the pliability of the Constitution's federalism principles, a pliability that Americans had exploited since the nation's founding. Henry Clay, for example, born in Virginia in 1777 and sent to Congress from Kentucky in

1806, avidly embraced what became known as the "principles of '98," the extreme states' rights propositions Jefferson and Madison set forth in the Virginia and Kentucky Resolutions. Clay told the House of Representatives in 1818 that he had "imbibed those constitutional principles" as a young man and followed them throughout his career. Those principles, he continued, were entirely consistent with his proposed "American System," the elaborate project to spur American economic development with protective tariffs, federal funding for internal improvements, and a strong Bank of the United States. If a construction of the Constitution was beneficent "in all its effects and consequences," he declared, then it was consistent with the "principles of '98."[70] Thus, in Clay's hands the agrarian-based, states' rights constitutional theory that Jefferson and Madison had shaped to oppose Federalist centralization was magically transformed into a handy justification for an elaborate program of federally supported and commercial-oriented nationalism that would have made Hamilton beam with pride.

The southerner John C. Calhoun was equally adept. When he opposed President Andrew Jackson's bill to distribute excess funds from the U.S. Treasury to the states, he relied on federalism to undergird his position. Such a distribution plan, Calhoun insisted, was a tool of presidential aggrandizement that would enhance national power and corrupt the states. When he reversed himself, however, and supported a similar distribution proposal that the anti-Jackson Clay subsequently advanced, Calhoun was still able to anchor his position on solid federalism grounds. Then, he insisted that the distribution plan would increase the interest of the states in serving as vigilant "sentinels of economy" and thereby expand their role in monitoring the operations of the national government.[71]

Calhoun, in fact, towers as a paradigmatic figure in the history of American federalism. By the 1830s he stood as the unquestioned champion of the South's antebellum doctrine of state sovereignty and sharply limited national powers. In 1810, however, when he began his political career in the House of Representatives, he had been an ardent nationalist. Then, feeling no threat to the South and its peculiar institution, Calhoun had enthusiastically supported war with Great Britain, a protective tariff, the second Bank of the United States, the use of federal funds to finance internal improvements, and a broad construction of the Necessary and Proper

Clause. When Madison, in his last presidential act in 1817, vetoed a bill that provided federal funding for internal improvements, he vetoed a bill that Calhoun had pushed through the House.[72] Between 1810 and 1830, of course, not a word of the Constitution had been changed.

Indeed, Calhoun's monumental accomplishment as a constitutional theorist lay neither in articulating a clear line between federal and state power—which he failed to do—nor in protecting the slaveholding South that he so dearly loved—an effort in which he proved spectacularly unsuccessful. Rather, his distinctive achievement lay in devising, and elaborately defending, a constitutional theory with an institutional mechanism that could produce operationally definitive answers to specific "federalism" questions while, at the same time, guaranteeing as a practical matter the exact substantive result he desired. With respect to the American federal structure, that was the seal of his theoretical genius.

Twentieth-century figures, of course, proved equally adept. Justice George Sutherland, a conservative Republican from Utah, believed passionately in limited government and a substantive Tenth Amendment. He also believed that the United States should play a strong and aggressive international role and that the president should have ample power to conduct the nation's foreign policy with vigor. He resolved the resulting constitutional tension between his ideas of limited government and his desire for a robust executive power by distinguishing neatly "between the powers of the federal government in respect of foreign or external affairs and those in respect of domestic or internal affairs." The two types of powers, he maintained, were "different, both in respect of their origin and their nature."[73] Consequently, all traditional constitutional principles that imposed restraints on national power in "internal" affairs—such as the doctrines of reserved rights and delegated powers—were simply irrelevant to the nation's "external" powers. Like Clay and Calhoun, Sutherland showed that federalism could be molded to any purpose or policy. He freed national executive power where he wished it free and shackled it where he wished it shackled.[74]

Modern liberals were no less adroit. In the 1960s, Justice William Brennan, an outspoken liberal from New Jersey, argued that the federal system was no longer sufficient to enforce the Constitution's guarantees of individual rights. Repeatedly, he insisted that the federal judiciary was the "primary" institution charged by the Constitution with "vindicating" the fundamental rights of Americans.[75] Federalism, he noted, was a "vague" concept lacking in "content."[76] As national politics and the Court's membership shifted rightward, however, Brennan responded deftly. In 1977 he proclaimed himself "a devout believer" in "our concept of federalism"[77] and called on the state courts to become the new "Guardians of Individual Rights" by construing their own constitutions with breadth and vigor.[78] Brennan's commitment to liberal politics and individual rights remained constant, but the processes of political change compelled him to find new instruments within the federal structure to serve his purposes. When he found the instrument he needed not in the federal courts but in the courts of the states, he was easily able to shape the doctrinal grounds necessary to support state judicial independence and authority.[79]

Clay. Calhoun. Sutherland. Brennan. Masters of American federalism.

5

FEDERALISM AS CONTINGENT

Although the founders established a federal structure and set out certain guiding principles and limiting provisions, they also summoned succeeding generations to adapt their creation to the demands of an unknown future. "'Tis time only," Hamilton ventured, "that can mature and perfect so compound a system."[1] Madison put the point more cautiously. "All new laws, though penned with the greatest technical skill, and passed on the fullest and most mature deliberation," he explained, "are considered as more or less obscure and equivocal until their meaning be liquidated and ascertained by a series of particular discussions and adjudications."[2] It was essential to design a frame of government capable of adapting to the demands of an unknowable future. "In framing a system which we wish to last for ages," Madison counseled the Philadelphia Convention, "we shd. not lose sight of the changes which ages will produce."[3]

The federal structure was contingent, however, not merely because many of the Constitution's provisions were "obscure and equivocal" but also for two additional and equally fundamental reasons. First, the Constitution incorporated principles designed to ensure that its governmental system would evolve over time. Some changes it mandated, and others it authorized. Second, the Constitution embraced many provisions that invited or necessitated pragmatic adaptations to changing times and conditions. Moral ideals such as "Justice" and "Liberty,"[4] collective purposes such as "common Defence" and "general Welfare,"[5] and empirically referential concepts such as "Commerce" and "Progress of Science and useful

Arts"[6] all infused the document with inherent principles of vitality. The Constitution was a charter designed to evolve as much as to endure; indeed, it was designed to endure precisely because it was authorized to evolve.

So, too, was the federal system. Both the "federal and State governments are in fact but different agents and trustees of the people," Madison explained, and therefore the people were to determine whether either level of government would "be able to enlarge its sphere of jurisdiction at the expense of the other." As the "confidence" of the people shifted between the two levels, they would expand or contract the "sphere of jurisdiction" of each as they thought desirable. "Truth, no less than decency, requires that the event in every case should be supposed to depend on the sentiments and sanction of their common constituents."[7] The Constitution's inherent principles of vitality—its many mandates, authorizations, and invitations to change—gave "the people" numerous openings and opportunities to reshape the spheres of jurisdiction in their federal structure. The "framers and ratifiers created institutional space for pluralism, and they left much of the Constitution's construction to normal politics," Daniel J. Hulsebosch wrote. "Consequently, there were institutional pockets in which multiple understandings of the Constitution could develop at any given time and that gave ample room for changes in those understandings over time."[8]

Adaptations Mandated and Authorized

The Constitution established a governmental structure premised on the necessity and desirability of certain kinds of change. It mandated regular elections for president, vice president, and members of Congress,[9] and it provided that representation in the House of Representatives and the Electoral College be apportioned among the states "according to their respective Numbers." Moreover, in a striking requirement, it mandated a decennial census to ensure that representation in the two bodies would be regularly reapportioned as the nation's population grew in numbers and shifted in location.[10] Thus, it offered sparsely settled regions and rising social interests opportunities to increase their influence in the institutions of government. All of those provisions guaranteed that national policy would be subject to periodic shifts and innovations.

Further, the Constitution ensured that those shifts and innovations would reverberate through the national government and reshape its operations. Periodic and popular elections were in varying ways to determine the composition of the executive and legislative branches, and the executive and the Senate were in turn to determine the composition of the judiciary. Changing popular views and values, if manifested in relatively consistent voting patterns over several elections, would consequently find voice in all three national branches and eventually place on the Supreme Court judges who shared those new views and assumptions and who would infuse them into the nation's constitutional law.[11] Thus, with unpredictable spurts, setbacks, and lags, the law of the Constitution itself would evolve in rough accord with the changing views and values of the American people.

The Constitution, moreover, made the three national branches subject to substantial and largely discretionary restructuring by the legislature.[12] It gave Congress sweeping powers to organize itself and to conduct its internal business as it saw fit. Subject to certain prescriptions about basic structure and membership, it authorized the legislative branch to control the election of its members, judge their suitability for office, provide times and places for assembling, establish its own internal rules of procedure, provide funding for itself and its members, and create such supportive agencies and institutions as were necessary for its operations.[13] With respect to the executive branch, the Constitution created only two offices, those of "President" and "Vice President."[14] All other structural elements it left to Congress. It conferred on the legislature the power to decide what "Executive Departments" were necessary, organize them as it wished, and determine which offices and positions in those departments should be subject to senatorial approval and which should lie within the discretion of the president, the courts, or the "Heads of Departments."[15] Indeed, when the First Congress established the three original executive departments— those for foreign affairs, treasury, and war—it structured them differently, making the secretary of the treasury in effect an agent of the legislature by requiring that he provide certain information to the Congress and submit specified reports at the request of either chamber.[16] With respect to the judiciary, the Constitution mandated the existence of only "one supreme Court" and but a single office, that of "Chief Justice."[17] As with the executive branch, it left all other structural arrangements to Congress. It granted the legislature broad authority to staff and structure the Supreme Court and to make "Exceptions" to its constitutionally ordained appellate jurisdiction.[18] It conferred even wider authority to create whatever lower courts the legislature wished and to organize their operations, select their locations, and fix their jurisdiction.[19] Those provisions contemplated a wide range of possible structural variations in the nation's legal system and, consequently, a wide range of possibilities in developing and enforcing national law as times and needs evolved.[20] Indeed, the provisions concerning all three branches, especially the executive and judiciary, contemplated a national government that was organizationally flexible, open to periodic and substantial alterations, and subject to the controlling and largely discretionary judgment of the legislature.

In addition, the Constitution authorized the admission of new states,[21] a reflection of both the founders' belief that their "empire of liberty" should expand and their intention that the federal structure should evolve in size and operation. New states would inevitably introduce new issues and interests, reduce the power of the original thirteen states, and disrupt old sectional alliances and create new ones.[22] Still, in spite of scattered opposition, the founders adopted provisions for organizing the nation's territories into new states for admission to the Union as equals. "We are representatives, sir, not merely of the present age but of future times," James Wilson told the Philadelphia Convention: "not merely of the territory along the sea-coast, but of regions immensely extended westward."[23]

The results flowing from those provisions reverberated through the nation's history and helped spur an ever-widening circle of changes in the relationship of the states both to one another and to the different federal branches. Most obviously, it was the battle over the admission of new states, whether they would be free or slave, that generated an unbridgeable gulf between the sections, and it may well have been the admission of three fertile cotton and sugar states—Louisiana (1812), Mississippi (1817), and Alabama (1819)—that ultimately forged the South into the aggressive and intransigent "slave power" that northerners came to hate and fear.[24] As ex–Supreme Court justice Benjamin Curtis declared, by 1861 the territorial question had become one of "such stupendous magnitude that the national experience must be staked on it."[25] Westward expansion and the admission of new states culminated in the Civil War, and that in turn led to the three Reconstruction amendments that fundamentally altered the constitutional relationship between the states and the national government.

Finally, the Constitution authorized its own amendment,[26] a provision that represented a radical innovation in the theory of constitutionalism and demonstrated the founders' acceptance of the idea that changes in government and society were not only unavoidable but also desirable.[27] Indeed, the founders' embrace of change was apparent when the First Congress approved twelve amendments, and the states swiftly ratified ten. Over the next two centuries Americans added seventeen more that covered a range of subjects but fell into three principal groups.[28] The first, the three Civil War amendments, abolished slavery, created rights of national citizenship, and barred the states from denying the vote "on account of race, color, or previous condition of servitude."[29] The second, the Progressive Era amendments, authorized a federal income tax, provided for the direct election of senators, instituted national prohibition, and barred the states from denying women the vote.[30] The third group, from the twentieth-century era of "the Sixties," extended the right to vote in a variety of ways. The amendments allowed citizens of the District of Columbia to cast ballots for president, prohibited poll taxes and similar franchise-denying devices, and lowered the minimum voting age to eighteen.[31]

Collectively, the amendments expanded national rights and powers broadly, but they also failed—as had the original Constitution—to identify with precision the resulting scope of many of those rights and powers. The Fourteenth Amendment transformed the constitutional relationship between states and nation most broadly and profoundly, for example, but from the moment of its adoption judges and commentators disputed its scope and offered the widest possible variety of interpretations. The Supreme Court was uncertain and inconsistent in construing it,[32] and the one principle on which the justices agreed with relative consistency—that it reached only "state action"[33]—posited a line between "public" and "private" behavior that was both uncertain and unstable.[34] Further, the

Fourteenth Amendment and six of the others expressly granted Congress power to enforce their provisions by "appropriate" legislation,[35] a criterion that was as elastic as one could imagine. Small wonder, then, that the Court swung wildly in its decisions.[36] In one notorious episode, it insisted on the need to remain "loyal to the ideals and dreams of Our Federalism" that were established in 1787[37] and then, the very next year, proclaimed that the Civil War amendments had caused "a vast transformation from the concepts of federalism that had prevailed in the late 18th century."[38] Although the amendments radically broadened national rights and powers, they confirmed that the federal structure remained doubly blurred as well as contingent.

Adaptations Invited

Beyond the Constitution's provisions that mandated or authorized change, many others invited change. Some incorporated fundamental moral and political concepts that had evolved over more than two millennia and would, as the founders knew, continue to evolve: "Justice," "Union," "Liberty," "property," "public use," "Citizens," "due process," "equal protection," "Privileges and Immunities," and "the Obligation of Contracts."[39] Other provisions established collective goals whose meanings and requirements would necessarily vary over time: "common Defence," "general Welfare," "domestic Tranquility," and "Progress of Science and useful Arts."[40] Finally, many established standards or categories that required practical judgments that could only be made with reference to specific historical contexts and conditions: "imminent," "excessive," "on account of," "unreasonable," "cruel and unusual," "absolutely necessary," "Commerce" carried on "among" states and nations, and legislation "appropriate" to protect identified rights and purposes.[41] Such words and provisions guided, empowered, and limited state and national governments, but each was subject to changes in meaning and application as American society developed. Such altered meanings and applications would inevitably reshape the operations of the federal structure.[42]

The story of the nation's historical development and the Constitution's consequent doctrinal evolution has often been told. From a small, rural, scattered, and predominantly Anglo-Protestant society huddled along the shores of the Atlantic Ocean,[43] the colonies grew into a centralized commercial, industrial, and technological colossus that spanned a continent, embraced an astonishingly heterogeneous population of three hundred million people, produced goods in varieties and wealth in amounts that stunned the imagination, and extended its military might, economic power, and cultural influence to the most distant regions of the globe. It was the vibrant terms of the Constitution, both ideal and pragmatic, that allowed Americans to adapt their federal structure to that sweeping transformation and to bear their system of republican self-government through the decades and into the radically transformed world of the twenty-first century.[44]

The course of that evolution was long and complex. Massive economic changes spurred by scientific discovery, technological innovation, bureaucratic organization, and capital concentration transformed the United States into an industrialized and urbanized nation with an open, lucrative, and expanding national market.[45] Law stimulated and helped direct the changes, but the changes also pressed against the institutions of American law and government, compelling them at all levels to adapt to new circumstances and challenges.[46] As industrialization and urbanization disrupted established patterns of life, people across the land found themselves in an increasingly interdependent world where social causality no longer seemed traceable to local forces. Rather, distant institutions and events appeared ever more commonly to determine the social and economic conditions of daily life.[47] Those developments eroded and then destroyed the "island communities" of the eighteenth and early nineteenth centuries, linking the fates of scattered localities ever more closely to the fates of distant entities and remote forces.[48] When Mississippi responded to the depression of 1837 by repudiating its financial obligations, for example, European lenders quickly retaliated by refusing to grant a congressionally authorized loan to the U.S. government.[49] Economic expansion and changes in state laws encouraged the rise of national corporations, and the corporate form enabled promoters and investors to "lock in" capital and thereby create powerful and enduring legal entities—institutions whose immortal status, bureaucratized administrative apparatus, and wide-ranging influence over politics, culture, and social life gave them the capacity to rival governments in directing the course of national affairs.[50] In reaction, drawing on the inspiration of science and a growing belief in the power of expertise, Americans increasingly came to see government as an instrument capable of ameliorating the harsh excesses of industrialization and rationally improving the conditions of life for all.[51] A nationalized market, a centralizing corporate economy, and a burgeoning faith in the possibilities of scientific regulation and administration inexorably shifted power, politics, and attention to the national level while profoundly altering ideas about both the proper limits of government action generally and the desirability of expanded efforts at the national level in particular.[52]

Those changes reoriented relationships in the federal structure. The processes of national "state building" accelerated after the Civil War and generated new laws, ideas, doctrines, and institutions that realigned and further centralized American government.[53] From a disjointed government "of courts and parties,"[54] the United States developed gradually and unevenly into a centralized modern nation-state with rapidly expanding administrative capacities. "Undoubtedly the recent economic development of the country, particularly the development of the last two decades," Woodrow Wilson wrote in 1908, "has obliterated many boundaries, made many interests national and common, which until our own day were separate and local."[55] By the end of World War I the relationships among the levels and branches had been transformed. "In short, modern American state building progressed," Stephen Skowronek declared, "by replacing courts and parties with a national bureaucracy."[56] When Jefferson became president, the federal government had some twenty-five hundred nonmilitary employees; two centuries later it had more than 2.7 million, a thousandfold increase.[57]

In the eighteenth century, when "Commerce" remained in many ways "local" and "Welfare" was seldom functionally "general," Congress held limited authority over both. As the world changed, however, Americans were compelled to apply the contingent provisions of the Constitution to unimagined and revolutionary new realities. Sweeping social changes made commerce functionally national and the people's welfare effectively "general," and in that new context those contingent provisions authorized Congress to act. The Progressive activist Jane Addams spoke for a new generation that came of age in the late nineteenth century when she noted that "the center of [reform] effort had shifted to Washington." The "sanitary regulation of sweatshops by city officials, and a careful enforcement of factory legislation by state factory inspectors will not avail," she explained, "unless each city and State shall be able to pass and enforce a code of comparatively uniform legislation." The nationalization of the economy meant that higher safety and welfare standards could be effective only if they applied across the land, and thus improved conditions could be achieved "only by federal legislation."[58] John Marshall's landmark opinion in *Gibbons v. Ogden*,[59] which had first sketched the reach of the commerce power, made "the scope of federal power turn upon facts in the world,"[60] and a half-century later the Court announced that congressional powers were sufficient to "keep pace with the progress of the country, and adapt themselves to the new developments of time and circumstances."[61] Such a statement, then-professor Felix Frankfurter declared in 1936, demonstrated the Court's "recognition that policy, especially in the economic aspects of modern legislation, is largely a function of fact."[62]

The statements of Marshall and Frankfurter echoed Madison's advice in the *Federalist* about the "extensive information" and "knowledge of the affairs, and even of the laws, of all the States" that would be necessary to enact wise federal legislation. "How can foreign trade be properly regulated by uniform laws, without some acquaintance with the commerce, the ports, the usages, and the regulations of the different States?" he asked. "How can the trade between the different States be duly regulated without some knowledge of their relative situations in these and other respects?"[63] As those "relative situations"—the real-world conditions that the Constitution referenced—changed, so too did the meaning and application of its contingent provisions.

As the perceived "facts" of social and economic life grew increasingly interrelated and nationalized, then, the reach of federal power necessarily expanded. While as late as 1869 the Supreme Court held to the doctrine that the Constitution delegated no "police power" to the federal government,[64] that proposition began to crumble in the late nineteenth century. As Americans came to recognize that many of the social and moral evils they perceived transcended state lines and could therefore be dealt with effectively only by national action, Congress responded by using its authority over taxing, interstate commerce, and the postal system to combat them. Gradually, its varied efforts came to be recognized as proper exercises of what was, in effect if not in name, a national "police power." Because congressional power over interstate commerce was "complete in itself," the Court declared in 1913, the national legislature could "adopt not only means necessary but convenient to its exercise, and the means may have the quality of police regulations."[65] By World War I Congress had extended the reach of its regulatory measures—with the Court's repeated approval—to such matters as liquor, gambling, prostitution, diseased livestock, and the labeling of food and drugs.[66]

When the Great Depression brought an even more acute appreciation of the interconnectedness of twentieth-century life, the Supreme Court accepted the same reality. It construed the commerce power to reach any activity that, in the aggregate, had some significant effect on interstate commerce,[67] and it construed the "general Welfare" clause to sanction massive new federal taxing and spending programs.[68] The "concept of the general welfare," it announced in 1937, could not be "static."[69] As the Rehnquist Court readily acknowledged, "our interpretation of the Commerce Clause has changed as our Nation has developed."[70]

As the nation's economic transformation proceeded, other complex developments compounded its massive and rippling social effects. Changes in demographics, immigration patterns, cultural assumptions, social and economic mobility, and mass communications technology as well as pressures arising from wars and foreign involvements combined to generate powerful social movements and underwrite sweeping shifts in public attitudes on such fundamental subjects as race, gender, family, religion, ethnicity, and sexuality. Challenging older attitudes and sometimes establishing radical new ones, those profound and invariably contested developments contributed to reshaping the nation's values and thereby redirecting its politics.[71]

As Americans adapted to those changes in complex and varied ways, many of the Constitution's pivotal terms slowly took on new meanings and generated new implications.[72] "The great generalities of the constitution," Judge Benjamin N. Cardozo of the New York Court of Appeals acknowledged in 1921, "have a content and a significance that vary from age to age."[73] Ideas of "justice" shifted from a focus on relationships between individuals to a focus on interrelationships among social groups and institutions. Increasing numbers of Americans began to accept the idea of "social justice," the belief that the conditions of modern society drew people into complex webs of interconnected relationships and that the responsibilities imposed on individuals to provide for themselves should be matched by new responsibilities assumed by society and its government to assist those unable to do so on their own.[74] Similarly, ideas of "liberty" expanded from narrow concepts about individual rights of autonomy, independence, and property to broader conceptions of "liberty" that recognized the wide variety and complex social nature of human "liberties." Those new conceptions heightened awareness of the practical problems that prevented many individuals from either exercising their formal legal rights in practice or achieving minimally satisfactory outcomes by doing so. Finally, ideas of "equality" shifted along two distinct but related lines. First, they moved beyond the limited category of white, property-holding males to include all individuals regardless of race, gender, ethnicity, economic status, and eventually sexual orientation. Second, they moved beyond the realm of formal legal rights and into the world of social practices where unequal conditions and differential social and economic power often underwrote extreme de facto inequalities and abuses.[75]

Infusing new significance into many of the Constitution's pivotal terms, and thereby expanding the scope of national authority and responsibility, those developments realigned the operations of the federal structure.[76] The most striking changes came in matters of race, an issue that had from the nation's beginning shaped the workings of the federal structure.[77] During the late nineteenth century a virulent antiblack racism—as well as other deeply embedded ideas about gender roles, marriage and family, and the intrinsic worth of various religious, racial, and ethnic groups—helped determine the significance of the Fourteenth Amendment by shaping dominant ideas about the nature of justice, liberty, and equality.[78] When the courts dealt with American Indians and peoples from Eastern Europe, Africa, and Asia, Lawrence Friedman wrote, "the popular idea of race was dominant."[79] During the twentieth century, however, new and different ideas about "race" and other fundamental concepts and categories began to alter American assumptions and eventually helped reshape conceptions of justice, liberty, and equality, continuing the social process of infusing new meanings into the Fourteenth Amendment and other constitutional provisions.[80]

Culminating in the decades after World War II, those developments brought major changes to the federal structure. They led the federal judiciary to expand the reach of the Due Process and Equal Protection clauses, impose more stringent limits on the states, and provide protections for many traditionally disfavored social groups.[81] Similarly, they led to broadened interpretations of congressional power that expanded national regulatory authority over ever-widening areas of social and economic life. Further, they helped induce Congress to enact, and both the executive and judicial branches of the national government to enforce, a monumental series of civil rights laws intended to secure for all Americans equal rights in both law and practice.[82] The efforts ended legalized racial segregation and disenfranchisement, while gradually expanding the rights of women, workers, homosexuals, the disabled, political dissidents, racial and ethnic minorities, non-mainstream religious groups, criminal defendants and prison inmates, and those injured or abused by unlawful government actions.[83]

The processes of social and political change proceeded relentlessly, however, and in the late twentieth century social and political groups that opposed many of those developments began to coalesce and gather strength. Fostered by turmoil at home and abroad, reacting against what they saw as the excesses and outrages of "the Sixties," and influenced by the growing power of evangelical Protestantism and a vigorous revival of neoclassical economics, many Americans turned toward a new "conservatism" that struggled to redefine the conceptions and remake the policies that had dominated the national government for the previous half-century. Heralding the goal of returning to the Constitution's "original meaning," they revived and broadened concepts of the "local" and construed the ideas of justice, liberty, and equality more narrowly in an effort to limit national power, restrict or terminate certain disfavored national "rights," strengthen and protect other and more favored rights, and curtail a variety of federal regulatory and social welfare programs.[84] Thus, at the beginning of the twenty-first century the nation's enduring debate over the meaning of the Constitution and the proper working of its federal structure—driven by new social, political, and ideological values and attitudes—shifted directions but continued unabated.

While the new "conservative" movement was able to effectuate some specific changes and reshape parts of the nation's constitutional law, it nonetheless failed—and for the most part made no serious effort—to reverse the more general social, economic, and cultural changes that had transformed relationships and operations in the federal structure since the early nineteenth century.[85] Indeed, its adherents embraced for the most part the very values and goals that had largely driven those complex processes of institutional transformation—libertarian individualism, market freedom, corporate enterprise, technological innovation, and the nationalization and globalization of the economy. In effect, the centralizing changes of the preceding two centuries had destroyed the life conditions that had underwritten earlier ideas about state and national powers. In the eighteenth century ordinary life had remained traditional, small-scale, rural, and local. Political attitudes and cultural understandings had been drawn largely from firsthand experience with a limited number of relatively familiar people, places, objects, events, and ideas.[86] An authentically lived experience in a particular location—and usually in a particular and well-recognized social status—had nourished distinctive local values and attitudes, and the composite of those lived experiences had given roughly determinable, if often implicit and contested, specifications to many of the Constitution's parchment lines that limned the boundaries between national and state power. Life, however, changed drastically. The nation's population grew in size and diversity while sustaining "extraordinarily high" levels of geographical mobility.[87] National and then global transportation and communications grew swift, while cultural meanings and political views were increasingly shaped by a rushing flood of information and disinformation from distant media about a seemingly infinite variety of people, places, objects, events, and ideas that were diverse, remote, confusing, and often strange or ominous. Traditional habits were disrupted, small-scale institutions displaced, rural life and attitudes supplanted, and local concerns subordinated. Cohesive forces weakened, closely knit communities fragmented, and distinctively "local" values and attitudes withered and blended into broader views that wider numbers of Americans shared.[88] As part of the process, the ingrained understandings that had underwritten certain generally accepted ideas about the boundaries between national and state authority shifted, faded, and often disappeared.

The point, of course, is not that differences between geographical locations ceased to exist. Rather, the point is threefold. First, those differences declined substantially in political importance while ever larger parts of American culture became relatively more homogenized. Second, the differences that existed and intruded into national politics—whether new or familiar—were generally not identified so much with "states" or even with specific localities as with identifiable social strata or distinctive population segments that could be found scattered across the land. Third, and most important for the purposes of understanding the changes that occurred in American federalism, those differences translated much less frequently and easily into any consistent set of prescriptions for a proper division between state and national power.

By the early twenty-first century, then, the lived experience of most Americans made "federalism" an increasingly abstract and unrooted concept. Ambiguous and contingent from the beginning, and ever more remotely linked to the early days of the nation's lengthening past, the lines of division between state and national power had become ever more indistinct and ever more easily manipulable. The true nature of the federal structure—its doubly blurred, fractionated, instrumental, and contingent character—had never been so apparent.

II

CONSEQUENTIAL DYNAMICS

6

KALEIDOSCOPIC POLITICS

The federal structure's four intrinsic characteristics—that it was doubly blurred, fractionated, instrumental, and contingent—made its operations inherently elastic, dynamic, and underdetermined; and together they rendered it impossible either to identify or to maintain a definitive boundary between state and national authority. The four characteristics shaped a structure that produced not stagnation or deadlock but adjustment and accommodation, not "stasis" but "intertemporal equilibria."[1] Such "equilibria" were dynamic and adaptive, continuously regauging and rebalancing the pressures of multiple and conflicting forces that were themselves constantly shifting in nature, strength, and direction. The history of American federalism demonstrated the wisdom of Madison's recognition that "theoretic reasoning," even of the highest quality, "must be qualified by the lessons of practice."[2]

The dynamic effect of those four characteristics was nowhere more apparent or crucial than in the nation's opportunistic and volatile interstate politics. Four levels of institutional conflicts crosscut the Constitution's formal division between "national" and "state" governments. On one side, the states quickly multiplied in numbers, diversified in interests, subdivided in internal organization, and embraced increasing varieties of conflicting domestic interests. States and state interests competed with other states and their interests; substate units and interests competed with substate units and interests in other states; and coalitions of states and substate units and interests competed with one another, with states often arrayed against some of their own internal elements.[3] On the national side, the three federal branches—four, really, given the division of Congress into two chambers—often split among themselves, especially in addressing the issues that pitted states and substate units and interests against one another. Those crosscutting levels of conflict fragmented both the "national" and "state" sides of the Constitution's formal binary divide and inspired the continuous creation and dissolution of interstate alliances that stretched across the levels and branches of government in ever-changing combinations.

From that complex structure and that institutional dynamic, Americans created a distinctively kaleidoscopic national politics. Almost immediately, they organized political parties to broker their interstate alliances and seek control of as many of the levels and branches as possible.[4] As issues changed and interests proliferated, alliances across the four crosscutting levels disintegrated and reformed, while national parties adopted ever more innovative, extensive, and aggressive practices to hold their components together and extend their influence over the institutions of government. The resulting dynamic generated a fluid and pragmatic interstate politics that repeatedly subverted the formal binary divide between states and nation. It generated pressures, interests, and alliances that consistently pressed against the doubly blurred lines of constitutional authority, and it prevented both "the nation" and "the states" from acting as monolithic entities capable of upholding and maintaining a consistent divide between their respective "spheres" of authority.

State-Level Interstate Politics

From the nation's beginning the states competed for trade, investments, immigrants, entrepreneurial projects, transportation connections, access to western lands, and whatever else seemed as a practical matter desirable and advantageous. In 1781 Pennsylvania established a state bank to help finance the Revolutionary War, and between 1784 and 1790 New York, Massachusetts, and Maryland followed suit, hoping to strengthen their positions as centers of commerce and finance.[5] In the 1780s Pennsylvania, Delaware, Virginia, and New York sought similar preeminence by granting steamboat monopolies on their waters, while newer states—including Kentucky, Tennessee, Ohio, and Indiana—subsequently opposed the practice, largely because their geographical locations made them particularly vulnerable to such monopolies. Indeed, when the Orleans Territory granted an eighteen-year steamboat monopoly for the use of its port at the mouth of the Mississippi River, states across the West protested vigorously and turned quickly to the national government for relief.[6] Similarly, states devoted millions of dollars to improve their access to markets and to draw regional commerce into their territories. In 1785 South Carolina sponsored the construction of the Santee Canal to improve connections between its major port and local rivers that led into the interior; in the 1790s Connecticut and Rhode Island improved their roads in an effort to divert westward movement from Massachusetts; and in 1804 Georgia began building a wagon trail to Tennessee to expand its commercial reach and political influence.[7]

With equal vigor the states competed for population, offering immigrants a variety of inducements to settle within their borders. As rivalries intensified, moreover, the methods of competition escalated.[8] Indiana introduced competition on marital grounds. In 1824 it began offering relatively easy divorces to those who lived in the state, and in 1852 it strengthened its competitive position by offering divorces to any "bona fide" resident without requiring proof that the person had lived in the state before filing his or her petition.[9] Wisconsin barged into the population grab with another innovation, establishing a commissioner of immigration with an office located in New York City. In its first year of operation the agency printed more than twenty-five thousand pamphlets in three languages and distributed them to prospects throughout the city, at the port of entry, on arriving vessels, and even in Europe.[10] Collectively, Harry N. Scheiber concluded, the states' wide-ranging efforts constituted an elaborate system of "rivalistic state mercantilism."[11]

As the states fought for regional standing and larger roles in the nation's growing economy, their most extended competition during the early republic involved efforts to breach the Alleghenies and tap the anticipated riches of the interior. Surveys identified five relatively promising routes, and New York, Pennsylvania, Maryland, Virginia, North Carolina, South Carolina, and Georgia struggled for decades to establish inland connections that would draw the West's promised wealth into their coffers. Seek-

ing advantages over their rivals and support from both the national government and other states with mutual interests, their various projects involved both competition and cooperation. In 1806 Congress authorized
construction of a "National Road" over one Allegheny route that would
link Cumberland, Maryland, to the Ohio River at Wheeling, then in Virginia. Completed in 1818, the road was extended to Terre Haute, Indiana,
in 1838 and then to Vandalia, Illinois, in 1852, linking the fortunes of the
five states along its path. To compete, Pennsylvania responded by building
the "Pittsburgh Pike" to connect Philadelphia with the West and enable it
to hold its own against Maryland and the states to its south. The most
spectacular early success in the Allegheny competition, however, belonged
to New York. When it completed its Erie Canal in 1825, commercial traffic
surged. The achievement turned a handsome and steady profit for the
state, linked its fortunes to the economies of half a dozen states along the
Great Lakes, and boosted New York City to a position of national commercial dominance.[12]

The scrambling efforts of the states were not only extensive but shrewd
and sophisticated. While Pennsylvania competed with Maryland for the
east-west trade, for example, it did not hesitate to cooperate with the same
state—and to enlist the aid of both Delaware and the U.S. government as
well—in constructing a canal that linked the three states and improved
their mutual positions in the north-south trade.[13] Similarly, when South
Carolina entered the trans-Allegheny competition with its plan to build a
railroad from Charleston to the Mississippi River, the state's leaders—including Senators John C. Calhoun and Robert Y. Hayne—hoped not only
to stimulate their state's economy but also to join the slaveholding South
with large parts of the West. The railroad, they hoped, would draw Kentucky, Tennessee, and Ohio into slavery's sphere of influence.[14]

In the decades after 1815 national politics evolved into a well-recognized
trisectional conflict. New England and the mid-Atlantic states were industrializing, and they sought higher protective tariffs, cheaper raw materials,
and a restrictive policy toward western land sales. Southern states distrusted industrialism, opposed the tariff and federally financed internal improvements, sought higher cotton prices in international markets, and
committed themselves to the defense and expansion of slavery. The western states, with little manufacturing outside of Ohio and Kentucky, saw

their wealth and future in their rich natural resources, and they sought federally financed internal improvements and greater control over the vast stretches of federally owned lands within their borders. For more than a quarter of a century the three sections pressed their distinct interests and jockeyed over a series of proposed and sometimes consummated compromises, while the leading figures of the day—Calhoun, Andrew Jackson (Tennessee), Daniel Webster (Massachusetts), Henry Clay (Kentucky), and Martin Van Buren (New York)—made their careers and reached for the presidency by attempting to broker sectional alliances that could carry them, their region, and their disjointed parties to victory.[15]

During the 1830s, the nature of the sectional conflict began slowly to shift as the issue of slavery nudged the states toward a two-camp realignment divided along north-south lines. Although commitment to the Union, willingness to compromise, a shared antiblack racism, Jackson's triumph over South Carolina nullification, and the equal balance between free and slave states in the Senate held the nation together, the bonds of union began stretching perilously thin with the Mexican War and the resulting acquisition of new western territories in the 1840s. The rancorous and shaky Compromise of 1850 gave the South a new and more ruthless fugitive slave law but allowed California into the Union as a free state, ending the equal sectional balance in the Senate. Thereafter, events tumbled over one another in quickening succession. Northern states made repeated efforts to block the capture and return of fugitive slaves; the Kansas-Nebraska Act fired a vicious border war over the expansion of slavery into Kansas; the *Dred Scott* case outraged the North by extending the right to hold slaves into the territories and across the nation; the Democratic Party divided along sectional lines while the Whig Party disintegrated; and the election of 1860 brought Abraham Lincoln and the Republicans to power and drove an unbridgeable wedge between the sections. Eleven southern states seceded and formed their own Confederacy, leading to the Civil War—the ultimate extension of the interstate competition that had driven the politics of the federal structure since its birth.

Union victory ended the war and abolished the institution of slavery, but it could hardly dampen competition among the states. The underlying struggle over race continued to divide them deeply and often bitterly. Conflict was acute during Reconstruction, declined substantially thereafter when northern states allowed their southern counterparts to establish new institutions of white supremacy, and then began to escalate again in the twentieth century as the movement for black civil rights gathered new strength, in significant part because of growing black voting strength in the North. The political history of the conflict was largely the story of a southern state coalition that exploited its power in the national branches and its influence in the Democratic Party to keep African Americans in a socially inferior and politically subservient position. For some three-quarters of a century the coalition held together tightly, and only late in the twentieth century did its efforts begin to fail and its member states to alter their "local" racial practices.[16]

Beyond the racial struggle, conflict and competition among the states continued across the board in the everyday battles of American politics. In the 1890s New Jersey and Delaware enacted general incorporation laws that offered provisions especially attractive to promoters and managers, and their efforts sparked competition to attract corporate registrants. Seeking chartering fees and increased tax revenues, states offered ever more favorable terms to those who would incorporate in their jurisdiction.[17] On another front, Illinois, Rhode Island, Iowa, South Dakota, and Utah were among the states that joined the competition for the "migratory divorce business,"[18] while in the early twentieth century Nevada sought its fortune by escalating moral competition, offering itself as a "divorce mill," a gambling center, a location for legalized prostitution, and a supplier of "quickie" marriages.[19] Similarly, during the Great Depression Mississippi pioneered new techniques for attracting business with its "Balance Agriculture with Industry" plan, which authorized local bond initiatives to finance the construction of manufacturing facilities for companies willing to move into the state. After World War II other states copied the plan, and by the early 1960s nine southern states and a handful of northern ones had adopted industrial bond programs and raised more than $440 million for businesses willing to relocate.[20] In the 1950s North Carolina originated yet another new approach. It competed for population, prestige, and wealth by heralding the area around its three major universities as the high-technology "North Carolina Research Triangle." Supporting its campaign with substantial public funding, the state transformed a previously rural region into a prosperous and booming center of intellectual, scientific, and commercial activity.[21]

The states, of course, also cooperated, though often only to compete more effectively against some rival groups of states. As early as 1785 Maryland and Virginia ratified a Potomac River and Chesapeake Bay trade agreement and invited Pennsylvania and Delaware to join,[22] and by 1925 Congress had approved thirty-nine such interstate agreements under the Constitution's Compact Clause.[23] As American life nationalized, the number of such agreements quickly multiplied. By the beginning of the twenty-first century Congress had approved some two hundred of them, with the number of states participating in each ranging from two to fifty. As of 2001, the states had entered into an average of 23.4 interstate compacts each, with those at the low end—South Dakota and Wisconsin—participating in 14 each and those at the top—Colorado, Vermont, and New Hampshire—in 32.[24] The scope and subject matter of the compacts, moreover, grew increasingly wide and varied, falling by one estimate into at least twenty-five different types and covering interstate issues involving health, energy, agriculture, corrections, fisheries, natural resources, sanitation, civil defense, parks and recreation, flood control, crime prevention, emergency management assistance, and river basin control.[25] The agreements established literally dozens of interstate boards, agencies, and commissions to administer their provisions and exercise the powers they granted. In addition, at least five other interstate compacts included the U.S. government as a party, bringing together both federal and state powers to deal with special problems involving interstate rivers and mountain ranges.[26]

Beyond formal interstate compacts, the states found other ways to join forces when cooperation served their mutual purposes. One was the use of agreements that did not require congressional approval. In 1893 the Supreme Court suggested in *Virginia v. Tennessee*[27] that congressional approval was not required for interstate agreements that did not encroach on national power or alter the nature of the federal structure, and over the years the states entered into a large number of such unratified agreements, which the Court subsequently upheld.[28] A second method was to enact uniform statutes that eliminated differences between state laws and thereby simplified interstate business planning. Pressed by nationalizing commercial interests and led by the American Bar Association, the states in 1892 established the National Conference of Commissioners on Uniform State Laws, an organization that drafted model statutes and proposed them to the states for adoption. By the 1930s the commissioners had succeeded in drafting seven such laws that a majority of states accepted, and in the second half of the twentieth century they enjoyed their greatest triumph, adoption of the Uniform Commercial Code by all fifty states.[29] A third cooperative method was to adopt informal executive and administrative understandings, frequently without formal authorization from the legislatures of the participating states. Offering flexibility and discretion, such interstate understandings proliferated in the twentieth century and, like interstate compacts and formal but unratified agreements, covered a wide range of governmental actions. New York, for example, sought interstate assistance in identifying and prosecuting those who violated its gun-control laws, and it entered into memoranda of understanding with Florida, Georgia, Ohio, Texas, and Virginia—the principal sources of the unlicensed firearms arriving in the Empire State.[30] Informal agreements and understandings were also used to establish and maintain literally thousands of de facto working arrangements between states and a wide variety of federal agencies and departments.[31] By the late twentieth century such informal understandings facilitated cooperation among the states and with the U.S. government in such areas as agriculture, crime, education, emergency assistance, pollution, pest control, waste management, insurance, taxation, welfare fraud, and road and vehicle safety.[32]

Such state-level interstate politics affected almost all national issues. In the late twentieth century, for example, it proved particularly significant in environmental politics. Interests in eastern and western coal-producing states divided sharply on a range of regulatory issues while steadily pushing the national government to the center of environmental politics;[33] seven mining states forced the issue of strip mining onto the national scene and eventually led Congress to adopt the compromise Surface Mining Control and Reclamation Act of 1977;[34] and a coalition of northeastern and midwestern states simultaneously battled a coalition of western states over the use and control of federally owned public lands in the West.[35]

Illustrating the complexity and variety of state coalitions, the federal Endangered Species Act[36] divided the states along lines largely determined by the number and location of endangered species that existed within their respective borders.[37] One of the principal reasons the act generated and then sustained majority support in Congress was that its effect was concentrated in only six states—California, Texas, Florida, Alabama, Washington, and Utah—which together accounted for 90 percent of the habitat conservation plans that the government adopted to control land development under the statute. Congressional delegations from those six states consistently opposed the act and repeatedly voted to weaken it, while delegations from the far more numerous states that were largely unaffected continued to support it. The striking geographical spread among the six seriously affected states—ranging, as they did, from the East to the West Coast and from the Gulf of Mexico to the Canadian border—suggested the extent to which new issues could forge novel state coalitions that differed radically from the more familiar and often contiguous regional alliances of the past.

Substate and Mixed-Level Interstate Politics

As states jockeyed for advantage, so too did cities, towns, counties, and substate regional groups and interests across the nation. Initially, they fought for preferences and benefits from their states. Above all, cities and towns sought to become state capitals, and well into the nineteenth century local rivalries compelled states to shift their capitals from one to another under the spur of shifting populations and differential economic growth. The competition, moreover, was not confined to new states west of the Appalachians, for between 1777 and 1810 nine of the original thirteen states transferred their capitals to new locations while two others rotated theirs between rival claimants.[38] In addition, larger towns as well as smaller ones—and even villages and crossroads—competed to become county seats and to obtain the rewards of housing local governmental offices and courthouses. "Every town expected to become the county seat," Lewis Atherton wrote. "In several counties official records were captured by violence with that in mind."[39] Further, cities and towns competed for the honor and opportunities that came from hosting state prisons, land offices, universities, agricultural colleges, and institutions for the poor, blind, deaf, and insane.[40] Finally, they fought to obtain funding necessary for promising local projects. Massachusetts towns, for example, competed for state support and authorization to build bridges over the three rivers that obstructed local traffic around Boston, and in 1785 an alliance between Boston, Medford, and Charlestown secured state approval for the construction and operation of what became the famous Charles River Bridge.[41] Cities and towns, in fact, became increasingly active as political centers and public service providers in the late eighteenth and early nineteenth centuries.[42]

Beyond benefits directly available from their states, towns and cities across the land also struggled for another even more tantalizing prize—statewide, regional, or even national place and prominence. Competition among merchant towns had grown since the middle of the eighteenth century,[43] and by the beginning of the nineteenth it routinely reached across state lines, accelerating sharply as western expansion and the admission of new states created both breathtaking new opportunities and audacious new rivals.[44] Chambers of commerce and boards of trade began to flourish as the spearheads of methodical campaigns for local and regional economic expansion. In 1801 there were four such organizations in the new nation, but the numbers jumped to several dozen by the 1840s and then skyrocketed by the 1890s to almost three thousand. In 1913 the number stood at 3,356 and included 243 interstate, national, and international associations.[45]

For the politics of federalism, the salient point was that the process united and divided states and substate units in ever-changing combinations. After 1810, for example, Baltimore established its dominance over several local rivals in the Chesapeake region and began to challenge Philadelphia. It forced its way into the latter's southern coastal trade, secured overland routes into the Ohio Valley, and seized control of the grain and tobacco trade of Virginia, Maryland, and even much of central Pennsylvania itself.[46] When Baltimore decided in 1827 to compete with New York and its Erie Canal by building a railroad westward, Philadelphia turned anxiously to its state government to save it from being crushed between its two powerful rivals. The state responded by constructing a series of canals and portage roads that reached Pittsburgh in 1835, barely holding the state's principal western city in the economic orbit of its principal eastern city.[47]

Pennsylvania, like the other states, was riven by local and regional rivalries.[48] Its southeastern counties were continually pulled toward Baltimore through the Susquehanna Valley, while its northern counties were drawn toward the Great Lakes, the Erie Canal, and New York City.[49] Similarly, its western region repeatedly sought to establish its independence from Philadelphia and the East by linking itself to Baltimore. In the 1840s Pittsburgh led a bruising campaign to force the state legislature to authorize an extension of Maryland's powerful instrument, the Baltimore & Ohio Railroad, that would link the western city more efficiently to markets in the South. When Philadelphia merchants stalled the effort in 1846, western Pennsylvania threatened to secede and establish "a new trans-Alleghenian commonwealth" consisting of twenty-two counties, an effort that Philadelphia's supporters branded as "treason" and derided as "The Pittsburgh Lunacy."[50] While the western city eventually won its connection to the Baltimore & Ohio, the state's eastern interests retaliated by securing the state's support for extending their own instrument, the Pennsylvania Railroad, through Pittsburgh and on to Chicago and the West.

Rivalries between cities and towns grew equally intense in the Midwest. Chicago used its new rail connections with the East to challenge St. Louis, an older and wealthier regional center, for economic dominance of the Mississippi Valley.[51] Gradually it overtook the latter and then surpassed it, largely because it could exploit both the water route that ran from the Great Lakes through the Erie Canal and the increasingly efficient rail lines that linked it with major cities in the East. St. Louis, in contrast, suffered from a decline in its lucrative Mississippi River trade and the shrinking advantages it could obtain, especially after the Civil War, from its long-established connections with the markets of New Orleans and the South.[52]

Smaller cities and towns also joined the struggle for profitable interstate positions. Kansas City, Missouri, and Leavenworth, Kansas, fought for control of trade along the Missouri River, and the former eventually prevailed because in 1869 it secured rail links to both Chicago and St. Louis.[53] Typical of the volatility of substate alliances, only a decade earlier Kansas City had regarded St. Louis as a rival, and the two cities had battled for intrastate supremacy. Kansas City threatened to develop a northern rail connection to Chicago through cities in Iowa, while St. Louis considered financing a rail line westward that would bypass Kansas City to the south in favor of Pleasant Hill, Missouri, and allied interests in Kansas.[54] Similarly, Cincinnati made strenuous efforts in the 1840s to expand its early success in the river trade by forging rail links with St. Louis. Subsequently, however, it found itself threatened by Louisville, which had cut into its southern trade by allying with the aggressive Louisville and Nashville Railroad. In 1874 Cincinnati responded by building its own railroad, the Cincinnati Southern, and forging an alternate route that avoided Louisville and linked it to Chattanooga, Tennessee, and eventually to New Orleans and the Gulf.[55]

Those developments not only illustrated the energy driving interstate competition and cooperation among substate units, but they also spotlighted a pivotal institutional development, the urbanization of America and the emergence of dozens of metropolitan centers as relatively independent and increasingly powerful political and economic actors.[56] Backed by ambitious local or regional interests, cities often took the lead in promoting interstate political and economic alliances.[57] They did so not only because of self-interest but also because intrastate rivalries often deadlocked state governments, preventing the states from promoting one of their cities or regions over others and frustrating state efforts to maintain a unified economic development policy.[58] During the nineteenth century cities mushroomed in number and size, and by the twentieth century they had transformed the way Americans lived, worked, and thought. Their governments grew elaborate and complex as they built, operated, and regulated water and sewage systems, bridges and tunnels, comprehensive lighting services for streets and other public places, massive transportation networks, recreational facilities and cultural institutions, health and emergency medical services, and increasingly critical police, fire, and sanitation departments.[59] Cities became, in short, major governmental institutions with interests quite distinct from those of their states and often quite inconsistent with those of the other cities and regions in their home states. Indeed, in the early twenty-first century a number of cities across the country began to authorize marriages between same-sex couples, an action that challenged the laws of their states, raised serious questions of national constitutional law, and gave new salience to the ideas of local diversity and autonomy that were associated with the values of the federal structure.[60]

For American federalism, the growing size and power of cities created special complications. American law embraced what became known as "Dillon's Rule," the principle that local government entities were wholly creatures of state law.[61] "Municipal corporations owe their origin to, and derive their powers and rights wholly from, the [state] legislature," the eponymous Judge John F. Dillon declared. The state "breathes into them the breath of life," and it could consequently "abridge and control" or even "destroy" their powers.[62] Thus, the rise of cities disjointed the federal structure, creating magnetic centers of economic, political, cultural, and social power that had no formal constitutional place. Regardless of Dillon's Rule, however, such dynamic centers of de facto power could hardly be stopped from effectively pressing their interests on both state and national governments. Their growing power and persistent pressure eventually pushed most states to enact "home rule" laws that granted their cities and counties substantial autonomy and authority to deal with many "local" matters. In 1875 Missouri took the further step of amending its constitution to grant its cities power to draft their own independent "home rule" charters, and by the middle of the twentieth century approximately half the states had adopted similar constitutional provisions.[63] By the 1980s that number had jumped to forty, while several other states had conferred similar independent powers on their cities by statute.[64] Thus, even with Dillon's Rule, the rise of the cities helped further fragment the state half of the federalism divide, creating political units with power and interests separate from those of their states, not only as de facto matters but also increasingly as de jure matters.[65]

The rise of the cities, however, was only one phase in the complex story of substate fragmentation that confused the federal structure's binary division. As cities grew in size and importance, they soon spurred a countermovement—the rise of incorporated and independent suburbs that halted the territorial expansion of growing central cities. In 1874 Brookline, Massachusetts, blocked Boston's annexation effort, and during the following half-century most large cities that sought to expand their geographical bases—Chicago, Oakland, St. Paul, Cleveland, Birmingham, Louisville,

Pittsburgh, Atlanta, and St. Louis among many others—suffered defeat at the hands of independent, and often relatively well-to-do, suburban communities.[66] By the 1950s, in fact, eighteen of the nation's twenty-five largest cities began to lose population steadily, while over the subsequent three decades independent suburbs gained more than sixty million residents. By 1970 more people lived in suburbs than in either cities or rural areas, and a decade later the nation's fourteen largest metropolitan areas housed an overwhelming majority of their populations outside their original central cities. In seven of those metropolitan areas more than 70 percent of the population lived in suburbs, and in another five more than 60 percent did so.[67]

The proliferation of independent suburbs did not merely limit urban territorial expansion but also created yet more intrastate geographical divisions that spurred new varieties of social and political conflicts. Racial, ethnic, and economic differences exacerbated a growing divide between cities and suburbs, spurring frequent and often sharp conflicts. By the late nineteenth century central cities were coming to be associated with recent Southern and Eastern European immigrants, blacks migrating from the South, the industrial working class, and the relatively poor and benighted who were often seen as living in environments marked by vice, crime, corruption, and radicalism of all varieties. The suburbs, conversely, tended to attract whites and those in the middle and upper-middle classes, and they projected images of order, tranquility, prosperity, and security.[68] By the 1960s, after decades of migration from the South, a majority of African Americans lived in northern central cities, and the demographic shift led to sharpened racial tensions, growing urban poverty, and a "complex and pervasive racial discrimination" that frustrated black hopes for advancement. For the federal structure, it also erected sharply etched and often bitterly contested geographic borders between contiguous areas in the same states and interstate metropolitan areas.[69] While patterns of conflict varied over the decades, the urban-suburban divide came to mark a major fault line in national politics.[70]

Further, the suburbanization process combined with population growth and the multiplying complexities of modern life to spawn a luxurious proliferation of substate governmental units. By the late twentieth century there were 18,000 organized municipalities in the United States in addition to some 3,000 counties, 18,000 townships, approximately 21,000 school districts, and some 30,000 other special purpose districts. The greater Boston metropolitan region, for example, included 101 separate towns and cities.[71] To complicate matters even further, approximately 81,000 of those governmental units held the power to levy taxes, while some 38,000 incorporated in their institutional structures some form of separation of powers. The creation and multiplication of such local government units spread institutional fragmentation across the land, infused it into the smallest units of local government, and mixed private and public elements and related interstate regional interests in literally thousands of diverse and shifting combinations.[72]

Interstate Politics and the National Government

In their continuous efforts to compete and cooperate, states and substate elements repeatedly sought to induce the federal government to advance their interests. Indeed, the very process of admitting new states to the Union frequently divided the older states and their interests, with some pressing Congress and the president for early action and others seeking delay or even rejection. To deprive their adversaries of electoral votes, for example, the Federalists sought to delay the admission of pro-Republican states until after the presidential elections of 1796 and 1804.[73] More notoriously, from 1819 to the Civil War the entire admission process was dominated by the overarching struggle for national power between two blocs of states, the free and the slave.

More ordinary and far more pervasive, competition for federal favors among states and substate elements quickly became the mark of the nation's quotidian politics. Even before ratification the Confederation Congress had begun to use land grants to support public education, and the new government under the Constitution continued the practice and increased its generosity until by the early nineteenth century such grants had come to seem a matter of entitlement. From the nation's earliest years, that federal largesse spurred intense competition for favors among "settlers, squatters, veterans, eastern economic interests, state governments, townships, and political parties that used land policies to capture votes."[74] By 1792 Washington, Jefferson, and Madison had all joined Hamilton in finding legal theories that allowed them to approve congressional funding to support New England's cod fishing industry,[75] and pleas for similar assistance from other groups began to pour into Congress. "Military veterans, squatters on the public domain, victims of natural disaster, deranged Army officers, and even state and territorial legislatures," Laura Jensen found from her study of early American social policy, "prayed for tangible forms of congressional assistance."[76] With increasing frequency Congress responded, and by the early years of the nineteenth century the national government was fostering a variety of diverse state and substate interests with tariffs, land grants, ship subsidies, procurement policies, restrictive trade regulations, geographical and engineering surveys, and medical care for those who became sick or disabled while sailing the seven seas or navigating the nation's lakes, rivers, and canals.[77] As early as 1790, for example, Congress began to provide financial relief to disaster victims, and by 1822 it was enacting general relief bills for the benefit of states and localities that had suffered damage from floods, fires, and storms. "By the time of a devastating fire in Alexandria, Virginia, in 1827," another study found, "Congress had already granted twenty-seven separate claims for relief, encompassing thousands of claimants and millions of dollars."[78]

More frequent and persistent were the efforts of states and localities to secure federal funding for internal improvements. In 1803 Congress agreed to devote federal funds from land sales in the new state of Ohio to local road building, and shortly thereafter it authorized construction of a "National Road" to link the Atlantic Coast with the nation's expanding interior. In 1808 Jefferson's secretary of the treasury, Albert Gallatin, proposed a general federal program to construct roads, bridges, and canals, and the issue of federal funding for internal improvements established itself as a pivotal issue in national politics. Henry Clay and John Quincy Adams urged congressional adoption of an "American System"—protective tariffs providing revenues for "internal improvements"—that encouraged states and towns to compete for federal grants,[79] and Congress repeatedly responded favorably with money and land grants. While three presidents—James Madison, James Monroe, and Andrew Jackson—vetoed such bills on the constitutional ground that they funded merely "local" projects, Congress continued to approve, and presidents to sign, measure after measure financing internal improvements. Indeed, the amount of federal funding for internal improvements increased in every successive administration, including those of Madison, Monroe, and Jackson.[80]

The advent of the railroad spurred states and substate units to redouble their efforts to obtain federal support and funding. The heavy costs of construction and fears of the promotional schemes of their rivals fostered a new willingness of states and substate units to join more extensive interstate coalitions in efforts to reorient national policy and secure for themselves more ample federal funding. Bills to finance construction projects inundated Washington, and five times during the 1850s Congress passed responsive legislation that granted a total of more than eighteen million acres of land to thirteen states for the benefit of forty-five separate railroad companies.[81]

Those bills, however, like their predecessors, were hostage to the fractionated politics of the federal structure. Geographical and economic rivalries among states and substate units blocked more funding schemes than they allowed, for each individual measure seemed likely to help only a few while imposing relative disadvantages on many. The New England states enjoyed comparatively good roads and easy access to the sea, and they saw no benefit for themselves from improved transportation that would stimulate westward migration and lower their competitors' costs. After opening its Erie Canal, New York shared New England's views, as did Pennsylvania after it completed its own "Main Line" system of canals and portage roads that crossed the state. Similarly, southern states were convinced that improved transportation would only strengthen the competitive position of the North and West while providing a justification for revenue-raising tariffs and loose constitutional construction, both of which they saw as threats to their peculiar institution.[82]

When secession eliminated critical opposition and war made interstate railroad construction imperative, however, the politico-geographical calculus was transformed. Congress responded with the Pacific Railway Acts of 1862 and 1864, providing lavish support for the construction of a transcontinental railroad.[83] The new availability of federal funding and the prospects of burgeoning western markets encouraged complex new interstate alliances and quickly forged two major competing state and substate blocs. For the most glittering prize—the first transcontinental connection—interests in New York City, the states along the Great Lakes,

Chicago, Iowa, and Omaha, Nebraska, joined forces to compete for federal largesse against a coalition promoting the linked interests of Baltimore, Philadelphia, Cincinnati, St. Louis, Kansas City, and Leavenworth,
Kansas.[84] Interstate politics among state and substate coalitions, and the
rampant corruption they encouraged, had seldom been so comprehensive
or vicious.[85]

Although the period of massive railroad subsidies lasted little more than
a decade, federal funding for internal improvements became an increasingly accepted part of American government. In 1906, for example, midwestern organizations and interests from Chicago to New Orleans formed
the Lakes-to-Gulf Deep Waterway Association and sought federal funding
to build a continuous waterway linking Chicago and the Great Lakes
with New Orleans and the Gulf of Mexico. Among their adversaries were
northern and eastern interests that favored an expansion of the St. Lawrence River and the construction of an improved water route through the
Great Lakes to the Atlantic Ocean. With substantial state support and ultimately decisive funding from the federal government, especially in the
Rivers and Harbors Act of 1930, the Chicago–New Orleans project finally
reached fruition. Critical to its success was the work of Illinois congressman Henry T. Rainey, an influential thirty-year member of the House who
became Democratic majority leader in 1931 and Speaker in 1933. Rainey
represented the Twentieth Congressional District in the state's southeast
corner, the district through which the Illinois River—a major link in
the planned waterway—flowed and then joined the Mississippi River just
above St. Louis. The new Lakes-to-Gulf waterway was expected to bring
substantial business to the district where it was widely popular, especially in
its southernmost county, which shouldered the junction of the two
rivers.[86] The project exemplified the classic dynamic of the American federal system, the synergism that arose from local congressional districting,
state and substate competition, and the exercise of the national government's powers.[87]

In the late nineteenth century, moreover, interstate competition escalated sharply as states and substate entities began more commonly to seek
not just federal funding but also federal regulation. After Massachusetts established the first state railroad commission in 1869 and other states
quickly followed, interests disadvantaged under the resulting regimes be-

gan pushing for national legislation. St. Louis, for example, had long enjoyed a lucrative trade in products from Latin America—especially sugar, molasses, crockery, and coffee—that were shipped through New Orleans and up the Mississippi. The railroads enabled Chicago to subvert that pattern by joining with Baltimore importers and trunk lines willing to cut their rates to attract much-needed westbound freight. Profiting from discounts of up to 90 percent, Baltimore and Chicago won the western trade in Latin American products from New Orleans and St. Louis. Merchants in the latter two cities quickly came to support national legislation that would prohibit such "unfair" discounts.[88] Such economic disruptions and local vulnerabilities combined to spur passage of the first federal law seeking to regulate the railroads, the Interstate Commerce Act of 1887.[89] The statute was the beginning of a long and exceptionally complicated story, but the politics of the act's origins and implementation—as with the stream of similar national regulatory statutes that soon followed—continued to be driven, in large part, by the dynamics of economic growth and the complex competition and cooperation between states and substate units that drove the politics of the federal structure.

Those complexities inevitably produced their special ironies, perhaps most strikingly for the South. Forced by military defeat to return to a Union newly dominated by the forces of northeastern capital, southern states immediately found themselves struggling to resuscitate their ravaged economies and regain a share of power from the nation's wealthy and highly productive states in the North and Midwest. Although they remained passionately committed to states' rights, intensely so in racial matters, they nonetheless began to support substantial exertions of federal power to regulate business as a "defensive reaction" against the powerful northern commercial and financial interests that controlled the national economy and the Republican Party. Thus, it was southern votes that proved critical in enacting the Interstate Commerce Act and many of the other national regulatory measures that followed.[90] Indeed, the drastic expansions of federal power that subsequently came with Progressivism and the New Deal were made possible only with the support of substantial numbers of southern votes. The trade-off, of course, was agreement that the national government would not interfere with southern racial practices.[91]

Racial and economic issues, however, were hardly alone in driving the interaction between mixed-level interstate politics and federal regulation. The temperance movement illustrated the structure's complex dynamics in the area of moral reform.[92] In the 1880s the Woman's Christian Temperance Union and the Prohibition Party focused their campaigns against alcohol at the national level. Promising eventual success, they invoked the analogy of abolitionism and its victorious campaign to end slavery. "Needless to say," Richard F. Hamm noted, "such an approach was poorly adapted for Texas, and, indeed, all of the South."[93] Southern congressmen fought national prohibition vigorously, and the reformers' campaign failed in 1890 when Congress passed the Wilson Act, allowing states to control or prohibit the importation of liquor from interstate sources.[94] Those actions stalled national prohibition for a quarter of a century and reshaped the political context of temperance reform. By compelling advocates to shift their efforts to the state and county levels, they freed the movement in the South from the specter of "federal control." With the availability of alcohol thus defined officially as a "state" matter, Prohibition began its march across the South, transforming the region into the movement's stronghold. Beginning in the late 1890s, southern prohibitionists rolled to one victory after another, and by the second decade of the twentieth century most of the South was legally dry by state or county action.[95] Then, when the movement's growing strength combined with the onset of World War I to revive the hopes of national action, southern fervor and southern votes pushed for a structural result quite the opposite of the one they had supported in 1890. Determined to extend their own "local" practices across the land, they helped drive the successful campaign to nationalize Prohibition by adopting the Eighteenth Amendment.[96]

The issue of water resources, a major concern in the West, similarly illustrated the shifting interests and alliances that marked the politics of the fractionated federal structure.[97] On the state level, western states cooperated in their quest for federal aid to fund dams, irrigation projects, hydroelectric plants, and urban aqueducts, while battling among themselves for larger shares of scarce water resources.[98] On the substate level, conflicts over water rights between urban and agricultural interests in the same state frequently brought opposed intrastate interests into alliances with their counterparts in other western states. The results of the Newlands Act of

1902 were typical. In the summer of 1901 thirty senators and representatives from seventeen western states caucused in Cheyenne, Wyoming, and agreed to back a proposal drafted by Senator Francis G. Newlands of Nevada that called for the use of federal revenues from land sales to finance the construction of dams and irrigation systems in the West. Eastern and midwestern agricultural interests, fearing sharpened competition from western farmers, opposed the measure, but President Theodore Roosevelt helped secure its passage by rallying nonagrarian interests from those regions in support of western Republicans and Democrats.[99] Once established, however, the program forced its recipients to compete for the limited federal funds available, and within a decade of the act's passage the western states were fighting bitterly among themselves.[100] To complicate matters further, the agricultural interests that the statute was designed to assist found themselves also competing against western cities that needed new water projects to satisfy the thirst of their growing populations.[101] The split between intrastate agricultural and urban interests intensified over the following decades, and by the middle of the twentieth century cities such as Denver, Houston, Phoenix, Dallas, and Los Angeles shared critical water interests that often united them with one another and against the interests of farmers and rural interests in their own states.[102]

The complex and extended battle over the reapportionment of federal, state, and local electoral districts revealed another element of the structural dynamic, the appeal of state and substate elements from one national branch to another. By the end of World War II urbanization and other demographic changes had caused grievous representational disparities among intrastate regions. In Vermont, the town of Victory, with 49 residents, elected the same number of state representatives as did Burlington with its 33,155 inhabitants. Similarly, the 34,423 residents of New Jersey's rural Sussex County elected one state senator, the same number metropolitan Essex County elected with its 905,949 citizens. By the mid-twentieth century only two states provided essentially equal representation to their urban residents. Underrepresentation was undeniable in the rest, moderate in seven states, serious in another nine, and substantial or severe in the remaining thirty.[103] As a consequence, urban representatives across the nation combined against their rural counterparts to urge equitable reapportionment plans, and the United States Conference of Mayors identified unequal apportionment as the paramount obstacle that municipal governments faced in attempting to deal with their pressing problems.[104]

Legislative malapportionment not only united and divided substate entities across the nation but affected the operations of the federal government as well. It prevented Congress from accurately reflecting popular needs, and it intensified separation-of-powers conflicts between a legislature shaped by one electoral scheme and an executive responsive to a distinctly different one.[105] Pressed by a variety of conflicting forces, including the immediate self-interest of many of its members, Congress refused to act. That refusal, however, did not necessarily settle the matter, for the tripartite federal government contained another branch that could, and eventually did, take action. Responding favorably to the urban coalitions, the Supreme Court intervened to resolve the apportionment battle in the early 1960s by issuing a series of decisions that imposed a "one person, one vote" rule on electoral districting at all levels of government.[106]

President Lyndon Johnson's "Great Society" illustrated yet another aspect of the dynamic that drove the federal structure's interstate politics, the struggle between states and their own substate components for influence within the national government. Johnson's programs expanded the influence that local government units enjoyed in Washington and bypassed the states in funneling large amounts of federal funds directly to substate units. The policy weakened state control over funding, enhanced the power of local officials, and favored different sets of interest groups.[107] State officials, not surprisingly, resented the power shift and fought tenaciously to reverse it. In 1978 the National Governors' Association protested publicly against what it termed "the ongoing attempts to bypass state governments in the implementation of domestic programs."[108] Beginning in 1981 Presidents Ronald Reagan and George H. W. Bush acceded to their pleas. Their administrations cut back substantially on both the access of substate units to federal agencies and their control over the federal grants they received.[109]

The Supreme Court exacerbated such intrastate conflicts, too, by complicating the legal relationship between states and their local government units. Although the former were privileged with constitutional standing and the latter were mere creatures of state law under Dillon's Rule,[110] the Court sometimes relied on concepts of federalism to protect local government units as well as states.[111] In *National League of Cities v. Usery*,[112] for example, it cited the Tenth Amendment in protecting local as well as state governments from a congressional statute that arguably intruded into their structure and operations. More striking, in *Washington v. Seattle School District No. 1*[113] the Court allowed a local school district to raise the Fourteenth Amendment to void a state statute that blocked the district's local busing program, and in *Lawrence County v. Lead-Deadwood School District No. 40-1*[114] it allowed a South Dakota county to invoke the Supremacy Clause to invalidate a state law that limited the county's discretion in using federal funds. Thus, in spite of the constitutional principle that states exercised complete control over the organization and powers of local government units, the Court gave those local entities some degree of federal constitutional autonomy and freed them to challenge the laws of the very states that created and empowered them.[115]

Finally, during the twentieth century states and their thousands of substate units added yet another level to the complexities of interstate politics. Organizing their own separate national lobbying instruments, they formed dozens upon dozens of such groups, including the National League of Cities, the National Governors' Association, the National Conference of State Legislatures, the United States Conference of Mayors, and the National Association of Counties as well as many narrower and more specialized groups. The National Assembly of State Arts Agencies, for example, was established to lobby Congress on behalf of state agencies devoted to fostering the arts. All of those organizations enabled states and their innumerable substate entities to develop cooperative programs among themselves, form coalitions to push mutually advantageous policies, and lobby in support of interests held in common with other public and private organizations.[116] They, of course, lobbied the national government—or at least whichever branch or agency seemed in the circumstances either the most promising target of opportunity or the only available point of access. Even gathered together for mutual lobbying purposes, however, states and localities frequently found their interests divided. Financial grants to cities could undermine the authority of states, for example, while proposed federal funding schemes could be relatively advantageous for some states but disadvantageous to others.[117] Thus, the various national associations of state and local governments not only lobbied against one another on many issues, but they also had to mediate conflicts, rivalries, and disagreements among their own members, sometimes finding themselves deadlocked in their efforts to take united action and sometimes supporting compromise positions that failed to command the unanimous approval of their members.

Private Organizations and the Multiple and Intersecting Layers of Interstate Politics

Cooperation and conflict among states and substate units involved far more than formal and public government actions. As Madison emphasized, the units of government were invariably backed, and commonly driven, by interests that actuated their citizens and by the resources those citizens brought to the public arena. Thus, the dynamic that drove the fractionated politics of the federal structure arose in large part from the efforts of an ever-widening range of private groups seeking to achieve their goals through government action. Organizations representing those private groups added another even more fractionated and complex level to the politics of the federal structure, for their interests and connections were not only conflicting but also extensive, stretching across local, state, regional, national, and international levels.[118]

From the earliest days of the republic interstate associations formed around state and local groups, often structuring themselves on the Constitution's "federal" model and usually pursuing political objectives through governments at multiple levels. In the early nineteenth century such private associations spread southward and westward from New England and the Atlantic seaboard cities until by the 1850s they covered the entire United States east of the Mississippi River. The rising tide of moral reform that swept the nation in the decades before the Civil War was driven in large part by organizations that "inspired the creation of thousands of interlinked local and state societies."[119] Before 1790 such associations invariably began as local operations, but by the 1820s most new ones were founded as national organizations with expressly national ambitions. A decade later four such associations—the Freemasons, the American Temperance Society, the American Anti-Slavery Society, and the General Union for Promoting Observance of the Christian Sabbath—had spread so widely that each enrolled as members more than 1 percent of the nation's entire population.[120] In the decades after the Civil War the number of such national associations multiplied even more rapidly.

Like the national, state, and local governments they sought to influence, those national organizations both cooperated with and struggled against one another. Their political values and goals often conflicted on bitterly divisive issues involving race, ethnicity, religion, economics, and education. "Unsurprisingly, peak periods of nativist association building and political agitation," Theda Skocpol noted, generally occurred during "the same periods when large numbers of ethnic American groups were launched or expanded."[121] Sometimes those associational conflicts divided states and substate units along similar lines; sometimes they divided them by region; and sometimes they divided them in erratic and crazy-quilt patterns. Pennsylvania's notorious internal divisions were exacerbated by the fact that its settled eastern region was controlled by Germans while Scotch Irish dominated its west, for example, while ethnic divisions between "Yankees" from New England and Dutch "Yorkers" deepened the split between New York's upstate and southern regions.[122] Although the nature of associational cooperation and conflict changed over the centuries, such activities continuously drove the nation's politics and molded the operations of its federal structure.

Another interstate institution, the private business corporation, contributed similarly to reshaping the operations of the federal structure. Like the national political parties, business corporations were unrecognized by the Constitution but became central to the workings of American government. Like municipalities and other local government entities, business corporations were created by state law, entrusted to the control of elected officials, and empowered to make rules controlling the lives of thousands and then tens and hundreds of thousands of people. Also like local government units, they were allowed to carry on their affairs freely across state and national borders and to conduct their affairs with private corporations as well as with local, state, federal, and foreign governments. Exerting enormous and wide-reaching powers, they became by the late nineteenth century institutions of far greater importance than most of the thousands of government entities to which Americans owed formal allegiance.[123] Law, habit, custom, interest, organization, and the messages of mass culture combined not only to legitimate them but also to obscure their role as de facto institutions of government.[124]

Thus, from its beginning the American constitutional enterprise was multipolar and multidimensional, a cooperative institutional project criss-crossed with a seemingly infinite number of diverse and conflicting private interests and governmental entities. The enterprise sought to conduct democratic government on a national scale by giving place to interacting levels and branches, voice to multitudes of private groups and interests, and opportunities for all to compete, cooperate, and combine in any reasonable manner that seemed to them useful. That, according to Bernard Bailyn, was implicit in the founders' plan. "Tensions—networks of tensions—were the fundamental necessity for free states," he noted, and what the Constitution created was "a great web of tensions."[125] The American people—an inexhaustible cornucopia of diverse social, economic, religious, ethnic, geographic, and political interests and values—produced their own great web of individual and group tensions, and they undertook the collective enterprise of living with and mediating those tensions by working through the complex web of institutional tensions that the Constitution and its federal structure established. The result was a luxuriously fractionated and inherently dynamic institutional politics that continually pressed new demands and new meanings on the federal structure's doubly blurred lines of authority and effectively prevented both national and state governments from consistently and continuously maintaining any rigid or definitive boundary between their respective powers.

7

READJUSTING COMPONENTS

As the Constitution left the states free to organize themselves internally, so it conferred similar powers on the central government. It gave Congress power to establish the institutional capacities necessary for the operation of the national government, and it made the three branches largely independent of one another in exercising their powers, pursuing their goals, and arranging many of their internal procedures. Holding such powers and enjoying such independence, the national branches—animated by their officeholders' diverse interests and ambitions, operating in a rapidly changing world environment, and interacting with other components of the doubly blurred federal structure—could hardly stand immutable.

At the beginning of the twenty-first century "Congress," "the Presidency," and the "Supreme Court" all existed, just as they had in 1789. The institutions that originally bore those names, however, had long faded from the scene, replaced by radically different ones. As the nation developed and its needs changed, the national branches evolved in size, role, operation, internal complexity, and scope of authority. As of 2006, in fact, the three national branches were divided, by the federal government's own count, into some 495 separate "Departments and Agencies."[1] That triple-tracked institutional transformation reverberated through the federal structure and profoundly altered its operating system.

Congress

More complex than the other two national branches, and more fully specified on paper, Congress evolved from a small and unstructured deliberative body closely connected to local and state government into a complex and highly bureaucratized institution with its own national orientation, agenda, and values.[2] Some changes occurred relatively quickly, evidencing both the Constitution's lack of specificity and the legislature's quick departure from the founders' vision. Other changes occurred more slowly or came much later, demonstrating both the flexibility of the Constitution's provisions and the pressures of external social and political developments. In reshaping the national legislature, all contributed to remolding the operations of the federal structure.

Early on, the Senate shifted away from the role the founders had envisioned and "reconstituted" itself.[3] Looking to the British House of Lords as their model, the founders had conceived of the upper house as a body aloof from the people, bound to the states, reactive to the "popular" lower house, and committed to supporting and counseling the executive.[4] From the beginning, however, the Senate conformed to that role only imperfectly,[5] and in the two decades after the War of 1812 it rejected the original role almost completely. As political parties, the national electorate, and the problems facing the nation changed, so did the Senate's own "institutional vision." In 1816 the body adopted for the first time a system of standing committees, distributing essentially independent powers among its members and conferring on committee chairs substantial authority and prestige both in and out of Congress. Over the following decade it established internal rules that increased its autonomy from the executive, enhanced its ability to enact legislation, and strengthened the power of internal majorities to control the body's business. Senators became intimately involved in popular electoral politics at both state and national levels, and the body's institutional role grew more removed from state influence, proactive with respect to the House and legislative matters generally, and stubbornly independent of the executive. Significant though less substantial changes subsequently reshaped the Senate at the beginning of the twentieth century and then again during the 1960s and 1970s.[6]

One early change the Senate made in its rules brought particularly significant and long-term consequences. In 1806 the body discarded the "previous question" motion—the parliamentary device that allowed majorities to terminate debate and force measures to a vote. Fairly termed "the most critical procedural choice in the history of the Senate," the decision transformed the upper house into an institution that allowed virtually unlimited debate.[7] The change put the Senate at the mercy of small minorities and even individual senators who, if sufficiently determined, could exact inordinate concessions and sometimes prevent the body from acting.[8] Eliminating the "previous question," moreover, seemed to flout the framers' commitment to majority rule in representative assemblies and create a Senate distinctly different from the one they had sought to establish.[9]

The House of Representatives changed only a bit more slowly. As late as 1800 it remained relatively unorganized and without significant internal hierarchies, reflecting some of the loftiest republican ideals of the founders. Originally, it had few standing committees, and those that did exist exercised quite limited power.[10] Further, no formal party leadership structure existed; few rules restricted the right of members to bring matters to the floor; and substantive debates were common and often extended. A series of major rule changes over the next century—establishing standing committees, granting extensive power to committees and their chairs, and placing business under the control of a hierarchical and sometimes authoritarian leadership structure—gradually transformed the House into a more streamlined, majoritarian, and partisan body.[11] In 1811, for example, it turned away from the Senate's path and adopted a "previous question" motion allowing majorities to terminate debate, and in the following decade it spawned a party caucus system that helped embed the practice of disciplined party government in its internal organization and procedures.[12] The developments contradicted some of the founders' highest hopes about republican government, violating in particular their deep conviction that "parties" were dangerous and that free and open debate should be the norm.

By the early nineteenth century, moreover, a communications revolution was transforming the political context in which both houses operated. The means of transportation improved substantially with the construction of roads, canals, and railways, while methods of transmitting news and information were revolutionized.[13] The Post Office Act of 1792, for example, not only laid the foundation for an effective national postal service but also incorporated two provisions that helped transform the politics of the early republic. It provided exceptionally favorable terms for carrying newspapers, and it prohibited public officials from screening or otherwise interfering with the newspapers' use of the mails. "Few institutions," wrote Richard R. John, "were more profoundly shaped by this event than Congress."[14] The act encouraged the rapid expansion of the free press and underwrote a remarkable extension of the public sphere, reducing the political advantages of the Atlantic seaboard and its principal cities, linking hinterland communities to the discussion of national issues, and providing unprecedented amounts of current and diverse information to Americans across the land. By the 1830s the nation's postal system boasted 2,476 separate routes, and the number of newspapers had jumped from 106 in 1790 to 1,258, many of which circulated far beyond their cities and towns of origin.[15] Congress had become the "popular" branch of government in a distinctly new way, not only in theory but in fact. Members used their franking privilege to flood their constituencies with favorable publicity; adversaries exploited vastly expanded informational sources as a basis for launching their assaults; and ordinary citizens were increasingly able both to inform themselves about national issues and to press their views on their representatives.[16] The Congress of worthy gentlemen that the founders had envisioned quickly dissolved into memory, replaced by a rowdier and more volatile Congress of "common men" in close and regular contact with their constituencies.

As the political context and internal workings of the two chambers changed, so did the balance of power between them. Originally, the House was considered the more powerful and republican body, "dependent on the people alone."[17] The Senate, in contrast, smacked of aristocracy and, until 1795, compounded its suspect nature by conducting its business in secret.[18] The relationship, however, was gradually reversed, and by the 1820s the Senate had become the more prestigious body.[19] Population growth affected the chambers differently, and the Senate's smaller size and statewide electoral districts magnified its prestige compared with the more unwieldy and locally oriented House. Moreover, the Senate's six-year term promised greater security and more opportunities for members to achieve national recognition and hence made the upper house especially attractive to the talented and ambitious. Finally, two of the Senate's exclusive powers—to advise and consent on treaties and major federal appointments[20]—proved particularly important when foreign policy issues or major presidential nominations for office erupted into national controversies. Alexis de Tocqueville marked the change that had occurred by the 1830s. The House was filled largely with "village attorneys, those in trade, or even men belonging to the lowest class," he wrote, while the Senate was packed with "eloquent attorneys, distinguished generals, skillful magistrates, or well-known statesmen." The former appeared "vulgar," the latter "illustrious."[21]

Indeed, developments during the nineteenth century further expanded the role of the Senate and essentially negated a fundamental constitutional prerogative that the Constitution allocated to the House. Article I conferred on the government's authentically "popular" branch the exclusive right to originate all revenue-raising bills.[22] That provision, Madison believed, was pivotal: "This power over the purse may, in fact, be regarded as the most complete and effectual weapon with which any constitution can arm the immediate representatives of the people." It was responsible for the "continual triumph" of the British House of Commons, and it would enable the American House of Representatives to prevail even against the "utmost degree" of opposition from the Senate or the executive.[23] Initially, the Senate deferred to the lower chamber's initiation power,[24] but it soon began to challenge and subvert the power's significance. By the early nineteenth century the Senate was using its bicameral veto and its authority to amend[25] to become, in effect, an equal partner in shaping revenue measures, and by century's end it had become the dominant partner. In both 1883 and 1894, for example, the Senate "amended" House tariff bills by essentially striking every substantive provision they contained and replacing them with its own entirely new bills. On each occasion, the House acquiesced. As of the mid-twentieth century, one scholar concluded, "the Senate has dominated most of the revenue-raising legislation of the past fifty years."[26] Thus, over the course of some two centuries Madison's "complete and effectual weapon" shrank for the most part to a mere formality of timing.

In spite of the Senate's broader powers and greater prestige, the relationship between the two bodies remained flexible, and the dynamics of American politics periodically returned the House to center stage. In the 1860s Radical Republicans under Thaddeus Stevens of Pennsylvania dominated national Reconstruction policy, while House Democrats drove the major reform achievements of Woodrow Wilson's highly successful first term.[27] Similarly, in the late twentieth century the House again returned to prominence. During the 1980s House Democrats played a particularly powerful role as the institutional base of opposition to the "Reagan Revolution," while in the following decade House Republicans carried the assault on what became the Clinton interregnum. The revival of the House in the late twentieth century led one political scientist to suggest that "[t]oday, the House and Senate are virtually political equals—a rare, possibly unique condition among the world's national bicameral legislatures."[28]

As the internal structures and power relationships of the two houses changed, so did the roles they played in the federal structure. Most obvious, alterations in election procedures substantially reoriented both chambers. The House changed first. At the Philadelphia Convention the delegates had rejected George Mason's argument that the existence of "different interests and views" counseled that the popularly elected branch "be taken not only from different parts of the whole republic, but also from different districts of the larger members of it."[29] Accordingly, the Constitution gave the states the power, subject to congressional override, to determine the manner in which their representatives would be chosen.[30] Although the states initially adopted a variety of schemes, most—especially the small states—preferred statewide elections in order to unify their delegations and concentrate their voting strength. During the first half of the nineteenth century, however, as the states grew in population and their internal cohesion fragmented, pressures for district voting grew. Eventually, changing political calculations in some of the small states provided the votes necessary for Congress to pass the Reapportionment Act of 1842, which required districting in all House elections.[31] The change accentuated intrastate divisions, reduced the power of states as unified entities, and increased the influence of substate governmental units and private local interests in the national legislature.[32]

The analogous change in the Senate waited another seventy years. The Constitution provided that senators would be "chosen" by the legislatures of the states, and for more than a century the body had remained, relative to the House, more closely tied to state governments and their dominant interests. In 1913, however, as pressures for more direct democracy swept across the land during the Progressive Era, the nation adopted the Seventeenth Amendment, which mandated the direct popular election of senators.[33] The amendment further weakened the power of the states in the national government and helped forge a Senate that would become ever more responsive to national issues, opinions, and interest groups.[34]

Compounding those centralizing effects, alterations in committee rules and procedures tended over time to encourage Congress to spend more generously and to accept deficits in the federal budget. During the late nineteenth and early twentieth centuries changes in House committee rules decentralized authority to appropriate funds. The changes apparently stemmed from members' desires to funnel more money to their individual districts, and the altered rules induced Congress to increase federal spending in a number of areas. Moreover, other evidence suggests that, to the extent Congress gave its committees authority over multiple programs as opposed to single programs, the committees spent more freely and accepted budget deficits more readily.[35] Needless to say, the willingness of Congress to increase federal spending and incur larger deficits was a major factor in extending the reach of federal power and expanding the regulatory burdens it imposed on state and local governments.

More generally, the nature of the "representative" function of the two houses also changed. Population growth by itself had a major effect on both. First, the number of senators quadrupled, while the number of representatives jumped sevenfold. Thus, as a general matter, the voice and influence of individual members of Congress shrank steadily over the decades, reducing the responsibility of each for his or her chamber's actions and increasing incentives for more narrowly self-interested behavior. Second, and more important, each member came to "represent" vastly multiplied numbers of citizens. In 1789 House members represented an average of 50,000 people, a number that grew more than tenfold by the late twentieth century. More striking, senators originally represented an average of 115,000 people, while two hundred years later they represented an average of some 3 million, approximately as many people as lived in the entire United States in 1789. With such massive population growth, the substance of the representational function of the two houses and their individual members slowly shifted. Increasingly, members of Congress came to "represent" not just specific geographic regions or even states but, rather, amorphous ideologies with national resonance backed by national organizations pushing their own distinctive national interests, a development that did not require—or often even allow—them to follow any clear or consistent position on issues of "federalism."

Over the past century, moreover, the representative function of the House evolved away from the founders' vision in another way. The Constitution mandated two-year terms for representatives[36] because, as Madison maintained, it was "particularly essential" that the House "should have an immediate dependence on, and an intimate sympathy with, the people."[37] Yet, by the late twentieth century a lengthening history of party initiatives, legislative innovations, shifts in voting behavior, changes in campaign funding and electioneering practices, and increasingly sophisticated gerrymandering—both partisan and nonpartisan—had transformed the two-year term into what was, for most members, an almost unlimited tenure in office.[38] Political analysts reported that methodical gerrymandering had reduced the number of the House's 435 seats that were seriously contested to about 100 in 1994 and then to only about 40—less than 10 percent of the body's membership—in 2006.[39] Biennial elections remained as an institutional form, but the many de facto advantages of incumbency reduced it for most members of the House to little more than an expensive and time-consuming ritual.[40]

The de facto representative function of the Senate changed even more significantly. The Constitution mandated that the upper house "shall be composed of two Senators from each State,"[41] thereby ensuring the overrepresentation of smaller states. Although that representational principle remained unaltered, its social and political significance did not. The founders tended to equate territory with population, but the growth of large industrialized cities in geographically smaller states and the admission of western states with vast territories and small populations severed that connection.[42] In the early nineteenth century 33 percent of the nation's population could elect a majority of the Senate, a percentage that dropped to 26 in the 1860s and then to 17 a century later. By the opening decade of the twenty-first century it stood at only 16.3 percent.[43] Thus, the Senate came to overrepresent geographical size and underrepresent population far beyond the expectations of the founders.

Further, as the nation's population grew and shifted, so did the relative advantage or disadvantage that the individual states derived from the Senate's representational structure.[44] Virginia and Massachusetts—originally disadvantaged—increasingly gained relative influence in the Senate, for example, while Georgia, North Carolina, Florida, Texas, and California—long advantaged there—gradually lost relative influence. In addition, the political culture of the South and some sparsely populated states brought frequent reelection to their senators, and their longer individual tenures combined with the Senate's seniority system to give those states a heavily disproportionate influence over the chamber's committees and, consequently, over its agenda and decision making. In the years after Reconstruction committee control shifted "from the urban and industrial states of the North and East to the rural and agricultural or mining states of the South and West."[45] By 1934 not one of the thirteen largest committees in the upper house was headed by a senator from a state east of the Mississippi River or north of the Mason-Dixon Line.[46]

Finally, by the second half of the twentieth century the representational significance of the Senate had changed in yet another way, less directly related to the states as states but nonetheless significant for the operations of the federal structure. As of the mid-1990s, Lynn Baker and Samuel H. Dinkin found, "fully fifty percent of the nation's persons of color reside in the five largest states."[47] With their voting strength concentrated in states already relatively disadvantaged in the Senate, such minority groups lost proportional influence in the upper house and, consequently, in the national arena as well. Thus, the Senate's representation structure increasingly disadvantaged the racial and ethnic minority groups that tended to avoid smaller and more rural states and gather in the larger and more urbanized ones.

During the twentieth century, moreover, the two houses altered their organizational structures in ways that removed them even further from the deliberative bodies the founders had envisioned. Members increasingly surrounded themselves with large numbers of aides and issue specialists, while staffing literally hundreds of committees and subcommittees, most with relatively narrow jurisdictions and charges. In the Senate the number of personal and committee staffers stood at 470 in 1931, a number that grew to 3,250 in 1972 and then to 7,200 in 1991.[48] Congress also established a number of special agencies to support its work, including the Congressional Budget Office, the Government Accountability Office, and the Medicare Payment Advisory Commission.[49] Multiplying complexities, both in the issues that senators and representatives faced and in the nature of their own bureaucratized institutions, forced those in both houses to specialize, and often members knew relatively little or nothing about many of the bills their chambers considered or the activities they conducted.[50] Indeed, to monitor the critical operations of the Central Intelligence Agency, Congress formally divided its own membership into two distinct groups, adopting "an elite model of legislative oversight" that placed supervision in the hands of small and secretive committees and ensured that "most members of Congress would learn almost nothing of agency activities."[51] By the late twentieth century, one political scientist concluded, Congress had become a "collection of interacting bureaucracies."[52] Such working conditions bore little relationship either to the founders' image of a deliberative republican assembly or to the legislative body that had existed in the 1790s.

In addition, during the late twentieth century new internal reforms—limiting the power of committee chairs, strengthening party caucuses, opening proceedings to television, adopting ethical and financial reporting rules, and enhancing the opportunities of individual members to influence legislation—further reshaped the practices, behavioral norms, and public perceptions of both houses. Members of Congress were increasingly absorbed by the need to secure favorable media attention, amass ever larger campaign chests, protect against political attacks launched outside the normal election cycle, assess the dangers and opportunities created by new congressional ethics rules, and give heed to an expanding and increasingly aggressive array of activists, lobbyists, interest groups, and ideological partisans who enjoyed expanding access to the lawmaking process. Those developments, Julian E. Zelizer concluded, "fundamentally altered the national political experience."[53] Among their consequences, they further strengthened the national orientation of those who served in Congress and tied them tightly to the demands of national media, national interest groups, and national funding sources.

Those later changes even altered the basic legislative process itself, making it more complex and no longer entirely consistent with the standard procedure sketched in the Constitution's formal provisions. By the beginning of the twenty-first century, congressional lawmaking often required consideration by multiple committees in both houses, the merger of numerous and sometimes unrelated proposals, the development and adoption of procedural rules specially tailored for individual bills, endless informal negotiations with private groups, technical oversight by the Office of Management and Budget, bargaining with executive-branch wranglers wielding the threat of a presidential veto, the use of "holds" and "earmarks," the threat of filibusters and other delaying or obfuscating tactics, and the involvement of dozens or even hundreds of members as active participants and interchamber conferees, many or most of whom were often interested in only one particular provision or clause in sprawling measures that occupied hundreds of pages of text.[54] While "states" were, or could be, intimately involved in the legislative work, the process was increasingly sensitive to organized economic interests and activist political groups, an overall governmental process that seemed far more responsive to the nation's dynamic and fractionated politics than to any formal requirements of its binary federal structure.

Finally, beginning in the years after World War II, Congress as an institution substantially reoriented its general role within the federal government. Confronting the massive expansion of federal administrative agencies that resulted from the New Deal and the war effort, it enacted several innovative statutes, starting with the Administrative Procedure Act and the Legislative Reorganization Act of 1946, that began to reconceptualize the national administrative state as an arm of the legislature.[55] A cascade of similar statutes and amendments soon followed, accelerating the process of reorientation. Together with a growing readiness to delegate legislative power, distribute federal funds generously, and focus members' efforts on "case work" and constituent services—especially on matters within the jurisdiction of federal administrative agencies—the statutes inaugurated a new era of congressional involvement in the administrative process.[56] No longer was the national legislature simply a deliberative, consulting, and lawmaking body. Rather, it had become something new, a pluralistic and bureaucratized institution whose numerous and often uncoordinated parts sought to supervise and exploit a massive federal administrative state. As the twentieth century entered its second half, Congress became increasingly engaged in what seemed to be "executive" functions, while its delegation and funding practices led it toward ever more expansive efforts to impose national standards and policies on the states.[57]

The Federal Executive

The executive branch of the national government changed even more radically than did the legislative, in significant part because the Constitution left its nature and powers so vague that presidents through the years were able to remake the office as times and occasions demanded. The Constitution granted a variety of powers to "a President of the United States" and "vested" in the office an unadorned and unexplained "executive Power,"[58] an ambiguous grant that proved capable of underwriting an endless and seemingly uncabinable variety of claims to authority, discretion, and independence. The ratification debates did little either to explain the executive's specific powers or to clarify the meaning of the "vesting" clause.[59] Anti-Federalists tossed out "a grab bag of interpretations, charges, fears, and analyses," while few Federalists even attempted a general account of the office or its powers.[60] The most elaborate discussion appeared in eleven essays that Hamilton contributed to the *Federalist*, essays that predictably argued for an "energetic" executive with expansive powers and vast discretion.[61] Most Americans, however, including some Federalists, viewed Hamilton's interpretation with suspicion or even hostility.[62] "The office that emerged from the Philadelphia convention was incomplete and unformed," concluded one student of the presidency. "Thus, Washington, the first president, ventured into largely uncharted territory."[63]

In one respect the presidency was like the houses of Congress, for it, too, was profoundly reshaped by alterations in election procedures. The Constitution required state legislatures to provide a method of appointing "Electors" and directed that those chosen should meet in their states and cast votes to select the president and vice president.[64] The scheme was designed to serve as a refining device that would place the selection of president and vice president in the hands of respected individuals capable of making wise judgments. "The framers," Jethro Lieberman explained, "envisioned independent electors, beholden to no one, not even the people, in choosing the president."[65] Experience revealed technical difficulties in the process, however, and in the early nineteenth century democratic sentiments swept the country. In 1800 a quarter of the states, four of sixteen, had made provisions for selecting their presidential electors by popular vote; by 1828 three-quarters, eighteen of twenty-four, had done so.[66] The remainder quickly fell in line, and by the mid-nineteenth century all of the states had accepted the practice of holding popular elections for slates of electors pledged to party candidates, a consensus that in effect negated one of the founders' most distinctive constitutional inventions. As the Electoral College atrophied into a formality and the presidency became the prize of a nationwide popular vote, the office won new legitimation, independence, and status, while a growing mystique began to envelop its occupants. The development altered the dynamics of the constitutional plan and demonstrated that the framers had failed to anticipate what became a dominant fact of American politics, "that control of the government would depend on control of the presidency."[67]

Indeed, from the nation's beginning innovative presidential actions repeatedly expanded the role and power of the office.[68] Washington, Jefferson, and Jackson stretched its effective reach,[69] and the crisis of the Civil War forced Lincoln to abandon the traditional view that the executive held only those powers expressly granted by the Constitution.[70] Although his immediate successors reverted to more restrictive conceptions, at the beginning of the twentieth century Theodore Roosevelt advanced the dramatic new view that the president was the "steward of the people" who possessed not only the authority but the duty to do anything the national welfare required unless it was explicitly forbidden by the Constitution.[71] Thereafter, conceptions of the office continually expanded through the twentieth century, and by the 1970s Richard Nixon was prepared to claim that executive power essentially had no limit. When asked whether the president could authorize illegal actions if they were taken in the national interest, he replied candidly, "Well, when the President does it, that means it is not illegal."[72]

Beginning in the late nineteenth century, moreover, changes in politics and party organization gave new political muscle to the presidential office and underwrote its expansive and centralizing role. As the post-Reconstruction party system became entrenched in an industrializing and urbanizing world, presidents worked ever more assiduously to become the recognized and unquestioned leaders of their party. They worked to control disparate and local party elements, forge permanent and well-organized national party organizations, focus political debate on their own carefully selected national issues, and articulate an ideology and program that would unify the party and secure a national electoral majority. Increasingly, presidents concentrated on gaining reelection, orchestrated unified national campaigns, and demanded loyalty and "regularity" from the party's members in Congress and the states. The fate of the nation's nine vice presidents who succeeded to the highest office because of death or resignation reflected the striking emergence of the president as national party leader. In the nineteenth century not one of the four ascending vice presidents was able to gain his party's presidential nomination for the next election; in the twentieth century all five easily did so.[73] By the twentieth century, in other words, holding the presidential office essentially guaranteed renomination because it guaranteed control over a powerful national party organization and its networks of money, influence, and workers.

As the conception of the office expanded, and its power and mystique grew, the resources at its command multiplied exponentially. Not until the administration of James Buchanan did Congress appropriate money for a presidential assistant,[74] but the executive branch expanded markedly during the Civil War and continued a somewhat erratic growth through the late nineteenth and early twentieth centuries. The New Deal sharply accelerated the pace. In Franklin Roosevelt's first term alone sixty new executive agencies were established, and the branch expanded to 824,259 employees, a 42 percent jump in only four years.[75] Then, in 1939 Congress reorganized and enlarged the branch, creating the Executive Office of the President and bringing the White House Office, the Bureau of the Budget, and the National Resources Planning Board under its authority.[76] By 2005 the number of total federal civilian employees had more than tripled to 2.72 million,[77] while "the executive branch" had grown to include fifteen cabinet-level departments together with seventy-three "Boards, Commissions and Committees," sixty-four "Independent Agencies and Government Corporations," and four "Quasi-Official Agencies."[78] As the branch grew, presidents labored methodically—though often with only limited success—to centralize authority in the White House, seeking to control its ever-expanding bureaucratic apparatus and marshal its massive resources to serve their political agendas. Nixon's presidency was a turning point. "Nixon's systematic efforts to centralize authority in both the White House and the Executive Office of the President and to use them to pursue presidential goals," two students of the office concluded, "have for the most part been followed, and in some cases intensified, by his successors."[79]

The expanding size and power of the executive branch, together with the president's escalating ability to capture the public imagination and establish the national agenda, made the office an irresistibly centralizing force that altered both the balance and dynamics of the federal structure.[80] Presidents increasingly found it essential to propose national solutions for almost every problem that captured national or even regional attention.[81] They became the nation's legislative leaders, expected to formulate policies and proposals to remedy all ills. Despite his fervent attacks on "big government" and his proposals to "return power to the states," for example, Ronald Reagan continued the process of strengthening the presidency by magnifying its celebrity status and exemplifying the ideal of the "strong" president. His major achievements did not include limiting the federal government—which, in fact, grew during his administration—but did include increasing federal military spending, highlighting the centrality of national rather than state policy, and bringing America to a position of unrivaled international dominance.[82] Similarly, George W. Bush, who pledged "to make respect for federalism a priority in this administration,"[83] claimed unprecedented and unchecked powers to wiretap and imprison American citizens, asserted growing control over state and local law enforcement agencies as part of a "war" on terror, and sponsored dramatically centralizing legislation including the USA PATRIOT Act, the No Child Left Behind Act, the Class Action Fairness Act, and the truly extraordinary Military Commissions Act of 2006.[84]

For the federal structure, the expanding powers of the executive steadily tilted the governmental balance toward ever greater national direction and control. Establishment of a Department of Justice in 1870, a federal prison system in the 1890s, and the first federal "Bureau of Investigation" in 1909 expanded the executive's law enforcement capabilities and began shifting prosecutorial power to the national government.[85] The potential consequences became apparent in the aftermath of World War I. Fearing political radicalism as the "most terrible menace of danger since the barbarian hordes overran West Europe and opened the Dark Ages," the bureau's chief, J. Edgar Hoover, was able to compile secret dossiers on more than eighty thousand individuals whom he suspected of some form of political dissent.[86] Between 1900 and 1929 the number of federal criminal statutes tripled, doubled again over the next two decades, and then tripled once more during the following half-century.[87] The drastic expansion of the federal criminal law broadly extended the prosecutorial reach of the executive branch, pushed it into areas previously under exclusive state authority, and magnified its discretion in selecting targets on which to concentrate national enforcement efforts.

During the second half of the twentieth century, moreover, presidents of both parties increasingly resorted to de facto lawmaking through "executive direct action." One study, for example, found that more than half of 427 separate federal agencies established between 1946 and 1996 had been created without congressional action. Direct presidential orders established 43 of them, and cabinet members authorized the remaining 177.[88] Even more striking, the executive was increasingly using such devices as executive orders, national security directives, and presidential memoranda, proclamations, and legislative signing statements to make law. The purpose of such documents, explained Samuel A. Alito Jr., then assistant attorney general in the Reagan administration, was simply to "increase the power of the executive to shape the law."[89] Those presidential devices shared three common characteristics that altered the president's constitutional role. They allowed the executive to negate or alter statutory provisions that he disliked but refused to veto, to announce and enforce rules of "law" that had little or no basis in enacted legislation, and to shape domestic politics more directly by advancing or retarding the interests of those groups he wished to reach.[90]

As such executive lawmaking became increasingly common, it also became increasingly insulated from the checking power of the legislative branch. For the most part, Congress simply acceded to executive orders, either ratifying their provisions by subsequent legislation or in effect sanctioning them by silence. In any event, executive orders generally stood as law. Further, when Congress did try to overturn such orders, it rarely succeeded. Between 1945 and 1998 it considered forty-six bills specifically intended to reverse or substantially alter executive orders. The great majority—74 percent—failed to get out of committee, and only five passed both houses, one of which was struck down by presidential veto.[91] Finally, even when executive orders required funding, and legislative support seemed essential as a constitutional matter, presidents frequently found indirect ways to obtain the necessary funds by diverting or otherwise shifting appropriations made for other purposes.[92] An increasing amount of "law" was thus made not by the "lawmaking branch" but by the executive.[93]

As executive power grew in domestic matters, it expanded exponentially in foreign affairs.[94] From the nation's earliest years the executive branch sought to reduce or avoid the Senate's treaty power,[95] and by 1815 it had excluded the upper house from negotiations with foreign countries. In the late nineteenth century it began to limit the Senate's power even further by avoiding formal "treaties" and conducting foreign policy through informal "executive agreements" that required no legislative ratification.[96] A series of Supreme Court decisions between 1920 and 1942 sanctioned and enhanced the practice. After holding that treaties were the supreme law of the land even if they contained provisions not otherwise within the constitutional authority of the federal government, the Court ruled that informal executive agreements had the legal status of formally adopted treaties and that those informal agreements could displace state law and even authorize confiscation of private property otherwise protected by the Fifth Amendment.[97] Between 1939 and 1989 the United States signed and ratified 702 treaties, but during the same years it entered into 11,698 executive agreements.[98] At the same time, the Court further enhanced the power of the executive by increasingly deferring to its interpretations of treaty language and reducing reliance on the interpretative canons of international law.[99]

The president's powers over foreign policy were "plenary and exclusive," the Court ruled in 1936, and they conferred "a degree of discretion and freedom from statutory restriction which would not be admissible were domestic affairs alone involved." Indeed, it declared, those executive powers existed independent of the Constitution and operated free from any restrictions based on the reserved rights of the states. In the area of foreign affairs, the Court announced, the principles of federalism were simply irrelevant.[100]

The president's authority as "Commander in Chief" came to underwrite even more sweeping expansions of executive power.[101] With rare and generally ineffective exceptions, Congress acquiesced in executive decisions to commit the nation's armed forces abroad.[102] As two political scientists concluded, "the President stands virtually unchallenged in his unilateral ability to commit the United States to war."[103] That, of course, seemed inconsistent with one of the specific propositions on which both the constitutional text and the intent of the founders appeared clear—that Congress, not the executive, held the power to declare war. Beginning in the 1790s, however, governmental practice and judicial opinions combined to gradually transfer that awesome power, in effect, to the executive,[104] one part of the uneven but continuous shift of power within the national government from the legislative to the executive branch.[105]

The steady and massive expansion of executive authority not only altered the balance of power among the national branches but also diminished state power, helping to drive the increasing centralization of American government that occurred in the twentieth and early twenty-first centuries. The synergism between the nation's growing international role and the power of the executive had become apparent by the 1890s, and it was displayed clearly in 1901 when the president used an executive order to establish the Army War College and simultaneously began to push measures designed to tighten presidential control over the war department and expand federal authority over the militias of the states.[106] Expanded naval construction and increased professionalization in the armed services followed, and World War II and the subsequent cold war led to the creation of vast, permanent, and hugely expensive national military, intelligence, and security establishments that came to influence many of society's basic institutions—legal, economic, medical, cultural, educational, and even religious. To ensure the country's technological dominance during the cold war, for example, the federal government began funding national laboratories and essentially took control over many areas of scientific research and development. Within decades, the work of government laboratories extended beyond military and nuclear technology into a wide range of scientific fields with the broadest potential applications and the widest possible influence on American life.[107] The continuously expanding and increasingly powerful executive institutions commanded a swelling share of national resources, conducted massive numbers of extensive and sometimes legally dubious operations that were held secret from the American people, and magnified the importance of areas in which state and local officials had no legal authority.[108]

Growing executive power, moreover, directly affected domestic life and the affairs of the states in multiple and substantial ways. Its impact ranged from the selection of National Guard and Reserve units called for full-time duty to the prosperity of innumerable localities with economies closely tied to either the production of military weapons and supplies or the operation of military bases and related facilities.[109] Presidential power also intruded into both state authority and individual rights insofar as it began to serve as a constitutional justification for the executive to engage in warrantless wiretaps and other seizures and to detain, interrogate, and imprison people who were citizens of a state or were arrested within a state.[110] Further, many foreign policy decisions, however much directed toward "national security," responded in significant part to domestic pressures and served some domestic interests at the expense of others. When Franklin Roosevelt issued Executive Order 9066 directing the internment of Japanese Americans in early 1942, for example, he was responding not only to a perceived national security threat but also to domestic political pressures: an orchestrated and racist campaign by white farmers and California politicians to "kick the Japs out." Working through such organizations as the White American Nurserymen of Los Angeles, those groups sought to eliminate tenacious economic competitors and to seize their fertile and finely cultivated lands.[111] Whatever Roosevelt's knowledge or intentions, his executive order allowed them to do both.[112]

Thus, the growth of executive power, regardless of the constitutional bases offered in justification, profoundly altered the operation and dynamics of the federal structure. It centralized the political system, drew power away from the states, focused public attention on national issues, created a new and often unchecked source of national lawmaking authority, and allowed the federal executive to benefit some domestic groups and interests while excluding or harming others. Further, in an age when air travel, economic globalization, international population movements, instantaneous worldwide communications, and the threat of international terrorism blurred or erased lines between "domestic" and "foreign" matters, the elastic rationale of national security and the abstract principle that the executive held "plenary power" in conducting the nation's foreign affairs combined to provide a justification for the exercise of unlimited and unchecked presidential powers. Together, those developments—increasingly rationalized and defended by aggrandizing constitutional theories that often employed the misleading label of "the unitary executive"—created a kind and degree of centralization that undermined everything the federal structure was designed to prevent. The founders had neither contemplated nor intended anything remotely like that result.[113]

Indeed, by the beginning of the twenty-first century the executive branch would no longer have been recognizable to eighteenth- and nineteenth-century Americans. Not to John Adams in 1789, who thought it "almost impossible" to believe that "a president should ever have the courage to make use of his partial negative."[114] Nor to the old Jeffersonian constitutionalist St. George Tucker, who wrote in 1803 that "the part assigned" the president with respect to Congress "is strictly preventive, and not creative."[115] Nor even to the young political scientist Woodrow Wilson, who as late as 1893 concluded that in the nation's governmental structure the executive branch occupied a "really subordinate position."[116]

The Federal Judiciary

The federal judiciary underwent changes almost as drastic as those that remade the executive branch.[117] From a Supreme Court with uncertain authority and no guaranteed lower court system to enforce its mandate, it expanded into an elaborate three-tiered system headed by an unquestionably authoritative Supreme Court backed by a nationwide enforcement apparatus of more than a dozen appellate courts, ninety-four district courts, almost a thousand life-tenured judges, and tens of thousands of officers and employees, including magistrate judges, bankruptcy judges, law clerks, marshals, and other supporting personnel. To that elaborate structure, Congress added a collection of other "legislative" courts—tribunals staffed by judges lacking the constitutional protections of life tenure and financial independence[118]—to deal with a wide variety of relatively specialized subjects such as taxes, veterans' claims, charges arising from the national military services, and disputes between private parties and many of the federal government's regulatory and administrative agencies. Subject to varying levels of review by the Article III judiciary, such "legislative" courts handled a rapidly increasing share of national judicial business in the twentieth and twenty-first centuries.[119] From its humble early years as a scattered handful of courts lacking general jurisdiction over matters of national law and devoted largely to run-of-the-mill private-law disputes, then, the national judiciary evolved into a powerful and bureaucratized system incorporating hundreds of courts and deciding hundreds of thousands of cases each year, a system that exercised a general jurisdiction over all issues of federal law, controlled essentially all litigation involving either foreign governments or the government of the United States, and authoritatively developed and enforced an ever more pervasive and truly supreme national law.[120]

In the twentieth century, moreover, the federal judiciary grew increasingly centralized and developed its own administrative and even political policies. In 1922 Congress established the Conference of Senior Circuit Judges (changing its name to the Judicial Conference of the United States in 1948), an organization headed by the chief justice of the United States and exercising limited administrative control over the lower courts and their judges. In 1939 Congress authorized the Administrative Office of the United States Courts and in 1967 added a research-oriented adjunct, the Federal Judicial Center, both of which strengthened the judiciary's internal administrative capacities.[121] As federal dockets ballooned in the latter half of the twentieth century, the Judicial Conference expanded its horizons. It adopted more centralized administrative measures to increase the system's efficiency, developed and promoted its own views on the problems facing the national judiciary, and ultimately intruded into issues of substantive legislative policy. By the late twentieth century, under the leadership of Chief Justice William Rehnquist, the conference became an influential advocacy group not only in seeking to improve the judicial system but also in lobbying Congress on controversial social and political issues, perhaps most notoriously urging, in the name of "traditional principles of federalism," that a proposed Violence Against Women Act be scuttled.[122] When Congress ignored the advice and enacted the statute, the five "profederalism" justices on the Rehnquist Court backed the opinion of the Judicial Conference by voiding the legislation at the first opportunity.[123] Thus, by the beginning of the twenty-first century the federal judiciary had become an extensive, powerful, and centrally administered judicial system, no longer a mere passive and neutral adjudicator but an active—and on occasion partisan—participant in the nation's governing process.[124] While its legal and practical reach was limited, and the other branches carried on numerous activities and made innumerable decisions that never came before the courts, the national judiciary nonetheless exercised sweeping powers and held final authority to decide the most critical legal and constitutional issues that divided the nation.

While the federal judiciary grew ever more centralized in its organizational structure, however, it also proved unwieldy and uneven in its application of national law. As the number of its courts and judges multiplied and their caseloads skyrocketed, the Supreme Court was increasingly unable to review more than the tiniest fraction of lower court decisions. By the early twenty-first century, for example, it reviewed less than one-fifth of I percent of the decisions of the circuit courts, while those intermediate appellate courts reviewed only about a quarter of the final decisions of the federal trial courts.[125] The circuit courts, moreover, frequently disagreed among themselves on the questions they addressed. In four years around the turn of the twenty-first century, for example, the circuits were divided on more than a thousand issues of federal law.[126] Further, evidence suggested that variations in federal trial courts were even more striking, with the great majority of their rulings on preliminary, but often practically decisive, procedural matters receiving no appellate review and individual judges frequently able to determine the results of cases by exercising their formal or de facto discretion in shaping both the relevant facts and the controlling law.[127] Thus, while the authority and prestige of the federal judiciary rose over the centuries, the uniformity of its decisions on federal law matters did not necessarily follow suit.

Sitting atop the national judicial system, the Supreme Court itself also changed markedly. "So lightly was the Court regarded, and so slight was its prestige," one of John Marshall's biographers noted, "that when the government moved to Washington [in 1800], no provision was made for it to be housed."[128] For some seventy years the Court was relegated to the gloomy basement of the Capitol Building, and it was able to move above-ground to the old Senate chamber only when the upper house abandoned its early home in favor of the expanded facilities that awaited it in the Capitol's newly completed north wing. Finally, in the 1930s, nearly a century and a half after the founding, Congress decided to provide the Court with its own building. By that point, Americans had come to believe that the Court's position merited an imposing monument, and they designed for the justices a white "marble palace" and placed it prominently in the center of Capitol Hill. The Court's sequential homes aptly symbolized its rise in the American constitutional system from the depths to the heights.

The course of its rise was long and complicated. Marshall started the transformation in the early nineteenth century, outlining broad and nationalizing constitutional principles, unifying the justices through turbulent political times, and projecting an image of the Court as a forum of reason and law. He persuaded the justices, for example, to abandon their prior practice of issuing diffusive seriatim opinions and to stand, instead, behind a single "opinion of the Court," a practice that conveyed an image of judicial unanimity, objectivity, and authority.[129] Challenges, however, regularly recurred, and during Jackson's presidency and again through the Civil War era the Court's position seemed particularly vulnerable.[130] Better days, however, were ahead. The power of the Court's mandate and the authority of its voice grew steadily, and in the late nineteenth century it rose to a position of clear primacy in construing the Constitution and in the twentieth century ascended to its current position as the truly "supreme" authority on constitutional issues.[131] Although the founders had been familiar with the idea of judicial review, they considered it a far more tentative and limited power than the sweeping authority the Court came to assert and most Americans to accept.[132] Beginning in the late nineteenth century the Court exercised its equity powers with growing breadth and invalidated both state and federal measures with increasing frequency; and, after defeating Franklin Roosevelt's "Court-packing plan" in 1937, it began extending its authority and reach even further, first for "liberal" purposes during the Warren era and then for "conservative" ones during the Rehnquist years. Under both regimes, however, the Court formally announced its position as the ultimate authority on the Constitution's meaning and application.[133] When it asserted its jurisdiction to decide the contested presidential election of 2000, a dubious and bitterly disputed action, no government institution—not the federal executive, not the House or Senate, and not a single state, including the state whose judgment was overruled—moved in any way to oppose its action.[134] The entire society and all its governmental institutions acquiesced in the decision and the result it brought.

While over the centuries the Court's efforts were varied and sometimes contradictory, its cumulative rulings, especially since the late nineteenth century, gradually and steadily expanded the powers of the national government.[135] Under a variety of clauses, most centrally the Commerce and General Welfare clauses, it allowed Congress to legislate directly or indirectly over most aspects of American life, while it construed the vague provisions of Article II to allow the executive vast, unprecedented, and sometimes wholly unchecked powers. So, too, it expanded its own power and, often, that of the lower federal judiciary as well. Beginning in the late nineteenth century, the Court used a variety of tools—equity, preemption, statutory construction, the "dormant" Commerce Clause, incorporation of the Bill of Rights, and a "general" and then "special" federal common law—to forge the national judiciary into a major and sometimes decisive force in American government. Similarly, it used its own far-reaching and discretionary appellate jurisdiction, a comprehensive "supervisory" power over the lower federal courts, and an increasingly muscular practice of judicial review to ensure that it, and it alone, would speak the final constitutional word on whatever national issues it chose to address.[136]

The Court's ascension since the late nineteenth century roughly paralleled that of the executive. Facing the complexities of the twentieth century, Congress—though still the most powerful branch on parchment—too frequently proved itself politically fragmented and institutionally cumbersome.[137] A Senate coalition of one-third plus one—less than 7 percent of the legislature's total membership—could prevent Congress from acting to check executive or judicial actions, and there were usually thirty-four senators who supported any action taken by the Court or by any but the most fiercely unpopular of presidents. In contrast, both the executive and the judiciary—or at least the president as an individual and the Court as a nine-person body—stood as relatively more unified, efficient, and authoritative, and they projected far more positive images in both the actual governing process and general public opinion. In terms of quick, decisive, and galvanizing action the decisive advantage lay beyond question with the president, while in terms of ultimately persuasive constitutional authority the advantage seemed to lie, in the long run at least, with the Court. In spite of the de facto shifts in power relations among the three branches, however, Congress did continue to rival the others in one respect. It, too, sometimes made law.

An Invented Fourth Branch: The Federal Administrative Apparatus

While federal administrative capacities existed from the beginning in the cabinet departments and such agencies as the land and post offices, the national government in the late nineteenth century began establishing what became, in effect, almost a new fourth branch of government, an apparatus of "independent" regulatory agencies that was nowhere mentioned in the Constitution.[138] Congress created the agencies; the executive approved them; and the Court upheld their legitimacy. After establishing the Interstate Commerce Commission in 1887, the national government added a variety of other agencies such as the Food and Drug Administration (1906), the Federal Reserve Board (1913), and the Federal Trade Commission (1914). The Great Depression and the New Deal spawned dozens more, including the Social Security Administration, the Securities and Exchange Commission, the National Labor Relations Board, and the Federal Housing Administration. World War II further accelerated the trend, and from the 1940s the federal administrative apparatus extended its reach until it touched, at least indirectly, most areas of economic and social activity.[139]

The operations of federal administrative agencies provoked a series of constitutional problems. In the first instance, they raised questions about whether and under what conditions Congress could "delegate" its powers, for its statutes commonly authorized the agencies to promulgate rules that carried the force of law. Further, they raised questions about the separation of powers, for Congress frequently delegated not only power to make rules but also power to enforce the rules and to adjudicate disputes arising under them. It conferred on the same agencies, in other words, what seemed legislative, executive, and judicial powers. From 1887 the Court struggled with those problems, gradually extending the scope of allowable delegation to the broadest reaches and minimizing separation-of-powers restrictions as long as the agencies followed certain prescribed procedures and their final decisions remained subject, at least in theory, to judicial review.

The new national administrative apparatus[140] stretched the effective reach of the central government. It extended federal power into areas that previously had been under the primary or exclusive control of the states, and it expanded the practical capacities of the national government to influence and control ever wider areas of life. Further, its sustaining rationale—that experts could apply neutral and objective scientific methods to make government actions more rational and efficient—readily encouraged the use of uniform nationwide rules and standards.[141] As congressional delegations of power grew broader and vaguer, moreover, they increasingly generated concerns about the constitutional legitimacy of the rules and adjudications that the administrative apparatus produced. Thus, administrative government not only expanded national authority but did so in ways that seemed to undermine the idea that constitutional principles constrained the central government and limited its power to preempt state authority.[142]

Sporadic and diverse efforts to limit the administrative state after the middle of the twentieth century failed to check the centralizing trend. When criticism of federal agencies intensified during the 1960s, reformers sought to restrict agency discretion by expanding federal judicial review of their actions. Such broadened review, however, did not limit national power but merely shifted it to another national branch.[143] Similarly, disputes over the administrative apparatus increasingly became battlegrounds between Congress and the executive, with each seeking to assert control over the agencies while insulating them from the influence of the other.[144] Thus, even when the federal administrative apparatus drew criticism and provoked efforts to reform or limit it, the efforts still kept both attention and authority riveted at the national level.

The States

As the elements on the national side of the federal structure changed, so did those on the state side. The states quadrupled in number; their institutions multiplied; and their interests proliferated, becoming increasingly diverse on one hand and interconnected on the other. Indeed, as early as the mid-nineteenth century, many states had grown so populous and heterogeneous that, by themselves, they far exceeded the limits of the traditional "small" republic that the Anti-Federalists had invoked in opposing Madison's "extended republic." By the beginning of the twenty-first century more than half the states contained populations larger than that of the entire United States in 1789.

In the eighteenth and most of the nineteenth centuries state and local governments conducted the overwhelming amount of the nation's public business. Their extensive activities ranged from substantial efforts to stimulate economic development to relatively continuous supervision of many of the most basic areas of daily life. The idea of "*salus populi*," the right and power of the people to secure their general welfare, underlay political debate and legal regulation. With little or no national involvement, state and local governments enforced "minute and ubiquitous regulations shaping the most important public policy concerns of the nineteenth century: public safety, public economy, public property, public morals, and public health."[145]

As the nineteenth century progressed, however, the role and status of the states relative to the central government began to decline.[146] Nationalization of the economy weakened the ability of states to identify and control the forces that affected the lives of their citizens, and increasingly complex interstate problems strained their institutional resources and administrative capacities. As the federal government began to expand its activities and enjoyed new successes in meeting the nation's social and economic problems, the states entered a period of lowered visibility and shrinking relative importance.

Three other developments accelerated the trend. One was the rise of cities and suburbs as driving political forces and major suppliers of essential new government services.[147] A second was the emergence of foreign policy as a paramount concern—especially the galvanizing effect of World War II, the frightening dangers of the cold war, and the specter of international terrorism—which inevitably moved the states toward the political background. The third was the spread of new and more expansive ideas of personal freedom that began to force limits on many traditional state regulatory activities involving public health and morality. "The period from 1940 to the early 1960s," Jon C. Teaford concluded, "was therefore a dark age for the image of state government, an era when the prestige of the states dipped to its lowest point."[148] Philip Kurland, a great admirer of decentralization, lost hope. Federalism, he declared in 1968, was "moribund if it is not dead."[149]

As usual, however, change was ceaseless, and by the late twentieth century the relative decline of the states began to slow and, in some areas, reverse itself. In part because of electoral redistricting schemes forced on them by the federal government, the states entered a new era of rising accomplishments and prestige. Although they had struggled for a century to modernize their governments, by the 1980s they were making progress that was rapid, widespread, and substantial. They streamlined their lawmaking procedures, professionalized their legislatures, expanded institutional support staffs, and gave their governors longer terms and greater powers with which to establish and implement their programs. Further, they funded their judiciaries more generously, raising their quality by appointing judges on the basis of merit and unifying their operations with centralized rule-making procedures and more effective administrative structures.[150] By the 1980s state governments seemed newly accountable, effective, and respected.

Perhaps of greatest importance, the states—principally those in the South—were ending their brutal and centuries-old practices of racial abuse and discrimination. Persistent and often intense federal pressure over several decades had compelled them to abandon legalized racial segregation and disenfranchisement, while expanded electorates that included African Americans as well as growing numbers of Hispanic and Asian Americans—together with broad changes in popular attitudes about race and ethnicity—led many to enact laws prohibiting public and even some types of private discrimination based on race, religion, ethnicity, and national origin. As a growing number of states became more active in protecting politically vulnerable groups, the image of the states improved and public confidence in their fairness and effectiveness rose.[151] Beginning at last to break the iron link between "federalism" and southern racial oppression, the changes began to stimulate a new faith in both the possibilities and virtues of decentralized government.[152]

Ironically, however, the expanding activities of the states and renewed public faith in their ability to govern fairly led to increasing centralization at the state level and a relative decline in the influence of cities and other substate elements. Municipal governments, for example, had exerted strong influence in Congress over federal budget allocations from 1957 to 1977, but during the century's last quarter their position weakened. A variety of factors—tax indexation, fiscal deficits, increasing congressional control over appropriations, and Republican administrations determined to enhance state authority—reduced both their independence from state government and their political clout in Washington.[153] Thus, at the beginning of the twenty-first century, the trend at the state level was toward increasing activism and centralized control over the units of local government.[154]

That state-level trend largely matched the continuing trend at the national level. In spite of the Rehnquist Court's "federalism revolution," which gave some protections to state governments while depriving disfavored social groups of national rights, the federal government—though changing its selection of beneficiaries—continued its activist and centralizing course. The national orientation of Congress, the vastly swelling power of the executive, and the determination of the federal judiciary to make national law in its chosen areas[155] continued to drive the evolution of the federal structure relentlessly and push it ever farther from the system of government that had existed in 1789.

8

CONTESTED AUTHORITIES

Upon election to the House of Representatives in 1789, James Madison considered the overwhelming challenges that lay ahead and admitted how little the Constitution had actually settled. "We are in a wilderness without a single footstep to guide us," he confessed.[1] Of the many things the Constitution had not settled, perhaps the most important was the locus of authority in construing the Constitution and resolving conflicts between the central government and the states. The matter had not been settled for an obvious reason. The founders harbored too many vague, incomplete, and conflicting ideas on the subject to underwrite any clear consensus.

Original Uncertainties

The delegates to the Philadelphia Convention considered a variety of possible mechanisms for authoritatively construing and applying the Constitution. The original "Virginia Plan" introduced by Governor Edmund Randolph called for the president and members of the judiciary to form a "council of revision" that would be empowered to negate acts of both national and state legislatures.[2] Madison, James Wilson, Oliver Ellsworth, George Mason, and others argued in favor of one or another form of such an executive-judicial "Revisionary power."[3] Pursuing an alternative path to the same goal, Madison subsequently urged the delegates to give Congress a negative in "all cases" where state laws contravened the

Constitution. "This prerogative of the General Govt.," he insisted, "is the great pervading principle that must controul [*sic*] the centrifugal tendency of the States."[4] Repeatedly, however, the convention rejected such proposals.[5]

In the end, the delegates finessed the issue with another ambiguous compromise, adopting the Supremacy Clause and the Oath Clause.[6] The first mandated that the Constitution "shall be the supreme Law of the Land," and the second that members of the legislative, executive, and judicial branches of state and federal governments "shall be bound by Oath or Affirmation, to support this Constitution."[7] What the provisions did not do was confer authority on any specific level or branch to say definitively what the Constitution meant when disputes arose. Indeed, by requiring all state and federal officials to swear an oath of allegiance, the provision rather plausibly suggested that all were equally responsible for interpreting and enforcing the new charter. Such a compromise promised little but future contestation.

Following ratification, questions about the Constitution's meaning erupted immediately, and the founders advanced a variety of theories to identify loci of interpretative authority. One view was termed "departmentalism," the idea that each of the three national branches was authorized to construe the Constitution in performing its duties and that none could override the constitutional judgments of the others. Irresolvable conflicts between the three, and between nation and states as well, were to be settled ultimately by the people themselves.[8] Madison and Jefferson articulated the departmentalist theory in the earliest years of the new government, while Presidents Andrew Jackson and Abraham Lincoln subsequently advanced their own versions in fighting the Court's definitions of national power. Jackson rejected the broad power that *McCulloch v. Maryland*[9] upheld, while Lincoln castigated the narrow restrictions that *Dred Scott v. Sandford*[10] imposed. Departmentalism remained an influential theory through the Civil War but faded during the late nineteenth century and reappeared only sporadically thereafter.[11]

A second view, associated most closely with Hamilton,[12] maintained that the Supreme Court was required to construe the Constitution and that its supervision would ensure that the proper lines of constitutional authority would be honored. "The interpretation of the laws is the proper and peculiar province of the courts," Hamilton declared in the Seventy-Eighth *Federalist*. "A constitution is, in fact, and must be regarded by the judges, as a fundamental law."[13] The Philadelphia Convention had produced "a limited Constitution" that "contains certain specified exceptions to the legislative authority," and those limitations "can be preserved in practice no other way than through the medium of courts of justice, whose duty it must be to declare all acts contrary to the manifest tenor of the Constitution void."[14] Subsequently blessed by Chief Justice John Marshall's opinion in *Marbury v. Madison*,[15] Hamilton's view gradually gathered support, especially after the Civil War, and helped legitimize the power of judicial review and underwrite the Supreme Court's growing authority from the late nineteenth century onward.[16]

A third view came from the Anti-Federalists and was advanced most forcefully by a particularly able pamphleteer known only as "Brutus." Agreeing, at least as a prediction of fact, that the national judiciary would become the authoritative interpreter of the Constitution, Brutus maintained that its rulings would ultimately destroy the federal structure. Because the national judiciary was an integral part of the new central government, he predicted, it "will lean strongly in favour of the general government, and will give such an explanation to the constitution, as will favour an extension of its jurisdiction."[17] Thus, the Constitution was dangerous precisely because Hamilton was right about the institutional role of the federal judiciary but dreadfully wrong about its consequences. "The judicial power will operate to effect, in the most certain, but yet silent and imperceptible manner, what is evidently the tendency of the constitution," Brutus charged: "—I mean, an entire subversion of the legislative, executive, and judicial powers of the individual states."[18] His warning sounded ominously during the ratification debates, reverberated loudly through the antebellum years, and continued to echo periodically thereafter among those who strongly opposed the nation's growing centralization.[19]

A fourth view emerged in the 1790s and came to dominate the Federalist Party by decade's end. The federal judiciary was the authoritative interpreter of the Constitution, and its duty was not to protect the states or the federal structure but to protect a strong central government and, further, to ensure that the central government remained in the hands of its true adherents. Convinced that they were the virtuous and authentic party of the

Constitution, the Federalists of the late 1790s "could not picture them-selves as an 'alternative' to anything."[20] Thus, as their hold on power be-gan to slip after Washington's retirement, they "imagined themselves in a state of siege,"[21] established and then expanded a provisional army,[22] en-acted the oppressive Alien and Sedition Acts, and turned to the national courts—packed with Federalist appointees—to enforce the laws and re-press their opponents.[23] During the next two years, the Federalists made a concerted effort to ensure victory in the presidential election of 1800 by charging some two dozen Republican activists with seditious libel, indict-ing seventeen of them, and convicting ten. Not one Federalist judge ques-tioned the constitutionality of the repressive measures, and the Supreme Court did not review a single conviction under them.[24] Indeed, all the Federalist judges who heard prosecutions treated the statutes favorably, and two Supreme Court justices—William Patterson and Samuel Chase—presided over successful prosecutions while making their Federalist politi-cal sympathies glaringly apparent.[25] Finally, when the Federalists lost the election of 1800, they used their lame-duck control of Congress and the executive to expand the jurisdiction of the national judiciary and pack more Federalists onto its bench. Upon taking power, the Jeffersonian Republicans repealed the measures and attempted to impeach the most unrestrained of the Federalist judges.[26] Thus, despite the fact that many of the founders—including Hamilton, Patterson, John Adams, and perhaps both Washington and Marshall[27]—accepted the later Federalist Party view, the election of 1800 and the political developments that followed wholly discredited it. By 1815 the Federalist Party had crumbled to in-significance, and Americans regarded its view of the Court's role as im-properly partisan and antithetical to the very idea of ordered constitutional government.

Finally, rallying opposition to the attempted Federalist repression, Jef-ferson and Madison articulated a fifth view in the Virginia and Kentucky Resolutions of 1798. In constitutional disputes, they argued, the states were the ultimate institutions charged with ensuring that the national gov-ernment remained cabined within its delegated sphere. In the Virginia Resolutions Madison warned that the federal judiciary could usurp "dan-gerous powers, not delegated," and invoked the compact theory to argue that the states retained "the ultimate right" as parties to the Constitution "to judge whether the compact has been dangerously violated."[28] The resolutions declared the states "duty bound" to "interpose" themselves against unconstitutional acts and appealed to the other states to "concur with this Commonwealth" in declaring the Federalist statutes void.[29] In the more radical Kentucky Resolutions, Jefferson invoked the same compact theory and announced that each party to the agreement "has an equal right to judge for itself" on matters of constitutionality, but he went beyond Madison's position in drawing his legal conclusions. The Kentucky Resolutions directly pronounced the Federalist statutes "not law" and flatly declared them "altogether void and of no force."[30] The ideas in the resolutions were subsequently developed by a long line of primarily southern antebellum spokesmen, and they underwrote the hard-line states' rights position that began to coalesce in the 1820s and remained vital until the Civil War. Thereafter, they continued to attract scattered adherents among those adamantly opposed to the dominant policies of the national government, especially in racial matters.[31]

While those five views were distinct, they were also frequently blended and blurred in the minds of the founders. Madison and Jefferson, for example, reflected the fluid and unsettled nature of the ideas the founding generation launched. At different times both not only articulated "departmentalist" and "states' rights" ideas, but each on occasion also advanced ideas that sounded quite "Hamiltonian." In the Philadelphia Convention Madison suggested that the courts would be able to declare laws contrary to the Constitution "null & void,"[32] and in the *Federalist* he acknowledged that the Supreme Court was to be the authoritative voice in drawing the line between federal and state power. "It is true that in controversies relating to the boundary between the two jurisdictions," he declared, "the tribunal which is ultimately to decide, is to be established under the general government."[33] Similarly, in 1787 Jefferson agreed that there should be "an appeal from the state judicatures to a federal court" to settle "all cases where the act of Confederation controuled," and the following year he praised the idea of federal judicial review as a protector of constitutional rights.[34] After ratification, warning against the dangers of legislative and executive tyranny, Jefferson urged adoption of a bill of rights because of "the legal check which it puts into the hands of the judiciary."[35] Similarly, even Hamilton himself did not always sound "Hamiltonian." In the *Federalist* he affirmed a distinctly "Jeffersonian" proposition. "It may safely be received as an axiom in our political system," the arch-nationalist wrote, "that the State governments will, in all possible contingencies, afford complete security against invasions of the public liberty by the national authority." State legislatures "can discover the danger at a distance; and possessing all the organs of civil power, and the confidence of the people, they can at once adopt a regular plan of opposition, in which they can combine all the resources of the community."[36] Whether Hamilton's statement reflected his actual expectations or merely exhibited tactical shrewdness, it exemplified the founding generation's deep uncertainty as to how disputes between national and state authority would and should be resolved.[37]

While the Federalist Party view disappeared, the other four evolved and remained in relatively continuous use throughout the antebellum decades.[38] Hamilton's ideas were largely adopted by the Marshall Court[39] and increasingly found their strongest support in the North, while departmentalism, the arguments of Brutus, and the theories espoused in the Virginia and Kentucky Resolutions blended into a variety of anti-Court and "states' rights" positions that attracted sporadic support in many states but exerted their strongest and steadiest appeal in the South.[40] By 1819 when Spencer Roane, a judge on the Virginia Court of Appeals, attacked Marshall's nationalist opinion in *McCulloch v. Maryland,* he was able to draw on an overflowing reservoir of arguments and quotations from a range of commentators—including Brutus, Madison, Jefferson, and even Hamilton—to defend the contention that "the ultimate redress against unconstitutional acts of the general government" lay with the "*state legislatures,*" which would "sound the alarm to the people, and effect a change." In any event, Roane insisted, "the *judiciary* is *not,* in such cases, a competent tribunal."[41]

By the 1820s and 1830s opposition to the Court and its assertions of national authority was relatively widespread, but the most concerted and virulent attacks came from southerners who flatly rejected the idea that the national judiciary was the ultimate arbiter of disputes over the line between state and national authority. Determinations about the scope of governmental powers "were not intended to be surrendered" to a handful of judges, John Taylor of Caroline protested, for "the universal idea of judicial power confined its operation to individuals, and had never extended it to political departments." The Supreme Court's power "may, without control, disorder and subvert the primary division of power" in the federal structure and become a "gradual and piecemeal mode of destroying it."[42] As the sectional split widened, southern theorists blended older ideas into a sweeping assault on the national judiciary. Federal judges were merely "the judicial representatives" of a "united majority," John C. Calhoun charged, echoing Brutus. Granting them power to determine the constitutionality of laws "would be, in reality, to confide it to the majority, whose agents they are."[43] Thus, "it would seem impossible to deny to the States the right of deciding on the infractions of their powers," for the "right of judging, in such cases, is an essential attribute of sovereignty."[44] Calhoun drew a bright line. "We contend, that the great conservative principle in our system is in the people of the States, as parties to the Constitutional compact, and our opponents that it is in the Supreme Court," he declared. "This is the sum total of the whole difference."[45]

In his famous Senate debate with Daniel Webster in 1830, Robert Y. Hayne of South Carolina etched the southern states' rights position sharply.[46] "It is clear that questions of sovereignty are not the proper subjects of *judicial investigation*," he maintained. "They are much too large, and of too delicate a nature, to be brought within the jurisdiction of a Court of justice."[47] As the U.S. Supreme Court had never assumed jurisdiction over questions arising under international treaties between "sovereigns," so it could not "assume jurisdiction over questions arising between the individual States and the United States." Guided by Calhoun and borrowing from Brutus, Hayne insisted that the Court was inherently "disqualified from assuming the umpirage between the States and the United States, because it is created by, and is indeed merely one of the departments of the Federal Government."[48]

In opposition, ardent nationalists—increasingly northerners—rejected the states' rights position and drew on Hamilton and Marshall to defend the claim that the Court was the ultimate constitutional authority. "The harmony, and perhaps the stability of the union, depends in a very material degree, upon the just and discreet exercise of the judicial power," New York's chancellor James Kent declared in 1824, and the "judicial power of the union is the ultimate expounder of the constitution."[49] Justice Joseph Story made Herculean efforts as both scholar and justice to counter southern arguments and develop a nationalist jurisprudence that placed a vibrant federal judicial power at the center of the constitutional system.[50] There was "a final and common arbiter provided by the constitution itself, to whose decisions all others are subordinate," he insisted, "and that arbiter is the supreme judicial authority of the courts of the Union."[51] Replying to Hayne on the Senate floor, Webster gave the nationalist theory its most famous and eloquent voice, identifying the South with nullification and the North with union and the Court. By creating the federal judicial power and mandating the supremacy of federal law, Webster thundered, the Constitution created "the key-stone of the arch" and mandated that "all questions of constitutional power" be resolved by "the final decision of the Supreme Court."[52]

Webster's powerful defense of the Court did more than embrace and extend the Hamiltonian view. It also illustrated the fluid and dynamic nature of ideas about the Court and its role in the federal structure. Webster's oration, after all, was designed not merely to identify New England with the Union and the South with division but also to achieve a further purpose: to erase from national memory New England's own ill-fated invocation of "state sovereignty" and secessionism during the War of 1812 and the infamous Hartford Convention.[53]

The constitutional debates grew so bitter that they drove the aging Marshall to the edge of despair. "I yield slowly and reluctantly to the conviction that our Constitution cannot last," he confessed privately to Story. The commitment to "a firm and solid government" had grown "doubtful" even in the northern and western states, while the situation in the South was "desperate." Discord and division loomed. "The Union has been prolonged thus far by miracles," the chief justice concluded. "I fear they cannot continue."[54]

For three decades the debate raged. Emotions intensified; political lines hardened; and the problem of the territories grew ever more acute. Appeals to the Constitution's "original" meaning provoked only deeper and ever more bitter disagreements, and on both sides demands and threats escalated. Ultimately, no miracle was forthcoming. Only an appeal to arms, it turned out, could resolve some of those original constitutional conflicts and uncertainties.

Partial Resolutions

As a constitutional matter, the Civil War was decisive, but only in part. It determined that states could not secede, nullify federal law, or act as final authorities in construing the Constitution. Repudiated by Union victory, rejected by the Court, and then effectively buried by a century and a half of national history, the antebellum southern states' rights position withered and disappeared as a viable constitutional theory, surfacing in later decades for the most part only as a last-ditch justification for legalized racial discrimination and oppression.

War, however, could hardly decide everything. Even with the three constitutional amendments it spurred, it did not decide which part or parts of the national government properly held the ultimate right to construe the Constitution, nor what standards or principles of interpretation existed to guide whoever was empowered to construe it authoritatively.[55] Nor, of course, did it determine how far the reach of national power had been extended. Thus, the war decided that battles over constitutional authority and the line between federal and state power would be waged at the national level, but it did not end the battles themselves. Waged on new fronts, those battles would continue, refocused but unabated.

In the post–Civil War decades versions of Hamilton's view grew into orthodoxy. The idea of constitutional judicial review had become increasingly accepted by the state courts during the previous half-century; the efforts of Marshall, Story, and Webster had forged a nationalist doctrine as the banner of the booming North; and Union victory had driven its great rival from the field.[56] As the century advanced, the Court began playing a more central role in the processes of American government, expanding the jurisdiction of the lower courts, broadening their equity powers, and invalidating state and federal legislation with increasing frequency.[57] Americans had long portrayed the Constitution as the nation's "anchor," but in the late nineteenth century they began to shift their focus by conferring that high metaphorical honor directly on the Court itself. Chief Justice Morrison Waite recognized the change. "The Court," he announced in

1876, "is now looked upon as the sheet anchor."[58] Two decades later Justice David J. Brewer spoke what had become a commonplace, at least among the nation's conservative elements, when he identified the Court as "The Nation's Anchor."[59]

As the Court's role and authority expanded, constitutional thinkers began to advance the idea that it was not only the voice of the Constitution but also, at least by default, the defender of the states and the federal structure. Thomas M. Cooley, perhaps the most influential constitutional theorist of the late nineteenth century, acknowledged the change the war had wrought. The "effectual checks upon the encroachments of federal upon state power must be looked for, not in state power of resistance" but in the federal electoral process and "in a federal supreme court with competent power to restrain all departments and all officers within the limits of their just authority."[60] Woodrow Wilson sounded the same idea a few years later. It was "quite evident" that the national courts were "the only effectual balance-wheel of the whole system," he announced. "The federal judges hold in their hands the fate of state powers, and theirs is the only authority that can draw effective rein on the career of Congress."[61] Thus, the idea that the Court was the constitutional defender of the states moved toward national acceptance only belatedly, a product of the Civil War, the massive and disruptive social changes that followed, and the gradual rise of the Court to an ever more powerful position in an industrializing and centralizing nation. For states' rights advocates, it was a last-ditch expedient, a fallback position thrust on them by military defeat and political necessity.

While the emerging new orthodoxy stood in sharp contrast to the views that many of the founders had advanced, it also differed significantly even from Hamilton's theory, the one "original" theory that it most closely resembled. First, Hamilton and many of those who supported ratification believed that the national courts were necessary not to protect the states but to protect the new central government. More to the point, they believed that the national courts were necessary for the precise purpose of securing the national government against defiance and subversion by the states.[62] Indeed, when Madison proposed his "federal negative" on state laws before and during the Philadelphia Convention, he too saw its purpose as protecting the national government and limiting the states.[63] In the nation's early years, moreover, Federalist judges in the national courts scrutinized state laws carefully, invalidating some even when "there was colorable argument for the statutes' validity."[64] In the original Hamiltonian view, then, the Court's role in the federal structure was the opposite of the one that rose toward orthodoxy during the late nineteenth century. Second, the early Federalists saw the Senate, not the judiciary, as the constitutional institution specifically designed to safeguard the states and guarantee their sovereignty. The Senate "will derive its powers from the States, as political and coequal societies," Madison explained,[65] and their equal vote in the upper house was "a constitutional recognition of the portion of sovereignty remaining in the individual States, and an instrument for preserving their residuary authority."[66] Another Federalist pamphleteer put the point more concisely. "The federal Senate," he maintained, "are *the representatives of the sovereignties of their respective states.*"[67] Thus, when Americans in the late nineteenth century began to conceive of the Court as the protector of the states, they drew on but one of many divergent theories the founders had advanced and, equally important, substantially modified the particular theory on which they drew.

There was, too, an embarrassing quadruple irony in the spreading post–Civil War view that the Court was the protector of the states. First, the idea resonated awkwardly with the infamous *Dred Scott* decision. In the antebellum context marked by explosive population growth in the North and an intensifying sectional conflict over slavery, the Constitution's provision for admitting new states had transformed the Senate from the protector of the states generally into the protector of the slave states in particular.[68] Fearing that it would be unable to control the presidency or the House of Representatives, the South clung tenaciously to its equality in the upper chamber. For decades it insisted on the admission of a new slave state to balance each newly admitted free state. Then, when the balance stood at fifteen states apiece, Congress attempted to resolve the escalating sectional dispute with the desperate Compromise of 1850, one element of which admitted California as a free state and ended forever the equality of the slave states in the Senate. Quickly, the South turned from relying on a Senate veto to advancing an audacious constitutional argument that made slavery a national institution and compelled the federal government to protect its existence everywhere in the Union and its territories. In 1857 the Supreme

Court outraged the North by its decision in *Dred Scott*,[69] holding that the plaintiff remained a slave even in a free state and adopting—at least in the sweeping opinion of Chief Justice Roger B. Taney—the South's aggressive and nationalizing proslavery constitutional theory.[70] At that crucial point, then, the Court suddenly made itself the de facto defender of slavery and the South. Thus, to even the most recalcitrant postwar southerner, the idea that the Court could be the protector of the states and their rights evoked the memory of *Dred Scott* and gave the idea a hint of plausibility.

Second, the war changed the law radically by inspiring three sweeping constitutional amendments that imposed severe new limitations on the states and added substantially to the powers of Congress. The amendments gave the states no new constitutional basis for claiming special protection from the Court, and they suggested no special role for the Court in either protecting the states or limiting Congress. Indeed, as late as 1880 the Court declared that the federal courts, absent congressional authorization, lacked power to enforce the Fourteenth Amendment. "It is not said," the justices reasoned in *Ex parte Virginia*, "that the *judicial power* of the general government shall extend to enforcing the prohibitions and to protecting the rights and immunities guaranteed."[71] Thus, the new role of the Court as defender of the states not only lacked foundation in the Civil War amendments but also seemed oblique to, if not inconsistent with, their language and purpose.

Third, the three Civil War amendments were intended to protect the freed slaves and to guarantee them liberty, equality, and the rights of national citizenship.[72] Yet, as the Court began to construe them, it constrained their meaning stringently and in the process sacrificed the rights they were intended to protect. After Reconstruction, when the Court emerged in some part as the de facto protector of the states, it did so by in effect condoning the concerted and violent efforts of the South to disenfranchise, segregate, and oppress its black citizens.[73] The Court's role as protector of the states, in other words, was not only unauthorized by the three Civil War amendments, but its practice contradicted the fundamental values and purposes that had inspired them. Small wonder, then, that some southern commentators—the gentleman racist Woodrow Wilson being a classic example[74]—were able to reconcile themselves in some part to the emerging idea that the Court was the defender of the states and the federal structure.

Finally, less obvious but more significant in long-range terms, the political dynamics of the federal structure were changing. American experience, especially in the decades after the Civil War, generated a growing sense that the Court was a particularly powerful and effective instrument for resolving serious interstate disputes and for controlling the divergent tendencies and conflicting interests of the states. The political parties and electoral coalitions that triumphed in the nation's kaleidoscopic politics and thereby gained control of the central government came to see the Court as an exceptionally valuable ally, one that they could either use to enforce their policies immediately or remake over time to do so in the future.[75] As a matter of the nation's political and institutional dynamics, in other words, the Court's steadily expanding constitutional role after the Civil War was rooted ultimately not in any widespread desire to protect the states but in the shared desire of national officials, national political parties, and national electoral coalitions to enforce the national policies that they favored. Thus, the political and institutional sources driving the Court's steadily expanding role after the Civil War sprang from nationalizing and centralizing forces that undermined any possibility that it could consistently and reliably serve as the protector of the states or of any particular, state-centered vision of American federalism.[76]

Continuing Disputes

The Civil War determined that constitutional authority in the United States lay at the national level. That newly definitive principle lent additional support to the corollary that the Supreme Court was the specific national institution designed to serve as the Constitution's authoritative voice, and that corollary supported in turn a subsidiary inference that the Court was also the protector of the states. Compared with the two premises on which it rested, however, that last inference was highly problematic for a readily apparent reason. The Civil War and its three constitutional amendments expanded national power and reconfigured the federal structure, but they did not abolish the structure's four inherent characteristics. Thus, even assuming that the Court was the final authority on federalism issues, the Constitution still furnished inadequate direction in deciding most specific issues about the structure's proper limits and operations.

By itself, the structure's doubly blurred nature confronted the Court with an intractable problem: if it was the defender of American federalism, that role charged it not with one but with two counterpoised duties. The role made it responsible not only for protecting state powers and rights but also for vindicating national powers and rights. Not surprisingly, then, after the Civil War the Court turned periodically, and sometimes quite energetically, to protecting the authority of the central government and enforcing national rights. As it had asserted national authority over state courts and sanctioned the doctrine of implied powers in the early republic,[77] so in the late nineteenth century it began to expand national power once more. Haltingly and somewhat irregularly the Court sanctioned enlargements of congressional power; more broadly and consistently it asserted national judicial authority to protect corporate enterprise and the expanding national market, and it did so by limiting legislative efforts to regulate economic activities, especially those undertaken by the states.[78] Then, in the 1930s, it expanded federal executive power,[79] extended the powers of Congress dramatically, and began laying the groundwork for even broader extensions of national judicial power.[80] Subsequently, the Warren Court again stretched the powers of Congress while asserting sweeping federal judicial authority to create a range of new federal rights and to impose a wide range of new restrictions on the states.[81] The idea that the Supreme Court was the defender of the federal structure, in other words, was a concept that offered neither a determinate norm nor a substantive guarantee.

The Court's role vis-à-vis the federal structure, then, remained necessarily uncertain and contested. From Reconstruction to the early twenty-first century judges and commentators advanced a variety of conflicting theories intended to define its proper role, but all seemed to have only two things in common. None was explicitly prescribed by the Constitution, and all were practical devices shaped by the political context in which they were deployed and by the ideological commitments of those who deployed them.

With the racial and constitutional settlement that followed Reconstruction, debate over the Court's role in the federal structure entered a new phase. Responding to the emergence of complex new political and social issues that arose from the nation's rapid industrialization, disputes increasingly raised not just questions of federalism but, more importantly, questions of separation of powers. The dominant constitutional issue of the new era focused on the extent to which the courts, especially the national courts, could properly invalidate laws adopted by the legislative branches of both states and nation.

As the new urban and industrial world began taking shape, the state governments expanded their efforts to regulate a widening variety of economic activities, while the national government enacted its first substantial measures designed for the same purpose. In response, the courts limited or invalidated many of their efforts, and after a period of hesitancy the U.S. Supreme Court decided in the 1890s to assert its authority to act as the ultimate arbiter in determining which of those regulations were constitutional.[82] For the next half-century, constitutional debate centered on two related issues: first, the scope of state and federal power to regulate economic activities, and second, the judiciary's proper role and authority in imposing limits on such legislative efforts.[83]

The new phase of constitutional debate came into sharper focus in 1893 when Harvard professor James Bradley Thayer published what would become one of the most influential essays ever written on the nature and standards of federal judicial review. Concerned about the growing social problems created by industrialization and wary of the Court's increased readiness to impose limits on governmental actions, Thayer sought to limit the scope of judicial review generally and, in particular, to guarantee Congress a wide discretion in exercising its powers. In "The Origin and Scope of the American Doctrine of Constitutional Law," he suggested that the Court's principal function lay not in protecting federalism and the states but in maintaining national power and, where necessary, limiting the states. The federal judiciary, Thayer wrote, properly voided executive or legislative acts only when their unconstitutionality was "so clear that it is not open to rational question."[84] That highly deferential "rule of the clear mistake" applied, however, only when the federal courts reviewed "the work of a co-ordinate department," that is, another branch of the national government.[85] In contrast, when they reviewed state actions, they were to apply the "true and just construction" of the Constitution—a more stringent standard that allowed the states little leeway.[86] Thus, his theory directed the Court to allow ample flexibility to Congress and the president while supervising state actions more rigorously. It was hardly surprising that Thayer would advance such a double standard, for he was a Yankee who worshiped John Marshall and spent the Civil War spreading propaganda for the Loyal Publication Society. Above all else, he cherished the North's triumph in the Civil War, the preservation of the Union, and the full vindication of national authority.[87]

Thayer's theory was widely influential, and its subsequent history illustrated how ideas about the Court's role in the federal structure continued to evolve in response to changing times and politics. Many of the great figures of legal Progressivism—including Louis Brandeis, Felix Frankfurter, and Learned Hand—hailed Thayer's "American doctrine" as the summit of constitutional wisdom, but they remolded it adroitly to serve their own new and quite different political purposes. Quietly, they jettisoned Thayer's strict "true and just" standard and extended his deferential "rule of the clear mistake" to federal review of state actions. Unlike Thayer, those legal Progressives were part of a younger generation, emotionally removed from the passions of the Civil War and able to assume easily the Union's triumph and preservation. They saw not nullification and secession but industrialization and social reform as their generation's overriding challenge. Inspired by faith in science, progress, and popular government, they distrusted the courts as biased and ill-informed, and they embraced the legislature as the popular instrument of science, expertise, and rational progress. Consequently, they sought to prevent the courts from voiding legislative reforms, and in Thayer's "rule of the clear mistake" they found a highly useful device—once they had suitably redesigned it—to free the legislatures of the states as well as the nation from close judicial oversight.[88]

Thayer's original theory and its Progressive reformulation implied strikingly different roles for the federal judiciary vis-à-vis the states. The two versions demonstrated not only that theories about judicial review and the Court's role in the federal structure evolved over time but also that their inspiration lay in the changing social and political purposes of their advocates. Theories prescribing the Court's role and the standards applicable to its work were contingent ideas shaped not by unchanging principles of either federalism or judicial review—much less by any version of "original-ism"—but by the shifting values and interests of those who struggled to direct the course of the nation's ongoing constitutional enterprise.

As the social changes of the nineteenth and early twentieth centuries generated new prescriptions for the Court's role in the federal structure, so the decades after World War I brought new conditions that nourished their own new and distinctive theories. The Great Depression, the New Deal, World War II, and the stunning postwar economic boom expanded the size of the federal government and cast on it primary responsibility for overseeing the economy and sustaining the nation's prosperity.[89] Combined with the threat of "totalitarianism," the dangers of the cold war, and the emerging movement for black civil rights, however, those developments also brought unnerving new anxieties. If bigger government was necessary, but if government at all levels could threaten individual liberties, then some institutional bulwark was essential to preserve democracy and protect the rights of individuals. Like the defenders of the states after the Civil War—but unlike their Progressive forebears—post–World War II liberals transferred their institutional commitments to the federal judiciary, and they did so with the stereotypical ardor of converts.[90]

Their basic intuition was simple, yet sweeping. If all governments could endanger individual rights and liberties, then constitutional rights needed special protection, and a national judiciary with economically independent and life-tenured judges seemed the best available institution to shoulder the responsibility. Thus, they argued, the judiciary should enforce the Bill of Rights vigorously and apply its guarantees not only to the national government but also to the states. From hesitant beginnings in the 1920s and 1930s, the Court began increasingly to fulfill that prescription by expanding the reach of the Equal Protection and Due Process clauses and by enforcing the guarantees of the first eight amendments against the states as well as the federal government.[91]

Like their Progressive forebears, mid-twentieth-century liberals designed their theories to preserve wide areas of democratic lawmaking for the legislative branch, especially its power to regulate the economy. Unlike those ancestors, however, they also designed their theories to carve out a special and active role for the national courts in protecting individual noneconomic rights and liberties. More particularly, in terms of the federal structure, they designed their theories to discount the role of the Court as the protector of the states and to enhance its contrary role as the vindicator of national law and national rights.[92] As Progressives had reshaped Thayer's theory in order to expand the ability of the states to enact the social reform measures they favored, so mid-twentieth-century liberals reshaped their Progressive heritage to limit the ability of the states to abuse the civil rights and liberties that they had come to cherish.

In 1954 two events crystallized the new liberal conviction about the Court's role in the federal structure. First, on the level of theory, Herbert Wechsler, an ex–New Dealer who taught at the Columbia Law School, published an essay titled "The Political Safeguards of Federalism."[93] The Constitution, Wechsler argued, protected the states by making them constituent elements of the federal government with equal representation in the Senate, authority to select the president through the Electoral College, and the right to control voting and districting for the House.[94] Because those "political safeguards" ensured that the federal government would heed the states and respect their interests, he reasoned, the Supreme Court need not do so. Indeed, recognition of the "political safeguards" showed that the Court's distinctive constitutional task was not to protect the federal structure but, rather, to protect those constitutional values that the "political safeguards" failed to guarantee: first, the supremacy of national law, and second, the rights of individuals and minorities enshrined in the U.S. Constitution.[95]

Second, on the level of constitutional law, the Court handed down its monumental decision in *Brown v. Board of Education*.[96] Ruling racial segregation in public schools unconstitutional, the decision invalidated *Plessy v. Ferguson*,[97] one of the landmarks of the post-Reconstruction settlement. With respect to the federal structure, it seemed to repudiate the post–Civil War idea that the Court was the protector of the states and to inspire a contrary new image of the national judiciary as the protector of the national constitutional rights and liberties of all Americans. During the next fifteen years, under the leadership of Chief Justice Earl Warren, the Court issued a series of bold centralizing decisions in a variety of areas that expanded noneconomic rights and liberties while imposing sharp constraints on the power of the states. Soon the Warren Court came to stand as a symbol of liberalism, nationalism, and a new judicial sympathy for the weak, disadvantaged, and systemically abused.[98]

While the liberal view of the Court's proper role remained vibrant,[99] the underlying political consensus that underwrote it began to fragment in the late 1960s under a fierce combination of internal and external pressures. Beginning with the presidential election of 1968 national politics began a long and slow drift rightward, and opponents increasingly began to level a burgeoning variety of criticisms at the Court and the liberal nationalist values that inspired it. Abandoning his earlier views, Alexander Bickel chastised the Warren Court for creating new constitutional rights instead of deferring to the democratically elected branches of both nation and states.[100] Philip Kurland revived the warnings of Brutus, charging that the Court supported "a constant attrition of state power" because it was "an integral part of the central government."[101] Raoul Berger scoured the historical record for evidence showing that the founders intended the Court to impose clear constitutional limits on the national government and to protect the states by enforcing a substantive Tenth Amendment.[102] Lewis Kaden probed the weaknesses of the "political safeguards" theory, showing how changes over time had eroded the institutional ability of states to protect themselves through their constitutive roles in the national government.[103] Regardless of the founders' original intentions, he suggested, historical changes might have made it necessary for the Court to become the defender of the federal structure. More directly political, Richard Epstein argued that the Warren Court erred not in being "active" but in enforcing the wrong substantive values. The Court should abandon its liberal policies and promote conservative and free market principles across the board, including the protection of the states against extensions of national power.[104]

As Republican appointments slowly transformed the Court after 1968, its orientation began haltingly to change, exhibiting a fading concern with civil rights and a growing concern for states' rights. As early as 1976 five justices invoked the Tenth Amendment to limit congressional power,[105] seemingly reversing some forty years of post–New Deal case law that ignored the amendment.[106] Less than a decade later, however, five justices invoked the "political safeguards" idea to again reverse course,[107] though

their effort drew scathing fire from four conservatives who vehemently rejected the liberal theory. The "political safeguards" idea, one of the dissenters declared, was "an outright rejection" of "the intention of the
Framers of the Constitution."[108] Finally, by the early 1990s, Republican
appointments had created a solid five-justice conservative bloc. Under
Chief Justice William Rehnquist, the Court began to invoke the values and
principles of federalism, enhance the independence of the states, and limit
the powers of Congress and the lower federal courts.[109] In the process it
struck down more than twenty federal statutes, construed federal civil
rights laws narrowly, and pronounced itself forthrightly as the constitutional protector of the states and the federal structure.[110]

The actions of the Rehnquist Court forced liberals to rethink their positions once again. While a few attempted to update and strengthen the "political safeguards" argument,[111] others began developing theories designed to limit the constitutional role of the national courts on more
fundamental grounds. Some began to explore such familiar ideas as "originalism," "departmentalism," and "popular sovereignty" in order to argue
that the newly conservative national judiciary was acting beyond its assigned role and improperly interfering with the judgments of Congress
and the nation's democratic processes.[112] "The Constitution does not
mean only what the judges say it means," Cass Sunstein declared in 1993.
Rather, the meaning that nonjudicial government officials and "citizens in
general" gave it over the years "has been more important than its meaning
within the narrow confines of the Supreme Court building."[113] Richard
Parker agreed. "[T]he authority of constitutional argument by judges is
defeasible—indeed, it ought to be challenged periodically," he argued.
Ultimately, judicial decisions "must appeal to ordinary people," for the
people retained the right to make final decisions on disputed constitutional questions.[114]

To those new liberal arguments the majority justices on the Rehnquist
Court countered with unqualified assertions of both federal judicial supremacy and the Court's duty to limit Congress and protect the states.
"The power to interpret the Constitution in a case or controversy," it insisted, "remains in the judiciary."[115] Notwithstanding the broad constitutional powers of Congress, "it is the responsibility of this Court, not Congress, to define the substance of constitutional guarantees."[116] The Court

backed its assertions—somewhat erratically to be sure[117]—with a series of decisions limiting the commerce power, reviving a substantive Tenth Amendment, expanding state sovereign immunity under the Eleventh Amendment, and restricting the authority of Congress to protect civil rights and liberties under the Fourteenth Amendment.[118]

Thus, at the beginning of the twenty-first century the question of the Court's proper role in the federal structure remained bitterly contested. Spurred by broad political, cultural, ideological, and institutional changes, judges and commentators cleverly reworked the available fund of ideas to serve their distinctive purposes in a changing social and political context. Despite massive amounts of historical research and the elaboration of ever more sophisticated "theories" of constitutional interpretation, however, they seemed unable to convince those with differing political and ideological commitments. On one level, of course, the reason for their failure was simple. Neither the Constitution nor any other authoritative "originalist" source defined a clear and complete line of division between national and state power, nor did they specify either the exact role the Court should play in the constitutional system or the authoritative methods it should use in fulfilling that role.

9

EVOLVING UNDERSTANDINGS

While ideas about the locus of authority in the federal structure shifted abruptly after the Civil War, general ideas about the nature of American federalism itself evolved more slowly. By the middle of the twentieth century, however, as the processes of social change accelerated ever more sharply under the intensifying pressures of centralization, globalization, and technological innovation, Americans experienced a growing uncertainty about the federal structure's utility as well as its nature. Searching for direction in a rapidly changing world, they increasingly looked to the structure's basic purposes in an effort to identify its consequences and assess its worth. Their efforts only highlighted the structure's inherently dynamic, elastic, and underdetermined nature.

The "Values of Federalism"

Doubts about the utility of the federal structure were nowhere more obvious than in the numerous discussions about the "values of federalism" that began to proliferate in the late twentieth century.[1] The discussions were curious and revealing. Often they were almost tautologically abstract, treating the "values of federalism" as logical inferences from general prescriptive theories rather than as actual historical results that were—or were not—attributable to the federal structure and its actual operations. Further, the discussions were frequently based on dubious premises. Commonly, for example, they implied that such "values" as "political accountability" and "popular participation" were better served at the state than the national level on the basis of the facially inaccurate assumption that state governments were small-scale institutions interacting face-to-face with their citizens rather than impersonal bureaucracies that governed millions of people from great social and political, if not always geographical, distances.[2] Consistently, too, the discussions advanced "values" that were amorphous, contested, and nondirective. Commentators agreed that "diversity" was one of the "values of federalism," for example, but few agreed on just how much and what type of "diversity" was desirable or even constitutionally allowable. "Diversity" was a "value" capable of infinite variation in interpretation and practice, and as such it conveyed no clear or determinate meaning.

Most striking, discussions about the "values of federalism" revealed an acute, if often implicit, awareness that the federal structure had changed drastically over the years and that the role of the states had in many ways grown uncertain, unsatisfying, and perhaps even unnecessary. Thus, the implicit premise that drove such discussions seemed to be an anxious sense that the lines purportedly separating national and state powers were no longer practicable or even consistently detectable. "Does federalism retain substantial value in the 20th century," asked a leading casebook on constitutional law in 1997, "or is it an obsolete obstruction to be dismissed with minimal lip service?"[3] To many, some kind of functional analysis seemed necessary, first, to identify intelligible lines that could be drawn between national and state authority, and second, to explain why it was useful to draw such lines.

The substance of the discussions, however, only magnified the structure's uncertainties because they highlighted the ambiguous nature of the "values" that federalism was supposed to serve. The most fundamental and widely accepted of those values, for example, was "preserving liberty." As Justice Lewis F. Powell Jr. voiced the standard claim, the constitutional power of the states was "designed to protect our fundamental liberties" by creating checks on the national government.[4] Although Powell's statement was incontestable as a general matter, it provided little guidance as a matter of theory and fostered little confidence as a matter of experience.

As for theory, the value of "protecting liberty" simply ignored the ambivalent nature of the federal structure, the fact that the national government was also designed to protect liberty—for its part, to protect liberty from abuses by the states.[5] The "irregular and mutable legislation" of the states had become "odious to the people," Madison declared, and they would "never be satisfied till some remedy be applied to the vicissitudes and uncertainties which characterize the State administrations."[6] The new national government was the remedy the Constitution provided for such local abuses, and hence the value of "protecting liberty" pointed to the virtues of centralization at least as much as it did to those of decentralization. Indeed, after the three Civil War amendments, the value weighed heavily in favor of national authority and responsibility. More generally, too, the abstractly considered value of "protecting liberty" ignored the fact that "liberty" was seldom, if ever, protected absolutely and across the board. Rather, liberty was a complex, changing, and pluralistic concept, and protecting it in practice invariably meant protecting only some liberties, to some extent, in some contexts, and against some restrictions. Thus, as an abstract and theoretical matter, the value of "protecting liberty" was as incontestable as it was nondirective.

As for experience, the states had repeatedly proved themselves unreliable protectors of liberty. Over more than two centuries they had not been relatively more successful at the task than either local or national governments, and after the Civil War and the passage of the three resulting amendments the federal government emerged, gradually and unevenly, as the most effective governmental force protecting and expanding the constitutional liberties of American citizens.[7] It is "the federal government, not the states, that appears to be our system's primary protector of individual liberties," Michael McConnell explained. "This seems to be the premise of the Fourteenth Amendment and of much New Deal legislation."[8] The nation's long and painful history of racial oppression, moreover, unequivocally identified the states—especially some fifteen southern and border states—as the nation's most persistent and egregious oppressors of "fundamental liberties."[9]

Equally important, when the federal government did fail to protect constitutional liberties and itself became an oppressor—as it did, for example, in the years around World War I, in the aftermath of Pearl Harbor, and during the McCarthy era—the states not only failed to act as checks but indulged in parallel abuses that equaled or exceeded those of the national government.[10] During World War I at least eleven states and dozens of cities passed sedition laws prohibiting disloyal speech, for example, while most states established special "councils of defense" that pressured citizens to buy war bonds and used threats or punitive sanctions against those who refused.[11] Further, in the succeeding "Red Scare" numerous states passed criminal syndicalism statutes, and thirty-two adopted laws that prohibited anyone from flying the Red flag. By the end of the 1920s the states had arrested more than fourteen hundred people under those statutes, convicting more than three hundred and imposing sentences that ranged up to twenty years in prison.[12] Similarly, when the federal government sent more than one hundred thousand Japanese Americans to concentration camps during World War II, the states posed no opposition. Worse, the West Coast states vigorously encouraged the effort.[13] Indeed, California's attorney general, future chief justice Earl Warren, led a conference of the state's law enforcement officials in urging that all "alien Japanese" be "forthwith evacuated" from the state.[14] Again during the McCarthy era, state and local governments once more failed to check national abuses and, instead, readily piled on. Forty-four states criminalized speech that advocated the overthrow of government, while forty-two—plus well over two thousand local and municipal governments—required public employees to sign loyalty oaths. Every state in the Union banned Communists and their alleged sympathizers from admission to the bar, while thirty-five prohibited Communist Party candidates from running for office. For mere membership in the party, moreover, Texas imposed a twenty-year prison term, while Michigan outdid the Lone Star State by mandating a life sentence. Tennessee, however, took the prize. The Volunteer State decided that party membership warranted death.[15]

More recently, the U.S. government enacted the USA PATRIOT Act[16] and committed egregious violations of constitutional rights by wiretapping American citizens without lawful warrant, imprisoning and holding American citizens and thousands of others for years without legal counsel or access to a judicial forum, and torturing untold numbers of those imprisoned individuals in violation of both national and international law.[17] Notwithstanding the proclaimed "values of federalism" and the hypothesized role of the states in protecting "liberty," the states failed to "check" those actions of the national government. They could not intervene in any direct way to counter or obstruct the policy of the national government, and the protest resolutions that some states and literally hundreds of local governments adopted seemed unavailing and, in the short run at least, futile.[18] Thus, while "protecting liberty" was a fundamental and unquestionable constitutional value, its relationship to the federal structure was, at best, dubious and unproven.

Another proffered "value of federalism" was the ability of states to benefit the nation by serving as independent "laboratories" for social "experiments." The idea, as Justice Oliver Wendell Holmes Jr. phrased it in 1921, was that states were "insulated chambers" that could conduct "social experiments that an important part of the community desires."[19] If successful, such experiments would redound to the benefit of the nation; if unsuccessful, only one state, not the whole nation, would suffer. The concept became popular, and the majority justices on the Rehnquist Court embraced it as a justification for their "profederalism" agenda.[20] The idea, however, was both nondirective and nonauthoritative.

First, like the value of "protecting liberty," the idea of the states as "laboratories" conducting "experiments" offered no help in identifying specific lines between state and national authority, between "experiments" that the Constitution allowed and those that it barred. Indeed, the idea invariably provoked an automatic and, in the abstract, unanswerable response. As Chief Justice William Howard Taft phrased it in *Truax v. Corrigan,* the "Constitution was intended—its very purpose was—to prevent experimentation with the fundamental rights of the individual."[21] Thus, the laboratory idea merely rerouted normative evaluation back to the original doubly blurred nature of the federal structure.

Second, the idea of the states as laboratories was not a premise of the Constitution. Although the founders were well aware of both the dangers of state rivalries and the value of state experience in constitution making,[22] they did not consider state power as part of any beneficent scheme to encourage localized social experimentation. To the contrary, they deplored many of the legislative expedients the states adopted after independence and sought precisely to limit their ability to conduct such "experiments." Most assiduously, the founders strove to bar the states from enacting measures that would disrupt the social and economic order, such as local tariffs, debtor relief acts, and paper money laws.[23] "The loss which America has sustained since the peace, from the pestilent effects of paper money," Madison protested, caused catastrophic damage and "constitutes an enormous debt against the States chargeable with this unadvised measure." Such folly, he declared, could be "expiated" only by the "voluntary sacrifice" of state power.[24] If "the sovereignty of the states cannot be reconciled to the happiness of the people, the voice of every good citizen must be, Let the former be sacrificed to the latter."[25] Reviewing the debates at the Constitutional Convention, Jack Rakove concluded that "[n]othing in these arguments suggested that [the drafters] regarded the states as laboratories of liberty or nurseries of republican citizenship."[26]

Although nineteenth-century Americans came to recognize that states sometimes competed by adopting novel social policies,[27] only at the dawn of the twentieth century did they generalize the idea, begin employing it widely, and adopt the distinctive "laboratory" metaphor. That striking conceptual development was the product of Progressivism and its buoyant faith in science, expertise, and rational social improvement.[28] The idea of the states as "laboratories" was quite different, for example, from the eighteenth-century view of Hamilton, Madison, David Hume, and John Adams that history contained the record of "experiments" that allowed "the politician or moral philosopher" to understand "the principles of his science."[29] It was different, too, from the founders' idea that government under the Constitution would serve as a test for the possibility of republican self-government,[30] and it was different still from their belief that the Constitution could be improved over time by a process of trial and error.[31] Those eighteenth-century ideas shared the assumption that human nature and the principles of politics were unchanging and that the goal of "science" was to discover a balanced form of government that would allow "energetic" action while preserving individual liberty. In contrast, the twentieth-century idea of the states as "laboratories" sprang from profoundly different assumptions: that rapid and far-reaching changes were destroying an older social world and creating a radically new one; that novel methods and institutions were essential to meet the unprecedented disruptions and dangers of the new industrial order; and that modern experimental science was capable of understanding social evolution, controlling its course and direction, and methodically improving the lives of all people.

Given the distinctive origins and assumptions of the "laboratory" metaphor, it was no surprise that it was the Progressive activist Louis D. Brandeis who popularized it most widely. "There is a great advantage in the opportunity we have of working out our social problems in the detached laboratories of the different states," he counseled in 1912. With "the full benefit of experiments in the individual states,"[32] reformers could design effective laws establishing minimum wages, maximum hours for factory labor, compensation programs for injured workers, and a wide variety of other salutary public health and safety measures. After his successful argument before the Supreme Court in *Muller v. Oregon*,[33] which upheld a state statute regulating the hours of female factory workers, Brandeis praised the law and portrayed the Oregon legislature as a methodical social scientist applying modern experimental methods to solve the problems of industrialism.[34] When sitting on the Court in 1932, he articulated the idea in what became its classic formulation. "It is one of the happy incidents of the federal system," he wrote, "that a single courageous State may, if its citizens choose, serve as a laboratory and try novel social and economic experiments without risk to the rest of the country."[35]

The power of the metaphor grew out of the same Progressive faith in science and social reform that led Brandeis to recast Thayer's "rule of the clear mistake" in his effort to open the constitutional gates more widely to social reform efforts in the states.[36] Given the idea's resoundingly Progressive political resonance, then, it was no surprise that Taft rejected it so bluntly. Indeed, in launching his classic rejoinder in *Truax v. Corrigan* Taft was responding directly to Brandeis himself. There, the chief justice sought to counter the latter's brash Progressive dissent that dismissed the common-law rules of master and servant as "merely experiments in government" that "must be discarded when they prove to be failures."[37]

With respect to federalism, moreover, the "laboratory" metaphor had dubious and even insidious implications. As Earl M. Maltz pointed out, it undermined, rather than supported, other ideas about the structure's values. Implicitly, the metaphor of laboratory experimentation challenged both the autonomy and diversity of the states by conceiving of their "experimental" legislation "as a vehicle for eventually developing a national consensus on 'correct' social and economic policies" that would demand nationwide adoption.[38] When Brandeis spoke of the states as laboratories for resolving social problems, he also spoke of identifying "the ultimate right solution of the problem."[39] The idea behind the laboratory metaphor, then, was not only novel to the twentieth century but inconsistent with other "values of federalism."

Another quality of Brandeis's laboratory metaphor was even more revealing. It was a sometime thing. When the states passed statutes restricting noneconomic rights involving free speech, he and many other Progressives immediately objected, arguing that such state actions were unconstitutional.[40] The states' "laboratory" function, in other words, was not a substantive "value" but a pragmatic tool, an instrument whose desirability depended—as Taft had readily and rightly understood—on the nature of the experiment at issue.[41] It was for that reason in large part that the metaphor dropped from vogue almost immediately after World War II, when the idea of "social experiments" suddenly came to summon images not of benevolent Progressive reforms but of Nazi death camps and Stalinist labor colonies.

Finally, the idea of states as "laboratories" was not only an invention of the twentieth century but also a radical departure from the idea of states that dominated the antebellum era. Then, the laboratory idea was not only absent but anathema. Instead, states were regarded as clones of rival social orders, expected to remain loyal at all costs to the values and institutions of the system that spawned them. Along the Mason-Dixon Line and into the battleground of the western territories, states were nothing so much as border fortresses, outposts for extending and protecting the counterpoised realms of free and slave labor. Calhoun fought to protect slavery in the District of Columbia, he announced to the Senate, because the nation's capital constituted the "outworks" of the South.[42] When the Kansas-Nebraska Act repealed the Missouri Compromise in 1854 and created two potential new states, the result was "Bleeding Kansas," not a rational experiment in social policy but a free-fire zone of cultural imperialism, a stem-cell territory waiting to take on the characteristics of whichever region could impose its will. Missouri, the bordering slave state, became the base for proslavery military incursions, while Lawrence, the territory's antislavery center, quickly became known throughout the North as "the Free State Fortress."[43]

Thus, to see the states as "laboratories" was to see a federal structure different from the one the founders had established and different from the one that existed through most of the nineteenth century.[44] It was, in fact, to see a novel and distinctly twentieth-century federalism. The Progressives' use of the "laboratory" metaphor illustrated the way that new generations infused new ideas and values into the complex structure of American federalism, and those who subsequently adopted their metaphor illustrated the way that later generations absorbed such changes while forgetting that they were, in fact, changes.[45]

A third "value of federalism," the protection that decentralized government offered to distinctly "local" values and interests, suggested yet another problem. In the seventeenth century, and well into the eighteenth, the states remained diverse geographical communities with their own relatively homogeneous populations and distinctive habits, attitudes, traditions, and religions. "Virginia," Patrick Henry announced proudly during the ratification debates, "has certain scruples."[46] Washington's Revolutionary army faced "overwhelming difficulties," Daniel Boorstin wrote, because an "intense separatism" generated fierce "determination to keep local resources to defend [local] homes and towns."[47] That colonial sense of separateness was the result of rural conditions, small and scattered populations, the slowness and difficulty of transportation and communication, and a narrow social and political provincialism that gave little heed to the affairs of the other colonies and that, when it did look outward, looked toward Great Britain or the Continent.[48] As late as 1800, when Thomas Jefferson was elected president, 96 percent of the nation's population lived in small towns or rural areas, while only six cities claimed more than ten thousand inhabitants.[49] When the founders drafted and ratified the Constitution, an "entrenched localism" was the "predominant factor" in American life.[50]

The ratification debates reflected those realities. Anti-Federalists repeatedly appealed to the value of small republics that enabled independent citizens to conduct their public affairs by dealing with known and trusted neighbors.[51] The "Federal Farmer" explained that "the state governments will possess the confidence of the people" because they "will have a near connection, and their members an immediate intercourse with the people."[52] Brutus made the same point. Only when someone was "a neighbor" with whom one was "intimately acquainted" would a person "commit his affairs into his hands with unreserved confidence."[53] Federalists generally accepted the same assumption while cleverly turning its significance. Madison used the predominance of localism to argue that the new central government would not be able to overpower the states because the "greater proportion of the people have the ties of personal acquaintance and friendship" with local officials, and therefore "the popular bias may well be expected most strongly to incline" toward them.[54] Hamilton, cleverly but more disingenuously, simply snuck an ambiguous new element onto the standard list of intimate acquaintances. "Where, in the name of common-sense," he asked, "are our fears to end if we may not trust our sons, our brothers, our neighbors, our fellow-citizens?"[55]

During the century following ratification, however, Americans "fundamentally altered their society and their social relationships," abandoning the assumption that in a proper society "most people were bound together by personal ties of one sort or another."[56] Always a relatively mobile people, Americans spread out across the land, moving between farm and city and from state to state. By the 1830s the average citizen appeared to Tocqueville as someone "always in a hurry" who "settles in a place from which he departs soon after so as to take his changing desires elsewhere."[57] A burgeoning culture and ideology of democracy compounded the leveling effect of such geographical movement. "Mobility, the challenge democracy set out to meet, turned out to be one of its greatest assets in unifying American society," Robert Wiebe noted. As Americans adventured from their homes, the "first principles" of democratic government "slipped easily into their bags" and provided "a citizen's ticket that was good for admission to public life wherever they might go."[58] Further, the proliferation and spread of private organizations across the land accelerated and institutionalized the process of social and cultural nationalization. In 1760, excluding church and commercial organizations, fewer than forty such associations existed in the colonies; their activities were local, and not one had been founded as a national organization. By the 1830s there were more than thirteen hundred such associations, most with extensive interstate affiliations, and many transformed into—or initially founded as—national associations espousing openly national goals.[59] Revolutions in transportation and communication, expansion to the Pacific, industrialization and urbanization, and the influx of ethnically and

religiously diverse immigrant groups combined to spread a rapidly growing and increasingly heterogeneous American people across the continent.[60] By the mid-nineteenth century, if not before, the comfortable idea
that Americans dealt with familiar neighbors known to tightly knit communities had given way to the unnerving idea that they were all too commonly compelled to deal with strangers who were unknown and often unknowable. The founders' classic image of social stability and the local
citizen known on personal knowledge to be virtuous had given way to
Herman Melville's disturbing image of pervasive risks posed by an ever-
reappearing but ever-different "Confidence Man."[61]

From the Civil War onward the movement toward unification, nationalization, and cultural homogenization accelerated. The integration and triumph of the national market and the rise of ever more pervasive and powerful mass media shaped a national culture that led Americans—however
much they might disagree in beliefs and values—to consume the same
products, consider the same subjects, share the same concerns, and rely on
the same sources for information, education, and entertainment. Radio,
movies, television, airplanes, and the Internet created an ever-expanding,
-pervading, and -dominating national culture that was unimaginable in
the eighteenth century. In the process the authentically "local" in America—values, habits, ideas, and practices distinctive to specific geographical
locations—weakened, disintegrated, and often disappeared, either blending into widely shared national attitudes or fading into the exotic, eccen-
tric, and peripheral.

The decline of consensual "local" values and attitudes was strikingly apparent in the changing role of the jury, that most fundamental institution
of the common law and the Constitution. Through the end of the eighteenth century common-law juries represented the authentic voice of their
communities, and the law empowered them not only to find "the facts"
but "the law" as well. Such juries "had been able to arrive at verdicts in individual cases and to apply law consistently over a long series of cases,"
William E. Nelson explained, "largely because men selected to juries
shared a common set of ethical values and assumptions that facilitated the
attainment of unanimity and consistency in the application of the rules of
common law." But during the early nineteenth century, under pressures
from a changing society and a mobile population, "ethical unity broke

down," and jurors increasingly brought to their task divergent values and interests that fragmented consensus and made their judgments erratic and unpredictable.[62] Because an expanding national commerce required stability and predictability in the law, state after state sought to meet that demand by replacing its reliance on the local communal knowledge of the jury with the generalized and formalized standards of judges and treatise writers. Courts and legislatures withdrew from juries the power to find the law and imposed a range of restrictions on their discretion, giving judges broader powers to determine applicable legal rules, create presumptions and distribute burdens of proof, control the admission and use of evidence, and set aside jury verdicts and order new trials. The breakdown of distinctive consensual communities meant that legal stability and predictability could no longer rest on fragmenting and erratic "local" judgments but required, instead, the "objective" and uniform standards that only general rules and trained professionals could provide. The new attitude toward the jury, Lawrence M. Friedman noted, was "appropriate to mobile societies and big cities where it was easy to be unknown and anonymous."[63]

The dissipation of the authentically "local" was similarly evident in the evolution of the substantive laws of the states. With the development of an integrated and expanding national market, business and financial interests pressed to increase the law's predictability and improve its facilitative role by eliminating divergent and conflicting "local" state laws and replacing them with "uniform" national rules.[64] In 1842 the Supreme Court responded in *Swift v. Tyson*,[65] holding that the federal courts need not follow the decisions of the state courts in "general" common-law matters but could, instead, render their own independent judgments on such issues. The decision was designed to underwrite the development of an independent "federal common law" that would enable the federal courts across the nation to apply uniform rules and induce state courts to abandon their "idiosyncrasies" and adopt the same rules.[66] Although *Swift* met with only mixed success, practical pressures for commercial uniformity continued to intensify, and during the twentieth century business organizations and bar associations combined to induce the states to adopt a growing number of "model" statutes that codified and unified the law across the nation in a wide range of areas.[67] The demands of an interstate economy based on the mass production and mass consumption of standardized goods and services steadily shrank, and largely extinguished, the spaces where distinctively "local" commercial laws and practices could survive.

Indeed, the American West, often pictured as the land of "rugged individualism" and deeply ingrained local values, was secured, opened, settled, and nourished by the continuous support and supervision of the national government. From the farsighted provisions of the Northwest Ordinance to the methodical removal of American Indian tribes, and from the construction of internal improvements to commercial linkages with national and international markets, the federal government shaped the law, culture, politics, and economies of both the "old" and "new" West. Even the most ruggedly "local" western values were underwritten by national policies and national authority.[68]

Equally important, some of the "local" values that were held most firmly in the eighteenth century—those involving race, gender, religion, ethnicity, and the proper hierarchy of social deference—were later repudiated by constitutional provisions, national legislation, Supreme Court rulings, and the development of a national culture of democracy. Far and away the most distinctive, deeply embedded, and passionately defended "local" institution in America, after all, was slavery, and as late as 1861 even Lincoln and his Republican Party accepted the principle that "the proper division of local from federal authority" precluded the national government from abolishing the peculiar institution in the states where it existed.[69] The Thirteenth Amendment, however, extinguished that "local" value. Similarly, other subjects often considered "local"—including marriage, divorce, child rearing, and matters involving the health, safety, and morality of communities—came to be shaped by national policy, in some cases directly and in others indirectly through federal laws involving taxes, pensions, welfare, bankruptcy, and immigration.[70] Indeed, the institution of marriage, which was often portrayed as a quintessentially "local" matter,[71] repeatedly created practical problems involving interstate relations and the meaning of the Full Faith and Credit Clause, and it provoked a series of vigorous debates about the desirability of unifying the nation's marriage laws.[72] The late nineteenth century, moreover, brought national regulation in response to polygamy and the Mormon control of Utah,[73] while the movement for gay rights in the late twentieth century spurred a vigorous campaign to extend national authority by constitutionalizing the law of marriage, a campaign supported by many who claimed on other issues to be ardent supporters of decentralized government or proponents of the states as "laboratories."[74]

Finally, the authentically "local" had long been subordinated to national party demands and the politics of gerrymandering. "The people of Pennsylvania are about one-third Federalist, yet all their new members of Congress are Democrats," the *Salem Gazette* complained in 1802; "the legislature took great care in laying out the districts, to make the elections as sure for the Democrats as if they had voted by a ticket at large."[75] Rather than seeking to provide representation for cohesive geographical areas, the political parties that controlled state legislatures shifted district lines and divided or merged "local" populations to enhance their statewide and national power. By the late twentieth and early twenty-first centuries, moreover, the availability of sophisticated computer programs and increasingly refined tools of analysis enabled national parties controlling state legislatures to shift "local" populations from district to district ever more methodically in the effort to create for themselves larger numbers of "safe" seats. Their efforts underscored the truth that Alexander Bickel noted more than forty years ago: "Any given neighborhood is, after all, an arbitrary construct, the trace at some time of somebody's pencil on a map."[76] The methodical redrawing of district lines, and the calculated use of neighborhoods as population chips in a larger national political contest, highlighted the arbitrary quality of "local" political boundaries and underscored the decisive role that national goals, values, and interests played in ostensibly "local" politics.[77]

The central point, of course, was not that "local" conditions and controversies became unimportant. Quite the contrary. The well-being of their geographical homes was vital to Americans, and geographically specific concerns remained dominant at most times and places. Indeed, states, counties, cities, towns, and suburbs consistently sought to control their own "local" affairs and, often at least, to control the "local" administration and operation of "national" programs within their borders.[78] Indeed, that typical "local" goal was one of the driving forces behind the nation's kaleidoscopic politics, the persistent effort of states and localities to shape national policy in ways that would favor their own interests. Rather, the point was that social and economic change had revolutionized the meaning and significance of the "local." To the extent that "federalism" protected the "local" in the twenty-first century, it protected values and benefits that were quite different from those it had protected in the eighteenth century.

In contrast to the "local" concerns of earlier times, the "local" issues that absorbed Americans by the twentieth century increasingly reflected geographically specific manifestations of problems common to everyone across the nation—or at least common to the de facto nationwide or worldwide socioeconomic groups to which various local residents belonged. The most pressing "local" issues, in fact, seldom involved matters unique to a particular place. Rather, they were geographically particularized versions of generic national problems related to jobs, crime, medical care, education, immigration, environmental degradation, standards of public morality, global economic competition, the threat of international terrorism, the content and orientation of national media, and recurring eruptions of the kinds of racial, ethnic, religious, and gender-based conflicts that simmered across the nation and the world. Critical to most of those problems, moreover, were policies and politics rooted in national or international conditions or specific decisions made by the U.S. government, by one or more foreign governments, or by "private" corporations chartered elsewhere in the world and conducting global operations. Sometimes those decisions stemmed from sweeping policies that shaped world affairs. More commonly, they grew from relatively mundane matters centering on either the commodities and services provided by national and international commerce or the opening, operation, or closing of nearby plants, stores, clinics, offices, military bases, housing projects, or other such facilities. At the beginning of the twenty-first century, then, the typical "local" issue seldom involved values or habits peculiar to a particular location but rather questions raised by the relationship between specific geographical areas and powerful institutions and interests rooted in other parts of the nation or world.[79]

The transformation of the "local" had a dramatic effect on the idea of federalism. As the constitutional line between the "local" and the "national" grew increasingly hypothetical and arbitrary in the lived experience of Americans, efforts to define its nature and specify its location increasingly became verbal formulations of largely arbitrary and often imaginary divisions. Even some of federalism's most avid supporters readily conceded that the concept had lost its power to capture reality. "Where is the philosopher's stone of federalism, the demarcation principle between central and state functions that would rationalize a division of labor within the American federal system?" Aaron Wildavsky asked. His answer was blunt. "Nowhere." His reason was compelling. "Every offer to specify what is local and what is national, I believe, will founder on these facts of life: every national activity has its local aspects and every local activity has a national perspective."[80] As early as 1819 Madison himself had come to recognize the same truth. "In the great system of Political Economy having for its general object the national welfare," he noted, "everything is related immediately or remotely to every other thing."[81] The challenge, then, was to draw a line between the national and the local that would produce the most desirable practical results, a line that was necessarily artificial, mutable, and pragmatic. By the beginning of the twenty-first century the concepts of the "local" and the "national" had become little more than conclusory labels serving overt or covert instrumentalist purposes, much as the counterpoised concepts of "manufacturing" and "commerce" had been a century earlier.[82]

Thus, ideas about the "values of federalism" proved exceptionally problematic and largely unavailing. New "values" were invented, and old ones given new content. More important, insofar as "values" remained unchanged, they did so as abstract concepts with only uncertain and fluctuating connections to the federal structure itself.[83] While "values" such as protecting liberty, encouraging diversity, ensuring accountability, and promoting participation properly remained in the constitutional pantheon, they justified only one conclusion about the federal structure: that, under the right circumstances, divided government might foster them. That conclusion said nothing, however, about the nature of those "right circumstances," nor did it explain how the conflicting demands of the various "values of federalism" should be balanced against one another or how the relationships among the levels and branches could be adjusted to achieve such a balance.[84] Like other questions about federalism, none of those could be answered in the abstract. Nor, of course, could they be answered from the text of the Constitution or any "original" intent or understanding of the founders.

The Nature of Federalism

As the proffered "values of federalism" changed over the years, the very concept of "federalism" itself did the same. The "original" federal structure was simply an expedient, a working compromise necessary to allow the founders to forge a new and more "energetic" central government. Unlike the separation of powers, a structural device the founders freely chose to utilize, federalism was a de facto condition thrust upon them by political reality, a historical fait accompli they were compelled to accept and the principal obstacle they were challenged to overcome. Designed both to recognize and to curtail state "sovereignty," the Constitution sketched lines between state and national powers that were ambiguous and contested from the outset; and, to the extent that areas of consensus existed, they were defined far more by custom, convenience, and existing conditions and technologies than by text, theory, or any generally accepted set of meanings.[85]

The early operations of the federal structure, moreover, were uncertain and varied, as individuals and groups considered its possibilities and staked out tentative positions on unanticipated issues. Sometimes the founders used national powers boldly and broadly, as in Hamilton's financial program, Washington's Neutrality Proclamation, Jay's Treaty, the Alien and Sedition Acts, Jefferson's Louisiana Purchase, the Embargo and Non-Intercourse Acts, the beginnings of the "American System," and the decisions of the Marshall Court. Sometimes, conversely, those same founders constrained national power sharply and insisted that state authority was broad and fundamental. Further, the constitutional views of the founders shifted as issues changed and their own positions vis-à-vis the national government rose or fell. Jefferson's vigorous actions as president contradicted many of the positions he had taken while standing in opposition to Federalist rule,[86] and Madison's rejection of the first Bank of the United States in 1791 changed into support for a second Bank of the United States in 1816.[87] From the first days of Washington's presidency, the members of the founding generation demonstrated that they shared no determinate and comprehensive agreement on the nature of the federal structure or the lines of division between national and state powers.[88] Indeed, one of the few things that was clear, ironically, was the immediate need for administrative cooperation between the states and the new central government. As a practical matter, the federal structure required the state and central governments to conform their operations in a number of areas, and with the formation of Washington's first administration state and federal officials set about to do just that.[89]

Over the decades, however, as the new constitutional structure proved workable and its practices grew relatively settled, commentators began to develop general theories that purported to identify or prescribe the structure's "true" nature. The culture and politics of the nineteenth century gave rise to the idea that the Constitution ordained a system of "dual federalism," while developments of the twentieth century strengthened the idea that it created a system of "cooperative federalism." The former assumed that the national government was one of limited and delegated powers and that the states were independent sovereigns with exclusive authority over clearly identifiable "local" matters. In theory, "dual federalism" preserved liberty and democracy by ensuring that each level of government was confined to its "separate sphere" and continually checked the expansionist efforts of the others.[90] The latter conceived the system in a radically different manner. The idea of "cooperative federalism" assumed that federal power was elastic and that the various levels of government had overlapping interests and shared functions.[91] In theory, the structure of "cooperative federalism" remained decentralized and democratic because no single governmental unit held exclusive power and because numerous gaps in governmental powers guaranteed wide areas of individual freedom.[92] The idea of "dual federalism" assumed the existence of clear constitutional borders and, especially after the Civil War, their enforcement by the Supreme Court; the theory of "cooperative federalism" relied on the existence of political parties and pressure groups to maintain the system's working boundaries. Both nicely reflected the dominant needs, values, practices, and politics of the respective centuries that embraced them most fully.[93]

The two labels, in turn, served as both jurisprudential guides and ideological weapons. Those who opposed national action tended to invoke the theory of "dual federalism" to demonstrate that their views were consistent with the "authentic" federalism of the founders, while those who advocated expanded national action increasingly adopted the idea of "cooperative federalism" to demonstrate that "dual federalism" was inaccurate as historical description and outmoded as constitutional prescription. In spite of disagreements, however, by the middle of the twentieth century few disputed that American government showed little resemblance to a system of "dual" federalism and considerable similarity to a more centralized type of "cooperative"—or, as some critics of centralization began to call it, "coercive"[94]—federalism.

Not surprisingly, then, as the social and cultural dynamics of American politics began to change drastically after the 1960s and critics of post–New Deal liberalism sought more convincing grounds on which to condemn its "cooperative federalism," new theories crystallized and rose to prominence.[95] Rooted intellectually in an exceptional collection of works published within little more than a decade after 1951,[96] theories of "competitive federalism" sprouted from the same revitalized interest in neoclassical economics that gave nearly simultaneous birth to such approaches as "law and economics" and "rational choice theory."[97] What was new in "competitive federalism" thinking was not the recognition that states and localities competed with one another, for that had been apparent from the nation's beginning. What was new, rather, was the effort to minimize the extent to which the founders had established the Constitution precisely to limit state competition and to ensure that harmony and uniformity prevailed in many areas of national life. What was new, too, was the sustained effort to "theorize" state and substate competition in terms of neoclassical economics and "free market" principles and to use the resulting theories to urge strict limits on the national government and "market-based" policies on all governments. What was also new, finally, was the implicit parallel effort to minimize or ignore complex social and economic realities: the cultural construction of markets, the prevalence of market failures, and the fundamental differences between the moral and political ideals of American constitutionalism and the operations and pressures of the international corporate economic system. Thus, "competitive federalism" theorists tended to advance values, policies, and interests associated with the economic policies of the post-Reagan Republican Party. As theories of "dual" and "cooperative" federalism had rationalized earlier political and constitutional orders, so theories of "competitive federalism" sought to rationalize an emergent and radically different "conservative" political and constitutional order.[98]

The new theories of "competitive federalism" were both "positive" and normative. They began by assuming that individuals were self-seeking and utility-maximizing actors, that their preferences were highly varied, and that the proper function of government was to protect their freedom to seek satisfaction of those diverse preferences. Federalism, then, was highly desirable, the argument ran, because it entailed a multitude of relatively equal and geographically limited governments, a structural condition that compelled those governments to compete for citizens by structuring attractive "packages" of costs and benefits that, in turn, enabled individuals to satisfy their preferences more fully by freely selecting their homes from an extensive and varied menu of jurisdictions. Consequently, the theories concluded, it was essential to preserve many local governmental units, to ensure that individuals retained the right to "exit" jurisdictions and move to others, and to keep the powers of the central government limited so that it would not be able to suppress competition and enforce dysfunctional uniformities among the states.[99] In the last quarter of the twentieth century those ideas spread widely and seemed to exert a growing influence on political and constitutional debate.[100]

Like the predecessor theories of "dual" and "cooperative" federalism, theories of "competitive federalism" readily served ideological purposes. Michael S. Greve, for example, a leading scholar at the conservative American Enterprise Institute, castigated "cooperative federalism" as "a rotten idea" while elaborating the contrasting virtues of "competitive" or "market-preserving" federalism.[101] Yet, he did not accept all competition and markets as good. He bitterly attacked the Court's decision in *Erie Railroad Co. v. Tompkins*,[102] for example, even though it abolished the centralized national common law of *Swift v. Tyson*[103] and directed the federal judiciary to enforce the varied common-law rules of the separate states. Acknowledging that *Erie* seemed like "a profederalism decision," Greve argued that it was actually "the opposite" because it allowed "parochial state courts" to encourage the "systematic exploitation of out-of-state corporations in franchise disputes and, most egregiously, in products liability litigation." Similarly, Greve indicted "plaintiffs' lawyers" on the ground that they tended to "shop" among states "for a hospitable court and jury" that would "sock it to out-of-state defendants."[104] Thus, the "competitive" right of states to establish their own distinctive menus of values and laws had sharp limits, as did the citizens' right to "exit" one jurisdiction to find in others more attractive "packages" of legal rules to better satisfy their preferences.[105]

Like predecessor theories, then, "competitive federalism" ultimately relied for many, if not most, of its specific conclusions and policy recommendations on the social, political, and ideological commitments of its advocates.[106] Commonly, "competitive federalism" theories were shaped by, and drew their strongest support from, those who were hostile to national regulation and who rejected the policies and programs of New Deal and post–New Deal liberalism.[107] Their appearance and use in the late twentieth century exemplified once again the way in which theories of federalism emerged from the processes of social change and reflected the ideas, values, and interests of new generations confronting new historical contexts and new political alignments. As Lawrence M. Friedman wrote, over the course of more than two centuries the "culture of federalism," like "the reality of federalism," had been "drastically altered."[108]

Indeed, the spread of "competitive federalism" theories illustrated just how "drastically altered" both the culture and reality of federalism had become, for that theory was noticeably different from those that had preceded it. Both "dual" and "cooperative" federalism purported to be rooted in the Constitution and to derive their specific propositions from it. "Competitive federalism," in contrast, rested on an overtly extraconstitutional economic theory. Although its advocates claimed that their theory was consistent with the Constitution, they also acknowledged that it was neither explicitly mandated by the Constitution nor, as a factual matter, derived from it.[109] Thus, "competitive federalism" reflected the assumptions of the late twentieth and early twenty-first centuries in yet another way. It implicitly accepted the proposition that the operations of the federal structure were not for the most part directed by the Constitution itself but by values, ideas, and interests that lay beyond the document's provisions.[110]

The Nature and Meaning of the Constitution

On the broadest level, shifts in cultural and intellectual assumptions over more than two hundred years also changed the way that lawyers, judges, and the educated public thought about law and the Constitution. "[T]he word 'constitution' did not mean in the eighteenth century what it means now—at least, not what it means in the twentieth century," John Phillip Reid pointed out. Then, the "word 'constitutional' was not synonymous with 'legal.'"[111] It carried, rather, a much broader, more amorphous, and custom-based meaning. During the late eighteenth century, that relatively fluid, custom-based meaning evolved into the modern meaning of a constitution as a fundamental law that was beyond the power of the legislature to alter. After 1787, however, the rise and spread of utilitarianism, naturalism, positivism, and relativism altered many traditional "legal" and "constitutional" ideas, while philosophical skepticism, pragmatism, cognitive indeterminism, and later "postmodernism" deepened doubts about the human capacity to know while highlighting the seemingly infinite malleability of words, sounds, symbols, and images. As the wildly inventive professions of advertising, public relations, and political consulting rose to prominence in the twentieth century, they confirmed the scope of that malleability and magnified the reasons for doubting expanding portions of the nation's public discourse. Together, those forces undermined many previously shared cultural understandings and inspired ever more audacious efforts to exploit the nation's apparently crumbling consensus on meanings and values. Such developments implicitly and sometimes explicitly challenged the basic Enlightenment assumptions that underwrote the very idea of a written constitution.[112]

Moreover, while eighteenth-century Newtonian assumptions had led the founders to see the Constitution as a machine both powered and checked by the forces of ambition, that conception gave way in the nineteenth century to evolutionary assumptions that understood the Constitution as a "living" organism adapting to a changing social environment.[113] The "chief strength" of the Constitution was its "elasticity and adaptability," Woodrow Wilson maintained in 1885, for any "governmental system would snap asunder a constitution which could not adapt itself to the new conditions of an advancing society."[114] That adaptive process, Wilson reaffirmed two decades later, created a "national consciousness" that drove "a slowly progressive modification and transfer of functions as between the States and the federal government along the lines of actual development."[115] In the early twentieth century many Progressives embraced the idea of a "living" Constitution in their efforts to combat the conservative federal judiciary,[116] and by midcentury it had become a widely shared idea,[117] especially popular among the liberal heirs of Progressivism[118] though sharply disputed by their adversaries.[119]

From the mid-twentieth century on, in the wake of the New Deal "Constitutional Revolution"[120] and *Brown v. Board of Education*,[121] Americans struggled with the challenge of reconciling the undeniable facts of social and legal change with traditional jurisprudential ideas about the nature and purpose of a written Constitution. While theories proliferated, none seemed able to command substantial, let alone majority, support. Scholars and judges opposed to the liberal decisions of the Warren Court surged to the forefront by reenergizing and reorienting theories of "originalism,"[122] which, they claimed, could provide clear norms and authoritative interpretations of the Constitution. Their conclusions often varied among themselves,[123] however, and their methods raised grave analytical problems.[124] One was the difficulty of establishing any clear and applicable "original" meaning for many constitutional provisions; a second was the fact that whatever "original" meanings could be reliably ascertained often provided little unambiguous direction on contemporary controversies; a third was the spreading recognition that any authoritative guidance attributed to "original" meanings depended in large part on the level of generality at which interpreters chose to construe those meanings.[125] Originalism, in other words, although commonsensical and widely accepted as a general idea, was simply inadequate as a sole, or even primary, method for interpreting the Constitution.[126] Its practical use, moreover, opened constitutional interpretation to a range of potentially arbitrary, discretionary, and simplistic historical judgments. Beyond those analytic problems, finally, loomed the embarrassing fact that, as a practical matter, originalist theories served primarily as purposeful instruments of constitutional change and doctrinal innovation.[127] Originalism was the natural tool of those who sought justification for overthrowing the precedents and practices of the relatively recent past, for it allowed them to appeal to the precedents and practices of a more distant, and therefore allegedly more "authentic," past.[128]

The revitalization of originalism highlighted rather than resolved the problems of interpreting constitutional federalism. It spurred the development of rival liberal and progressive originalisms and demonstrated that a conviction, however passionate, that constitutional government demanded clear, established, and unchanging norms was simply not sufficient to produce clear, established, and unchanging norms. Indeed, relied on as a sole or primary guide, originalism seemed to exacerbate rather then minimize problems of constitutional uncertainty.[129] To the extent that commentators denied the doubly blurred nature of the federal structure, ignored its elastic and dynamic nature, and sought to discard the innumerable markers and guides that its history had generated, they distorted the structure's essential nature and threatened to cast aside much of the nation's invaluable and hard-earned political, social, and moral wisdom.[130] To the extent that they attempted to replace that national experience with preemptive claims of some "originalist" truth, moreover, they expanded the realm of discretion in constitutional interpretation because they relied on a method and standard incapable of fulfilling their promises.[131] Efforts to apply originalism consistently and exclusively demanded the impossible and threatened to produce not merely continual compromise but also, and far worse, continual pretense.[132]

Indeed, originalism was plagued by the deepest of ironies. Purporting to be based on the study of "history," it usually proved ahistorical and presentist. Its normative goals regularly led its practitioners into a fundamental error of historical analysis—ignoring or minimizing the fact that "the past" was different from the present, and usually quite complexly so. Moreover, to provide the specific normative guidance it purported to offer, originalism was usually compelled to disregard or minimize essential elements of the historical record. It was compelled, that is, to scant the obvious fact that the available evidence was frequently inadequate or unrepresentative and the further fact that whatever evidence did exist often revealed flux, doubt, vagueness, confusion, avoidance, deception, novelty, variety, inattention, obfuscation, uncertainty, disagreement, incompleteness, partisanship, opportunism, ambiguity, inconsistency, and accommodation. Failing to give those qualities their due weight, originalism proved itself for the most part not only inadequate and artificial but also subjective and manipulable.[133] Indeed, too often it did little but inspire the production of ever more fully weaponized versions of the nation's legal, political, and constitutional history.

In truth, originalism had from the beginning failed to produce clear and determinate answers to the constitutional questions that divided Americans, especially those involving the nature and limits of the federal structure.[134] As early as 1793, for example, the Court issued its first major ruling on the federal structure in *Chisholm v. Georgia*,[135] a decision that was particularly revealing because it followed closely on the heels of ratification, raised a fundamental issue of federal-state relations, and came from a five-justice Court made up quite literally of nothing but the most authentic of "founders." The four justices in the majority included a chief justice who had been a member of his state's ratifying convention as well as one of the authors of the *Federalist,* a second justice who had served as the presiding officer of his state's ratifying convention, and two justices who had served as delegates to both their states' ratifying conventions and the Philadelphia Convention itself.[136] Yet the fifth justice, an equally authentic founder who had led the fight for the Constitution in his own state's ratifying convention, disagreed with them.[137] More striking perhaps, a large number of Americans also disagreed with the four founders in the majority, and within a bare five years they secured the adoption of a constitutional amendment that overturned the decision.[138] Had four out of five founders simply been "wrong"? An unanswerable, and ultimately unhelpful, question. What the episode demonstrated was that a few founders disagreed with a few other founders and that the rest of them—the overwhelming majority—had simply "given the matter no thought at all" until the specific question in the case arose shortly after ratification.[139]

Another factor, too, was surely involved in *Chisholm* and its repudiation. As the founders themselves recognized so keenly, by the mid-1790s things had changed, and changed quite substantially. Many of the founders had reoriented their thinking or changed their minds on a variety of issues. Whatever they thought about the question that *Chisholm* presented, however, it was most likely not quite the same as what they had thought about it—had they thought about it at all—in 1787 and 1788. Indeed, the fact that ideas and politics changed so quickly in the decade after ratification meant that even evidence from the early 1790s could be a dubious, if not wholly unreliable, guide to any "original" understanding of the Constitution itself.[140]

From *Chisholm* on, as subsequent controversies about the federal structure arose, originalism continued for the most part to play a similarly inconclusive, contested, and partisan role. In their debate over the constitutionality of the Bank of the United States in 1819, for example, both John Marshall and Spencer Roane advanced their contrary positions by avidly embracing originalism and pleading fidelity to the authentic Constitution of the founders. Marshall proclaimed that those, like Roane, who rejected his view, were animated by "unfounded jealousies" and "deep-rooted and vindictive hate."[141] Roane announced that anyone who accepted Marshall's view "must be a deplorable idiot."[142]

10

THE "ARDUOUS ENTERPRISE"

This inquiry examines the original nature of American federalism. It argues that, from its founding, the federal structure was doubly blurred, fractionated, instrumental, and contingent and that those four characteristics made the structure's resulting governmental system inherently elastic, dynamic, and underdetermined. The inquiry suggests, consequently, that the claim that the federal structure provides specifically directive constitutional norms is deeply problematic and for the most part simply inaccurate. It suggests equally that the Constitution and other "originalist" sources fail to provide specifically directive norms capable of authoritatively resolving contested federalism issues. Its fundamental point, then, is not that federalism "changed" over the years but that the nature of the original constitutional structure made change inevitable.[1]

Before proceeding further, it is necessary to identify four propositions that this inquiry neither rejects nor questions. First, the inquiry does not doubt that the Constitution can furnish a foundation for normative theories of federalism. The Constitution obviously can, for it has done so repeatedly in every age and for every political interest that seriously competed for power. Indeed, its four intrinsic characteristics made the federal structure inherently vulnerable to theorists who sought to impose on it their own particular values, meanings, and purposes. Thus, the inquiry readily acknowledges that the Constitution has helped spawn countless normative theories of federalism; it merely argues that none of those theories identified any "original" version that was "true" or "correct." Second, this inquiry does not doubt that the Constitution contains some provisions that are relatively clear and that it establishes worthy principles of law and government.[2] It suggests only that establishing institutions of government is not the same as clearly defining the powers and proper relationships of those institutions and that establishing fundamental principles of government is not the same as prescribing the proper application of those principles in an unknown future. Third, this inquiry does not doubt that ideas about the lines between national and state power were in some ways clearer—though still vague, incomplete, and contested—during the nation's earlier decades or that as a general matter changes in those ideas occurred more slowly during those earlier times than during later ones. It acknowledges, moreover, the obvious fact that the operations of the federal structure evolved through a series of relatively coherent "systems" or "regimes" of government and that, during much of the nation's history, those sequential forms were accompanied by a series of reasonably specific and, for a time, generally accepted sets of constitutional doctrines and assumptions.[3] Finally, this inquiry does not doubt that those who pledged fealty to "federalism" and its "principles" over the years were sincere and honorable. If the nation's history demonstrates anything, it shows that Americans held reverent, passionate, and often quite well considered views about the federal structure. It was a series of disputes involving such views, after all, that hewed the path to a civil war in which millions fought and more than six hundred thousand died. Thus, the inquiry does not suggest that beliefs and theories about federalism lacked either profound intellectual commitments or deep emotional allegiances.

This historical inquiry, then, advances only one primary claim and three principal corollaries. Most fundamentally, it argues that the nation's federal structure was from its beginning characterized by four inherent qualities: it was doubly blurred, fractionated, instrumental, and contingent. From that premise, the inquiry draws three major conclusions. The first is that those characteristics made the federal structure flexible and its working system of government inherently elastic, dynamic, and underdetermined. As a consequence, the operative lines of the federal system were consistently contested and necessarily malleable. The second conclusion is that no authentic "original" authority exists—neither the text of the Constitution nor any intent or understanding of the founders—that is capable of providing specifically directive norms for the "correct" operation of the federal structure. The third is that, even had some such "original" authority actually prescribed a "true" or "correct" federal system, the structure's four inherent characteristics would have made it impossible for Americans to maintain that system unchanged over time.

The Indeterminate Nature of American Federalism

The structure's doubly blurred quality caused normative uncertainty from the republic's earliest days. The Constitution sketched imprecise lines between state and federal powers, and it failed to mark their limits clearly or completely. Further, it compounded that uncertainty by giving the two levels of government overlapping authority to govern the same territories, the same people, and many of the same activities. Finally, the Constitution conceived of both levels of government as counterpoised forces protecting the same vague and contested values—liberty, property, and republicanism. Its design thus placed the powers of states and nation in purposeful tension and subjected them to inevitable and persistent conflicts. At any given time and on any given issue, both state and national governments could be seen as protectors of those fundamental values. Indeed, because there was widespread disagreement about the specific meaning and implications of those values, Americans were able to claim that protective role for both state and national governments on any and all contested issues. The structure was thus inherently blurred in two distinct ways. The Constitution was ambiguous in drawing the lines of authority between the two levels, and it was ambivalent in allocating to both the responsibility for protecting the nation's fundamental values.

Fragmenting both sides of the governmental divide, the structure's fractionated quality added another destabilizing and dynamic principle. On the "national" side, the central government was split into three distinct branches—one of which was internally divided and all three of which evolved into complex bureaucracies—that exercised different powers, possessed different capabilities, and affected state and local affairs in different ways. The three national branches could, and frequently did, disagree with one another, thereby often rendering "national" policy diffuse, inconsistent, or even nonexistent. On the "state" side, the individual components were even more numerous, and they were doubly divided: first, divided from one another, and second, divided within themselves. Consequently, the controversies that roiled American law and politics seldom, if ever, pitted "the states" against "the central government" as monolithic entities. Rather, they pitted some states and substate elements and interests against other states and substate elements and interests, with one or more of the three national branches sometimes lending support to one or another of the various sides. Thus, to speak of conflicts over state and national powers in general or in the abstract was to force constitutional analysis into a procrustean divide that ignored the kaleidoscopic nature of the nation's shifting and intricately layered interstate politics. The intrinsic dynamism of that kaleidoscopic politics continuously generated changing matrices of pressures on the doubly blurred constitutional lines between state and federal power and prevented either side of the binary divide, states or nation, from maintaining those lines clearly and consistently.

The structure's instrumental nature meant that human purposes properly drove the actions of its levels and branches. The structure's "checks and balances," however, did not quite channel and control those actions as the founders had planned. The structure's lines of authority were drawn inadequately and incompletely, and its architecture failed to make individual interests and institutional duties fully "coincide." It was impossible, moreover, for the Constitution either to prevent alliances across the levels and branches or to prescribe with precision when, how, and to what extent its components should properly "check" one another. As the structure's components responded to changing human purposes, then, their actions provoked the other levels and branches to respond. Those responses, however, took a variety of forms, not merely "checking" the actions of other levels and branches but also ignoring, deflecting, accepting, abetting, and compounding those actions. As factional pressures constantly drove the levels and branches to adapt, their interactions brought periodic shifts in their respective goals and periodic fluctuations in the ways they exercised their imprecisely defined powers. The structure's instrumental nature, consequently, made its operative system of government inherently dynamic and adaptive.

Finally, the structure's contingent quality meant that fundamental legal changes were authorized and often invited and that both the federal structure's individual components and its overall operations were necessarily mutable and malleable. Periodic elections, population growth and movement, the admission of new states, the exercise of branch discretion, formal constitutional amendments, and a variety of incremental changes in legal rules and institutional practices combined to reshape the structure's components and operations, while extrinsic social, cultural, political, economic, ideological, and intellectual pressures remolded the meaning, significance, and application of many constitutional provisions. Such changes reverberated through the structure, altering the powers of its components, shifting their areas of operation, and recalibrating their functional relationships.

Together, those four characteristics meant that American federalism was, by its very nature, incapable of either reaching permanent equilibrium or serving as a determinative constitutional norm. That conclusion does not imply that all constitutional interpretation is "subjective" or that the Constitution itself is nondeterminative in all of its parts and provisions. The conclusion applies only to federalism, and it rests solely on the inherent nature of the original structure that the Constitution ordained and established. That structure simply incorporated far too many mutable and malleable parts divided by far too many murky and manipulable lines either to define or to sustain any single and true balance.

Those four characteristics, then, meant that any attempt to construe the Constitution's federalism provisions solely in light of their "original" meaning was doomed to failure because from the very beginning those provisions were unsettled and incomplete and because they created an intrinsically dynamic and underdetermined system of government. They meant, too, that even had there been some "true" original system of constitutional federalism, it could not be revived and followed by later generations.[4] The Constitution itself, the meaning of its pivotal words, the political context that shaped it, the nation's economic system and international role, the social and cultural composition of the American people, the size and operations of the national branches, the number and organization of the states and their myriad subunits, and the fundamental ways in which Americans conceived of law, government, the general welfare, and the nature of American federalism all changed profoundly. No act of will, neither the Court's nor the people's, could return the constitutional order to the conditions and practices of its birth. Thus, with respect to federalism, there is no "true" constitutional system or "correct" constitutional balance that has been "lost" or driven into "exile."[5] There is only the flexible and dynamic federal structure through which the American people managed their affairs over the centuries and sought faithfully to give life to their collective national enterprise in constitutional self-government.[6]

Further, the four characteristics also meant that the only essential structural requirement of American federalism was the independent existence, efficacious operation, and ultimate public accountability of the various levels and branches of the "compound republic." While the lines between federal and state authority were vague and elastic from the beginning, the independent existence and potential checking function of the levels and branches were constitutive and pivotal. Thus, the energy, autonomy, and efficacy of each were essential. In its widely criticized decision in *National League of Cities v. Usery*[7] the Court sought to protect the "states as states" by denying Congress the power "to directly displace the States' freedom to structure integral operations in areas of traditional governmental functions."[8] It was a vague and in many ways unsatisfactory line, and the Court struggled woefully to give it effect before finally abandoning it.[9] The root judicial instinct in the case, however, was sound, for it sensed the decisive point—that the states, like the three federal branches, must remain independent centers of political power and popular government. To put the matter bluntly and simply, the Court intuited well when it recognized the need to protect states from being "commandeered" by the federal government[10] but stumbled when it used their existence to limit congressional power under the Commerce Clause[11] and the Fourteenth Amendment.[12]

Finally, the four characteristics meant that specific theories and propositions that purported to draw clear and determinate lines of authority between states and nation were rooted ultimately not in the Constitution or other "originalist" sources but in the personal values, beliefs, interests, and purposes of those who articulated the theories and propositions.[13] That conclusion did not mean that individuals were necessarily insincere or duplicitous when they proclaimed deep and abiding commitments to the values and principles of federalism; it meant only that they failed to recognize the ambiguities in those values and principles and, consequently, failed to recognize the subtle and varied ways in which their own inclinations resolved the ambiguities in the constitutional structure and shaped the specific contours of their formal views.[14] The conclusion, in other words, does not deny that some people believed sincerely in their specific versions of federalism; nor does it deny that some genuinely believed that their conceptions were mandated by the Constitution itself. It just means that those people were, as a general matter, mistaken.[15] The key question in understanding the actual history and operation of American federalism, after all, is not what particular views individuals held on federalism issues but, rather, why it was that they came to hold those particular views and what consequences they expected from their adoption and implementation. The reality of the complex personal and social process by which theories and propositions about federalism were formed means, therefore, that in most cases the critical consideration in evaluating such theories and propositions is not simply the formal constitutional arguments offered in justification but the substantive values and purposes that animated their advocates and, most telling, the practical consequences—concrete and specific—they seemed likely to bring if accepted.[16]

Two immediate objections to that last point may jump to mind. One goes to the complexity of human values and the subjectivity of human purposes. How, possibly, could we judge why individuals articulated the propositions they did? Constitutional debate, after all, must be open and public, and the conflicting positions advanced must be readily accessible to reasoned examination and critical evaluation.[17] The other objection goes to the issue of justification and legitimacy. What difference should it make what substantive values and purposes informed different ideas and propositions about federalism? Constitutional debate is a normative practice that must turn on whether propositions are well grounded and well reasoned, whether they are consistent with known empirical facts and authoritative legal sources.

This historical inquiry suggests that neither of those objections is relevant to the conclusions it reaches. The first objection falls short because an analysis of arguments about federalism does not require us to plumb the ultimate depths of individual psyches. The standard tools of law, history, biography, and the social sciences are adequate to determine with sufficient reliability the values and purposes that inspired various ideas about federalism as well as the consequences they seemed likely to bring. Calhoun was a brilliant and sophisticated theorist, but it was quite clear why he shaped his ideas about federalism as he did and what consequences he hoped to achieve with them. Indeed, the overtly instrumental nature of the federal structure requires that we examine such motives and purposes; for, as the inquiry suggests, it would otherwise be impossible to understand its de facto history or wisely assess proposals for guiding its future course.

The second objection is equally irrelevant, but for a different reason. The inherent characteristics of the federal structure—that it is doubly blurred, fractionated, instrumental, and contingent—mean that the Constitution did not, and could not, provide either "correct" or foreordained answers to the federalism questions that seriously divided Americans over the years. Thus, regardless of the sincerity and depth with which individuals held their views about federalism and its principles, the specific form their views took and the specific applications they believed proper simply could not have found their defining source in the Constitution and related "originalist" sources. Such specific conclusions, consequently, could have been forged only in the specific personal experiences of individual lives as they were shaped in varying ways by elements of the nation's culture and its contested history of constitutional debate. Indeed, this historical inquiry suggests that the more fully specified and passionately held a person's views on federalism, the more directly and comprehensively those views must have been the product of compelling personal values and interests. Thus, because constitutional provisions and "originalist" sources did not, and could not, define "correct" or foreordained answers to most claims about federalism,[18] there is simply no reasonable and satisfactory alternative for judging their merits other than scrutinizing the values and purposes of their advocates and advancing well-grounded estimates of their likely practical consequences if adopted.[19]

Normative Principles and the American Constitutional Enterprise

To say that the Constitution fails to provide correct or foreordained answers to disputed federalism questions is not to say that it fails to provide *any* correct answers or that it fails to provide varying degrees of normative guidance on a range of questions, including some involving federalism. Rather, it is to set the stage for exploring the flexible and dynamic nature of the federal structure and assessing its place in the nation's constitutional enterprise. It is also to acknowledge that the challenge of constitutional self-government is, as Hamilton said of the drafting and ratification of the Constitution itself, "so arduous an enterprise."[20]

The American constitutional enterprise is "so arduous" because its contours are imprecise, its direction contested, its conduct burdensome, and its fate uncertain. Its course is not predetermined or automatic but contingent and open-ended. We might fervently wish it otherwise, but the wish would be in vain. The enterprise is an irreducibly human project, and its success demands, among other necessities, the solicitude of the American people and the sound judgment of their chosen agents.

To that arduous enterprise, the Constitution itself makes five paramount contributions.

First, it establishes the nation's familiar "compound" structure of limited and divided powers, a structure that creates multiple units of government capable of counterbalancing one another. Sometimes, and in the relatively short run, a single unit of government may check the others; more commonly, and in the longer run, a single unit may prevail only with the concurrence of at least some of the others. Such a system of divided powers, Madison insisted, was the "proper structure" to provide a "republican remedy for the diseases most incident to republican government."[21] That complex structure is fundamental and essential. Over time, and as a general matter, it tends—however imperfectly—to prevent the excessive accumulation of power in any one person or governmental unit, to provide rival institutional bases for monitoring and checking the uses of public power, and to encourage public officials to consult, negotiate, and compromise before carrying out their policy decisions. That structure, moreover, creates an institutional pluralism that helps foster a relatively diverse political culture and nourish relatively open processes of public discussion and decision making. It is a structure, as Hamilton noted, that tends to encourage "a spirit of accommodation" in government officials and to protect "the reasonable expectations of their constituents."[22] Such a structure, sustaining a culture and practice of republican self-government, tends to produce—again, and unfortunately, only over time and only as a general matter—decisions and policies that are pragmatic, consensual, and relatively just.

Second, the Constitution prescribes three paramount institutional principles. The first is the principle of elective and representative government, a principle that the Constitution shrewdly adapted both to strengthen its structure of divided powers and to diversify the responsiveness of its three branches by subjecting them to different electoral methods. Although formal amendments and evolving practices altered the nature of both the original electorate and the original electoral design, the Constitution embodied from the start the principle of popular sovereignty. It made the three national branches and the governments of the states dependent, ultimately if for the most part indirectly, on the votes of the people. The second principle is that individual rights and liberties should be recognized and effectively protected by law. As Hamilton pointed out, in both its structure and many of its provisions the Constitution explicitly protects a variety of individual rights.[23] Moreover, immediately after the new government convened the Federalists, led by Madison in the House, drafted and pushed to ratification ten rights-identifying and rights-protecting amendments that became the Bill of Rights, while subsequent generations wisely added yet more.[24] The third principle is that all governmental power is limited, that each level and branch holds only delegated powers, and that none can properly act beyond the limits of its granted powers. The Constitution ordains itself "the supreme Law of the Land,"[25] and its provisions limn broadly if imprecisely the nature and scope of the powers that the levels and branches may exercise. Its supremacy thus mandates and underwrites a particular, complex, ingrained, and highly institutionalized version of a "rule of law."[26]

Third, the Constitution stands as a commanding symbol of national unity and human community, proclaiming the ideals and goals that are to animate the nation's enterprise in self-government. It implies those goals and ideals in both its compound structure and its three foundational principles, and it inscribes many of them with greater specificity in individual provisions and amendments. Most broadly and succinctly, the Constitution proclaims them in its Preamble: its purpose is "to form a more perfect Union, establish justice, insure domestic Tranquility, provide for the common defence, promote the general Welfare, and secure the Blessings of

Liberty to ourselves and our Posterity." More particularly and explicitly, if far too belatedly, it proclaims them in subsequent amendments, especially in the great clauses of the Fourteenth Amendment: to protect the equal rights and privileges of all Americans and to guarantee fair and equal treatment to all persons who come within the jurisdiction of the United States.[27] However vague and contested those ideals and goals may be, they continue to shine as bright, worthy, and beyond challenge. They remain, as Carl L. Becker discovered when he confronted the terrifying triumphs of Nazism in the early and ominous days of World War II, "Some Generalities That Still Glitter."[28] They constitute the ultimate legal and moral touchstone of the nation's constitutional enterprise.

Fourth, the Constitution links the nation's governmental enterprise to the ennobling tradition of western constitutionalism that runs from ancient Greece to contemporary strivings around the globe to establish and maintain workable structures of decent and well-ordered self-government. It constitutes both a brilliant summing up and a shrewd leap forward, a hard-won synthesis that blends the political and moral wisdom of more than two millennia with sagacious eighteenth-century judgments about human nature, American society, and the practical dynamics of republican politics.[29] That linkage and synthesis gives the Constitution a profound intellectual and cultural resonance, implicitly incorporating a range of deeply embedded values and aspirations that amplify the meaning of its ideals and illuminate the purpose of its structure.

Finally, the Constitution implies an ethical mandate of honor, fairness, good faith, and reasoned discourse. The ideals of the Preamble assume those qualities, and the closing provisions of Article VI demand them.[30] Serving the government of the United States, the Constitution declares, is a "public Trust."[31] Indeed, the very idea of a written constitution—with its implicit assumptions about individual rights, limited government, and a "rule of law"—assumes honor, fairness, good faith, and reasoned discourse not only on the part of government officials but also on the part of all who purport to construe its meaning, apply its principles, and live the reasoned and public life it frames.[32] The Constitution's basic provisions, moreover, are designed to elicit those qualities. The structure of divided power warns officials that their actions will be monitored by powerful rivals, while the requirement of periodic elections guarantees that those officials can be removed from office and that their rivals might well be the ones who replace them. Those considerations also counsel restraint and fairness in office because abuses of power establish precedents that can easily be turned against their authors when elective offices change hands. Although the founders held deeply skeptical views of human nature, they also believed that a "proper structure" of government could encourage faithful administration and perhaps, in some part, even foster virtue.[33] They knew, too, that without some such leaven of honor, good faith, and genuine concern for the general welfare no form of popular self-government could endure. Benjamin Franklin made the point as the Philadelphia Convention prepared to adjourn. "Much of the strength & efficiency of any Government," he told the delegates, depends "on the general opinion of the goodness of the Government" and "the wisdom and integrity of its Governors."[34]

Those five contributions of the Constitution properly inform our understanding of the federal structure and provide general guidance, though not specific direction, for our informed practical judgments about its efficacious operation. Vague and elastic to be sure, those contributions nonetheless define the nation's animating ideals, shape its institutional structure, and clarify the working principles that underlie its ongoing enterprise in ordered and popular self-government. Thus, American federalism cannot be understood solely on the basis of textual provisions, "originalist" meanings, or independent structural features. It can only be understood properly, and construed wisely, as one congruent part of an inevitably dynamic, ever-rebalancing, culturally rooted, and intrinsically value-based institutional whole.[35]

Federalism and the Arduous Enterprise

This historical inquiry differs in its conclusions from those offered by many others who have examined the law and history of American federalism. It differs, for example, from Charles Black's conclusion that the constitutional law of federalism evolved in ways that left no clear lines or determinative principles.[36] The inquiry suggests, instead, that the Constitution was inherently incapable of providing specifically determinative principles of federalism or clear and unchanging lines of division between national and state power. The problem, in other words, was not merely partisan interpretations, judicial inconsistency, social pressures, or historical changes. The problem was the very nature of the Constitution and the governmental structure it created—the existence of the four intrinsic characteristics of American federalism.[37]

The inquiry also differs from Samuel Beer's claim that American federalism, in spite of its ambiguous and instrumental nature, may be properly understood in light of an authoritative "national theory of the Constitution and of the federal system."[38] Beer's argument is historically plausible and well reasoned, and it may point in directions that seem practically desirable to many. This inquiry, however, suggests that his theory, like other analogous theories, ultimately remains only one more effort to impose a particular and extrinsic normative order on the nation's federal structure.

Equally, the inquiry differs from Charles Fried's analysis of the Court's recent federalism jurisprudence, which acknowledges that politics, ideology, and conflicting social values influenced earlier Court decisions but denies that such factors played a role in the work of the Rehnquist Court.[39] This inquiry suggests, in contrast, that the Constitution provides no single and true conception of the federal structure and that all such conceptions are rooted in complex political, social, and ideological sources. Regardless, then, of the honest motives and good faith efforts of the Rehnquist Court—qualities that it presumptively shares with all prior Courts—there is no ground for believing that it was, or could be, an exception.[40]

Further, the inquiry differs from Herbert Wechsler's "political safeguards" thesis, which held that, because the Constitution gave the states place and power to defend themselves, the Court need not use its resources to protect their position in the federal structure.[41] The inquiry's rejection of Wechsler's conclusion may seem surprising, for at first glance it might be taken rather to support his conclusion, though on alternative grounds: the fact that the Constitution mandates no particular federalism "balance," provides no specifically directive federalism norms, and requires its interpreters to draw on their own personal values in construing its federalism provisions could point to the conclusion that the Court has no business deciding such open-ended and essentially "nonlegal" questions.[42] While such an inference would follow if one relied solely on certain abstract legal premises, it does not follow from the inquiry's historical and institutional analysis. First, the premise that would underlie a Wechsler-supportive conclusion—that the U.S. Supreme Court is simply a "court of law" and should not act in the absence of preexisting law—is false. In the American constitutional enterprise, the Supreme Court is not, and has never been, simply a "court of law." Second, the inquiry shows that the federal structure simply did not work as Wechsler claimed.[43] As a general matter, "the states" did not perceive their powers and limitations in a uniform manner nor assess the advantages and disadvantages of national actions in the same way. Nor, more importantly, did they act consistently and cohesively to control the branches of the central government. Instead, the federal structure produced a dynamic and kaleidoscopic politics that repeatedly divided the states from one another and fragmented them internally, a politics that prevented them from acting consistently as a cohesive constitutional unit and from seeking to preserve any particular constitutional balance. There seems no reason to believe that the structure's politics will operate differently in the future. Third, the inquiry suggests that over the centuries the Court has become an integral working component of a complex governmental structure, one that has evolved as the nation's operating system of democratic government has evolved. On one hand, its role in that structure has become specialized and constrained, cabined by a variety of cultural norms, political checks, doctrinal limitations, and professional constraints. On the other hand, its role has become broad and authoritative, extending at least potentially to any question that impinges on the integrity and operations of the nation's complex governmental structure or on the rights and liberties of those who come within the jurisdiction of the United States. The claim that the Supreme Court should "never" enforce federalism limits, then, is fundamentally inconsistent with the flexible, dynamic, and pragmatic principles that underlie the constitutional structure. It is inconsistent, in particular, with the Constitution's fundamental premise that each of the three national branches is independent, exercises a distinctive authority, and interacts in its own ways with the states, the citizenry, and the other national branches.

Thus, on the basis of the history and pragmatics of the American constitutional enterprise, the inquiry supports the proposition that the Court can properly act to protect "federalism" in a "case" or "controversy" within its "jurisdiction." The fact that the Constitution mandates no particular "balance," provides inadequate guidance, and compels the justices to draw on their own personal values surely means that the constitutional structure, properly understood, imposes a severely constraining institutional bias against such interventions. It also means, however, that the question of whether or not to intervene rests ultimately in the wisdom and judgment of the Court itself. Sometimes, it errs. The Constitution can provide no guarantees.

Finally, this historical inquiry differs from two diametrically opposed views that the Supreme Court itself has recently put forward. The first is the view—obviously contrary to the inquiry's conclusions—that the federal structure provides clear and objective prescriptions. In *New York v. United States* the Court held a federal statutory provision "inconsistent with the federal structure" and denied that practical considerations had any relevance to its analysis and decision. "Our task would be the same even if one could prove that federalism secured no advantages to anyone," it announced. "It consists not of devising our preferred system of government, but of understanding and applying the framework set forth in the Constitution."[44] Thus, the Court pictured its "task" as wholly distinct from either assessing practical consequences or implementing wise and authoritative policies. Instead, it portrayed its task as nondiscretionary and its process of judgment as a matter of sheer logic.[45] This inquiry suggests that such claims of a nondiscretionary judicial function and a specifically directive Constitution—when applied to questions of federalism, at least, as they were in *New York*—can be nothing but judicial smoke screens. Such claims serve only to obscure the practical problems at issue and mask the actual role of the Court and its individual justices in resolving them.[46]

The second of the Court's recently stated views asserts the exact opposite of the first. In *Garcia v. San Antonio Metropolitan Transit Authority* the Court declared that "the Constitution offers no guidance about where the frontier between state and federal power lies," and it ruled, consequently, that it held "no license to employ freestanding conceptions of state sovereignty when measuring congressional authority under the Commerce Clause."[47] This inquiry suggests that the Court did not quite hit the mark in either of those statements. First, the inquiry posits that "guidance"—in the sense of informed and aspirational counsel as opposed to clear and specific direction—is precisely what the Constitution does provide, at least on some federalism issues. Second, the inquiry suggests that the Court does, in fact, hold a "license" to employ constitutional values, concepts, and provisions in seeking to maintain the federal structure as an effective working feature of the nation's enterprise in self-government. Such judicial "lawmaking," in fact, has become a key component of that enterprise, a function that the Court may fulfill well or ill, properly or improperly, but a function nonetheless that has been firmly incorporated in American government for many generations, if not necessarily since 1789. Equally, however, the inquiry also suggests that the Court's "license" is severely limited because it confers an awesome, subjective, and necessarily discretionary power.[48] Thus, the exercise of that "license" prohibits the use of "freestanding conceptions" of any sort and mandates, instead, highly contextualized judgments informed by wisdom, decency, honesty, rectitude, and—perhaps essential for the operation of the other prerequisites—acute self-awareness.

Those last conclusions, the inquiry further suggests, capture the essence of the Court's role in federalism matters, a role that is consistent with the Constitution's theory as well as its text, compatible with principles of limited government and the nation's distinctive rule of law, and conducive to results that promise—only, unfortunately, in the long run and only with everything netted out—to be more salutary than not.[49] The nation's historical experience, it suggests, also supports those conclusions.[50] True, the Court has not always acted on its license, even when it should have; and, when it has acted, it has not always done so wisely. Like the other levels and branches of government and the nation's constitutional enterprise itself, the Court is ultimately a practical institution that is both human and majoritarian.[51]

While no institution can guarantee wise judgments, the Court can increase the likelihood of reaching such results in federalism cases by heeding three general cautions. First, it should recognize generally—as it sometimes does in individual cases[52]—that questions of federalism rarely if ever involve rules or principles with bright-line limits but, rather, that they require careful, flexible, and pragmatic line-drawing. Thus, the Court cannot properly claim that most of its federalism decisions, however draped they may be in "principles," are anything other than practical judgments. Indeed, the Rehnquist Court has unwittingly confessed as much by claiming that the critical issue in federalism cases is recognizing and enforcing "a distinction between what is truly national and what is truly local."[53] Those two ostensibly decisive terms appear nowhere in the Constitution, and they are, in fact, mere post facto conclusory labels. Thus, it is not the vacuous distinction between the truly "local" and the truly "national" that has determined the Court's judgments but, rather, the implicit assessments of relative values, conveniences, and consequences that its justices have made.

Second, acknowledging the pragmatic nature of its federalism jurisprudence would compel the Court to justify its specific decisions by carefully analyzing and explaining their likely practical consequences. Such an acknowledgment would mean that the Court could not claim that its judgments stemmed from general "principles" or abstracted "values of federalism." It would be required, instead, to explain its decisions on the basis of an ample factual record by providing a thorough analysis of the practical social and institutional considerations at issue.[54] If the Court can impose heavy evidentiary burdens on Congress to justify its legislative efforts, as it has repeatedly done, then it can accept equally heavy evidentiary burdens on the parties who seek its judgment and on its own exercise of power as well.[55] After all, the Court is making judgments that are based inevitably on the personal values of the justices, and therefore its "license" to supervise the operations of the federal structure is highly restrictive and the conditions of its exercise most exacting.

Third, the Court should acknowledge that federalism and its "values" can be protected not just by drawing lines between governmental units but also by drawing lines between governmental power and the American people. Federalism and its "values," in other words, are also implicated when the Court addresses questions of individual rights and the requirements of free and open democratic processes, for those fundamental values also help "maintain the Constitution's enumeration of powers" as essential limits on governmental action.[56] In determining whether any particular decision is consistent with the "values of federalism," it seems essential to determine whether and how the decision would affect both individual rights and open democratic processes. Federalism decisions, after all, are about more than the formal relationship between state and central governments: they are also about protecting individual liberty and preserving popular government. Indeed, federalism decisions never bring results that are *only* "structural." If the history of American federalism teaches anything, it is that such decisions also bring differential social and political consequences to individuals and groups. To cause such differential social consequences, the Court—shaped as it is by the personal values and interests of its members—must demonstrate quite clearly why its federalism decisions are both practically necessary and generally benevolent.

Thus, finally, the inquiry concludes that neither the Constitution nor its federal structure offers any guarantees. That conclusion may readily be acknowledged as both unsatisfying and unnerving. Perhaps deeply so. It remains, nonetheless, a fundamental aspect of the American constitutional enterprise where the question is never *whether* to honor the goals, values, and provisions of the Constitution but always *how* to fulfill the profound trust they impose. The founders did, after all, retain faith in the possibilities of human decency. "As there is a degree of depravity in mankind which requires a certain degree of circumspection and distrust, so there are other qualities in human nature which justify a certain portion of esteem and confidence," the *Federalist* declared. "Republican government presupposes the existence of these qualities in a higher degree than any other form."[57] Recognizing the elastic, dynamic, and underdetermined nature of the federal structure teaches the essential role not of general prescriptive theories or historical legal briefs but of sound and balancing institutions in the structure of government; fair and equitable relations among the society's groups and interests; and intellectual humility, political tolerance, moral sympathy, and public integrity in the nation's citizens and officials. It also teaches, for those who will listen, the ultimate truth that tenacious moral commitments to securing justice, freedom, human equality, and democratic government in the lived and living world are the redeeming leaven and sine qua non of that noble, if highly uncertain, national enterprise.

NOTES

Chapter 1. American Constitutional Federalism as a Normative Problem

1. There are varieties of "originalist" thinking, all claiming to offer methods for construing the Constitution "truly" and "objectively." All reflect an understandable desire for an authentic and rationally ascertainable constitutional law. All are inadequate, however, and subject to overlapping, if somewhat different, criticisms. The use of the term "originalism" in the text is meant to include all such theories, whether they use the language of "intent," "meaning," "understanding," or some other cognate term.

2. For a history of "originalist" thinking, *see* Johnathan O'Neill, *Originalism in American Law and Politics: A Constitutional History* (Baltimore, Md., 2005).

3. Antonin Scalia, *A Matter of Interpretation: Federal Courts and the Law* (Princeton, N.J., 1997), 28, 29.

4. Scalia, *Matter of Interpretation,* 38, 45.

5. Presidential Executive Order 13132, 64 F.R. 43255 (Aug. 4, 1999), 1.

6. *Alden v. Maine,* 527 U.S. 706, 748, 726 (1999) (Kennedy, J.). The five were Chief Justice William Rehnquist and Justices Sandra Day O'Connor, Antonin Scalia, Anthony Kennedy, and Clarence Thomas. Between 1994 and 1999 the Rehnquist Court voided twenty separate federal statutes and averaged four invalidations every year, a rate that was "exceptional" compared with the Court's average over the previous two centuries of one invalidation every fifteen months. The Committee on Federal Legislation of the Association of the Bar of the City of New York, "The New Federalism," 54 *The Record of the Association of the Bar of the City of New York* 712 (1999).

7. The four were Justices John Paul Stevens, David A. Souter, Ruth Bader Ginsburg, and Stephen G. Breyer. They dissented, *e.g.,* in *United States v. Lopez,* 514 U.S. 549, 602, 603, 615 (1995); *Seminole Tribe of Florida v. Florida,* 517 U.S. 44, 76, 100 (1996); *Idaho v. Coeur d'Alene Tribe of Idaho,* 521 U.S. 261, 297 (1997); *Printz v.*

United States, 521 U.S. 898, 939, 970, 976 (1997); *College Savings Bank v. Florida Prepaid Postsecondary Education Expense Board,* 527 U.S. 666, 691, 693 (1999); *Florida Prepaid Postsecondary Education Expense Board v. College Savings Bank,* 527 U.S. 627, 648 (1999); *Alden,* 527 U.S. at 760; *United States v. Morrison,* 529 U.S. 598, 628 (2000); *Board of Trustees of the University of Alabama v. Garrett,* 531 U.S. 356, 376 (2001); and *Federal Maritime Commission v. South Carolina State Ports Authority,* 535 U.S. 743, 772 (2002).

8. *Florida Prepaid,* 527 U.S. at 648, 664 (Stevens, J., dissenting, joined by Souter, Ginsburg, and Breyer, JJ.). *Accord Federal Maritime Commission,* 535 U.S. at 772, 788.

9. *See, e.g., City of Boerne v. Flores,* 521 U.S. 507 (1997); *Granholm v. Heald,* 544 U.S. 460 (2005).

10. For divisions among the five, *see, e.g., Kimel v. Florida Board of Regents,* 528 U.S. 62 (2000); *Tennessee v. Lane,* 541 U.S. 509 (2004); *Nevada Department of Human Resources v. Hibbs,* 538 U.S. 721 (2003); *City of Boerne,* 521 U.S. 507; *U.S. Term Limits, Inc. v. Thornton,* 514 U.S. 779 (1995); *Crawford v. Washington,* 541 U.S. 36 (2004); *Granholm,* 544 U.S. 460; *Gonzales v. Raich,* 545 U.S. 1 (2005).

11. *Coeur d'Alene Tribe,* 521 U.S. at 275 (Kennedy, J., joined by Rehnquist, C.J.).

12. *Id.* at 291 (O'Connor, J., joined by Scalia and Thomas, JJ., concurring).

13. *Morrison,* 529 U.S. at 627 (Thomas, J., concurring). *Accord Saenz v. Roe,* 526 U.S. 489, 521 (1991) (Thomas, J., dissenting, accusing three of the "profederalism" justices of adopting a view "contrary to the original understanding," at 527). Justice Thomas acknowledged that it might be "too late in the day" to adopt the "original understanding" on some issues. *Lopez,* 514 U.S. at 584, 601 (Thomas, J., concurring).

14. *Kelo v. City of New London,* 545 U.S. 469 (2005). The five "profederalism" justices also adopted an expansive view of federal preemption in frequently displacing significant elements of state law. *See* Richard H. Fallon Jr., "The 'Conservative' Paths of the Rehnquist Court's Federalism Decisions," 69 *University of Chicago L. Rev.* 429 (2002).

15. James Madison, "Outline Notes," Sept. 1829, in Gaillard Hunt, ed., *Writings of James Madison* (New York, 1910), Vol. 9, 357. *Accord* letter from James Madison to Thomas Jefferson, Oct. 24, 1787, in Robert A. Rutland *et al.,* eds., *The Papers of James Madison* (Chicago, 1977), Vol. 10, 208 [hereafter, "*Papers of James Madison*"].

16. For an excellent discussion of the arguments for and against centralized power and a persuasive defense of federalism, *see* David L. Shapiro, *Federalism: A Dialogue* (Evanston, Ill., 1995), and for a history of the operations of the federal system, *see* David B. Walker, *The Rebirth of Federalism: Slouching Toward Washington,* 2d ed. (New York, 1999).

17. *Morrison,* 529 U.S. at 620 (Rehnquist, C.J.). *Accord, e.g., Nevada v. Hall,* 440 U.S. 410, 432 (1979) (Rehnquist, J., dissenting) ("the Framers' careful allocation of responsibility among the state and federal judiciaries," at 441); *Garcia v. San Antonio Metropolitan Transit District,* 469 U.S. 528, 557 (1985) (Powell, J., dissenting) (a "constitutionally mandated balance of power between the States and the Federal Gov-

ernment was adopted by the Framers," at 572). *See* Robert Justin Lipkin, "Federalism as Balance," 79 *Tulane L. Rev.* 93 (2004).

18. This, of course, is not to deny that the founders sought to "balance" power in a way that would protect liberty, property, and republicanism. *See, e.g.,* John Phillip Reid, *Constitutional History of the American Revolution,* abridged ed. (Madison, Wisc., 1995), 103.

19. On early discussions of the separation of powers, *see* John Phillip Reid, *Constitutional History of the American Revolution: The Authority of Law* (Madison, Wisc., 1993), Vol. 4, 163–73; on its differences with federalism, *see* M. Elizabeth Magill, "The Revolution That Wasn't," 99 *Northwestern L. Rev.* 47 (2004).

20. *James B. Beam Distilling Co. v. Georgia,* 501 U.S. 529, 548, 549 (1991) (Scalia, J., concurring in the judgment).

21. The nature and content of that ideal, of course, evolved over the centuries: *e.g.,* U.S. Const. Amends. xiii–xv, xvii, xix, xxiv, xxvi.

22. This does not mean that particular interpretations of federalism necessarily reflect only their advocates' conscious pursuit of either specific sociopolitical objectives or simple self-interest. Both the psychology of human beings and the nature of the "original" federal structure are far too complex for such a simple and direct connection to hold in all cases. "There was scarcely a member of the [constitutional] convention whose views can be explained by any simple formula, economic or otherwise," in part because "it is all but impossible to differentiate private selfishness from public spirit." Edmund S. Morgan, *The Birth of the Republic, 1763–89,* 3d ed. (Chicago, 1992), 133, 132.

23. Pathbreaking work came from the so-called legal realists, and the proposition has been developed most methodically by political scientists using the "attitudinal" model. On the former *see, e.g.,* Morton J. Horwitz, *The Transformation of American Law, 1870–1960: The Crisis of Legal Orthodoxy* (New York, 1992). On the latter, *see, e.g.,* Jeffrey A. Segal and Harold J. Spaeth, *The Supreme Court and the Attitudinal Model* (New York, 1993); Lawrence Baum, *The Puzzle of Judicial Behavior* (Ann Arbor, Mich., 1997); Lee Epstein and Jack Knight, *The Choices Justices Make* (Washington, D.C., 1998).

24. Judges are cabined in their decision making by a variety of social, cultural, political, professional, and institutional constraints. *See, e.g.,* Karl N. Llewellyn, *The Common Law Tradition: Deciding Appeals* (Boston, 1960), 19–61; Terri Jennings Peretti, *In Defense of a Political Court* (Princeton, N.J., 1999), chs. 4–7; Ronald Kahn and Ken L. Kersch, "Introduction," in Kahn and Kersch, eds., *The Supreme Court and American Political Development* (Lawrence, Kans., 2006), 13–21.

25. Theorists debate the reasons why the Constitution properly commands authority from succeeding generations. Some rely on varieties of an original, even if entirely hypothetical, "social contract": *e.g.,* John Rawls, *A Theory of Justice* (Cambridge, Mass., 1971), 11; Jeremy Waldron, "Theoretical Foundations of Liberalism," 37 *Philosophical Quarterly* 127 (1987). Others advance theories that emphasize a continuing de

facto acceptance by the people: *e.g.*, Jed Rubenfeld, "Reading the Constitution as Spoken," 104 *Yale L. J.* 1119, 1154–63 (1995); Michael C. Dorf, "Integrating Normative and Descriptive Constitutional Theory: The Case of Original Meaning," 85 *Georgetown L. J.* 1765, 1772, 1796 (1997). A third group stresses the importance of moral principles embodied in the Constitution: *e.g.*, Christopher L. Eisgruber, "Justice and the Text: Rethinking the Constitutional Relation between Principle and Prudence," 43 *Duke L. J.* 1 (1993); Richard H. Fallon Jr., "Legitimacy and the Constitution," 118 *Harvard L. Rev.* 1787 (2005); Randy E. Barnett, *Restoring the Lost Constitution: The Presumption of Liberty* (Princeton, N.J., 2004).

Chapter 2. Federalism as Doubly Blurred

1. Alexander Hamilton, John Jay, and James Madison, *The Federalist*, ed. Edward Mead Earle (New York, 1937), No. 16, at 99 [hereafter, "*Federalist*"].

2. *Federalist*, No. 15, at 91. *Accord Federalist*, No. 16, at 98.

3. *Federalist*, No. 22, at 197 (legislation); *Federalist*, No. 29, at 176–77 (militia); *Federalist*, No. 32, at 195; No. 33, at 201; No. 34, at 209 (taxation); *Federalist*, No. 82, at 535, 536; No. 81 at 532 n. (judicial power). *See* G. Edward White, *The Marshall Court and Cultural Change, 1815–35* (New York, 1988), ch. 8.

4. *Federalist*, No. 32, at 194 (emphasis in original). State and federal jurisdiction would be "concurrent," Hamilton declared, unless "a similar authority in the States would be absolutely and totally *contradictory* and *repugnant*" to national authority. *Id.*

5. *Federalist*, No. 1, at 6 (Hamilton); No. 39, at 243 (Madison); No. 85, at 567, 568 (Hamilton). *See, e.g.*, Jennifer Nedelsky, *Private Property and the Limits of American Constitutionalism: The Madisonian Framework and Its Legacy* (Chicago, 1990); Jack N. Rakove, *Original Meanings: Politics and Ideas in the Making of the Constitution* (New York, 1996); Gordon S. Wood, *The Creation of the American Republic, 1776–1787* (Chapel Hill, N.C., 1969).

6. *Federalist*, No. 51, at 336; *Federalist*, No. 37, at 227.

7. Speech of Gilbert Livingston, in Jonathan Elliot, ed., *The Debates in the Several State Conventions on the Adoption of the Federal Constitution*, 2d ed., rev. (New York, 1987 [1836]), Vol. 2, 388 [hereafter, "Elliot, *Debates*"]. As Wilson Nicholas told the Virginia ratifying convention, the members of the House would protect "the interests of their constituents" by checking the national executive, while the state legislatures "will be a powerful check on them." *Id.*, Vol. 3, at 17–18.

8. Forrest McDonald, *Novus Ordo Seclorum: The Intellectual Origins of the Constitution* (Lawrence, Kans., 1985), 10, 13. *See* Wood, *Creation of the American Republic*, 608–09.

9. The theory of "popular sovereignty" responded to the common assumption of eighteenth-century political theory that "sovereignty" itself could not be divided. *See, e.g.*, John Phillip Reid, *Constitutional History of the American Revolution: The Authority to Legislate* (Madison, Wisc., 1991), Vol. 3, 74–78.

10. *Federalist*, No. 22, at 140–41.

11. *Federalist*, No. 46, at 305; No. 49, at 327. *See* U.S. Const. Preamble; Wood, *Creation of the American Republic*, esp. ch. 9.

12. *Federalist*, No. 46, at 304–05.

13. *Federalist*, No. 53, at 348.

14. James Wilson, speech in the Pennsylvania ratifying convention, Elliot, *Debates*, Vol. 2, 443. Wilson stressed his argument repeatedly. *See, e.g., id.,* Vol. 2, at 455–56, 478, 502.

15. *Id.,* Vol. 2, 443–44 (emphasis in original).

16. Wood, *Creation of the American Republic*, esp. ch. 13; Stanley Elkins and Eric McKitrick, *The Age of Federalism: The Early American Republic, 1788–1800* (New York, 1993), 12–13. Madison mocked the idea that the Revolution could have been fought to preserve "certain dignities and attributes of [state] sovereignty," and he equated such claims with "the impious doctrine" that "the people were made for kings, not kings for the people." *Federalist*, No. 45, at 298–99.

17. U.S. Const. Art. V.

18. "Uncertainty was the dominant mood," Joseph J. Ellis explained, and the Constitution's position on sovereignty "was anyone's guess." Joseph J. Ellis, *Founding Brothers: The Revolutionary Generation* (New York, 2000), 9–10. *Accord* Daniel A. Farber, *Lincoln's Constitution* (Chicago, 2003), 37.

19. On the ratification process and its problems, *see* Rakove, *Original Meanings*, ch. 5.

20. There was a sound legal reason why "the people" were properly required to ratify in the various states. Ratification meant not merely approval of the new Constitution but also approval of its new limitations on the constitutions of the separate states. While the entire American people were necessary to approve the national Constitution, then, the people of the individual states were necessary to accept the new limitations on the powers of each of their respective states. Madison recognized the point. It would be "essential" to require ratification by the people rather than by state legislatures, he noted, "as inroads on the *existing Constitutions* of the States will be unavoidable." Letter from James Madison to George Washington, April 16, 1787, in Robert A. Rutland *et al.*, eds., *The Papers of James Madison* (Chicago, 1975), Vol. 9, 385. Thus, ratification required "the people" to act in a double capacity: first, as "the people" of the individual states for the purpose of accepting the limitations the new Constitution would impose on their state constitutions; and second, as "the people" of the United States for the purpose of ratifying the national Constitution itself. *See* McDonald, *Novus Ordo Seclorum*, 280.

21. *Federalist*, No. 39, 246–47.

22. *Federalist*, No. 39, at 246.

23. *Federalist*, No. 39, at 250.

24. "The concept of federalism had been so imperfectly perceived by both sides of the revolutionary controversy that it was not part of any plan for resolving the constitutional crisis." John Phillip Reid, *The Constitutional History of the American Revolution*, abridged ed. (Madison, Wisc., 1995), 101.

25. John Phillip Reid, *Constitutional History of the American Revolution: The Authority to Legislate* (Madison, Wisc., 1991), Vol. 3, 227–33 (quotations at 228 and 230).

26. Letter from James Madison to James Monroe, May 13, 1786, *Papers of James Madison,* Vol. 9, 55.

27. *Federalist,* No. 15, at 89. Hamilton's usage remained vague and inconsistent. In his very next essay, for example, he referred to the Confederation as "the federal system." *Federalist,* No. 16, at 97. On Hamilton's and Madison's usage of the term, *see* Vincent Ostrom, *American Federalism: Constituting a Self-Governing Society* (San Francisco, 1991), ch. 4.

28. Max Farrand, ed., *The Records of the Federal Convention of 1787,* rev. ed. (New Haven, Conn., 1966 [1937]), Vol. 1, 283 [hereafter, "Farrand, *Records*"].

29. *See, e.g.,* Luther Martin, "Information to the General Assembly of the State of Maryland," in Herbert J. Storing, ed., *The Complete Anti-Federalist* (Chicago, 1981), Vol. 2, 47 [hereafter, "Storing, *Complete Anti-Federalist*"]. *Accord* "Essays by a Farmer," No. 3, in *id.,* Vol. 5, 29.

30. Charles R. King, ed., *The Life and Correspondence of Rufus King: Comprising His Letters, Private and Official, His Public Documents, and His Speeches* (New York, 1971 [1894]), Vol. 1, 300, 318.

31. Murray Dry, "Anti-Federalism in *The Federalist:* A Founding Dialogue on the Constitution, Republican Government, and Federalism," in Charles R. Kesler, ed., *Saving the Revolution:* The Federalist Papers *and the American Founding* (New York, 1987), 40, 53.

32. *E.g.,* David Broyles, "Federalism and Political Life," in Kesler, ed., *Saving the Revolution,* 80–81.

33. James Roger Sharp, *American Politics in the Early Republic: The New Nation in Crisis* (New Haven, Conn., 1993), 287.

34. "A Friend of the Constitution" [John Marshall], Essay No. 1, in Gerald Gunther, ed., *John Marshall's Defense of* McCulloch v. Maryland (Stanford, Calif., 1969), 159.

35. *Id.* at 159–60.

36. Herbert J. Storing, *Toward a More Perfect Union: Writings of Herbert J. Storing,* ed. Joseph M. Bessette (Washington, D.C., 1995), 88; Martin Diamond, "What the Framers Meant by Federalism," in Robert A. Goldwyn, ed., *A Nation of States: Essays on the American Federal System* (Chicago, 1974), 32–36; Richard B. Morris, *The Forging of the Union* (New York, 1987); Wood, *Creation of the American Republic,* chs. 7–11. Even many Anti-Federalists agreed on the need for a "supreme" central government in some areas. Saul Cornell, *The Other Founders: Anti-Federalism & the Dissenting Tradition in America, 1788–1828* (Chapel Hill, N.C., 1999), 63–64 and n. 27.

37. Letter from James Madison to Thomas Jefferson, Oct. 24, 1787, *Papers of James Madison,* Vol. 10, 212.

38. *Federalist,* No. 37, at 227. Both Madison and Wilson made the same point at the Philadelphia Convention. Farrand, *Records,* Vol. 1, at 166 and 356–58; Vol. 2, at 35.

39. *Federalist,* No. 45, at 299. *Accord* James Madison, "Vices of the Political System

of the United States," *Papers of James Madison,* Vol. 9, 345–58; Farrand, *Records,* Vol. 1, 356–58; letter from James Madison to Thomas Jefferson, Oct. 24, 1787, *Papers of James Madison,* Vol. 10, 209–14; Jack N. Rakove, "Constitutional Problematics, circa 1787," in John Ferejohn, Jack N. Rakove, and Jonathan Riley, eds., *Constitutional Culture and Democratic Rule* (Cambridge, U.K., 2001), 57–60. When Madison introduced his proposals for amending the Constitution in 1789, he could not resist commenting on the need for further restrictions on the states. *Papers of James Madison,* Vol. 12, 208.

40. *Federalist,* No. 33, at 200. Under the Constitution, he argued, "the laws of the whole are in danger of being contravened by the laws of the parts." *Id.,* No. 22, at 139.

41. Quoted in R. Kent Newmyer, *John Marshall and the Heroic Age of the Supreme Court* (Baton Rouge, La., 2001), 28.

42. Elkins and McKitrick, *Age of Federalism,* 702. *See, e.g.,* James Wilson, speech in the Pennsylvania ratifying convention, Elliot, *Debates,* Vol. 2, 486. *See id.* at 463.

43. Edmund S. Morgan, *The Birth of the Republic, 1763–89,* 3d ed. (Chicago, 1992), 134–38. *Accord* Rakove, *Original Meanings,* 162.

44. *E.g., Coleman v. Thompson,* 501 U.S. 722, 726 (1991) (O'Connor, J.).

45. *See, e.g.,* Larry Kramer, "Understanding Federalism," 47 *Vanderbilt L. Rev.* 1485, 1502 (1994); Kathleen M. Sullivan, "Dueling Sovereignties: *U.S. Term Limits, Inc. v. Thornton,*" 109 *Harvard L. Rev.* 78, 103 (1995).

46. *See, e.g., Gregory v. Ashcroft,* 501 U.S. 452, 456–58 (1991) (O'Connor, J.); Evan H. Caminker, "Judicial Solicitude for State Dignity," 574 *Annals of the American Academy of Political and Social Science* 81, 89 (2001).

47. Antonin Scalia, "The Two Faces of Federalism," 6 *Harvard Journal of Law and Public Policy* 19 (1982).

48. *See, e.g.,* Presidential Executive Order No. 13, 132 (Aug. 4, 1999), Sec. 2, "Fundamental Federalism Principles." *Compare, e.g.,* the opinions in *Alden v. Maine,* 527 U.S. 706 (1999): Justice Kennedy for the majority, at 748–54, and Justice Souter for four dissenters, at 798–803.

49. Harry N. Scheiber, "Federalism and Legal Process: Historical and Contemporary Analysis of the American System," 14 *Law and Society Rev.* 663, 669 (1980).

50. Aaron B. Wildavsky, *Federalism & Political Culture,* ed. David Schleicher and Brendon Swedlow (New Brunswick, N.J., 1998), 42.

51. Farrand, *Records,* Vol. 1, 529.

52. Farrand, *Records,* Vol. 1, 466.

53. Farrand, *Records,* Vol. 2, 7.

54. John Jay, "An Address to the People of the State of New York," in Henry P. Johnston, ed., *The Correspondence and Public Papers of John Jay, 1763–1826* (New York, 1971), Vol. 3, 304, 310.

55. Farrand, *Records,* Vol. 2, 667.

56. Quoted in Gordon S. Wood, *The Americanization of Benjamin Franklin* (New York, 2004), 221.

57. *Federalist,* No. 37, at 230–31. For Madison's doubts, *see* Rakove, "Constitutional Problematics, circa 1787," in Ferejohn *et al.,* eds., *Constitutional Culture,* 41–70.

58. Speech on the Bank Bill, Feb. 2, 1791, *Papers of James Madison,* Vol. 13, 378. *Accord* letter from James Madison to William Short, Oct. 24, 1787, Farrand, *Records,* Vol. 3, 136.

59. Lance Banning, *The Sacred Fire of Liberty: James Madison and the Founding of the Federal Republic* (Ithaca, N.Y., 1995), 200–01, 374, 394.

60. Calvin Jillson, *Constitution Making: Conflict and Consensus in the Federal Convention of 1787* (New York, 1988), 193.

61. *Federalist,* No. 37, at 226.

62. Elliot, *Debates,* Vol. 3, 94.

63. *Federalist,* No. 14, at 85.

64. Farrand, *Records,* Vol. 1, 167, 166. Both men supported the proposal, arguing that the impossibility of articulating a clear line meant that a congressional veto was essential.

65. Farrand, *Records,* Vol. 1, 170.

66. Farrand, *Records,* Vol. 1, 167.

67. Farrand, *Records,* Vol. 1, 169, 165. Dickinson agreed. *Id.,* Vol. 1, at 167.

68. Elliot, *Debates,* Vol. 3, 33.

69. *E.g.,* Rakove, *Original Meanings,* 179–80 (the phrase "direct taxes"); Luther Martin, "Information to the General Assembly of the State of Maryland," Storing, *Complete Anti-Federalist,* Vol. 2, 53 (provisions for originating revenue measures); Richard H. Kohn, *Eagle and Sword: The Federalists and the Creation of the Military Establishment in America, 1783–1802* (New York, 1975), 88 (military provisions); William E. Nelson, "The American Revolution and the Emergence of Modern Doctrines of Federalism and Conflict of Laws," 62 *Publications of the Colonial Society of Massachusetts: Law in Colonial Massachusetts* 419, 453 (1984) (judicial provisions).

70. U.S. Const. Art. I, Sec. 10, cl. 1.

71. Steven R. Boyd, "The Contract Clause and the Evolution of American Federalism, 1789–1815," 3d ser., 44 *William and Mary Quarterly* 529, 533 (1987).

72. Letter from James Madison to Thomas Jefferson, Oct. 24, 1787, *Papers of James Madison,* Vol. 10, 212.

73. Boyd, "Contract Clause," at 537, 531. *See* White, *Marshall Court and Cultural Change,* 11, 73, and ch. 9; Newmyer, *John Marshall,* 210–44.

74. 10 U.S. (6 Cranch) 87 (1810).

75. Leonard W. Levy, *Original Intent and the Framers' Constitution* (New York, 1988), 124, 132.

76. Farrand, *Records,* Vol. 1, 323.

77. Larry D. Kramer, *The People Themselves: Popular Constitutionalism and Judicial Review* (New York, 2004), chs. 4–5; Randy E. Barnett, "The Original Meaning of the Judicial Power," 12 *Supreme Court Economic Rev.* 115 (2004).

78. The Constitution's grant of powers to the national government was "a founda-

tion for endless confusion and discord." "Letters of Agrippa" [James Winthrop, Massachusetts], No. 12, part 2, in Storing, *Complete Anti-Federalist,* Vol. 4, 97. The Constitution's language "appears incomprehensible and indefinite." "Address by Denatus," *Virginia Independent Chronicle,* June 11, 1788, *id.,* Vol. 5, at 261. *Accord* Elliot, *Debates,* Vol. 2, 60 (Mr. Bodman, Massachusetts), 71 and 74 (Mr. Symmes, Massachusetts), 108 (General Thompson, Massachusetts), 338 (Mr. Williams, New York).

79. Letter of Edmund Randolph on the Federal Convention, Oct. 10, 1787, Storing, *Complete Anti-Federalist,* Vol. 2, 96. Randolph hoped that Virginia would be "seconded" by the other states "in causing all ambiguities of expression to be precisely explained." *Id.* at 97.

80. "Letters of Cato," No. 7, Storing, *Complete Anti-Federalist,* Vol. 2, 125; *id.,* No. 4, at 113. *Accord* "Essays by a Farmer," No. 1, *id.,* Vol. 2, 205 (the Constitution framed in "very general and extensive terms" and with "extensive latitude").

81. Elbridge Gerry to President of Senate and Speaker of House of Representatives of Massachusetts, Oct. 18, 1787, Farrand, *Records,* Vol. 3, 128. *Accord* A Federal Republican, "A Review of the Constitution Proposed by the Late Convention," in Storing, *Complete Anti-Federalist,* Vol. 3, 81 ("the present indefinite mode of expression in this constitution").

82. "Letters of Agrippa" [James Winthrop, Massachusetts], No. 16, in Storing, *Complete Anti-Federalist,* Vol. 4, 114. Anti-Federalists "penetrated the shade of mystery in which [the Constitution] was wrapped" and showed that it "excels all" frames of government "in darkness and ambiguity" and that "its mysterious veil was the fruit of deliberation and design." "The Fallacies of the Freeman Detected by A Farmer," in Storing, *Complete Anti-Federalist,* Vol. 3, 192.

83. George Clinton, "To the Citizens of the State of New York," Nov. 22, 1787, Storing, *Complete Anti-Federalist,* Vol. 6, 177. *See* Storing, *Toward a More Perfect Union,* 80–81.

84. George Mason, "Objections to This Constitution of Government," Robert A. Rutland, ed., *Papers of George Mason, 1725–1792* (Chapel Hill, N.C., 1970), Vol. 3, 992–93.

85. "Essays of an Old Whig," No. 2, in Storing, *Complete Anti-Federalist,* Vol. 3, 24 (emphasis in original). There were "no bounds to the new government." *Id.,* No. 4, at 41. *Accord* Elliot, *Debates,* Vol. 4, 55 (Samuel Spencer, North Carolina).

86. "Letters from the Federal Farmer," in Storing, *Complete Anti-Federalist,* No. 18, Vol. 2, at 340; No. 4, at 247; No. 16, at 325; No. 2, at 233. *Accord, e.g., id.,* No. 4, at 245, 246. "[T]here is no line of distinction drawn between the general, and state governments," and "the sphere of their jurisdiction is undefined." The Address and Reasons of Dissent of the Minority of the Convention of Pennsylvania to Their Constituents, in *id.,* Vol. 3, 155; the Constitution was "defective" in failing to draw "the precise boundary" between the state and national governments. James Monroe, "Some Observations on the Constitution," in *id.,* Vol. 5, 305.

87. "Essays of Brutus," in Storing, *Complete Anti-Federalist,* No. XI, Vol. 2, at 421; *id.,* No. I, at 367. *Accord* "Essays of an Old Whig," No. 2, in *id.,* Vol. 3, 23.

88. *E.g.*, Dry, "Anti-Federalism"," in Kesler, ed., *Saving the Revolution*, 40, 55.

89. Storing, *Toward a More Perfect Union*, 81.

90. Rakove, *Original Meanings*, 168. *See id.* at 201.

91. Joseph Story, "Address Delivered Before the Members of the Suffolk Bar, at Their Anniversary on the 4th September, 1821, at Boston," reprinted in Perry Miller, ed., *The Legal Mind in America: From Independence to the Civil War* (New York, 1962), 63, 73. Story bemoaned "the uncertainty and the untidiness of the Constitution as it left the hands of the framers." R. Kent Newmyer, *Supreme Court Justice Joseph Story: Statesman of the Old Republic* (Chapel Hill, N.C., 1985), 114.

92. Some of the Constitution's defenders denied or minimized the charge of ambiguity. *See, e.g.*, Elliot, *Debates*, Vol. 2, 24–25 (Mr. Strong, Massachusetts), 104 (Mr. Parsons, Massachusetts). *See* Peter J. Smith, "The Marshall Court and the Originalist's Dilemma," 90 *Minnesota L. Rev.* 612, 618–40 (2006).

93. Farrand, *Records*, Vol. 2, 666–67.

94. "A Landholder" [Oliver Ellsworth], "Essay 4," in Colleen A. Sheehan and Gary L. McDowell, eds., *Friends of the Constitution: Writings of the "Other" Federalists* (Indianapolis, Ind., 1998), 299.

95. Farrand, *Records*, Vol. 2, 25.

96. "A Countryman" [Roger Sherman], "Letter II," in Sheehan and McDowell, eds., *Friends of the Constitution*, 181–82.

97. *Federalist*, No. 65, at 428. In spite of the partial admission, Hamilton generally projected an image of greater certainty. *Federalist*, No. 82, at 534. *See* Rakove, *Original Meanings*, 50–51.

98. James Wilson, speech in the Pennsylvania ratifying convention, Elliot, *Debates*, Vol. 2, 424, 425.

99. Like the other founders, Madison was not entirely consistent. He declared in another essay, for example, that the powers granted "the federal government are few and defined," while those retained by the states were "numerous and indefinite." *Federalist*, No. 45, at 303.

100. Letter from James Madison to Thomas Jefferson, Oct. 24, 1787, *Papers of James Madison*, Vol. 10, 211. *See* Rakove, *Original Meanings*, 176–77.

101. *Federalist*, No. 37, at 228–30. Jefferson and John Adams similarly acknowledged the inadequacy of words. *See* letter from Thomas Jefferson to James Madison, Mar. 15, 1789, *Papers of James Madison*, Vol. 12, 13; John Adams, *Defence of the Constitutions of the United States of America* (1789), in John Patrick Diggins, ed., *The Portable John Adams* (New York, 2004), 325.

102. Storing, *Toward a More Perfect Union*, 111, 112. In introducing his proposed amendments, Madison repeatedly declared that he and his allies would support changes as long as they were "of such a nature as will not injure the constitution" and could be added "without weakening its frame, or abridging its usefulness." *Papers of James Madison*, Vol. 12, 198, 209.

103. Quoted in Mark R. Killenbeck, "No Harm in Such a Declaration?" in Mark R.

Killenbeck, ed., *The Tenth Amendment and State Sovereignty* (New York, 2002), 1, 2 n. 8. See *Federalist*, No. 44, at 294.

104. *See* Charles A. Lofgren, "The Origins of the Tenth Amendment: History, Sovereignty, and the Problems of Constitutional Intention," in Ronald K. L. Collins, *Constitutional Government in America* (Durham, N.C., 1980), 331; Killenbeck, ed., *The Tenth Amendment;* Walter Berns, "The Meaning of the Tenth Amendment," in *A Nation of States: Essays on the American Federal System* (Chicago, 1974), 139. For the argument that the Tenth Amendment imposed relatively clear and strict limits on national power, *see* Raoul Berger, *Federalism: The Founders' Design* (Norman, Okla., 1987), ch. 4.

105. "The whole point is that there was no common score, no assigned instruments, no blended harmonies. The politics of the 1790s was a truly cacophonous affair. . . . The political dialogue within the highest echelon of the revolutionary generation was a decade-long shouting match." Ellis, *Founding Brothers,* 16.

106. *Federalist,* No. 23, at 145.

107. *Federalist,* No. 33, at 198–99. Hamilton's belief in the broadest possible national powers was well known. *See* Farrand, *Records,* Vol. 1, 323; *Federalist,* No. 31, at 188–90; *Federalist,* No. 34, at 204–05.

108. Alexander Hamilton, "Final Version of an Opinion on the Constitutionality of an Act to Establish a Bank," in Harold C. Syrett *et al.,* ed., *The Papers of Alexander Hamilton* (New York, 1965), Vol. 8, 101, 100, 106, 102 (emphasis in original).

109. King, ed., *Life and Correspondence of Rufus King,* Vol. 1, 308. King was named one of the original twenty-five directors of the First Bank of the United States. *Id.* at 397.

110. Speech in the House of Representatives, Feb. 3, 1791, in Charles S. Hyneman and George W. Carey, eds., *A Second Federalist: Congress Creates a Government* (New York, 1967), 129.

111. H. Jefferson Powell, "The Principles of '98: An Essay in Historical Retrieval," 80 *Virginia L. Rev.* 689, 729 (1994). *Accord* Wythe Holt, "Separation of Powers? Relations between the Judiciary and the Other Branches of the Federal Government before 1803," in Kenneth R. Bowling and Donald R. Kennon, eds., *Neither Separate Nor Equal: Congress in the 1790s* (Athens, Ohio, 2000), 183–210.

112. *McCullough v. Maryland,* 17 U.S. (4 Wheat.) 316, 407 (1819).

113. Newmyer, *John Marshall,* 105. For Henry's attack on the Constitution during the ratification debate, *see* Storing, *Complete Anti-Federalist,* Vol. 5, 207 *et seq.*

114. *Federalist,* No. 44, at 293–94.

115. James Madison, remarks in the House of Representatives, Feb. 2, 1791, in Hyneman and Carey, eds., *Second Federalist,* 126.

116. Thomas Jefferson, "Opinion on the Constitutionality of the Bill for Establishing a National Bank," in Julian P. Boyd, ed., *The Papers of Thomas Jefferson* (Princeton, N.J., 1974), Vol. 19, 275, 276.

117. Powell, "Principles of '98," at 706–715.

118. St. George Tucker, *A View of the Constitution of the United States with Selected Writings,* ed. Clyde N. Wilson (Indianapolis, Ind., 1999 [1803]), 128.

119. Tucker, *View of the Constitution,* 227.

120. John Taylor, *Tyranny Unmasked,* ed. F. Thornton Miller (Indianapolis, Ind., 1992 [1822]), 219.

121. "Hampden" [Spencer Roane], Essay No. 1, in Gunther, ed., *John Marshall's Defense,* 108.

122. The founding generation agreed on "the urgency of their task" and the likelihood that "unless they came up with an acceptable, and at the same time, workable, scheme of national government, the union would dissolve." Morgan, *Birth of the Republic,* 134. They also agreed on the need to avoid clarity and comprehensiveness on many issues. Leonard W. Levy, *Emergence of a Free Press* (New York, 1985), 348.

123. "It was not a document that gave entire satisfaction to anyone." Morgan, *Birth of the Republic,* 143. *Accord* Storing, *Toward a More Perfect Union,* 34–36. See *Federalist,* No. 62, at 401 (Madison) and No. 85, at 571 (Hamilton).

124. Elliot, *Debates,* Vol. 4, 23 (William R. Davie).

125. Rakove, *Original Meanings,* 189, 196–98. Similarly, John Adams and Thomas Jefferson, exchanging letters from distant London and Paris, also disagreed on various points. Letter from Thomas Jefferson to John Adams, Nov. 13, 1787; letter from John Adams to Thomas Jefferson, Dec. 6, 1787, in Lester J. Cappon, ed., *The Adams-Jefferson Letters: The Complete Correspondence between Thomas Jefferson & Abigail & John Adams* (Chapel Hill, N.C., 1959), 212–14.

126. Alpheus Thomas Mason, "The Federalist—A Split Personality," 57 *American Historical Rev.* 625 (1952), 640–41. Hamilton and Madison disagreed, for example, on the rationale of the "large state" theory, the nature and role of judicial review, and the place of standing armies in the new republic. *Compare,* on factions, *Federalist,* No. 9 (Hamilton) *with* No. 10 (Madison); on judicial review, No. 78 (Hamilton) *with* Nos. 48–51 (Madison); and on the standing army, No. 26 (Hamilton) *with* No. 41 (Madison). *See* Robert A. Burt, *The Constitution in Conflict* (Cambridge, Mass., 1992), esp. ch. 2; Banning, *Sacred Fire of Liberty,* chs. 7 and 10, and "Appendix: The Personalities of 'Publius.'" For analyses that emphasize areas of agreement, *see* George Carey, "Publius—A Split Personality?" 46 *Rev. of Politics* 3 (1984). For a different view, *see* Morton White, *Philosophy,* The Federalist, *and the Constitution* (New York, 1987).

127. Burt, *Constitution in Conflict,* 46–47.

128. Sharp, *American Politics in the Early Republic,* 20, 66. For a detailed examination of the practical orientation of the founders and the changing ways in which they construed the Constitution during the 1790s, see Joseph M. Lynch, *Negotiating the Constitution: The Earliest Debates over Original Intent* (Ithaca, N.Y., 1999).

129. Quoted in Susan Dunn, *Jefferson's Second Revolution: The Election Crisis of 1800 and the Triumph of Republicanism* (Boston, 2004), 53, 58.

130. Newmyer, *John Marshall,* 70.

131. John R. Howe Jr., "Republican Thought and Political Violence of the 1790s,"

19 *American Quarterly* 147, 148, 149 (1967). *See* Marshall Smelser, "The Federalist Period as an Age of Passion," 10 *American Quarterly* 391 (1958).

132. Robert V. Remini, *The House: The History of the House of Representatives* (New York, 2006), 58, 62.

133. McDonald, *Novus Ordo Seclorum,* 4 (emphasis removed from original). "[I]t is meaningless to say that the Framers intended this or that: their positions were diverse and, in many particulars, incompatible." *Id.* at 224. On the changing and uncertain nature of American attitudes toward law and constitutionalism, *see* Wood, *Creation of the American Republic,* 259–305.

134. Gordon S. Wood, *The Radicalism of the American Revolution* (New York, 1991), 8. The experience reshaped "the culture of Americans" and "even altered their understanding of history, knowledge, and truth." *Id.* For examples of the profound transformations that occurred in American attitudes and values in the late eighteenth century, *see* Bruce H. Mann, *Republic of Debtors: Bankruptcy in the Age of American Independence* (Cambridge, Mass., 2002); Bernard Bailyn, *Ideological Origins of the American Revolution* (Cambridge, Mass., 1967), esp. chs. 5–6; Joyce Appleby, *Capitalism and a New Social Order: The Republican Vision of the 1790s* (New York, 1984); Michael Merrill, "Putting 'Capitalism' in Its Place: A Review of Recent Literature," 3d ser., 52 *William and Mary Quarterly* 315 (1995).

135. Wood, *Creation of the American Republic,* 525. *See id.* at 615; Daniel J. Boorstin, *The Americans: The National Experience* (New York, 1965), 416; Rakove, *Original Meanings,* 167.

136. Cass R. Sunstein, *Legal Reasoning and Political Conflict* (New York, 1996), 35. For the later development of such ideas into a broader relativist theory of democracy, *see* Edward A. Purcell Jr., *The Crisis of Democratic Theory: Scientific Naturalism and the Problem of Value* (Lexington, Ky., 1973), ch. 13.

137. Bernard Bailyn, *Faces of Revolution: Personalities and Themes in the Struggle for American Independence* (New York, 1990), 267.

Chapter 3. Federalism as Fractionated

1. Alexander Hamilton, John Jay, and James Madison, *The Federalist,* ed. Edward Mead Earle (New York, 1937), No. 51, at 339 [hereafter, *"Federalist"*]. *See* Jack N. Rakove, *Original Meanings: Politics and Ideas in the Making of the Constitution* (New York, 1996), 168, 180; Hanna Fenichel Pitkin, *The Concept of Representation* (Berkeley, Calif., 1967), 190–98.

2. *Federalist,* No. 51, at 339. *See* W. B. Gwen, *The Meaning of the Separation of Powers: An Analysis of the Doctrine from Its Origins to the Adoption of the United States Constitution* (New Orleans, La., 1965).

3. *Federalist,* No. 62, at 403 (Madison, or possibly Hamilton). *Accord* Max Farrand, ed., *The Records of the Federal Convention of 1787* (New Haven, Conn., 1966 [1937]), Vol. 1, 421, 584 [hereafter, "Farrand, *Records*"].

4. Jonathan Elliot, ed., *The Debates in the Several State Conventions on the Adoption of the Federal Constitution,* 2d ed., rev. (New York, 1987 [1836]), Vol. 2, 285 [hereafter, "Elliot, *Debates*"].

5. *See* M. Elizabeth Magill, "The Real Separation in Separation of Powers Law," 86 *Virginia L. Rev.* 1127 (2000); M. Elizabeth Magill, "Beyond Powers and Branches in Separation of Powers Law," 150 *University of Pennsylvania L. Rev.* 603 (2001).

6. *Federalist,* No. 51, at 336.

7. *Federalist,* No. 78, at 504.

8. Wythe Holt, "Separation of Powers? Relations between the Judiciary and the Other Branches of the Federal Government before 1803," in Kenneth R. Bowling and Donald R. Kennon, eds., *Neither Separate nor Equal: Congress in the 1790s* (Athens, Ohio, 2000), 87.

9. Barbara Aronstein Black, "Massachusetts and the Judges: Judicial Independence in Perspective," 3 *Law & History Rev.* 101 (1985).

10. Christine A. Desan, "The Constitutional Commitment to Legislative Adjudication in the Early American Tradition," 111 *Harvard L. Rev.* 1381 (1998); Christine A. Desan, "Remaking Constitutional Tradition at the Margin of Empire: The Creation of Legislative Adjudication in Colonial New York," 16 *Law and History Rev.* 257 (1998).

11. David P. Currie, *The Constitution in Congress: The Federalist Period, 1789–1801* (Chicago, 1997), 41–42 and n. 245.

12. Don Higginbotham, "The Federalized Militia Debate: A Neglected Aspect of Second Amendment Scholarship," 55 *William and Mary Quarterly* 39, 53 (3d ser., 1998).

13. *Federalist,* No. 37, at 229.

14. Letter from James Madison to Thomas Jefferson, Oct. 24, 1787, in Robert A. Rutland *et al.,* eds., *The Papers of James Madison* (Chicago, 1977), Vol. 10, 211 [hereafter, "*Papers of James Madison*"].

15. *Federalist,* No. 48, at 323. Madison's views on the separation of powers were themselves changing between 1787 and the early 1790s. Jack N. Rakove, "Constitutional Problematics, circa 1787," in John Ferejohn, Jack N. Rakove, and Jonathan Riley, eds., *Constitutional Culture and Democratic Rule* (Cambridge, U.K., 2001), 53–56.

16. Martin S. Flaherty, "The Most Dangerous Branch," 105 *Yale L. J.* 1725, 1755 (1996).

17. Gerhard Casper, "An Essay in Separation of Powers: Some Early Versions and Practices," 30 *William and Mary L. Rev.* 211, 261 (1989). *Accord* William Kristol, "The Problem of the Separation of Powers: *Federalist* 47–51," in Charles R. Kesler, ed., *Saving the Revolution:* The Federalist Papers *and the American Founding* (New York, 1987), 100, 101; Maeva Marcus, "Separation of Powers in the Early National Period," 30 *William and Mary L. Rev.* 269 (1989).

18. Currie, *Constitution in Congress: The Federalist Period,* esp. 28–54, 128–71.

19. *See, e.g.,* Michael Foley and John E. Owens, *Congress and the Presidency: Institutional Politics in a Separated System* (New York, 1996); Rebecca K. C. Hersman,

Friends and Foes: How Congress and the President Really Make Foreign Policy (Washington, D.C., 2000); Henry J. Merry, *Five-Branch Government: The Full Measure of Constitutional Checks and Balances* (Urbana, Ill., 1980); David C. King, *Turf Wars: How Congressional Committees Claim Jurisdiction* (Chicago, 1997).

20. Clinton Rossiter, *1787: The Grand Convention* (New York, 1966), 309.

21. Alexander Hamilton, "Pacificus No. I," in Harold C. Syrett *et al.*, eds., *The Papers of Alexander Hamilton* (New York, 1969), Vol. 15, 39, 42.

22. Letter from Thomas Jefferson to James Madison, July 7, 1793, *Papers of James Madison*, Vol. 15, 43.

23. James Madison, "Helvidius," No. 2, *Papers of James Madison*, Vol. 15, 72, 69, 66, 84, 81. *See generally* Richard Norton Smith, *Patriarch: George Washington and the New American Nation* (Boston, 1993), ch. 8.

24. U.S. Const. Art. I, Sec. 7, cl. 2 and 3; Art. II, Sec. 2, cl. 2.

25. *Federalist*, No. 48, at 321. *Accord id.*, No. 47, at 314–15; No. 51, at 336.

26. John Quincy Adams, "The Jubilee of the Constitution: A Discourse Delivered at the Request of the New York Historical Society," April 30, 1839, quoted in Forrest McDonald, *The American Presidency: An Intellectual History* (Lawrence, Kans., 1994), 179 n. 35.

27. For the variety of separation-of-powers issues that arose immediately in the First Congress, *see* Currie, *Constitution in Congress: The Federalist Period*, 20–32, 36–42.

28. U.S. Const. Art. I, Sec. 7, cl. 1.

29. James Roger Sharp, *American Politics in the Early Republic: The New Nation in Crisis* (New Haven, Conn., 1993), 127–33; Smith, *Patriarch*, 257–62, 264–65.

30. George Mason, for example, protested in the convention that "the office of Vice-President [was] an encroachment on the rights of the Senate." Farrand, *Records*, Vol. 2, 537.

31. U.S. Const. Art. I, Sec. 3, cl. 4. The vice president was also to succeed the president in the event of the latter's death, removal, or disability. U.S. Const. Art. II, Sec. 1, cl. 6.

32. Daniel Wirls and Stephen Wirls, *The Invention of the United States Senate* (Baltimore, Md., 2004), 184–85.

33. Letter from Thomas Jefferson to Elbridge Gerry, May 13, 1797, Paul Leicester Ford, ed., *The Writings of Thomas Jefferson* (New York, 1896), Vol. 7, 120.

34. Wirls and Wirls, *Invention of the United States Senate*, 119–20, 184–86.

35. The resolutions, written by Madison and Jefferson, respectively, challenged three statutes that were enacted to protect the Federalist Party and handicap their Republican opposition. *See generally* James Morton Smith, *Freedom's Fetters: The Alien and Sedition Laws and American Civil Liberties* (Ithaca, N.Y., 1956).

36. Letter from Alexander Hamilton to Theodore Sedgwick, Feb. 2, 1799, in Syrett *et al.*, eds., *Papers of Alexander Hamilton*, Vol. 22, 452, 453.

37. *See* Richard E. Ellis, *The Jeffersonian Crisis: Courts and Politics in the Young Republic* (New York, 1971), chs. 3 and 5; George L. Haskins and Herbert A. Johnson, *Foundations of Power: John Marshall, 1801–15* (New York, 1981), 151–63, 205–45.

38. Between 1856 and 1994, for example, there was a split in party control of the presidency and at least one house of Congress for sixty years, 42 percent of the total period. Charles O. Jones, *The Presidency in a Separated System* (Washington, D.C., 1994), 14, 19–23. For one example of the process, *see* Neal Devins, *Shaping Constitutional Values: Elected Government, the Supreme Court, and the Abortion Debate* (Baltimore, Md., 1996).

39. U.S. Const. Art. I, Sec. 3, cl. 1. *See, e.g., Federalist,* No. 62, at 401, 402.

40. Each of the branches had a different constituency, and each tended to offer different policy solutions to problems. *See, e.g.,* Theodore Lowi, *The End of Liberalism: The Second Republic of the United States* (New York, 1979); Richard Neustadt, *Presidential Power* (New York, 1976).

41. 14 U.S. (1 Wheat.) 304 (1816).

42. 19 U.S. (6 Wheat.) 264 (1821).

43. 22 U.S. (9 Wheat.) 1 (1824). *See* G. Edward White, *The Marshall Court and Cultural Change, 1815–35* (New York, 1988), 567–85, esp. 577–80.

44. 22 U.S. (9 Wheat.) 738 (1824).

45. Philip J. Weiser, "Towards a Constitutional Architecture for Cooperative Federalism," 79 *North Carolina L. Rev.* 663, 668–73 (2001); Alfred A. Marcus, *Promise and Performance: Choosing and Implementing an Environmental Policy* (Westport, Conn., 1980).

46. The "vesting" clause provides: "The executive Power shall be vested in a President of the United States of America." U.S. Const. Art. II, Sec. 1. The "take Care" clause appears in U.S. Const. Art. II, Sec. 3.

47. *Printz v. United States,* 521 U.S. 898, 923 (1997). *See* Jay S. Bybee, "*Printz,* the Unitary Executive, and the Fire in the Trash Can: Has Justice Scalia Picked the Court's Pocket?" 77 *Notre Dame L. Rev.* 269 (2001).

48. On separation-of-powers ideas interacting with federalism on civil rights issues, *see, e.g.,* William N. Eskridge, "Reneging on History? Playing the Court/Congress/President Civil Rights Game," 79 *California L. Rev.* 613 (1991).

49. Justice Scalia has been most closely associated with the theory. *Morrison v. Olson,* 487 U.S. 654, 697, 727 (1988) (Scalia, J., dissenting); *Lujan v. Defenders of Wildlife,* 504 U.S. 555, 557 (1992) (Scalia, J.). For defenses of the unitary executive idea, *see* Steven G. Calabresi and Christopher S. Yoo, "The Unitary Executive during the First Half-Century," 47 *Case Western Reserve L. Rev.* 1451 (1997); Saikrishna Bangalore Prakash, "Hail to the Chief Administrator: The Framers and the President's Administrative Powers," 102 *Yale L. J.* 991 (1993). For criticism, *see* Cass R. Sunstein, "The Myth of the Unitary Executive," 7 *Administrative L. J. of American University* 299 (1993); Lawrence Lessig and Cass R. Sunstein, "The President and the Administration," 94 *Columbia L. Rev.* 1 (1994); Martin S. Flaherty, "The Most Dangerous Branch," 105 *Yale L. J.* 1725 (1996).

50. Calabresi and Yoo, "Unitary Executive during the First Half-Century," 1451, 1452–53 (1997). The Court applied versions of the idea to statutes involving elements of the federal government: *Bowsher v. Synar,* 478 U.S. 714 (1986); *Immigration and*

Naturalization Service v. Chadha, 462 U.S. 919 (1983); and *Buckley v. Valeo,* 424 U.S. 1 (1976). The Court ignored the idea in *Morrison v. Olson,* 487 U.S. 654 (1988); *United States v. Nixon,* 418 U.S. 683 (1974).

51. *See* Evan Caminker, "*Printz,* State Sovereignty, and the Limits of Formalism," 1997 *Supreme Court Rev.* 199.

52. The theory of the "unitary executive," like federalism and other separation-of-powers ideas, is an instrument that can be used for a variety of purposes. While the label focuses attention on the issue of the president's authority over executive branch officials, the doctrine's far more important and dangerous uses involve efforts to expand the scope of executive power and eliminate checks on its exercise. *See* Weiser, "Towards a Constitutional Architecture."

53. *See generally* Martin H. Redish and Elizabeth J. Cisar, "'If Angels Were to Govern': The Need for Pragmatic Formalism in Separation of Powers Theory," 41 *Duke L. J.* 449 (1991).

54. *Chadha,* 462 U.S. 919 (1983); *Bowsher,* 478 U.S. 714 (1986).

55. *Morrison v. Olson,* 487 U.S. 654 (1988); *Mistretta v. United States,* 488 U.S. 361, 381 (1989).

56. *Compare, e.g., Allen v. Wright,* 468 U.S. 737 (1984) *with Lujan v. Defenders of Wildlife,* 504 U.S. 555 (1992). In *Lujan* both the majority and dissent relied on separation-of-powers principles to support their contrary conclusions. 504 U.S. at 557 (Scalia, J., for the majority) and 589 (Blackmun, J., dissenting).

57. Scholars have labeled the Court's separation-of-powers doctrines "incoherent" and "abysmal." Rebecca L. Brown, "Separated Powers and Ordered Liberty," 139 *University of Pennsylvania. L. Rev* 1513, 1517 (1991); E. Donald Elliott, "Why Our Separation of Powers Jurisprudence Is So Abysmal," 57 *George Washington L. Rev.* 506 (1989).

58. *Lujan,* 504 U.S., at 559–60.

59. *Federalist,* No. 22, at 132.

60. Art. IV, Sec. 3, para. 1.

61. *Federalist,* No. 14, at 83.

62. Rakove, *Original Meanings,* 165–66; Robert J. Berkhofer Jr., "Jefferson, the Ordinance of 1784, and the Origins of the American Territorial System," 3d ser., 29 *William and Mary Quarterly* 231 (1972).

63. Rakove, *Original Meanings,* 167.

64. The most extreme example was the partition of Virginia during the Civil War and the subsequent admission of West Virginia as a free state, an action the Supreme Court upheld in *Virginia v. West Virginia,* 78 U.S. (11 Wall.) 39 (1870).

65. On the influence of constituencies and constituent interests on congressional voting, *see* Morris Fiorina, *Representatives, Roll Calls, and Constituencies* (Lexington, Mass., 1974); John Kingdon, *Congressmen's Voting Decisions,* 2d ed. (New York, 1981); and Kenneth C. Martis, *Historical Atlas of United States Congressional Districts, 1789–1983* (Boston, 1982).

66. Competitions and coalitions were multiple and changing; they invariably in-

volved private interests; and they occurred in an infinite variety of combinations involving different private groups and different sets of governmental units at different levels and in different states. Thus, territorial boundaries became so interrelated that phenomena such as spillovers, coordination demands, and collective action problems proliferated endlessly and contingently. *Cf.,* Dennis C. Mueller, *Constitutional Democracy* (New York, 1996), ch. 6.

67. *Federalist,* No. 51, at 340. *See* Farrand, *Records,* Vol. 1, 136; *Federalist,* Nos. 10, 14, 44, and 51. Hamilton advanced a somewhat similar "large republic" theory: *e.g., Federalist,* Nos. 9 and 28. For the view they were refuting, *see, e.g.,* Elliot, *Debates,* Vol. 1, 352–53 (Luther Martin); *id.,* Vol. 3, 29–30, 33 (George Mason).

68. *Federalist,* No. 37, at 231.

69. *Federalist,* No. 51, at 340–41. *See also id.,* No. 14, at 85.

70. U.S. Const. Art. I, Sec. 2, cl. 2 and Sec. 3, cl. 3 (requiring members of Congress to be inhabitants of the state from which they are elected); Art. IV, Sec. 3, cl. 1 (guaranteeing territorial integrity of existing states); Art. V (guaranteeing "equal Suffrage in the Senate" to each state).

71. U.S. Const. Art. I, Sec. 10, cl. 3 (prohibiting interstate compacts without the consent of Congress).

72. U.S. Const. Art. I, Sec. 9, cl. 1 and Art. IV, Sec. 2, cl. 3 (protecting states that recognized slavery); Art. I, Sec. 10 (imposing a variety of restrictions on state powers, such as banning the coinage of money, impairing the obligation of contracts, and imposing trade duties); Art. IV, Sec. 1 (requiring states to give "Full Faith and Credit" to one another's public acts).

73. U.S. Const. Art. III, Sec. 2, cl. 1.

74. U.S. Const. Art. I, Sec. 10, cl. 3.

75. U.S. Const. Art. I, Sec. 10, cl. 3.

76. U.S. Const. Art. IV, Sec. 4.

77. U.S. Const. Art. IV, Sec. 4.

78. U.S. Const. Art II, Sec. 1, cl. 3.

79. U.S. Const. Art I, Sec. 3, cl. 1.

80. U.S. Const. Art I, Sec. 4, cl. 1. Madison regarded such national power as essential to "enable Congress to intervene against acts of injustice within the states." Rakove, *Original Meanings,* 224.

81. U.S. Const. Art. IV, Sec. 2, cl. 1.

82. U.S. Const. Art. III, Sec. 2, cl. 1. The latter provision was narrowed by the Eleventh Amendment in 1798.

83. *Federalist,* No. 46, at 309.

84. *Federalist,* No. 84, at 563. The assumption of state unity undergirded Hamilton's arguments in *Federalist,* No. 28, at 174, and No. 31, at 192. Madison and Hamilton were not alone in advancing the claim. *See, e.g.,* Farrand, *Records,* Vol. 1, 356 (William Samuel Johnson of Connecticut).

85. Charles Warren, *The Supreme Court in United States History* (Boston, 1922), Vol.

1, ch. 8; Vol. 2, chs. 13, 16, and 19. *See, e.g., Osborn v. Bank of the United States,* 22 U.S. (9 Wheat.) 738 (1824); *Ableman v. Booth,* 62 U.S. (21 How.) 506 (1859).

86. *See generally, e.g., Federalist,* No. 9 (Hamilton), and *Federalist,* No. 10 (Madison).

87. When the states did share the "same interest," they seldom faced substantial conflict with the national government, for in that situation the three federal branches generally reflected the same broad consensus.

Chapter 4. Federalism as Instrumental

1. Michael Kammen, *A Machine That Would Go of Itself: The Constitution in American Culture* (New York, 1986), 16–17.

2. Marci Hamilton, "The Elusive Safeguards of Federalism," 574 *Annals of the American Academy of Political and Social Science* 93, 101 (2001). *Accord* Harry N. Scheiber, "Federalism at the Bicentennial," in Harry N. Scheiber and Theodore Correl, eds., *Federalism: Studies in History, Law, and Policy* (Berkeley, Calif., 1988), 12.

3. Clarence Thomas, "Why Federalism Matters," 48 *Drake L. Rev.* 231, 234 (2000). Federalism and separation of powers, Thomas continued, "are not ends in themselves." His essay nicely illustrated the use of federalism as an instrument for advancing specific political and ideological values. The "ends" of federalism, the justice noted, were extremely limited: "to protect individual liberty and the private ordering of our lives." *Id.* at 234. The narrow ends he ascribed to the Constitution differed from, and contradicted, its text, which explicitly identifies the "ends" of the federal system in far broader and nobler terms: "to form a more perfect Union, establish Justice, insure domestic Tranquility, provide for the common defense, promote the general Welfare, and secure the Blessings of Liberty to ourselves and our Posterity." U.S. Const. Preamble.

4. For a similar view, *see* Jack N. Rakove, "American Federalism: Was There an Original Understanding?" in Mark R. Killenbeck, ed., *The Tenth Amendment and State Sovereignty: Constitutional History and Contemporary Issues* (New York, 2002), 107–29.

5. James Wilson, speech in the Pennsylvania ratifying convention, Jonathan Elliot, ed., *Debates on the Adoption of the Federal Constitution* (New York, 1987 [1888]), Vol. 2, 424, 425.

6. Madison defined a "faction" as "a number of citizens, whether amounting to a majority or minority of the whole, who are united and actuated by some common impulse of passion, or of interest, adverse to the rights of other citizens, or to the permanent and aggregate interests of the community." Alexander Hamilton, John Jay, and James Madison, *The Federalist,* ed. Edward Mead Earle (New York, 1937), No. 10, at 54 [hereafter, "*Federalist*"].

7. *Federalist,* No. 10, at 54, 55.

8. *Federalist,* No. 10, at 57 (emphasis in original). Although Hamilton accepted the ideas of "balances and checks" and the extended republic, *Federalist,* No. 9, at 48–49,

his emphasis differed from Madison's. He placed greater weight, for example, on the military power of a large state "to suppress faction and to guard the internal tranquility of States." *Id.* at 49.

9. *Federalist,* No. 10, at 60–61.

10. *Federalist,* No. 10, at 61. Madison articulated the theory at the Philadelphia Convention. Max Farrand, ed., *The Records of the Federal Convention of 1787* (New Haven, Conn., 1966 [1937]), Vol. 2, 452 [hereafter, "Farrand, *Records*"].

11. *Federalist,* No. 28, at 174.

12. *Federalist,* No. 51, at 336.

13. The "accumulation of all powers, legislative, executive, and judiciary, in the same hands" was "the very definition of tyranny." *Federalist,* No. 47, at 313.

14. *Federalist,* No. 48, at 321.

15. *Federalist,* No. 51, at 339. His argument is elaborated primarily in *id.,* Nos. 45–51.

16. *Federalist,* No. 51, at 337.

17. *Federalist,* No. 46, at 304–05, 311–12.

18. *Federalist,* No. 28, at 174.

19. *Federalist,* No. 57, at 370 (Madison, or possibly Hamilton).

20. *Federalist,* No. 10, at 60. Hamilton voiced similar views. *See Federalist,* No. 27, at 167. *See* Michael W. McConnell, "Federalism: Evaluating the Founders' Design," 54 *University of Chicago L. Rev.* 1484, 1513; Jack N. Rakove, *Original Meanings: Politics and Ideas in the Making of the Constitution* (New York, 1996), 201.

21. Historians disagree on the extent to which Madison and the Federalists relied on classical ideas of "republican virtue" as opposed to the balancing of selfish interests to secure the common good. *See, e.g.,* Gordon S. Wood, *The Creation of the American Republic, 1776–1787* (Chapel Hill, N.C., 1969), 505–06, 605–15 (Federalists relied on the idea of "virtue"); Joyce Appleby, "The American Heritage: The Heirs and the Disinherited," 74 *Journal of American History* 798 (1987) ("Self-interest was accepted as a functional equivalent to civic virtue," at 803); Bernard Bailyn, *Faces of Revolution: Personalities and Themes in the Struggle for American Independence* (New York, 1990), 259–68 (Federalists questioned classic idea but retained idea in a revised form); Jennifer Nedelsky, *Private Property and the Limits of American Constitutionalism: The Madisonian Framework and Its Legacy* (Chicago, 1990) (Federalists relied not so much on "virtue" or "self-interest" but sought to retain government in their own hands as a "competent elite" that would be capable of "discerning the public good," at 175–76).

22. Letter from James Madison to Edmund Pendleton, April 22, 1787, in Robert A. Rutland *et. al,* eds., *The Papers of James Madison* (Chicago, 1975), Vol. 9, 396.

23. *Federalist,* No. 48, at 321. Hamilton echoed the thought. *Federalist,* No. 73, at 476.

24. *Federalist,* No. 51, at 337.

25. *Federalist,* No. 72, at 470. *Accord Federalist,* No. 28, at 174.

26. For an account of the development of constitutional ideas in the process of polit-

ical contestation, *see* Keith E. Whittington, *Constitutional Construction: Divided Powers and Constitutional Meaning* (Cambridge, Mass., 1999).

27. Recent scholarship has emphasized the extent to which the three branches act "strategically" toward one another. *See, e.g.,* William N. Eskridge Jr., "Reneging on History? Playing the Court/Congress/President Civil Rights Game," 79 *California L. Rev.* 613 (1991); John A. Ferejohn and Barry R. Weingast, "A Positive Theory of Statutory Interpretation," 12 *International Rev. of Law & Economics* 263 (1992); William N. Eskridge Jr. and Philip P. Frickey, "Foreword: Law as Equilibrium," 108 *Harvard L. Rev.* 26 (1994).

28. For a recent consideration of the dynamic, *see* Daryl J. Levinson and Richard H. Pildes, "Separation of Parties, not Powers," 119 *Harvard L. Rev.* 2311 (2006).

29. Political scientists who discuss "regime politics" emphasize the extent to which political actors utilize and shape the judiciary in pursuing their policies. *See, e.g.,* George I. Lovell, *Legislative Deferrals: Statutory Ambiguity, Judicial Power, and American Democracy* (Cambridge, Mass., 2003); Mark A. Graber, "The Nonmajoritarian Difficulty: Legislative Deference to the Judiciary," 7 *Studies in American Political Development* 35 (1993); Keith E. Whittington, "'Interpose Your Friendly Hand': Political Supports for the Exercise of Judicial Review by the United States Supreme Court," 99 *American Political Science Rev.* 583 (2005); Howard Gillman, "How Political Parties Can Use the Courts to Advance Their Agendas: Federal Courts in the United States, 1875–1891," 96 *American Political Science Rev.* 511 (2002).

30. *See* Nobel E. Cunningham Jr., *The Jeffersonian Republicans: The Formation of Party Organization, 1789–1801* (Chapel Hill, N.C., 1957).

31. For changes in Madison's thinking, *see* Lance Banning, "The Practicable Sphere of a Republic: James Madison, the Constitutional Convention, and the Emergence of Revolutionary Federalism," in Richard Beeman, Stephen Botein, and Edward C. Carter II, eds., *Beyond Confederation: Origins of the Constitution and American National Identity* (Chapel Hill, N.C., 1987), 162–87; Marvin Meyers, ed., *The Mind of the Founder: Sources of the Political Thought of James Madison*, rev. ed. (Hanover, N.H., 1981). Madison was not alone in changing his views. Joseph M. Lynch, *Negotiating the Constitution: The Earliest Debates over Original Intent* (Ithaca, N.Y., 1999).

32. *Federalist*, No. 44, at 293.

33. Stanley Elkins and Eric McKitrick, *The Age of Federalism: The Early American Republic, 1788–1800* (New York, 1993), 263–70.

34. Although Madison approved the second bank, he retained a relatively limited view of implied powers. *See* James Madison, "Veto Message," March 3, 1817, *Compilation of the Messages and Papers of the Presidents*, Vol. 2, 569 (New York, 1897).

35. Ralph Ketcham, *James Madison: A Biography* (Charlottesville, Va., 1990), 640–46.

36. Letter from James Madison to George Washington, April 16, 1787, Rutland *et. al*, eds., *The Papers of James Madison*, Vol. 9, 383.

37. Examples are plentiful. The Federalists supported an embargo on American ship-

ping in 1794 but claimed that Jefferson's similar embargo of 1807 was unconstitutional. David P. Currie, *The Constitution in Congress: The Federalist Period, 1789–1801* (Chicago, 1997), 185.

38. Robert V. Remini, *The House: The History of the House of Representatives* (New York, 2006), 78, 87. *See generally* Alexander DeConde, *This Affair of Louisiana* (New York, 1976); Dumas Malone, *Jefferson the President: Second Term, 1805–1809* (Boston, 1974).

39. Arthur Meier Schlesinger, *New Viewpoints in American History* (New York, 1922), ch. 10.

40. Richard B. Bernstein, *Thomas Jefferson* (New York, 2003), 142–43, 147; Leonard W. Levy, *Jefferson and Civil Liberties: The Darker Side* (Cambridge, Mass., 1963), 57–67. Jefferson seemed equally cynical when he approved the Louisiana Purchase. Letter from Thomas Jefferson to Wilson C. Nicholas, Sept. 7, 1803, in Thomas Jefferson Randolph, ed., *The Writings of Thomas Jefferson* (Charlottesville, Va., 1829), Vol. 4, 2–3; letter from Thomas Jefferson to Levi Lincoln, August 30, 1803, *id.*

41. *Baltimore & Ohio Railroad Co. v. Baugh,* 149 U.S. 368, 390, 401 (1893). On Field *see* Paul Kens, *Justice Stephen Field: Shaping Liberty from the Gold Rush to the Gilded Age* (Lawrence, Kans., 1997).

42. Edward A. Purcell Jr., *Brandeis and the Progressive Constitution:* Erie, *the Judicial Power, and the Politics of the Federal Courts in Twentieth-Century America* (New Haven, Conn., 2000), 55–63.

43. H. N. Hirsch, *The Enigma of Felix Frankfurter* (New York, 1981), 191–93; Melvin I. Urofsky, *Felix Frankfurter: Judicial Restraint and Individual Liberties* (Boston, 1991), 165–70; Philip Hamburger, *Separation of Church and State* (Cambridge, Mass., 2002), 474–76.

44. *Bush v. Gore,* 531 U.S. 98 (2000).

45. Arthur Bestor, "State Sovereignty and Slavery: A Reinterpretation of Proslavery Constitutional Doctrine, 1846–1860," 54 *Journal of the Illinois State Historical Society* 117 (1961).

46. Richard Franklin Bensel, *Yankee Leviathan: The Origins of Central State Authority in America, 1859–1877* (New York, 1990), 95, 96. The constitution of the Confederate States rejected the right of secession and protected the institution of slavery by barring both the states and the new central government from taking action to restrict its growth or imperil its existence. Charles Robert Lee, *The Confederate Constitutions* (Chapel Hill, N.C., 1963); Alfred H. Kelly and Winfred A. Harbison, *The American Constitution: Its Origins and Development* (New York, 1976), 376–77.

47. Timothy S. Huebner, *The Southern Judicial Tradition: State Judges and Sectional Distinctiveness, 1790–1890* (Athens, Ga., 1999), 7. *Accord* Elizabeth Lee Thompson, *The Reconstruction of Southern Debtors: Bankruptcy after the Civil War* (Athens, Ga., 2004), 5.

48. *See* ch. 8, *infra. See also* Purcell, *Brandeis and the Progressive Constitution,* chs. 1–3, 9–11.

49. Samuel P. Huntington, *American Politics: The Promise of Disharmony* (Cambridge, Mass., 1981), 207.

50. Newt Gingrich, "Foreword," in Gordon S. Jones and John A. Marini, eds., *The Imperial Congress: Crisis in the Separation of Powers* (New York, 1988), x.

51. Gordon S. Wood, *The Americanization of Benjamin Franklin* (New York, 2004), 227–28.

52. The principal division between the states, Madison told the convention, lay in "their having or not having slaves." Farrand, *Records,* Vol. 1, 486.

53. U.S. Const. Art. I, Sec. 2, cl. 3 ("three-fifths" clause); Art. I, Sec. 9, cl. 1 (importation of slaves); Art. IV, Sec. 2, cl. 3 (fugitive slave clause). *See* Mark A. Graber, Dred Scott *and the Problem of Constitutional Evil* (New York, 2006), 91–114.

54. Edward A. Purcell Jr., "The Particularly Dubious Case of *Hans v. Louisiana:* An Essay on Law, Race, History, and 'Federal Courts,'" 81 *North Carolina L. Rev.* 1927, 2001–2038 (2003); Kerry Abrams, "Polygamy, Prostitution, and the Federalization of Immigration Law," 105 *Columbia L. Rev.* 641, 703–06 (2005); Robert J. Kaczorowski, "The Supreme Court and Congress's Power to Enforce Constitutional Rights: An Overlooked Moral Anomaly," 73 *Fordham L. Rev.* 153 (2004); Bartholomew H. Sparrow, *The Insular Cases and the Emergence of American Empire* (Lawrence, Kans., 2006), 58–64.

55. Letter from Joseph P. Bradley to Judge William B. Woods, Oct. 30, 1876, quoted in Charles Fairman, *Reconstruction and Reunion, 1864–1888,* Part II (New York, 1987), 564.

56. *Civil Rights Cases,* 109 U.S. 3 (1883). *See* Huebner, *Southern Judicial Tradition,* 189–91; Purcell, "Particularly Dubious Case of *Hans,*" 2021–28.

57. Woodrow Wilson, *Congressional Government: A Study in American Politics* (Boston, 1885), 27–28. For Wilson's hostility to the Civil War amendments, *see* Woodrow Wilson, *An Old Master and Other Political Essays* (New York, 1893), 146–48; Woodrow Wilson, *Constitutional Government in the United States* (New Brunswick, N.J., 2002 [1908]), 50, 195.

58. Arthur S. Link, *Woodrow Wilson and the Progressive Era, 1910–1917* (New York, 1954), 64–66; Henry Wilkinson Bragdon, *Woodrow Wilson: The Academic Years* (Cambridge, Mass., 1967), 249, 252; Arthur S. Link, *Wilson: The Road to the White House* (Princeton, N.J., 1947), 502; E. David Cronon, ed., *The Cabinet Diaries of Josephus Daniels, 1913–1921* (Lincoln, Neb., 1963), 32–33.

59. *See, e.g.,* Ira Katznelson, *When Affirmative Action Was White: An Untold History of Racial Inequality in Twentieth-Century America* (New York, 2005), chs. 2–5.

60. 347 U.S. 483 (1954). *See* Michael J. Klarman, *From Jim Crow to Civil Rights: The Supreme Court and the Struggle for Racial Equality* (New York, 2004); James T. Patterson, *Brown v. Board of Education: A Civil Rights Milestone and Its Troubled Legacy* (New York, 2001); Glenn Feldman, ed., *Before* Brown: *Civil Rights and White Backlash in the Modern South* (Tuscaloosa, Ala., 2004).

61. "Declaration of Constitutional Principles," 84th Cong., 2d Sess., 102 *Congressional Record* 4515–16 (1956).

62. Anne E. Kornblut, "Bush and Party Chief Court Black Voters at 2 Forums," *The New York Times,* Friday, July 15, 2005, A-12; Michal R. Belknap, *Federal Law and Southern Order: Racial Violence and Constitutional Conflict in the Post-Brown South* (Athens, Ga., 1987); Klarman, *From Jim Crow to Civil Rights,* esp. chs. 6–7.

63. James Jackson Kilpatrick, *The Sovereign States: Notes of a Citizen of Virginia* (Chicago, 1957), 304, 305, 281.

64. Charles L. Black, "The Lawfulness of the Segregation Decisions," 69 *Yale L. J.* 421, 424 (1960).

65. *Federalist,* No. 78, at 508 (Hamilton). On the role of property in developing judicial review, *see* Nedelsky, *Private Property and the Limits of American Constitutionalism,* esp. 189–95.

66. Alexander Bickel, *The Least Dangerous Branch: The Supreme Court at the Bar of Politics* (New York, 1962), 18, 16. Bickel was a strong supporter of *Brown,* but in reacting against its critics he magnified the claim that the Court's actions were problematic or dubious. *See generally* Barry Friedman, "The Birth of an Academic Obsession: The History of the Countermajoritarian Difficulty, Part Five," 112 *Yale L. J.* 153 (2002).

67. George M. Frederickson, "America's Original Sin," 51 *New York Rev. of Books,* 34 (March 25, 2004), reviewing David Brion Davis, *Challenging the Boundaries of Slavery* (Cambridge, Mass., 2003); Ira Berlin, *Generations of Captivity: A History of African-American Slaves* (Cambridge, Mass., 2003); and Don E. Fehrenbacher, *The Slaveholding Republic: An Account of the United States Government's Relations to Slavery,* ed. Ward M. McAfee (New York, 2001).

68. *Federalist,* No. 39, at 249.

69. *Alden v. Maine,* 527 U.S. 706, 714 (1999) (Kennedy, J.); *id.* at 800 n. 32 (Souter, J., dissenting).

70. Quoted in H. Jefferson Powell, "The Political Grammar of Early Constitutional Law," 71 *North Carolina L. Rev.* 949, 959 (1993). For Clay, *see* Merrill D. Peterson, *The Great Triumvirate: Webster, Clay, and Calhoun* (New York, 1987), and for Clay's explanation of his proposals *see* Henry Clay, "Defense of the American System," *The Life and Speeches of Henry Clay* (New York, 1843), Vol. 2, 9–67.

71. Peterson, *Great Triumvirate,* 254–55.

72. Madison believed that the bill went beyond congressional power. Drew R. McCoy, *The Last of the Fathers: James Madison & the Republican Legacy* (New York, 1989), 92–95.

73. *United States v. Curtiss-Wright Export Corp.,* 299 U.S. 304, 315 (1936).

74. *See* G. Edward White, *The Constitution and the New Deal* (Cambridge, Mass., 2000), 46–53, 69–77.

75. *See, e.g., Fay v. Noia,* 372 U.S. 391 (1963); *England v. Louisiana State Board of Medical Examiners,* 375 U.S. 411 (1964); *Dombrowski v. Pfister,* 380 U.S. 479 (1965); *Zwickler v. Koota,* 389 U.S. 241, 247 (1967).

76. *Francis v. Henderson,* 425 U.S. 536, 548–49 (1976) (Brennan, J., dissenting).

77. William J. Brennan Jr., "State Constitutions and the Protection of Individual Rights," 90 *Harvard L. Rev.* 489, 502 (1977).

78. William J. Brennan Jr., "The Bill of Rights and the States: The Revival of State Constitutions as Guardians of Individual Rights," 61 *New York University L. Rev.* 535 (1986).

79. *See* Robert C. Post, "Justice Brennan and Federalism," in Scheiber and Correl, eds., *Federalism,* 43.

Chapter 5. Federalism as Contingent

1. Alexander Hamilton, John Jay, and James Madison, *The Federalist,* ed. Edward Mead Earle (New York, 1937), No. 82, at 534 [hereafter, *"Federalist"*].

2. *Federalist,* No. 37, at 229.

3. Max Farrand, ed., *The Records of the Federal Convention of 1787,* rev. ed. (New Haven, Conn., 1966 [1937]), Vol. 1, 422 [hereafter, "Farrand, *Records"*].

4. U.S. Const. Preamble.

5. U.S. Const. Art. I, Sec. 8, cl. 1.

6. U.S. Const. Art. I, Sec. 8, cl. 3 and cl. 8.

7. *Federalist,* No. 46, at 304–06.

8. Daniel J. Hulsebosch, *Constituting Empire: New York and the Transformation of Constitutionalism in the Atlantic World, 1664–1830* (Chapel Hill, N.C., 2005), 258.

9. U.S. Const. Art. I, Sec. 2, cl. 1 (House); Art. I, Sec. 3, cl. 1 (Senate); Art. II, Sec. 1, cl. 2–4 (president and vice president).

10. U.S. Const. Art. I, Sec. 2, cl. 3 (House); Art. II, Sec. 1, cl. 2 (presidential electors).

11. *See, e.g.,* Robert A. Dahl, "Decision-Making in a Democracy: The Supreme Court as a National Policymaker," 6 *Journal of Public Law* 279 (1957); Lee Epstein, Jack Knight, and Andrew D. Martin, "The Supreme Court as a Strategic National Policy Maker," 50 *Emory L. J.* 583 (2001). *See* Bruce Ackerman, *We the People: Foundations* (Cambridge, Mass., 1991); Bruce Ackerman, *We the People: Transformations* (Cambridge, Mass., 1998).

12. "The Convention deliberately left most decisions about the nature of the judiciary and the executive to the First Congress." Kenneth R. Bowling, *Politics in the First Congress, 1789–1791* (New York, 1990), 273. For an itemization of changes in the structure and procedures of the national government since 1789, *see* Keith E. Whittington, *Constitutional Construction: Divided Powers and Constitutional Meaning* (Cambridge, Mass., 1999), 12

13. U.S. Const. Art. I, Secs. 2 through 6 contain the relevant provisions.

14. U.S. Const. Art. II, Sec. 1.

15. U.S. Const. Art. II, Sec. 2, cl. 1 and 2.

16. David P. Currie, *The Constitution in Congress: The Federalist Period, 1789–1801* (Chicago, 1997), 41–42.

17. U.S. Const. Art. III, Sec. 1; Art. I, Sec. 3, cl. 6. The significant powers, privileges, and prerogatives of the office are the results of historical development, congressional legislation, and internal judicial practices. *See* "Symposium: The Chief Justice and the Institutional Judiciary," 154 *University of Pennsylvania L. Rev.* 1323 (2006).

18. U.S. Const. Art. I, Sec. 8, cl. 9; Art. III, Sec. 1; Art. III, Sec. 2, cl. 2. The scope of congressional power is disputed. *See, e.g.,* Michael G. Collins, "The Federal Courts, the First Congress, and the Non-Settlement of 1789," 91 *Virginia L. Rev.* 1515 (2005).

19. Article III has been interpreted as identifying the outer limits to which Congress could extend the judicial power.

20. Madison stressed the fact that the law and the federal structure would develop differently depending on the existence and jurisdiction of a system of national courts. Farrand, *Records,* Vol. 1, 122; *Federalist,* No. 37, at 227.

21. U.S. Const. Art. IV, Sec. 3, cl. 1 and 2.

22. That assumption was implicit in Madison's concept of the "extended" republic. *See, e.g., Federalist,* No. 10. Expectations differed as to how the addition of new states would alter the federal system. *See, e.g.,* Drew R. McCoy, "James Madison and Visions of American Nationality in the Confederation Period: A Regional Perspective," in Richard Beeman, Stephen Botein, and Edward C. Carter II, eds., *Beyond Confederation: Origins of the Constitution and American National Identity* (Chapel Hill, N.C., 1987), 226–58.

23. James Wilson, speech in the Pennsylvania ratifying convention, in Jonathan Elliot, ed., *Debates on the Adoption of the Federal Constitution* (New York, 1987 [1888]), Vol. 2, 462.

24. Adam Rothman, *Slave Country: American Expansion and the Origins of the Deep South* (Cambridge, Mass., 2005); David Brion Davis, *Challenging the Boundaries of Slavery* (Cambridge, Mass., 2003), ch. 2; Don E. Fehrenbacher, *The Slaveholding Republic: An Account of the United States Government's Relations to Slavery,* ed. Ward M. McAfee (New York, 2001).

25. Quoted in Stuart Streichler, *Justice Curtis in the Civil War Era: At the Crossroads of American Constitutionalism* (Charlottesville, Va., 2005), 134.

26. U.S. Const. Art V.

27. The idea of incorporating a method of change in a constitution was "a totally new contribution to politics." Gordon S. Wood, *The Creation of the American Republic, 1776–1787* (New York, 1969), 613. *See* David E. Kyvig, *Explicit and Authentic Acts: Amending the U.S. Constitution, 1776–1995* (Lawrence, Kans., 1996); Richard B. Bernstein and Jerome Agel, *Amending America: If We Love the Constitution So Much, Why Do We Keep Trying to Change It?* (New York, 1993); and Sanford Levinson, ed., *Responding to Imperfection: The Theory and Practice of Constitutional Amendment* (Princeton, N.J., 1995).

28. One early amendment, the Eleventh (1798), limited the power of the federal judiciary over the states, while others addressed relatively technical issues of government organization: U.S. Const. Amend. XII (1804) (procedure for electing president and vice president), XX (1933) (presidential and congressional terms of office and presidential succession), XXII (1951) (limiting president to two terms), XXV (1967) (presidential succession), XXVII (1992) (compensation for members of Congress).

29. U.S. Const. Amend. XIII (1865) (abolishing slavery), XIV (1868) (creating na-

tional citizenship and substantial national citizenship rights), and XV (1870) (denying states the right to deny the vote on the basis of race).

30. U.S. Const. Amend. XVI (1913) (income tax), XVII (1913) (popular election of senators), XVIII (1919) (prohibition), XIX (1920) (women's vote). The Eighteenth Amendment was repealed in 1933 by the Twenty-First Amendment.

31. U.S. Const. Amend. XXIII (1961) (providing electoral votes to the District of Columbia in presidential elections), XXIV (1964) (banning the poll tax), and XXVI (1971) (guaranteeing the right to vote to people eighteen and older).

32. *Compare Ex parte Virginia*, 100 U.S. 339, 345 (1880) *with Ex parte Young*, 209 U.S. 123 (1908) and then *City of Boerne v. Flores*, 521 U.S. 507 (1997). On the amendment's vague terms, *see* William E. Nelson, *The Fourteenth Amendment: From Political Principle to Judicial Doctrine* (Cambridge, Mass., 1988).

33. *Civil Rights Cases*, 109 U.S. 3 (1883).

34. *See, e.g.*, Erwin Chemerinsky, "Rethinking State Action," 80 *Northwestern University L. Rev.* 503 (1985); Richard S. Kay, "The State Action Doctrine, the Public-Private Distinction, and the Independence of Constitutional Law," 10 *Constitutional Commentary* 329 (1993).

35. The seven were the three amendments enacted after the Civil War and four others that protected the right to vote. U.S. Const. Amends. XIII, XIV, XV, XIX, XXIII, XIV, and XVI.

36. *Compare, e.g., Katzenbach v. Morgan*, 384 U.S. 641 (1966) *with City of Boerne*, 521 U.S. 507.

37. *Younger v. Harris*, 401 U.S. 37, 44 (1971).

38. *Mitchum v. Foster*, 407 U.S. 225, 242 (1972).

39. U.S. Const. Preamble ("Justice," "Union," "Liberty"); Amend. V ("liberty," "property," "public use," "due process"); Amend. XIV ("liberty," "property," "due process," "equal protection"); Art. I, Sec. 10, cl. 1 ("the Obligation of Contracts"); Art. IV, Sec. 2, cl. 1 ("Privileges and Immunities," "Citizens"). Immediately after breaking with Hamilton and his ideas about "property," Madison began to redefine the concept by giving it a more inclusive, egalitarian, and essentially anti-Hamiltonian meaning. Susan Dunn, *Jefferson's Second Revolution: The Election Crisis of 1800 and the Triumph of Republicanism* (Boston, 2004), 51–52. Indeed, "property" was itself a doubly blurred concept that, like federalism, pointed in two different directions. G. Edward White, *The Marshall Court and Cultural Change, 1815–35* (New York, 1988), 59. For other examples of change, *see*, Garry Wills, *Lincoln at Gettysburg: The Words That Remade America* (New York, 1992), 121–47 ("Union" and "equality"); Paul C. Nagel, *One Nation Indivisible: The Union in American Thought, 1776–1861* (New York, 1964) ("Union"); T. Alexander Aleinikoff, *Semblances of Sovereignty: The Constitution, the State, and American Citizenship* (Cambridge, Mass., 2002) ("citizenship"); William M. Treanor, "The Original Understanding of the Takings Clause and the Political Process," 95 *Columbia L. Rev.* 782 (1995) ("property").

40. U.S. Const. Preamble ("common defence," "general Welfare," "domestic Tran-

quility"); Art. I, Sec. 8, cl. 1 ("common Defence," "common Welfare"); Art. I, Sec. 8, cl. 8 ("Progress of Science and useful Arts").

41. Amend. IV ("unreasonable searches and seizures"); Amend. VIII ("Excessive bail," "excessive fines," "cruel and unusual punishments"); Art. I, Sec. 10, cl. 3 ("imminent Danger"); Amend. 15, Sec. 1 ("on account of race, color, or previous condition of servitude"); Art. I, Sec. 10, cl. 2 ("necessary for executing [a state's] inspection laws"); Art. I, Sec. 8, cl. 3 ("Commerce with foreign Nations, and among the several states, and with the Indian Tribes"). The power to enact "appropriate" legislation was conferred in seven amendments: XIII, XIV, XV, XIX, XXIII, XXIV, and XXVI.

42. For one attempt to measure the extent of change, *see* William H. Riker, *Federalism: Origin, Operation, Significance* (Boston, 1964), 81–84. *See generally* Harry N. Scheiber, "Federalism and the Legal Process: Historical and Contemporary Analysis of the American System," 14 *Law and Society Rev.* 663, 677–82 (1980).

43. Rowland Berthoff, *An Unsettled People: Social Order and Disorder in American History* (New York, 1971), 129–34.

44. *E.g.,* Woodrow Wilson, *Constitutional Government in the United States* (New Brunswick, N.J., 2002 [1908]), 183.

45. *See, e.g.,* Charles Sellers, *The Market Revolution: Jacksonian America, 1815–1846* (New York, 1991); Walter Licht, *Industrializing America: The Nineteenth Century* (Baltimore, 1995); Stuart Bruchey, *Enterprise: The Dynamic Economy of a Free People* (Cambridge, Mass., 1990); Glenn Porter, *The Rise of Big Business, 1860–1910* (New York, 1973).

46. *See, e.g.,* Herbert Hovenkamp, *Enterprise and American Law, 1836–1937* (Cambridge, Mass., 1991); J. Willard Hurst, *The Legitimacy of the Business Corporation in the Law of the United States, 1780–1970* (Charlottesville, Va., 1970); William J. Novak, "The Legal Origins of the Modern American State," in Austin Sarat, Bryant Garth, and Robert A. Kagan, eds., *Looking Back at Law's Century* (Ithaca, N.Y., 2002), 249; Morton J. Horwitz, *The Transformation of American Law, 1780–1860* (Cambridge, Mass. 1977).

47. Thomas L. Haskell, *The Emergence of Professional Social Science: The American Social Science Association and the Nineteenth-Century Crisis of Authority* (Urbana, Ill., 1977). *See* Jackson Lears, *No Place of Grace: Antimodernism and the Transformation of American Culture, 1880–1920* (Chicago, 1981); Dorothy Ross, *The Origins of American Social Science* (New York, 1991).

48. Robert H. Wiebe, *The Search for Order, 1877–1920* (New York, 1967), 44. For the rapid spread of information in the early nineteenth century *see* Richard R. John, *Spreading the News: The American Postal System from Franklin to Morse* (Cambridge, Mass., 1995); James R. Beniger, *The Control Revolution: Technological and Economic Origins of the Information Society* (Cambridge, Mass., 1986); Richard DuBoff, "Business Demand and the Development of the Telegraph in the United States, 1844–1860," 54 *Business History Rev.* 459 (1980).

49. Streichler, *Justice Curtis,* 23.

50. Margaret M. Blair, "Locking in Capital: What Corporate Law Achieved for Business Organizers in the Nineteenth Century," 51 *U.C.L.A. L. Rev.* 387 (2003).

51. James T. Kloppenberg, *Uncertain Victory: Social Democracy and Progressivism in European and American Thought, 1870 –1920* (New York, 1986); Haskell, *Emergence of Professional Social Science;* Ross, *Origins of American Social Science;* Keith E. Whittington, "Dismantling the Modern State? The Changing Structural Foundations of Federalism," 25 *Hastings Constitutional Law Quarterly* 483, 489 – 503 (1998).

52. The needs of national and international business for both uniform and favorable conditions have repeatedly led large corporations and national trade associations to support federal regulation over state regulation when the states began to become active in a field. *See, e.g.,* Jonathan Walters, "'Save Us from the States!'" in Alan Ehrenhalt, ed., *Governing: Issues and Applications from the Front Lines of Government* (Washington, D.C., 2002), 120. Changing attitudes about the nature of "commerce" and the rights of workers pushed in the same direction. *See, e.g.,* James A. Wooten, *The Employee Retirement Income Security Act of 1974* (Berkeley, Calif., 2004).

53. Theda Skocpol, *Protecting Soldiers and Mothers: The Political Origins of Social Policy in the United States* (Cambridge, Mass., 1992); Laura Jensen, *Patriots, Settlers, and the Origins of American Social Policy* (New York, 2003).

54. The phrase is from Stephen Skowronek, *Building the New American State: The Expansion of National Administrative Capacities, 1877–1920* (New York, 1982), 46.

55. Wilson, *Constitutional Government,* 179–80.

56. Skowronek, *Building the New American State,* 287. For the transformation of American politics and public policy during the period, *see* Morton Keller, *Regulating a New Economy: Public Policy and Economic Change in America, 1900 –1933* (Cambridge, Mass., 1990); Richard L. McCormick, "The Party Period and Public Policy: An Exploratory Hypothesis," 66 *Journal of American History* 279 (1979); William R. Brock, *Investigation and Responsibility: Public Responsibility in the United States, 1865 –1900* (Cambridge, U.K., 1984); Morton Keller, *Affairs of State: Public Life in Late Nineteenth Century America* (Cambridge, Mass., 1977).

57. More precisely, in 1802 there were 2,597 civilian employees. Robert V. Percival, "Presidential Management of the Administrative State: The Not-So-Unitary Executive," 51 *Duke L. J.* 963, 975 (2001). In 2005 there were 2,720,462. U.S. Census Bureau, Federal Government Civilian Employment by Function, available at http://www.census.gov/govs/www/apesfed.html (last visited Sept. 25, 2006).

58. Jane Addams, *Twenty Years at Hull House* (New York, 1961 [1910]), 155. *Accord* Felix Frankfurter, *The Public and Its Government* (Boston, 1930), 32–33.

59. 22 U.S. (9 Wheat.) 1, 195, 203–04 (1824).

60. Lawrence Lessig, "Translating Federalism: United States v. Lopez," 1995 *Supreme Court Rev.* 125, 140. The Court extended the fact-based approach in construing the Commerce Clause in *Cooley v. Board of Wardens of the Port of Philadelphia,* 53 U.S. (12 How.) 299 (1851).

61. *Pensacola Telegraph Co. v. Western Union Telegraph Co.,* 96 U.S. 1, 8 (1877). The

Court recognized the growing interdependence of American life and attempted at various times to identify lines that would limit the expansion of federal authority. It justified one such line, that between "manufacturing" and "commerce," as an overt device of expedience. Unless the former was distinguished from the latter, the Court declared, there would be no limit on national power. "The result would be that Congress would be invested, to the exclusion of the states, with the power to regulate, not only manufacture, but also agriculture, horticulture, stock-raising, domestic fisheries, mining, in short, every branch of human industry. For is there one of them that does not contemplate, more or less clearly, an interstate or foreign market?" *Kidd v. Pearson,* 128 U.S. 1, 21 (1888).

62. Felix Frankfurter, *The Commerce Clause under Marshall, Taney and Waite* (Chicago, 1964 [1937]), 81–82.

63. *Federalist,* No. 53, at 350–51.

64. *United States v. DeWitt,* 76 U.S. (9 Wall.) 41 (1869). *See* Robert E. Cushman, "The National Police Power under the Commerce Clause of the Constitution," 3 *Minnesota L. Rev.* 289 (1919); Robert E. Cushman, "The National Police Power under the Taxing Power of the Constitution," 4 *Minnesota L. Rev.* 247 (1920).

65. *Hoke v. United States,* 227 U.S. 308, 323 (1913).

66. *Reid v. Colorado,* 187 U.S. 137 (1902); *Champion v. Ames,* 188 U.S. 321 (1903); *Hipolite Egg Co. v. United States,* 210 U.S. 45 (1911); *Hoke,* 227 U.S. 308; *Clark Distilling Co. v. Western Maryland Railroad Co.,* 242 U.S. 311 (1917).

67. The key decision was *Wickard v. Filburn,* 317 U.S. 111 (1942). *See* Barry Cushman, "Formalism and Realism in Commerce Clause Jurisprudence," 67 *University of Chicago L. Rev.* 1089 (2000); Lawrence H. Tribe, *American Constitutional Law,* 2d ed. (Mineola, N.Y., 1988), 305–18.

68. Key decisions were *United States v. Butler,* 297 U.S. 1 (1936); *Steward Machine Co. v. Davis,* 301 U.S. 548 (1937); *Helvering v. Davis,* 301 U.S. 619 (1937); and *Carmichael v. Southern Coal & Coke Co.,* 301 U.S. 495 (1937).

69. *Helvering,* 301 U.S. at 641. The concept, of course, had never been "static," and the Court had approved many special spending measures in the nineteenth century. *See, e.g., United States v. Realty Company,* 163 U.S. 427 (1896); Edward S. Corwin, "The Spending Power of Congress—Apropos the Maternity Act," 36 *Harvard L. Rev.* 548 (1922); Michele Landis Dauber, "The Sympathetic State," 23 *Law and History Rev.* 387 (2005); Jensen, *Patriots, Settlers.*

70. *United States v. Morrison,* 529 U.S. 598, 607 (2000). For recent assessments, *see* Barry Cushman and Richard D. Friedman, "The Sometimes-Bumpy Stream of Commerce Clause Doctrine," 55 *Arkansas L. Rev.* 981 (2003); Barry Cushman, "Continuity and Change in Commerce Clause Jurisprudence," 55 *Arkansas L. Rev.* 1009 (2003).

71. *See generally* Lawrence M. Friedman, *American Law in the Twentieth Century* (New Haven, Conn., 2002); Alison D. Morantz, "There's No Place Like Home: Homestead Exemption and Judicial Constructions of Family in Nineteenth-Century America," 24 *Law and History Rev.* 245 (2006); Austin Sarat, Bryant Garth, and

Robert A. Kagan, eds., *Looking Back at Law's Century* (Ithaca, N.Y., 2002); Reva B. Siegel, "Text in Context: Gender and the Constitution from a Social Movement Perspective," 150 *University of Pennsylvania L. Rev.* 297, 308–16 (2001); William E. Forbath, "Caste, Class, and Equal Citizenship," 98 *Michigan L. Rev.* 1 (1999); Lucas A. Powe Jr., *The Warren Court and American Politics* (Cambridge, Mass., 2000); William N. Eskridge Jr., "Some Effects of Identity-Based Social Movements on Constitutional Law in the Twentieth Century," 100 *Michigan L. Rev.* 2062 (2002); Harry Kalven Jr., *The Negro and the First Amendment* (Chicago, 1966); Ian F. Haney Lopez, *White by Law: The Legal Construction of Race* (New York, 1996).

72. *See, e.g.*, Mark Warren Bailey, *Guardians of the Moral Order: The Legal Philosophy of the Supreme Court, 1860–1910* (DeKalb, Ill., 2004); Earl M. Maltz, *The Fourteenth Amendment and the Law of the Constitution* (Durham, N.C., 2003), esp. ch. 1; Philip Hamburger, *Separation of Church and State* (Cambridge, Mass., 2002).

73. Benjamin N. Cardozo, *The Nature of the Judicial Process* (New Haven, Conn., 1921), 17.

74. *E.g.*, Herbert Croly, *The Promise of American Life* (Boston, 1989 [1909]), 20.

75. In addition to works previously cited, *see, e.g.*, John Fabian Witt, *The Accidental Republic: Crippled Workingmen, Destitute Widows, and the Remaking of American Law* (Cambridge, Mass., 2004); Michael McGerr, *A Fierce Discontent: The Rise and Fall of the Progressive Movement in America, 1870–1920* (New York, 2003); Barbara Young Welke, *Recasting American Liberty: Gender, Race, Law, and the Railroad Revolution, 1865–1920* (New York, 2001); Adam Fairclough, *Better Day Coming: Blacks and Equality, 1890–2000* (New York, 2001); Susan M. Sterett, *Public Pensions: Gender & Civic Service in the States, 1850–1937* (Ithaca, N.Y., 2003); Alan Dawley, *Struggles for Social Justice: Social Responsibility and the Liberal State* (Cambridge, Mass., 1991); Leonard W. Levy, *Emergence of a Free Press* (New York, 1985); Deborah L. Rhode, *Justice and Gender: Sex Discrimination and the Law* (Cambridge, Mass., 1989); James T. Patterson, *America's Struggle against Poverty, 1900–1980* (Cambridge, Mass., 1981).

76. The Court has often recognized the validity of the historical process that infuses constitutional provisions with a "broader principle" than originally considered. *E.g.*, *McDonald v. Santa Fe Trail Transportation Co.*, 427 U.S. 273, 296 (1976).

77. U.S. Const. Art. I, Sec. 2, cl. 3 (counting slaves as "three-fifths" of a person for purposes of apportioning representatives and direct taxes); Art. I, Sec. 9, cl. 1 (prohibiting abolition of the slave trade until after 1808); Art. IV, Sec. 2, cl. 3 (providing for the forcible return of runaway slaves captured in another state). *See generally* Derrick Bell, *Faces at the Bottom of the Well: The Permanence of Racism* (New York, 1992); Mark V. Tushnet, *Making Civil Rights Law: Thurgood Marshall and the Supreme Court, 1936–1961* (New York, 1994); John D. Skrentny, *The Minority Rights Revolution* (Cambridge, Mass., 2002); Robert H. Wiebe, *Who We Are* (Princeton, N.J., 2002), ch. 4.

78. Religion, for example, helped solidify the reign of racial segregation in the South after the Civil War and subsequently helped to lead the assault against it. *See* David L. Chappell, *A Stone of Hope: Prophetic Religion and the Death of Jim Crow* (Chapel Hill,

N.C., 2004); James B. Bennett, *Religion and the Rise of Jim Crow in New Orleans* (Princeton, N.J., 2005); Edward J. Blum, *Reforging the White Republic: Race, Religion, and American Nationalism, 1865–1898* (Baton Rouge, La., 2005).

79. Lawrence M. Friedman, *American Law in the 20th Century* (New Haven, Conn., 2002), 125. *See, e.g.,* Lopez, *White by Law;* Lucy E. Salyer, *Laws Harsh as Tigers: Chinese Immigration and the Shaping of Modern Immigration Law* (Chapel Hill, N.C., 1995); Erika Lee, *At America's Gates: Chinese Immigration during the Exclusion Era, 1882–1943* (Chapel Hill, N.C., 2003); John Higham, *Strangers in the Land: Patterns of American Nativism, 1860–1925* (New York, 1963).

80. Alice Kessler-Harris, *In Pursuit of Equity: Women, Men, and the Quest for Economic Citizenship in 20th-Century America* (New York, 2001); Reva Siegel, "Reasoning from the Body: A Historical Perspective on Abortion Regulation and Questions of Equal Protection," 44 *Stanford L. Rev.* 261 (1991); Sarah Barringer Gordon, *The Mormon Question: Polygamy and Constitutional Conflict in Nineteenth-Century America* (Chapel Hill, N.C., 2002), 119–45; Amy Dru Stanley, *From Bondage to Contract: Wage Labor, Marriage, and the Market in the Age of Slave Emancipation* (New York, 1998).

81. For a classic statement of the social theory of post–New Deal liberalism, *see West Virginia State Board of Education v. Barnette,* 319 U.S. 624, 639–40 (1943).

82. From the perspective of the dynamics of the federal system, the process represented the effort of the central government and the majority of the states to impose their "national" values on a recalcitrant South. *See, e.g.,* Powe, *Warren Court,* ch. 19.

83. *See generally* Michael J. Klarman, *From Jim Crow to Civil Rights: The Supreme Court and the Struggle for Racial Equality* (New York, 2004); Samuel Walker, *The Rights Revolution: Rights and Community in Modern America* (New York, 1998); Abraham L. Davis and Barbara Luck Graham, *The Supreme Court, Race, and Civil Rights* (Thousand Oaks, Calif., 1995); John E. Semonche, *Keeping the Faith: A Cultural History of the U.S. Supreme Court* (Lanham, Md., 1998); William E. Nelson, *The Legalist Reformation: Law, Politics, and Ideology in New York, 1920–1980* (Chapel Hill, N.C., 2001); Reva B. Siegel, "Text in Context"; William N. Eskridge, "Channeling: Identity-Based Social Movements and Public Law," 150 *University of Pennsylvania L. Rev.* 419 (2001); James Gray Pope, "Labor's Constitution of Freedom," 106 *Yale L. J.* 941 (1997).

84. On federalism, *see, e.g.,* Timothy Conlan, *From New Federalism to Devolution: Twenty-Five Years of Intergovernmental Reform* (Washington, D.C., 1998). On politics, *see, e.g.,* Sidney M. Milkis, *The President and the Parties: The Transformation of the American Party System since the New Deal* (New York, 1993); Robert Mason, *Richard Nixon and the Quest for a New Majority* (Chapel Hill, N.C., 2004); Matthew Dallek, *The Right Moment: Ronald Reagan's First Victory and the Decisive Turning Point in American Politics* (New York, 2000); Peter Steinfels, *The Neo-Conservatives: The Men Who Are Changing America's Politics* (New York, 1979). On constitutional change, *see, e.g.,* Dawn E. Johnsen, "Ronald Reagan and the Rehnquist Court on Congressional Power: Presidential Influences on Constitutional Change," 78 *Indiana L. J.* 363–412 (2003); "Symposium: Judicial Activism and Conservative Politics," 73 *University of*

Colorado L. Rev. 1139 (2002); J. Morgan Kousser, *Colorblind Injustice: Minority Voting Rights and the Undoing of the Second Reconstruction* (Chapel Hill, N.C., 1999); Martin H. Belsky, ed., *The Rehnquist Court: A Retrospective* (New York, 2002); Tinsley E. Yarbrough, *The Rehnquist Court and the Constitution* (New York, 2000). For a key galvanizing issue, *see* N. E. H. Hull and Peter Charles Hoffer, *Roe v. Wade: The Abortion Rights Controversy in American History* (Lawrence, Kans., 2001).

85. In many ways it accelerated those centralizing trends. *See, e.g.,* Samuel Issacharoff and Catherine M. Sharkey, "Backdoor Federalization," 53 *U.C.L.A. L. Rev.* 1353 (2006).

86. Berthoff, *Unsettled People,* 117, 122.

87. Patricia Kelly Hall and Steven Ruggles, "'Restless in the Midst of Their Prosperity': New Evidence on the Internal Migration of Americans, 1850–2000," 91 *Journal of American History* 829, 836, 844 (2006).

88. "Within the next century that still youthful but conservative social order was riven to the roots. The structure whose foundation had been laid by 1775 and which continued to rise for nearly another half century was broken off and never brought to maturity. By 1861, when it collapsed into civil war, it had lost almost all coherence." Berthoff, *Unsettled People,* 127.

Chapter 6. Kaleidoscopic Politics

1. The term is not used in any of its technical economic meanings, which generally relate to changes over time in the relationship between prices and rates of return on investment. *See* Edmund S. Phelps, "equilibrium: an expectational concept," *The New Palgrave: A Dictionary of Economics,* ed. John Eatwell, Murray Milgate, and Peter Newmen (New York, 1987), Vol. 2, 177–79; Murray Milgate, "equilibrium: development of the concept," *id.,* 179–83.

2. Alexander Hamilton, John Jay, and James Madison, *The Federalist,* ed. Edward Mead Earle (New York, 1937), No. 43, at 284 [hereafter, "*Federalist*"].

3. Intrastate conflicts and their political consequences arose from a seemingly infinite number of divisions. *See, e.g.,* John Swauger, "Regionalism in the 1976 Presidential Election," 70 *Geographical Rev.* 157 (1980); Walter Dean Burnham, "American Voting Behavior and the 1964 Presidential Election," 12 *Midwest Journal of Political Science* 1 (1968); Norman R. Luttbeg, "Classifying the American States: An Empirical Attempt to Identify Internal Variations," 15 *Midwest Journal of Political Science* 703 (1971); John Agnew, "Beyond Core and Periphery: The Myth of Regional Political Economic Restructuring and Sectionalism in American Politics," 7 *Political Geography Quarterly* 127 (1988); Fred M. Shelley and J. Clark Archer, "Sectionalism and Presidential Politics: Voting Patterns in Illinois, Indiana, and Ohio," 20 *Journal of Interdisciplinary History* 227 (1989).

4. On the role of political parties, *see, e.g.,* Clinton Rossiter, *Parties and Politics in America* (Ithaca, N.Y., 1960); Samuel H. Beer, "The Modernization of American Federalism," 3 *Publius* 49 (1973); Morton Grodzins, *The American System: A New View of*

Government in the United States (Chicago, 1966); Paul Kleppner *et al.*, *The Evolution of American Electoral Systems* (Westport, Conn., 1981); William H. Riker, *The Development of American Federalism* (Boston, 1987); Herbert Jacob and Kenneth N. Vines, eds., *Politics in the American States* (New York, 1965); William Nisbet Chambers and Walter Dean Burnham, eds., *The American Party Systems* (New York, 1967). On the influence of local constituencies on congressional voting, *see* Morris Fiorina, *Representatives, Roll Calls, and Constituencies* (Lanham, Md., 1974); John Kingdon, *Congressmen's Voting Decisions*, 2d ed. (New York, 1981); Kenneth C. Martis, *Historical Atlas of United States Congressional Districts, 1789–1983* (Boston, 1982); Warren E. Miller and Donald E. Stokes, "Constituency Influence in Congress," 57 *American Political Science Rev.* 45 (1963).

5. Ross M. Robertson, *History of the American Economy*, 2d ed. (New York, 1964), 155–56; Oscar Handlin and Mary Flug Handlin, *Commonwealth: A Study of the Role of Government in the American Economy: Massachusetts, 1774–1861* (New York, 1947), 107–08.

6. Maurice G. Baxter, *The Steamboat Monopoly: Gibbons v. Ogden, 1824* (New York, 1972), 7–8, 15–17.

7. Carter Goodrich, *Government Promotion of American Canals and Railroads, 1800–1890* (New York, 1960), 102, 115; Milton Sydney Heath, *Constructive Liberalism: The Role of the State in Economic Development in Georgia to 1860* (Cambridge, Mass., 1954), 234–35; Handlin and Handlin, *Commonwealth*, 117.

8. *See, e.g.*, Theodore C. Blegen, "The Competition of the Northwestern States for Immigrants," 3 *Wisconsin Magazine of History* 3 (1919).

9. Hendrik Hartog, *Man & Wife in America: A History* (Cambridge, Mass., 2000), 264–65. *See* Michael Grossberg, *Governing the Hearth: Law and the Family in Nineteenth-Century America* (Chapel Hill, N.C., 1985), 294–96.

10. Lewis Atherton, *Main Street on the Middle Border* (Bloomington, Ind., 1954), 4–5.

11. Harry N. Scheiber, "American Federalism and the Diffusion of Power: Historical and Contemporary Perspectives," 9 *University of Toledo L. Rev.* 619, 632–33 (1978). On the early development of the national market *see* Forrest McDonald, *We the People: The Economic Origins of the Constitution* (Chicago, 1958); Curtis Nettels, *The Emergence of a National Economy, 1775–1815* (New York, 1962); Charles G. Sellers Jr., *The Market Revolution: Jacksonian America, 1815–1846* (New York, 1991).

12. Goodrich, *Government Promotion*, ch. 3.

13. The federal government contributed $300,000 to the Pennsylvania-Maryland-Delaware project. Goodrich, *Government Promotion*, 63.

14. Merrill D. Peterson, *The Great Triumvirate: Webster, Clay, and Calhoun* (New York, 1987), 262–64.

15. *See, e.g.*, Charles M. Wiltse, *John C. Calhoun: Nullifier, 1829–1839* (New York, 1949), 41, 102; Robert V. Remini, *Daniel Webster: The Man and His Time* (New York, 1997), chs. 24–25; Elaine K. Swift, *The Making of an American Senate: Reconstitutive Change in Congress, 1787–1841* (Ann Arbor, Mich., 1996), 172.

16. *See, e.g.,* Adam Fairclough, *Better Day Coming: Blacks and Equality, 1890–2000* (New York, 2001); Laughlin McDonald, *A Voting Rights Odyssey: Black Enfranchisement in Georgia* (Cambridge, U.K., 2003); Richard C. Cortner, *Civil Rights and Public Accommodations: The* Heart of Atlanta Motel *and* McClung *Cases* (Lawrence, Kans., 2001).

17. James Willard Hurst, *The Legitimacy of the Business Corporation in the Law of the United States, 1780–1970* (Charlottesville, Va., 1970), 69–75; William L. Cary, "Federalism and Corporate Law: Reflections upon Delaware," 83 *Yale L. J.* 663, 664–70 (1974).

18. Hartog, *Man & Wife*, 265.

19. Lawrence M. Friedman, *American Law: An Introduction* (New York, 1984), 131–32.

20. Jon C. Teaford, *The Rise of the States: Evolution of American State Government* (Baltimore, Md., 2002), 141–43, 188. *See, e.g.* Advertisement, *The New York Times,* June 10, 2004, C-5; Mississippi Development Authority, "Why Mississippi?" http://www.mississippi.org/content/page/tortreform (last visited Sept. 28, 2006).

21. Teaford, *Rise of the States,* 190.

22. Joseph F. Zimmerman, *Interstate Cooperation: Compacts and Administrative Agreements* (Westport, Conn., 2002), 6.

23. Felix Frankfurter and James M. Landis, "The Compact Clause of the Constitution—A Study in Interstate Agreements," 34 *Yale L. J.* 685, 735–48 (1925). *See* Jane Perry Clark, *The Rise of a New Federalism: Federal-State Cooperation in the United States* (New York, 1965 [1938]), ch. 3; Vincent V. Thursby, *Interstate Cooperation: A Study of the Interstate Compact* (Washington, D.C., 1953), ch. 5; Frederick L. Zimmerman and Mitchell Wendell, *The Law and Use of Interstate Compacts* (Lexington, Ky., 1976).

24. Zimmerman, *Interstate Cooperation,* 41–42.

25. Zimmerman, *Interstate Cooperation,* 55–62. *See id.* chs. 4–5.

26. Zimmerman, *Interstate Cooperation,* 88–94.

27. *Virginia v. Tennessee,* 148 U.S. 503 (1893).

28. The Court expressly upheld the rule in *United States Steel Corp. v. Multistate Tax Commission,* 434 U.S. 452 (1978). *See* Christi Davis and Douglas M. Branson, "Interstate Compacts in Commerce and Industry: A Proposal for 'Common Markets among States,'" 23 *Vermont L. Rev.* 133, 137–39 (1998).

29. Lawrence M. Friedman, *American Law in the 20th Century* (New Haven, Conn., 2002), 379–80; William Twining, *Karl Llewellyn and the Realist Movement* (London, U.K., 1973), 270–301.

30. Zimmerman, *Interstate Cooperation,* 166.

31. Clark, *Rise of a New Federalism,* 12.

32. Zimmerman, *Interstate Cooperation,* ch. 6.

33. Richard H. K. Vietor, *Environmental Politics and the Coal Coalition* (College Station, Tex., 1980), 99–102, 119–22.

34. Chad Montrie, *To Save the Land and People: A History of Opposition to Surface Coal Mining in Appalachia* (Chapel Hill, N.C., 2003).

35. Harry N. Scheiber, "Federalism and Legal Process: Historical and Contemporary Analysis of the American System," 14 *Law and Society Rev.* 663, 688 (1980).

36. For a history of the act *see* Michael J. Bean and Melanie J. Rowland, *The Evolution of National Wildlife Law,* 3d ed. (Westport, Conn., 1997), 194–98.

37. This paragraph is drawn from Jason Scott Johnston, "The Tragedy of Centralization: The Political Economics of Natural Resource Federalism," 74 *University of Colorado L. Rev.* 487, 561–83 (2003).

38. Rosemarie Zagarri, *The Politics of Size: Representation in the United States, 1776–1850* (Ithaca, N.Y., 1987), 151.

39. Atherton, *Main Street,* 13.

40. Daniel J. Boorstin, *The Americans: The National Experience* (New York, 1965), 162–68.

41. Handlin and Handlin, *Commonwealth,* 109.

42. *See* Jon C. Teaford, *The Municipal Revolution in America: Origins of Modern Urban Government, 1650–1825* (Chicago, 1975), chs. 4–7.

43. Heath, *Constructive Liberalism,* 231–32; Kenneth Sturges, *American Chambers of Commerce* (New York, 1915), 16, 18.

44. *See generally* Rowland Berthoff, *An Unsettled People: Social Order and Disorder in American History* (New York, 1971), 127–73.

45. Sturges, *American Chambers,* 41, 44–45; Bayard Still, "Patterns of Mid-Nineteenth Century Urbanization in the Middle West," 28 *Mississippi Valley Historical Rev.* 187, 199 (1941); George Rogers Taylor, *The Transportation Revolution, 1815–1860* (Armonk, N.Y., 1951), 33–36.

46. Taylor, *Transportation Revolution,* 7–8.

47. Blake McKelvey, *The Urbanization of America, 1860–1915* (New Brunswick, N.J., 1963), 6–7.

48. Similar internal economic divisions fragmented the interests of merchants and towns in Ohio. Harry N. Scheiber, *Ohio Canal Era: A Case Study of Government and the Economy, 1820–1861* (Athens, Ohio, 1969), ch. 10.

49. Louis Hartz, *Economic Policy and Democratic Thought: Pennsylvania, 1776–1860* (Cambridge, Mass., 1948), 10–11.

50. Hartz, *Economic Policy,* 42–44.

51. William Cronon, *Nature's Metropolis: Chicago and the Great West* (New York, 1991).

52. Wyatt Winton Belcher, *The Economic Rivalry between St. Louis and Chicago, 1850–1880* (New York, 1947).

53. McKelvey, *Urbanization of America,* 24–26.

54. Charles N. Glaab, *Kansas City and the Railroads: Community Policy in the Growth of a Regional Metropolis* (Lawrence, Kans., 1993 [1962]), 63–76.

55. Goodrich, *Government Promotion,* 137, 239–41.

56. Economists, sociologists, and geographers have developed varieties of "central place theory" to explain the location, size, and function of cities. *See, e.g.,* Brian J. L. Berry, *Geography of Market Centers and Retail Distribution* (Englewood Cliffs, N.J.,

1967); John Friedmann and William Alonso, *Regional Development and Planning: A Reader* (Cambridge, Mass., 1964); Richard E. Preston, "The Structure of Central Place Systems," 47 *Economic Geography* 136 (1971). For historical analyses employing such concepts, *see* Cronon, *Nature's Metropolis,* and Richard Franklin Bensel, *Sectionalism and American Political Development, 1880–1980* (Madison, Wisc., 1984). The growing importance of cities in the nineteenth century was a change in the degree and nature of their importance, as cities had been significant actors from early colonial times. *See, e.g.,* Carl Bridenbaugh, *Cities in Revolt: Urban Life in America, 1743–1776,* rev. ed. (New York, 1970); Hendrik Hartog, *Public Property and Private Power: The Corporation of the City of New York in American Law, 1730–1870* (Chapel Hill, N.C., 1983).

57. McKelvey, *Urbanization of America,* 59.

58. Goodrich, *Government Promotion,* 163; Hartz, *Economic Policy,* 134.

59. *See, e.g.,* Jon C. Teaford, *Unheralded Triumph: City Government in America, 1870–1900* (Baltimore, Md., 1984); Stuart M. Blumin, *The Emergence of the Middle Class: Social Experience in the American City, 1760–1900* (New York, 1989); Zane L. Miller, *The Urbanization of Modern America: A Brief History* (New York, 1973); Jon C. Teaford, *City and Suburb: The Political Fragmentation of Metropolitan America, 1850–1970* (Baltimore, Md., 1979).

60. *E.g.,* Richard C. Schragger, "Cities as Constitutional Actors: The Case of Same-Sex Marriage," 21 *Journal of Law & Politics* 147 (2005); Roderick M. Hills Jr., "Is Federalism Good for Localism? The Localist Case for Federal Regimes," 21 *Journal of Law & Politics* 187 (2005).

61. The principle developed in the late eighteenth and early nineteenth centuries as "America's city fathers lost the battle for ascendancy" with their state governments. Teaford, *Municipal Revolution,* 90. Critical in the development was Chief Justice John Marshall's opinion in *Dartmouth College v. Woodward,* 17 U.S. (4 Wheat.) 518 (1819), denying that the protections of the Contract Clause reached municipal charters and stating that, insofar as such charters involved political powers, the "legislature of the State may act according to its own judgment." *Id.* at 629–30.

62. *City of Clinton v. Cedar Rapids and Missouri River Railroad Co.,* 24 Iowa 455, 475 (Sup. Ct. Iowa, 1868) (Dillon, J.). The rule was commonly traced to the work of Chancellor James Kent in the 1830s. Hartog, *Public Property,* 223.

63. Roscoe C. Martin, *The Cities and the Federal System* (New York, 1965), 30–31. For the origins of the "home rule" movement, *see* Teaford, *Unheralded Triumph,* ch. 5.

64. Robert C. Ellickson, "Cities and Homeowners Associations," 130 *University of Pennsylvania L. Rev.* 1519, 1569 and n. 211 (1982).

65. Scholars dispute the scope and effectiveness of "home rule" provisions. *See, e.g.,* Gerald E. Frug, "The City as a Legal Concept," 93 *Harvard L. Rev.* 1057 (1980); David J. Barron, "Reclaiming Home Rule," 116 *Harvard L. Rev.* 2255 (2003); Joseph F. Zimmerman, *Contemporary American Federalism: The Growth of National Power* (New York, 1992), ch. 8; Richard Briffault, "Our Localism: Part I—The Structure of Local Government Law," 90 *Columbia L. Rev.* 1 (1990).

66. Kenneth T. Jackson, *Crabgrass Frontier: The Suburbanization of the United States* (New York, 1985), 149–50, 153. There were exceptions, including Dallas, Houston, Indianapolis, Oklahoma City, and Jacksonville, Florida. *Id.* at 154. For an analysis of the urban-suburban dynamic, *see* Richardson Dilworth, *The Urban Origins of Suburban Autonomy* (Cambridge, Mass., 2005).

67. Jackson, *Crabgrass Frontier,* 283–84.

68. Jackson, *Crabgrass Frontier,* 150–55, 289–90.

69. Thomas J. Sugrue, *The Origins of the Urban Crisis: Race and Inequality in Postwar Detroit* (Princeton, N.J., 1996); Douglas S. Massey and Nancy A. Denton, *American Apartheid: Segregation and the Making of the Underclass* (Cambridge, Mass., 1993). For the earlier period *see* St. Clair Drake and Horace R. Clayton, *Black Metropolis: A Study of Negro Life in a Northern City* (New York, 1945); Kevin R. Cox, *Conflict, Power and Politics in the City: A Geographic View* (New York, 1973), 40–48.

70. *See, e.g.,* Agnew, "Beyond Core and Periphery"; G. Tomas Murauskas, J. Clark Archer, and Fred M. Shelley, "Metropolitan, Nonmetropolitan and Sectional Variations in Voting Behavior in Recent Presidential Elections," 41 *Western Political Quarterly* 63 (1988); Benjamin Walter and Frederick M. Wirt, "The Political Consequences of Suburban Variety," 2 *Social Science Quarterly* 746 (1970). Exemplifying the complexities of the federal system, the national government complicated and sharpened the division between urban and suburban areas. Beginning with the New Deal, its housing programs encouraged private home ownership and thereby nourished the growth of white middle-class suburbs, while at the same time creating large public housing projects that tended to concentrate minorities and the poor in relatively low-quality housing located within the cities. Jackson, *Crabgrass Frontier,* 229–30.

71. David J. Barron, Gerald E. Frug, and Rick T. Su, *Dispelling the Myth of Home Rule: Local Power in Greater Boston* (Cambridge, Mass., 2004), xi, 91.

72. Morton Grodzins and Daniel Elazar, "Centralization and Decentralization in the American Federal System," in Robert A. Goldwin, ed., *A Nation of States: Essays on the American Federal System* (Chicago, 1974), 1–2; Richard Briffault, "Who Rules at Home?: One Person/One Vote and Local Governments," 60 *University of Chicago L. Rev.* 339, 359 (1993); John Kincaid and Daphne A. Kenyon, "The Competitive Challenge to Cooperative Federalism: A Theory of Federal Democracy," *Competition among States and Local Governments: Efficiency and Equity in American Federalism* (Washington, D.C., 1991), 87, 98. *See* Richard Briffault, "A Government for Our Time? Business Improvement Districts and Urban Governance," 99 *Columbia L. Rev.* 365 (1999); Richard Briffault, "Localism and Regionalism," 48 *Buffalo L. Rev.* 1 (2000).

73. David P. Currie, *The Constitution in Congress: The Federalist Period, 1789–1801* (Chicago, 1997), 217–22; David P. Currie, *The Constitution in Congress: The Jeffersonians, 1801–1829* (Chicago, 2001), 88.

74. David Tyack, Thomas James, and Aaron Benavot, *Law and the Shaping of Public Education, 1785–1954* (Madison, Wisc., 1987), 33. For details, *see id.* 31–42.

75. Currie, *Constitution in Congress: The Federalist Period,* 168–69.

76. Laura Jensen, *Patriots, Settlers, and the Origins of American Social Policy* (New York, 2003), 224.

77. Taylor, *Transportation Revolution,* 19, 49, 352–71; Currie, *Constitution in Congress: The Jeffersonians,* 250–303.

78. Michele Landis Dauber, "The Sympathetic State," 23 *Law and History Rev.* 387, 394 (2005).

79. *See, e.g.,* Henry Clay, *The Life and Speeches of Henry Clay* (New York, 1843), Vol. 1, 55–78; 2 *id.* 9–67.

80. Taylor, *Transportation Revolution,* 18–21.

81. Taylor, *Transportation Revolution,* 94–96.

82. Taylor, *Transportation Revolution,* 20–22, 95; Goodrich, *Government Promotion,* 45–48, 288.

83. Goodrich, *Government Promotion,* 182–84.

84. Boorstin, *Americans: The National Experience,* 250–56; Goodrich, *Government Promotion,* 183; Glaab, *Kansas City and the Railroads,* 108–09.

85. Corruption was both interstate and international, and it easily transcended state lines. *See, e.g.,* Richard White, "Information, Markets, and Corruption: Transcontinental Railroads in the Gilded Age," 90 *Journal of American History* 19 (2003).

86. *See* Robert A. Waller, *Rainey of Illinois: A Political Biography, 1903–34* (Urbana, Ill., 1977), ch. 4.

87. For an interesting discussion of the relationship of local economic interests (and urban regional "trade areas") to congressional voting patterns, *see* Bensel, *Sectionalism,* ch. 2.

88. Edward A. Purcell Jr., "Ideas and Interests: Businessmen and the Interstate Commerce Act," 54 *Journal of American History* 561, 566 (1967).

89. On the passage of the Interstate Commerce Act *see* Stephen Skowronek, *Building a New American State: The Expansion of National Administrative Capacities, 1877–1920* (New York, 1982), 125–50; Gabriel Kolko, *Railroads and Regulation, 1877–1916* (Princeton, N.J., 1965); Lee Benson, *Merchants, Farmers, & Railroads: Railroad Regulation and New York Politics, 1850–1887* (Cambridge, Mass., 1955).

90. Richard Franklin Bensel, *Yankee Leviathan: The Origins of Central State Authority in America, 1859–1877* (New York, 1990), 14–17, 413–15 (quotation at 415).

91. *E.g.,* William E. Forbath, "Lincoln, the Declaration, and the 'Grisly, Undying Corpse of States' Rights': History, Memory, and Imagination in the Constitution of a Southern Liberal," 92 *Georgetown L. J.* 709, 755–58 (2004); Marc Linder, "Farm Workers and the Fair Labor Standards Act: Racial Discrimination in the New Deal," 65 *Texas L. Rev.* 1335, 1351–82 (1987); Ira Katznelson, *When Affirmative Action Was White: An Untold History of Racial Inequality in Twentieth-Century America* (New York, 2005).

92. On the Prohibition movement, *see, e.g.,* Jack S. Blocker Jr., *Retreat from Reform: The Prohibition Movement in the United States, 1890–1913* (Westport, Conn., 1976); James H. Timberlake, *Prohibition and the Progressive Movement, 1900–1920* (Cambridge, Mass., 1963); Joseph R. Gusfield, *Symbolic Crusade: Status Politics and the American*

Temperance Movement (Urbana, Ill., 1963); Ruth Bordin, *Women and Temperance: The Quest for Power and Liberty, 1823–1900* (Philadelphia, Pa., 1981); Joseph J. Rumbarger, *Profits, Power, and Prohibition: Alcohol Reform and the Industrializing of America, 1800–1930* (Albany, N.Y., 1989).

93. Richard F. Hamm, reviewing James D. Ivey, *No Saloon in the Valley: The Southern Strategy of the Texas Prohibitionists in the 1880s* (Waco, Tex., 2003), 91 *Journal of American History* 268–69 (2004).

94. *See* Richard F. Hamm, *Shaping the 18th Amendment: Temperance Reform, Legal Culture, and the Polity, 1880–1920* (Chapel Hill, N.C., 1995), ch. 2.

95. William A. Link, *The Paradox of Southern Progressivism, 1880–1930* (Chapel Hill, N.C., 1992), 96.

96. For similar complex regional and intrastate factors affecting the contemporaneous ratification of the Nineteenth Amendment, *see* Eileen L. McDonagh and H. Douglas Price, "Woman Suffrage in the Progressive Era: Patterns of Opposition and Support in Referenda Voting, 1910–1918," 79 *American Political Science Rev.* 415 (1985); Eileen L. McDonagh, "Issues and Constituencies in the Progressive Era: House Roll Call Voting on the Nineteenth Amendment, 1913–1919," 51 *Journal of Politics* 119 (1989).

97. *See, e.g.*, Daniel Tyler, *Silver Fox of the Rockies: Delphus E. Carpenter and the Western Water Compacts* (Norman, Okla., 2003); Douglas E. Kupel, *Fuel for Growth: Water and Arizona's Urban Environment* (Tucson, Ariz., 2003).

98. *E.g., Arizona v. California*, 373 U.S. 546 (1963). *See* Jack L. August Jr., *Vision in the Desert: Carl Hayden and Hydropolitics in the American Southwest* (Fort Worth, Tex., 1999).

99. George E. Mowry, *The Era of Theodore Roosevelt and the Birth of Modern America, 1900–1912* (New York, 1958), 124–25; Samuel P. Hays, *Conservation and the Gospel of Efficiency* (Cambridge, Mass., 1959), 12–14.

100. Hays, *Conservation*, 246–48.

101. Kupel, *Fuel for Growth*, 79–80.

102. Robert Gottlieb, *A Life of Its Own: The Politics of Water and Power* (San Diego, Calif., 1988); John Walton, *Western Times and Water Wars: State, Culture, and Rebellion in California* (Berkeley, Calif., 1992); Richard M. Bernard and Bradley R. Rice, eds., *Sunbelt Cities: Politics and Growth Since World War II* (Austin, Tex., 1983); Norris Hundley Jr., *Water and the West: The Colorado River Compact and the Politics of Water in the American West* (Berkeley, Calif., 1975); Norris Hundley Jr., *The Great Thirst: Californians and Water, 1770s–1990s* (Berkeley, Calif., 1992); Donald E. Worster, *Rivers of Empire: Water, Aridity, and the Growth of the American West* (New York, 1985).

103. Gordon E. Baker, *Rural Versus Urban Political Power: The Nature and Consequences of Unbalanced Representation* (New York, 1955), 11, 15–17.

104. Baker, *Rural Versus Urban*, 27.

105. James MacGregor Burns, *Congress on Trial* (New York, 1949), 65.

106. *E.g., Baker v. Carr*, 369 U.S. 186 (1962); *Gray v. Sanders*, 372 U.S. 368 (1963); *Westbury v. Sanders*, 376 U.S. 1 (1964); *Reynolds v. Sims*, 377 U.S. 533 (1964). *See*

Robert McKay, "Reapportionment: Success Story of the Warren Court," 67 *Michigan L. Rev.* 223 (1968).

107. Timothy Conlan, *From New Federalism to Devolution: Twenty-Five Years of Intergovernmental Reform* (Washington, D.C., 1998), 6–7; Scheiber, "American Federalism and the Diffusion of Power," 619, 647–48, 672–73. For a more favorable view from the 1960s, *see, e.g.,* Martin, *Cities and the Federal System,* chs. 6–8.

108. "A Letter to the President from the National Governors' Association," 9 *Publius* 91 (1978).

109. Kincaid and Kenyon, "Competitive Challenge to Cooperative Federalism," 87, 92–93.

110. *Hunter v. Pittsburgh,* 207 U.S. 161, 178–79 (1907).

111. *See, e.g.,* Joan C. Williams, "The Constitutional Vulnerability of American Local Government: The Politics of City Status in American Law," 1986 *Wisconsin L. Rev.* 83.

112. 426 U.S. 833 (1976).

113. 458 U.S. 457 (1982).

114. 469 U.S. 256 (1985).

115. *See* Richard Briffault, "'What About the 'Ism'?' Normative and Formal Concerns in Contemporary Federalism," 47 *Vanderbilt L. Rev.* 1303, 1328–35 (1994).

116. Paul H. S. Chen, "The Institutional Sources of State Success in Federalism Litigation before the Supreme Court," 25 *Law & Policy* 455 (2003); Elizabeth Garrett, "Enhancing the Political Safeguards of Federalism? The Unfunded Mandates Reform Act of 1995," 45 *University of Kansas L. Rev.* 1113, 1122 (1997).

117. Lynn A. Baker, "Putting the Safeguards Back into the Political Safeguards of Federalism," 46 *Villanova L. Rev.* 951, 955–56 (2001). For discussions of one such federalism issue and the problem of state diversity, *see* Garrett, "Enhancing the Political Safeguards of Federalism?"; David A. Dana, "The Case for Unfunded Environmental Mandates," 69 *Southern California L. Rev.* 1, 26 (1995).

118. Theda Skocpol, *Diminished Democracy: From Membership to Management in American Civil Life* (Norman, Okla., 2003), ch. 2, esp. 24–26, 32, 40, 50–51.

119. Skocpol, *Diminished Democracy,* 32.

120. *See* Clifford S. Griffin, *Their Brothers' Keepers: Moral Stewardship in the United States, 1800–1865* (New Brunswick, N.J., 1960).

121. Skocpol, *Diminished Democracy,* 59.

122. Hartz, *Economic Policy,* 22; Walter Dean Burnham, "American Voting Behavior and the 1964 Election," 12 *Midwest Journal of Political Science* 1, 21–23 (1968). Intrastate regional differences were often rooted in ethnic settlement patterns. *See* Frederick Jackson Turner, *The Significance of Sections in American History* (New York, 1932); V. O. Key and Frank P. Munger, "Social Determinism and Electoral Decision: The Case of Indiana," in Eugene Burdick and Arthur J. Brodbeck, eds., *American Voting Behavior* (Glencoe, Ill., 1959), 281–99.

123. *See, e.g.,* Arthur S. Miller, *The Modern Corporate State: Private Governments and the American Constitution* (Westport, Conn., 1976); Grant McConnell, *Private Power and American Democracy* (New York, 1966).

124. *See, e.g.*, Susan Strange, *The Retreat of the State: The Diffusion of Power in the World Economy* (Cambridge, U.K., 1996).

125. Bernard Bailyn, *To Begin the World Anew: The Genius and Ambiguities of the American Founders* (New York, 2003), 121. On the dynamic branch interrelationships characteristic of contemporary American government, *see* Stephen Skowronek, *The Politics Presidents Make: Leadership from John Adams to Bill Clinton* (Cambridge, Mass., 1997); Charles O. Jones, *The Presidency in a Separated System* (Washington, D.C., 1994); Neal Devins, *Shaping Constitutional Values: Elected Government, the Supreme Court, and the Abortion Debate* (Baltimore, Md., 1996).

Chapter 7. Readjusting Components

1. "A–Z Index of U.S. Government Departments and Agencies," available at http://www.firstgov.gov/Agencies/Federal/All_Agencies/index.shtml (last visited Sept. 25, 2006).

2. For suggestions about the general causes of such institutional change, *see* Joseph Cooper, "Organization and Innovation in the House of Representatives," in Joseph Cooper and G. Calvin Mackenzie, eds., *The House at Work* (Austin, Tex., 1981); Gerald Gamm and Kenneth Shepsle, "Emergence of Legislative Institutions: Standing Committees in the House and Senate, 1810–1825," 14 *Legislative Studies Quarterly* 39 (1989); Richard Fenno, *Congressmen in Committees* (Boston, 1973); Barbara Sinclair, *Legislators, Leaders and Lawmaking: The U.S. House of Representatives in the Postreform Era* (Baltimore, Md., 1995); Sarah A. Binder and Steven S. Smith, "Political Goals and Procedural Choice in the Senate," 60 *Journal of Politics* 398 (1998).

3. Elaine K. Swift, *The Making of an American Senate: Reconstitutive Change in Congress, 1787–1841* (Ann Arbor, Mich., 1996), esp. 160–79; George H. Haynes, *The Senate of the United States: Its History and Practice* (New York, 1960), Vol. 1, 38.

4. *See, e.g.*, Alexander Hamilton, John Jay, and James Madison, *The Federalist*, ed. Edward Mead Earle (New York, 1937), Nos. 62–66 [hereafter, "*Federalist*"].

5. Daniel Wirls and Stephen Wirls, *The Invention of the United States Senate* (Baltimore, Md., 2004), 203–04.

6. Swift, *Making of an American Senate*, 84–85, 179–82; William Riker, "The Senate and American Federalism," 49 *American Political Science Rev.* 452 (1955). For the later periods, *see* Barbara Sinclair, *The Transformation of the U.S. Senate* (Baltimore, Md., 1989); Fred R. Harris, *Deadlock or Decision: The U.S. Senate and the Rise of National Politics* (New York, 1993).

7. Binder and Smith, "Political Goals," 403–04.

8. Haynes, *Senate of the United States,* Vol. 1, 462. In 1917, under acute political pressures, the Senate finally adopted a form of the "previous question" motion, but it required a laborious procedure and a two-thirds vote to terminate debate. *See* Haynes, *Senate of the United States,* Vol. 1, 402–05. Currently, to cut off debate, Senate Rule 22 requires a two-thirds vote on proposals to change Senate rules and sixty votes on other nonrules proposals. John C. Roberts, "Majority Voting in Congress: Further Notes on

the Constitutionality of the Senate Cloture Rule," 20 *Journal of Law & Politics* 505, 506 (2004).

9. *Federalist*, No. 22 (Hamilton), at 134–36; No. 58 (Madison), at 382–83; Binder and Smith, "Political Goals," 398, 401–03.

10. The Ways and Means Committee was established as a standing committee in 1795, and its status was incorporated into the Standing Rules of the House in 1802 when there were a total of five standing committees. Robert V. Remini, *The House: The History of the House of Representatives* (New York, 2006), 61–62, 76. By the late 1790s the position of speaker of the House was becoming increasingly important, primarily because of its power to appoint committees and their chairs. *Id*. at 58–59.

11. *See* Nelson W. Polsby, "The Institutionalization of the U.S. House of Representatives," 62 *American Political Science Rev.* 144 (1968); Joseph Cooper, *Congress and Its Committees: A Historical Approach to the Role of Committees in the Legislative Process* (New York, 1960); Joseph Cooper and Cheryl D. Young, "Bill Introduction in the Nineteenth Century: A Study of Institutional Change," 14 *Legislative Studies Quarterly* 67 (1989); Gamm and Shepsle, "Emergence of Legislative Institutions," 39; Sarah A. Binder, "Partisanship and Procedural Choice: Institutional Change in the Early Congress, 1789–1823," 57 *Journal of Politics* 1093 (1995).

12. Gary W. Cox and Mathew D. McCubbins, "Bonding, Structure, and the Stability of Political Parties: Party Government in the House," 19 *Legislative Studies Quarterly* 215 (1994).

13. Ronald P. Formisano, *The Transformation of Political Culture: Massachusetts Parties, 1790s–1840s* (New York, 1983); Richard L. McCormick, *The Party Period and Public Policy: American Politics from the Age of Jackson to the Progressive Era* (New York, 1986); George Rogers Taylor, *The Transportation Revolution, 1815–1860* (New York, 1951).

14. Richard R. John, *Spreading the News : The American Postal System from Franklin to Morse* (Cambridge, Mass., 1995), 57.

15. Paul Starr, *The Creation of the Media: Political Origins of Modern Communications* (New York, 2004), 86, 88, 89–90.

16. John, *Spreading the News*, ch. 2.

17. *Federalist*, No. 52, at 342.

18. Harris, *Deadlock or Decision*, 18–19.

19. Richard Allan Baker, *The Senate of the United States: A Bicentennial History* (Malabar, Fla., 1988), 33.

20. U.S. Const. Art. II, Sec. 2, cl. 2.

21. Alexis de Tocqueville, *Democracy in America,* ed. Harvey C. Mansfield and Delba Winthrop (Chicago, 2000 [1835]), Vol. 1, 191.

22. "All Bills for raising Revenue shall originate in the House of Representatives, but the Senate may propose or concur with Amendments as on other Bills." U.S. Const. Art. I, Sec. 7, cl. 1.

23. *Federalist*, No. 58, at 380–81.

24. Wirls and Wirls, *Invention of the United States Senate*, 188–89.

25. U.S. Const. Art. I, Sec. 7, cl. 1 and 2.

26. Haynes, *Senate of the United States,* Vol. 1, 436–37, 442.

27. David R. Mayhew, *America's Congress: Actions in the Public Sphere, James Madison through Newt Gingrich* (New Haven, Conn., 2000), 133–34. See Nelson W. Polsby, *How Congress Evolves: Social Bases of Institutional Change* (New York, 2004).

28. Mayhew, *America's Congress,* 160.

29. Max Farrand, ed., *The Records of the Federal Convention of 1787* (New Haven, Conn., 1966 [1937]), Vol. 1, 49.

30. U.S. Const. Art. I, Sec. 4, cl. 1.

31. Rosemarie Zagarri, *The Politics of Size: Representation in the United States, 1776–1850* (Ithaca, N.Y., 1987), 106–31. By 1842 only ten of twenty-six states elected their representatives by statewide vote. *Id.* at 129.

32. David Brady, "Incrementalism in the People's Branch: The Constitution and the Development of the Policy-Making Process," in Peter F. Nardulli, ed., *The Constitution and American Political Development: An Institutional Perspective* (Urbana, Ill., 1992), 35, 40.

33. *Compare* U.S. Const. Art. I, Sec. 3, cl. 1, *with* U.S. Const. Amend. XVII (1913).

34. *See, e.g.,* Sara Brandes Crook and John R. Hibbing, "A Not-So-Distant Mirror: The 17th Amendment and Congressional Change," 91 *American Political Science Rev.* 845 (1997). *But see* Charles Stewart III, "Responsiveness in the Upper Chamber: The Constitution and the Institutional Development of the Senate," in Nardulli, ed., *Constitution and American Political Development,* 63, 71–77.

35. Elaine K. Swift and David W. Brady, "Common Ground: History and Theories of American Politics," in Lawrence C. Dodd and Calvin Jillson, eds., *The Dynamics of American Politics: Approaches and Interpretations* (Boulder, Colo., 1994), 92–93.

36. U.S. Const. Art. I, Sec. 2, cl. 1.

37. *Federalist,* No. 52, at 345. "Frequent elections are unquestionably the only policy by which this dependence and sympathy can be effectually secured." *Id.*

38. From 1789 to 1890 representatives sworn in for new Congresses had served an average of less than three years in the House, and in the late nineteenth century approximately 40 percent of members were first-termers. By the late 1960s representatives sworn in for new Congresses had served an average of more than nine years in the House, and fewer than 9 percent were first-termers. Richard Franklin Bensel, *Sectionalism and American Political Development, 1880–1980* (Madison, Wisc., 1984), 336–37. Between 1790 and 1798 only 62 percent of incumbent representatives were reelected. Rudolph M. Bell, *Party and Faction in American Politics: The House of Representatives, 1789–1801* (Westport, Conn., 1973), 7–9. In contrast, incumbents won reelection 90 percent of the time since 1945, 95 percent of the time since 1980, and 98 percent of the time since 1998. Since that last year, only about forty seats in the House have been seriously contested. C. Bryan Wilson, "What's a Federalist to Do? The Impending Clash between Textualism and Federalism in State Congressional Redistricting Suits under Article I, Section 4," 53 *Duke L. J.* 1367 n. 1 (2004); Michael P. McDonald and John Samples, "The Marketplace of Democracy: Normative and Empirical Issues," in

Michael P. McDonald and John Samples, eds., *The Marketplace of Democracy: Electoral Competition and American Politics* (Washington, D.C., 2006), 3. *See* Stephen Ansolabehere and James M. Snyder Jr., "Soft Money, Hard Money, Strong Parties," 100 *Columbia L. Rev.* 598 (2000); Gary C. Jacobson, "Competition in U.S. Congressional Elections," in McDonald and Samples, eds., *Marketplace of Democracy,* 27–52.

39. Robin Toner and Kate Zernike, "G.O.P. Faces Peril of Losing House, Strategists Say," *New York Times,* Sept. 4, 2006, A-1, A-11.

40. David H. Rosenbloom, *Building a Legislative-Centered Public Administration: Congress and the Administrative State, 1946–1999* (Tuscaloosa, Ala., 2000), ch. 4; Morris Fiorina, *Congress: Keystone of the Washington Establishment,* 2d ed. (New Haven, Conn., 1989); John Hibbing, *Congressional Careers: Contours of Life in the U.S. House of Representatives* (Chapel Hill, N.C., 1991); Glenn Parker, *Characteristics of Congress* (Englewood Cliffs, N.J., 1989), ch. 5; Brady, "Incrementalism in the People's Branch," in Nardulli, ed., *Constitution and American Political Development,* 35, 57.

41. U.S. Const. Art. I, Sec. 3, cl. 1. The Constitution further protects the states' interest in the Senate by providing that "no State, without its Consent, shall be deprived of its equal Suffrage in the Senate." U.S. Const. Art V.

42. Zagarri, *Politics of Size,* 4–7, 148–49.

43. Wirls and Wirls, *Invention of the United States Senate,* 216–17.

44. Lynn A. Baker and Samuel H. Dinkin, "The Senate: An Institution Whose Time Has Gone?" 13 *Journal of Law & Politics* 21, 24–29, 38–42 (1997).

45. Haynes, *Senate of the United States,* Vol. 2, 1056.

46. Haynes, *Senate of the United States,* Vol. 2, 1060–61.

47. Baker and Dinkin, "The Senate," 46 (emphasis in original deleted).

48. Harris, *Deadlock or Decision,* 129–30.

49. *See* FirstGov.gov at http://www.firstgov.gov/Agencies/Federal/Legislative.shtml (last visited Sept. 25, 2006).

50. Donald R. Matthews, *U.S. Senators & Their World* (New York, 1960), 95–96; Brady, "Incrementalism in the People's Branch," in Nardulli, ed., *Constitution and American Political Development,* 35, 41–43. For changes, *see* Steven S. Smith, *Call to Order: Floor Politics in the House and Senate* (Washington, D.C., 1989), 139–45; Harris, *Deadlock or Decision,* 109–12.

51. David M. Barrett, *The CIA & Congress: The Untold Story from Truman to Kennedy* (Lawrence, Kans., 2005), 22.

52. Roger H. Davidson, "Legislative Research: Mirror of a Discipline," in William Crotty, ed., *Political Science: Looking to the Future* (Evanston, Ill., 1991), Vol. 4, 28.

53. Julian E. Zelizer, *On Capitol Hill: The Struggle to Reform Congress and Its Consequences, 1948–2000* (New York, 2004), 263. *See* Polsby, *How Congress Evolves.*

54. Barbara Sinclair, *Unorthodox Lawmaking: New Legislative Processes in the U. S. Congress,* 2d ed. (Washington, D.C., 2000); Bruce Johnson, "The OMB Budget Examiner and the Congressional Budget Process," 9 *Public Budgeting & Finance* 5 (1989).

55. *See generally* Roger H. Davidson, "The Advent of the Modern Congress: The Legislative Reorganization Act of 1946," 15 *Legislative Studies Quarterly* 357 (1990).

56. Rosenbloom, *Building a Legislative-Centered Public Administration;* Charles Clapp, *The Congressman: His Job As He Sees It* (Washington, D.C., 1963), 84. *See* Mayhew, *Congress,* 31–33; Barry Weingast and William J. Marshall, "The Industrial Organization of Congress; or, Why Legislatures, Like Firms, Are Not Organized as Markets," 96 *Journal of Political Economy* 132 (1988); David Schoenbrod, *Power without Responsibility: How Congress Abuses the People through Delegation* (New Haven, Conn., 1993); Jonathan R. Macey, "Public Choice: The Theory of the Firm and the Theory of Market Exchange," 74 *Cornell L. Rev.* 43, 55 (1988).

57. *See* Fiorina, *Congress,* esp. ch. 5; Robert V. Percival, "Presidential Management of the Administrative State: The Not-So-Unitary Executive," 51 *Duke L. J.* 963 (2001).

58. U.S. Const. Art. II, Sec. 1, cl. 1.

59. Ralph Ketcham, *Presidents above Party: The First American Presidency, 1789–1829* (Chapel Hill, N.C., 1984), 8; Forrest McDonald, *The American Presidency: An Intellectual History* (Lawrence, Kans., 1994), 181.

60. McDonald, *American Presidency,* 190, 198.

61. *Federalist,* Nos. 67–77. Hamilton acknowledged limits on the executive power. *E.g., Federalist,* No. 77, at 497.

62. Gordon S. Wood, *The Creation of the American Republic, 1776–1787* (Chapel Hill, N.C., 1969), 519.

63. Michael A. Genovese, *The Power of the American Presidency, 1789–2000* (New York, 2001), 28.

64. U.S. Const. Art. II, Sec. 1, cl. 1–4.

65. Jethro K. Lieberman, *The Evolving Constitution: How the Supreme Court Has Ruled on Issues from Abortion to Zoning* (New York, 1992), 176. *See Federalist,* No. 68, at 441.

66. Susan Dunn, *Jefferson's Second Revolution: The Election Crisis of 1800 and the Triumph of Republicanism* (Boston, 2004), 275.

67. Jack N. Rakove, "Constitutional Problematics, circa 1787," in John Ferejohn, Jack N. Rakove, and Jonathan Riley, eds., *Constitutional Culture and Democratic Rule* (New York, 2001), 55. On the "management" of the modern president's "image," *see, e.g.,* Martin F. Wattenberg, "The Changing Presidential Media Environment," 34 *Presidential Studies Quarterly* 557 (2004); Jeremy D. Mayer, "The Contemporary Presidency: The Presidency and Image Management: Discipline in Pursuit of Illusion," 34 *Presidential Studies Quarterly* 620 (2004).

68. *See generally* Edward S. Corwin, *The President: Office and Powers, 1789–1957* (New York, 1957); Richard E. Neustadt, *Presidential Power: The Politics of Leadership* (New York, 1960); Richard E. Neustadt, *Presidential Power: The Politics of Leadership from FDR to Carter* (New York, 1980); Lewis L. Gould, *The Modern American Presidency* (Lawrence, Kans., 2003); Robert Dallek, *Hail to the Chief: The Making and Unmaking of American Presidents* (New York, 1996); James Pfiffner, *The Modern Presidency* (New York, 1998); Jeffrey Tulis, *The Rhetorical Presidency* (Princeton, N.J., 1987); Sidney M. Milkis and Michael Nelson, *The American Presidency: Origins and Development, 1776–2002* (Washington, D.C., 2003).

69. *See* Jack D. Warren Jr., "'The Line of My Official Conduct': George Washington and Congress, 1789–1797," in Kenneth R. Bowling and Donald R. Kennon, eds., *Neither Separate But Equal: Congress in the 1790s* (Athens, Ohio, 2000), 238–68.

70. *See, e.g.,* Daniel Farber, *Lincoln's Constitution* (Chicago, 2003).

71. Jon R. Bond and Richard Fleisher, *The President in the Legislative Arena* (Chicago, 1990), 7; Gould, *Modern American Presidency,* chs. 1 and 6.

72. Quoted in Alexander DeConde, *Presidential Machismo: Executive Authority, Military Intervention, and Foreign Relations* (Boston, 2000), 215. Earlier presidents had emphasized the need for the executive to take extraordinary actions to protect national interests, but the powers of the twentieth-century presidency have "incited subsequent presidents and their subordinates to operate outside the law in a sense that is qualitatively different from Locke's federative power or Jefferson's *salus populi.*" McDonald, *American Presidency,* 278.

73. Daniel P. Klinghard, "Grover Cleveland, William McKinley, and the Emergence of the President as Party Leader," 35 *Presidential Studies Quarterly* 736, 749 (2005). *See* Sidney M. Milkis, *The President and the Parties: The Transformation of the American Party System Since the New Deal* (New York, 1993); Sidney M. Milkis, *Political Parties and Constitutional Government: Remaking American Democracy* (Baltimore, Md., 1999).

74. Charles E. Walcott and Karen M. Hult, *Governing the White House: From Hoover through LBJ* (Lawrence, Kans., 1995), 1.

75. In addition, federal expenditures almost doubled to $8.5 billion. Matthew J. Dickinson, *Bitter Harvest: FDR, Presidential Power and the Growth of the Presidential Branch* (New York, 1996), 49–50.

76. Richard Polenberg, *Reorganizing Roosevelt's Government: The Controversy over Executive Reorganization, 1936–1939* (Cambridge, Mass., 1966), 188.

77. U.S. Census Bureau, "Federal Government Employment and Payroll Data," *Federal Government Civilian Employment by Function,* available at http://www.census.gov/govs/www/apesfed.html.

78. FirstGov.gov, The U.S. Government's Official Web Portal, available at http://www.firstgov.gov/Agencies/Federal/Executive.shtml; http://www.firstgov.gov/Agencies/Federal/Independent.shtml; and http://www.firstgov/Agencies/Federal/Quasi-Official.shtml (all last visited Sept. 25, 2006).

79. Walcott and Hult, *Governing the White House,* 9. *See* Charles E. Walcott and Karen M. Hult, "White House Structure and Decision Making: Elaborating the Standard Model," 35 *Presidential Studies Quarterly* 303 (2005).

80. Theodore J. Lowi, *The Personal President: Power Invested, Promise Unfulfilled* (Ithaca, N.Y., 1985), 97, 65; Stephen Skowronek, *The Politics Presidents Make: Leadership from John Adams to Bill Clinton* (Cambridge, Mass., 1997), 50.

81. The president's role as "legislative leader" was based, in constitutional theory, on the provision that authorizes the executive to recommend to Congress "such Measures as he shall judge necessary and expedient." U.S. Const. Art. II, Sec. 3.

82. Milkis, *President and the Parties,* 284.

83. George W. Bush, Remarks at the National Governors' Conference, Feb. 26, 2001, *Public Papers of the Presidents: George W. Bush* (Washington, D.C., 2001), Vol. 1, 132.

84. David E. Sanger, "In Address, Bush Says He Ordered Domestic Spying," *New York Times,* Dec. 18, 2005, A-1; Richard W. Stevenson and Adam Liptak, "Cheney Defends Eavesdropping without Warrants," *New York Times,* Dec. 21, 2005, A-36; William J. Stuntz, "Local Policing after the Terror," 111 *Yale L. J.* 2137 (2002); Susan N. Herman, "Collapsing Spheres: Joint Terrorism Task Forces, Federalism, and the War on Terror," 41 *Willamette L. Rev.* 941 (2005); Scott Shane and Adam Liptak, "Shifting Power to a President," *New York Times,* Sept. 30, 2006, A-1. For the statutes themselves, *see* Uniting and Strengthening America by Providing Appropriate Tools Required to Intercept and Obstruct Terrorism (USA PATRIOT Act), Act of 2001, Pub. L. No. 107-56, 115 Stat. 272 (2001); No Child Left Behind Act of 2001, Pub. L. No. 107-110, 115 Stat. 1425 (2001); Class Action Fairness Act of 2005, Pub. L. No. 109-2, 119 Stat. 4 (2005); Military Commissions Act of 2006, Pub. L. No. 109-366 (2006). For a relatively balanced assessment of the Bush administration's theory of executive power and its relevant foreign policy actions, *see* Michael D. Ramsey, "Torturing Executive Power," 93 *Georgetown L. J.* 1213 (2005).

85. McDonald, *American Presidency,* 283–85.

86. Richard Polenberg, *Fighting Faiths: The Abrams Case, the Supreme Court, and Free Speech* (New York, 1987), 165.

87. American Bar Association, Criminal Justice Section, *The Federalization of Criminal Law,* rep. James A. Strazzella (Washington, D.C., 1998), 9.

88. William G. Howell, *Power without Persuasion: The Politics of Direct Presidential Action* (Princeton, N.J., 2003), 126.

89. Quoted in Adam Liptak, "Presidential Signing Statements, and Alito's Role in Them, Are Questioned," *New York Times,* Jan. 14, 2006, A-11.

90. Phillip J. Cooper, *By Order of the President: The Use & Abuse of Executive Direct Action* (Lawrence, Kans., 2002). For examples of the domestic effect of such directives, *see id.* at, *e.g.,* 145, 162–66, 185–87, 195–96. In 2006 a special committee of the American Bar Association issued a report highly critical of the practice. American Bar Association, Task Force on Presidential Signing Statements and the Separation of Powers Doctrine, http://www.abanet.org/op/signingstatements. The *Wall Street Journal* derided the report as "a transparent political exercise." Editorial, "The ABA's Agenda," *Wall Street Journal,* July 31, 2006, A-10.

91. Howell, *Power without Persuasion,* 112–16.

92. Howell, *Power without Persuasion,* 120–26.

93. Henry P. Monaghan, "The Protective Power of the Presidency," 93 *Columbia L. Rev.* 1, 54 (1993) (emphasis added).

94. *See* Louis Henken, *Foreign Affairs and the United States Constitution,* 2d ed. (New York, 1996); Arthur M. Schlesinger Jr., *The Imperial Presidency* (Boston, 2004 [1973, 1989]).

95. U.S. Const. Art. II, Sec. 2, cl. 2.

96. McDonald, *American Presidency*, 386–90.

97. *Missouri v. Holland*, 252 U.S. 416 (1920); *United States v. Belmont*, 301 U.S. 324 (1937); *United States v. Pink*, 315 U.S. 203 (1942); *Dames & Moore v. Regan*, 453 U.S. 654 (1981). See Curtis A. Bradley, "The Treaty Power and American Federalism," 97 *Michigan L. Rev.* 390 (1998).

98. Cited in Jesse H. Choper, Richard H. Fallon Jr., Yale Kamisar, and Steven H. Shiffrin, eds., *Constitutional Law: Cases-Comments-Questions*, 9th ed. (St. Paul, Minn., 2001), 186, n. "c." The editors also note that a State Department study conducted before 1977 found that 86 percent of all executive agreements were approved by prior statutes or subsequent resolutions of Congress. *Id.* at 186, n. "d." Even Hamilton regarded the power to make treaties as too dangerous to commit solely to the authority of the president. *Federalist*, No. 75, at 487.

99. Evan Criddle, "The Vienna Convention on the Law of Treaties in the U.S. Treaty Interpretation," 44 *Virginia Journal of International Law* 431, 463, 471–73 (2004).

100. *United States v. Curtiss-Wright Export Corp.*, 299 U.S. 304, 318, 320 (1936).

101. U.S. Const. Art. II, Sec. 2 and 3. The scope of the power has never been fully delimited. *See* Henry P. Monaghan, "The Protective Power of the Presidency," 93 *Columbia L. Rev.* 1 (1993).

102. Congress "has never refused a president's initial request for support in employing force and has never declared war except when the executive requested it or already had engaged the armed forces in hostilities." DeConde, *Presidential Machismo*, 288.

103. John T. Rourke and Russell Farnen, "War, Presidents, and the Constitution," 18 *Presidential Studies Quarterly* 513 (1988). *See generally* John Lehman, *Making War: The 200-Year-Old Battle between the President and Congress over How America Goes to War* (New York, 1992); Louis Fisher, *Presidential War Power* (Lawrence, Kans., 1995).

104. *See* John Hart Ely, *War and Responsibility: Constitutional Lessons of Vietnam and Its Aftermath* (Princeton, N.J., 1993), 1–10; David P. Currie, *The Constitution in Congress: The Jeffersonians, 1801–1829* (Chicago, 2001), 123–29. For a thoughtful analysis of the legal issues, *see* William Michael Treanor, "The War Powers Outside the Courts," in Mark Tushnet, ed., *The Constitution in Wartime: Beyond Alarmism and Complacency* (Durham, N.C., 2005).

105. The de facto expansion of executive power altered the relationship between the president and Congress in a variety of ways. In practical terms congressional power "could decline and did." James L. Sundquist, *The Decline and Resurgence of Congress* (Washington, D.C., 1981), 11. The continuous processes of change and interaction meant that "no relationship between president and Congress is ever normal, for the country passes from one special pattern of association to another." *Id.*, 483. Examining the years from 1960 to the mid-1970s, another scholar identified eight noticeable changes in the relationship between Congress and the executive, most of which were traceable "not to laws but to accustomed practices or widespread expectations." They allowed the executive to deal with the other levels and branches "on his terms, not theirs." Richard Neustadt, *Presidential Power and the Modern Presidents: The Politics of*

Leadership from Roosevelt to Reagan (New York, 1990), 192, 199. For a detailed examination of the shifting relationship between Congress and the executive on foreign policy issues since World War II, *see* Robert David Johnson, *Congress and the Cold War* (New York, 2006).

106. Stephen Skowronek, *Building a New American State: The Expansion of National Administrative Capacities, 1877–1920* (New York, 1982), 215–16.

107. Peter J. Westwick, *The National Labs: Science in an American System, 1947–1974* (Cambridge, Mass., 2003); Stuart W. Leslie, "Playing the Education Game to Win: The Military and Interdisciplinary Research at Stanford," 18 *Historical Studies in the Physical Sciences* 55 (1987).

108. *See, e.g.,* Dana Priest, "Jet Is Open Secret in Terror War," *Washington Post,* Dec. 27, 2004, A-1; Patrick Radden Keefe, "Cat-and Mouse Games," 52 *New York Rev. of Books* 41 (May 26, 2005), reviewing William M. Arkin, *Code Names: Deciphering US Military Plans, Programs, and Operations in the 9/11 World* (Hanover, N.H., 2005); William G. Weaver and Robert M. Pallitto, "*The Law:* 'Extraordinary Rendition' and Presidential Fiat," 36 *Presidential Studies Quarterly* 102 (2006).

109. *See generally, e.g.,* Christopher N. May, *In the Name of War: Judicial Review and the War Powers Since 1918* (Cambridge, Mass., 1989). For a recent example, *see* Eric Schmitt, "Justice Department Backs Pentagon on Air Guard Changes," *New York Times,* Friday, Aug. 12, 2005, A-13 (Justice Department supports authority of Pentagon to move National Guard units without consent of state governors in spite of protests from two dozen states about the detrimental effects of the planned moves).

110. Adam Liptak, "Author of '02 Memo on Torture: 'Gentle' Soul for a Harsh Topic," *New York Times,* June 24, 2004, A-1; Adam Liptak, "Legal Scholars Criticize Memos on Torture," *New York Times,* June 25, 2004, A-14; David Johnston and James Risen, "Aides Say Memo Backed Coercion Already in Use," *New York Times,* June 27, 2004, A-1; letter from Hon. Alberto R. Gonzales, U.S. attorney general, to Hon. William H. Frist, majority leader, U.S. Senate (Jan. 19, 2006), transmitting U.S. Department of Justice, "Legal Authorities Supporting the Activities of the National Security Agency Described by the President" (Jan. 19, 2006), http://purl.access.gpo. gov/GPO/LPS66493. For a variety of legal analyses, *see* "Symposium: War, Terrorism, and Torture: Limits on Presidential Power in the 21st Century," 81 *Indiana L. J.* 1139 (2006).

111. Greg Robinson, *By Order of the President: FDR and the Internment of Japanese Americans* (Cambridge, Mass., 2001), 90–92.

112. Peter Irons, *Justice at War* (New York, 1983).

113. "Whatever other uncertainties may exist about the founding generation's vision of the American presidency, no reasonable doubt existed on one point: the President possessed no independent law-making power." Monaghan, "Protective Power of the Presidency," 15. *See, e.g.,* Stephen Grey, *Ghost Plane: The True Story of the C.I.A. Torture Program* (New York, 2007).

114. John Adams to Roger Sherman, July 17, 1789, Part III, reprinted in John

Patrick Diggins, ed., *The Portable John Adams* (New York, 2004), 401. *See* Lowi, *Personal President;* Cass R. Sunstein, "An Eighteenth Century Presidency in a Twenty-First Century World," 48 *Arkansas L. Rev.* 1 (1995).

115. St. George Tucker, *View of the Constitution of the United States with Selected Writings,* ed. Clyde N. Wilson (Indianapolis, Ind., 1999), 262. *See* Samuel P. Huntington, "Political Development and Political Decay," 17 *World Politics* 386 (1965).

116. Woodrow Wilson, *An Old Master and Other Political Essays* (New York, 1893), 160, 152.

117. The Judiciary Act of 1789, which established the federal judicial system, evidenced the extent to which attitudes about a national judiciary had changed in only two years since the Philadelphia Convention. Maeva Marcus and Natalie Wexler, "The Judiciary Act of 1789: Political Compromise or Constitutional Interpretation?" in Maeva Marcus, ed., *Origins of the Federal Judiciary: Essays on the Judiciary Act of 1789* (New York, 1992), 29, 30.

118. Article III judges "shall hold their Offices during good Behavior, and shall, at stated Times, receive for their Services a Compensation, which shall not be diminished during their Continuance in Office." U.S. Const. Art. III, Sec. 1

119. *See, e.g.,* Gordon G. Young, "Public Rights and the Federal Judicial Power: From *Murray's Lessee* through *Crowell* to *Schor*," 35 *Buffalo L. Rev.* 765 (1987); Richard Fallon Jr., "Of Legislative Courts, Administrative Agencies and Article III," 101 *Harvard L. Rev.* 916 (1988).

120. *See generally, e.g.,* Felix Frankfurter and James M. Landis, *The Business of the Supreme Court: A Study in the Federal Judicial System* (New York, 1928); Edward A. Purcell Jr., "Reconsidering the Frankfurterian Paradigm: Reflections on Histories of Lower Federal Courts," 24 *Law & Social Inquiry* 679 (1999); Judith Resnik, "History, Jurisdiction, and the Federal Courts: Changing Contexts, Selective Memories, and Limited Imagination," 98 *West Virginia L. Rev.* 171 (1995). Even when "state" law formally controlled an issue, the state courts frequently deferred to national law and adopted the views of the U.S. Supreme Court. Robert M. Howard, Scott E. Graves, and Julianne Flowers, "State Courts, the U.S. Supreme Court, and the Protection of Civil Liberties," 40 *Law and Society Rev.* 845 (2006).

121. *See* Peter Graham Fish, *The Politics of Federal Judicial Administration* (Princeton, N.J., 1973); Alpheus T. Mason, *William Howard Taft: Chief Justice* (New York, 1964).

122. Judith Resnik, "The Programmatic Judiciary: Lobbying, Judging, and Invalidating the Violence against Women Act," 74 *Southern California L. Rev.* 269, 275 (2000). *See* Judith Resnik, "'Uncle Sam Modernizes His Justice': Inventing the Federal District Courts of the Twentieth Century for the District of Columbia and the Nation," 90 *Georgetown L. J.* 607 (2002); Judith Resnik, "Trial as Error, Jurisdiction as Injury: Transforming the Meaning of Article III," 113 *Harvard L. Rev.* 924 (2000).

123. *United States v. Morrison,* 529 U.S. 598 (2000).

124. The judiciary's growing political salience in the twentieth century spurred both the executive and legislative branches to reconsider their roles in the appointment pro-

cess. *See, e.g.,* Henry J. Abraham, *Justices, Presidents, and Senators: A History of the U.S. Supreme Court Appointments from Washington to Clinton,* rev. ed. (New York, 1999); David Alistair Yalof, *Pursuit of Justices: Presidential Politics and the Selection of Supreme Court Nominees* (Chicago, 1999); Sheldon Goldman, *Picking Federal Judges: Lower Court Selection from Roosevelt through Reagan* (New Haven, Conn., 1997); Nancy Scherer, *Scoring Points: Politicians, Activists, and the Lower Federal Court Appointment Process* (Palo Alto, Calif., 2005).

125. In 2004, for example, the Supreme Court disposed of 85 cases; the courts of appeal terminated 56,243; and the district courts terminated 241,864. Chief Justice John G. Roberts Jr., "2005 Year-End Report on the Federal Judiciary," at 7, available at http://www.supremecourtus.gov/publicinfo/year-end/2005year-endreport.pdf; Administrative Office of the United States Courts, "Federal Judicial Caseload Statistics, March 31, 2005," at 6, available at http://uscourts.gov/caseload2005/contents.html (last visited Oct. 2, 2006).

126. John F. Preis, "An Empirical Assessment of Federal Question Jurisdiction," available at SSRN.com/author=591835, at 13–14 (last visited Sept. 21, 2006). *See* Arthur D. Hellman, "Never the Same River Twice: The Empirics and Epistemology of Intercircuit Conflicts," 63 *University of Pittsburgh L. Rev.* 81 (2001).

127. Purcell, "Reconsidering the Frankfurterian Paradigm, 724–27.

128. Jean Edward Smith, *John Marshall: Definer of a Nation* (New York, 1996), 284.

129. Smith, *John Marshall,* 292–95; G. Edward White, *The Marshall Court and Cultural Change, 1815–1835* (New York, 1988), 186–89.

130. The events brought the Court to "a new low point." Michael J. Klarman, "How Great Were the 'Great' Marshall Court Decisions?" 87 *Virginia L. Rev.* 1111, 1180 (2001).

131. Barry Friedman, "The History of the Countermajoritarian Difficulty, Part One: The Road to Judicial Supremacy," 73 *New York University L. Rev.* 333 (1998); Barry Friedman, "The Birth of an Academic Obsession: The History of the Counter-majoritarian Difficulty, Part Five," 112 *Yale L. J.* 153 (2002). The Court's claim to such authority remains contested. *See, e.g.,* Robert C. Post and Reva B. Siegel, "Legislative Constitutionalism and Section Five Power: Policentric Interpretation of the Family and Medical Leave Act," 112 *Yale L. J.* 1943 (2003).

132. *See, e.g.,* Sylvia Snowiss, *Judicial Review and the Law of the Constitution* (New Haven, Conn., 1990); Christopher Wolfe, *The Rise of Modern Judicial Review: From Constitutional Interpretation to Judge-Made Law,* rev. ed. (Lanham, Md., 1994); Robert Lowry Clinton, *Marbury v. Madison and Judicial Review* (Lawrence, Kans., 1989); William E. Nelson, *Marbury v. Madison: The Origins and Legacy of Judicial Review* (Lawrence, Kans., 2000); Larry D. Kramer, *The People Themselves: Popular Constitutionalism and Judicial Review* (New York, 2004).

133. *Cooper v. Aaron,* 358 U.S. 1 (1958); *Board of Trustees of the University of Alabama v. Garrett,* 531 U.S. 356 (2001).

134. *Bush v. Gore,* 531 U.S. 98 (2000).

135. As early as 1885 Woodrow Wilson blamed the Court for the excessive growth of congressional power. Woodrow Wilson, *Congressional Government: A Study in American Politics* (Boston, 1885), 23.

136. *See* Edward A. Purcell Jr., *Brandeis and the Progressive Constitution: Erie, the Judicial Power, and the Politics of the Federal Courts in Twentieth-Century America* (New Haven, Conn., 2000), 39–46, 51–63; H. W. Perry Jr., *Deciding to Decide: Agenda Setting in the United States Supreme Court* (Cambridge, Mass., 1991); Edward A. Hartnett, "Questioning Certiorari: Some Reflections Seventy-Five Years after the Judges' Bill," 100 *Columbia L. Rev.* 1643, 1731–33 (2000); Jonathan T. Molot, "Principled Minimalism: Restriking the Balance between Judicial Minimalism and Neutral Principles," 90 *Virginia L. Rev.* 1753, 1785–86 (2004); Amy Coney Barrett, "The Supervisory Power of the Supreme Court," 106 *Columbia L. Rev.* 324 (2006).

137. *E.g.*, Sinclair, *Transformation of the U.S. Senate*, 212.

138. *See* Gary Lawson, "The Rise and Rise of the Administrative State," 107 *Harvard L. Rev.* 1231 (1994).

139. *See generally* Lawrence M. Friedman, *A History of American Law*, 2d ed. (New York, 1985), Part III, ch. 5; Kermit L. Hall, *The Magic Mirror: Law in American History* (New York, 1989), ch. 10; Skowronek, *Building a New American State;* Robert L. Rabin, "Federal Regulation in Historical Perspective," 38 *Stanford L. Rev.* 1189 (1986); Morton Keller, *Regulating a New Economy: Public Policy and Economic Change in America, 1900–1933* (Cambridge, Mass., 1990); Robert Harrison, *State and Society in Twentieth Century America* (London, 1997).

140. The states, of course, were also expanding their own administrative capacities throughout the period. Friedman, *History of American Law*, Part III, ch. 5.

141. Felix Frankfurter, *The Public and Its Government* (Boston, 1964 [1930]), 161; G. Edward White, *Patterns of American Legal Thought* (Indianapolis, Ind., 1978), 227–87.

142. *See* Morton J. Horwitz, *The Transformation of American Law, 1870–1960: The Crisis of Legal Orthodoxy* (New York, 1992), ch. 8; Schoenbrod, *Power without Responsibility.*

143. Reuel E. Schiller, "Enlarging the Administrative Polity: Administrative Law and the Changing Definition of Pluralism, 1945–1970," 53 *Vanderbilt L. Rev.* 1389 (2000); Reuel E. Schiller, "Reining in the Administrative State: World War II and the Decline of Expert Administration," in Daniel R. Ernst and Victor Jew, eds., *Total War and the Law: The American Home Front in World War II* (Westport, Conn., 2002), 185–206.

144. David E. Lewis, *Presidents and the Politics of Agency Design: Political Insulation in the United States Government Bureaucracy, 1946–1997* (Stanford, Calif., 2003).

145. William J. Novak, *The People's Welfare: Law and Regulation in Nineteenth-Century America* (Chapel Hill, N.C., 1996), 235.

146. It is essential to note that the states were "in decline" only in a relative sense, compared with the expanding powers of the national government and the cities. *See,*

e.g., William R. Brock, *Investigation and Responsibility: Public Responsibility in the United States, 1865–1900* (New York, 1984). Throughout American history and into the twenty-first century the states remained energetic and powerful governmental forces, and they continued to hold extensive power and responsibility over many of the most significant areas of public life, including housing, education, social welfare, police and fire protection, use and conservation of natural resources, zoning and land development planning, and labor relations and employment practices. In addition, state law remained largely in control of critical areas of American life, including marriage and family, commercial transactions, estate planning and inheritance, use of automobiles and highways, criminal justice and corrections, and most broad common-law issues involving torts, contracts, and property.

147. *See, e.g.,* Jon C. Teaford, *Unheralded Triumph: City Government in America, 1870–1900* (Baltimore, Md., 1984); Stuart M. Blumin, *The Emergence of the Middle Class: Social Experience in the American City, 1760–1900* (New York, 1989); Zane L. Miller, *The Urbanization of Modern America: A Brief History* (New York, 1973); Jon C. Teaford, *City and Suburb: The Political Fragmentation of Metropolitan America, 1850–1970* (Baltimore, Md., 1979).

148. Jon C. Teaford, *The Rise of the States: Evolution of American State Government* (Baltimore, Md., 2002), 159.

149. Philip B. Kurland, "The Impotence of Reticence," 1968 *Duke L. J.* 619, 620.

150. Teaford, *Rise of the States,* ch. 8; Mavis Mann Reeves, "The States as Polities: Reformed, Reinvigorated, Resourceful," 509 *Annals of the American Academy of Political and Social Sciences* 83 (1990); Leon D. Epstein, "The Old States in a New System," in Anthony King, ed., *The New American Political System* (Washington, D.C., 1978), 325–69; David B. Walker, *The Rebirth of Federalism: Slouching toward Washington,* 2d ed. (New York, 2000), ch. 9.

151. On racial relations *see, e.g.,* Adam Fairclough, *Better Day Coming: Blacks and Equality, 1890–2000* (New York, 2001); Laughlin McDonald, *A Voting Rights Odyssey: Black Enfranchisement in Georgia* (New York, 2003); Michael J. Klarman, *From Jim Crow to Civil Rights: The Supreme Court and the Struggle for Racial Equality* (New York, 2004).

152. Although faith in such possibilities grew, many remained skeptical and wary. *See, e.g.,* Nate Blakeslee, *Tulia: Race, Cocaine, and Corruption in a Small Texas Town* (New York, 2005); Peter Irons, *Jim Crow's Children: The Broken Promise of the Brown Decision* (New York, 2002); McDonald, *Voting Rights Odyssey.*

153. Susan A. MacManus, "Federalism and Intergovernmental Relations: The Centralization versus Decentralization Debate Continues," in Crotty, ed., *Political Science,* Vol. 4, 212–15; Paul E. Peterson, *The Price of Federalism* (Washington, D.C., 1995), 83.

154. Developments included calls for broader intrastate regional cooperation and organization. *See, e.g.,* David J. Barron, Gerald E. Frug, and Rick T. Su, *Dispelling the Myth of Home Rule: Local Power in Greater Boston* (Cambridge, Mass., 2004); Richard Briffault, "Home Rule and Local Political Innovation," 22 *Journal of Law & Politics* 1 (2006).

155. In spite of its "profederalism" rhetoric, for example, the Rehnquist Court continued to expand the reach of national law. *E.g., United States v. Locke,* 529 U.S. 89 (2000); *Geier v. American Honda Co.,* 529 U.S. 861 (2000); *Crosby v. National Foreign Trade Council,* 530 U.S. 363 (2000). *See generally* Richard H. Fallon Jr., "The 'Conservative' Paths of the Rehnquist Court's Federalism Decisions," 69 *University of Chicago L. Rev.* 429 (2002); Ernest A. Young, "The Rehnquist Court's Two Federalisms," 83 *Texas L. Rev.* 1 (2004).

Chapter 8. Contested Authorities

1. Letter from James Madison to Thomas Jefferson, June 30, 1789, *The Papers of Thomas Jefferson,* Julian P. Boyd, ed. (Princeton, N.J., 1958), Vol. 15, 224.

2. Max Farrand, ed., *The Records of the Federal Convention of 1787* (New Haven, Conn., 1966 [1937]), Vol. 1, 21 [hereafter, "Farrand, *Records*"].

3. *E.g.,* Farrand, *Records,* Vol. 1, 73–74, 78.

4. Farrand, *Records,* Vol. 1, 165. *See id.,* Vol. 1, 164–68; *id.,* Vol. 2, 382. Madison argued that the congressional veto was "the most mild & certain means of preserving the harmony of the system." *Id.,* Vol. 2, 28.

5. Farrand, *Records,* Vol. 1, 131–40; *id.,* Vol. 2, 73–80, 294–95, 298, 382.

6. Farrand, *Records,* Vol. 2, 28–29.

7. U.S. Const. Art. VI, cl. 2 ("supreme Law") and cl. 3 ("bound by Oath").

8. Larry D. Kramer, *The People Themselves: Popular Constitutionalism and Judicial Review* (New York, 2004), 105–114; Larry D. Kramer, "Foreword: We the Court," 115 *Harvard L. Rev.* 5 (2001), 16–74; James Roger Sharp, *American Politics in the Early Republic: The New Nation in Crisis* (New Haven, Conn., 1993), 124–25, 130.

9. 17 U.S. (4 Wheat.) 316 (1819).

10. 60 U.S. (19 How.) 393 (1857).

11. *See generally* Kramer, *The People Themselves.* But see William Michael Treanor, "Judicial Review before *Marbury*," 58 *Stanford L. Rev.* 455 (2005).

12. *Accord* James Wilson, speech in the Pennsylvania ratifying convention, Jonathan Elliot, ed., *The Debates in the State Conventions on the Adoption of the Federal Constitution,* 2d ed. (New York, 1987 [1888]), Vol. 2, 445–46, 489 [hereafter, "Elliot, *Debates*"].

13. Alexander Hamilton, John Jay, and James Madison, *The Federalist,* ed. Edward Mead Earle (New York, 1937), No. 78, at 506 [hereafter, "*Federalist*"].

14. *Federalist,* No. 78, at 505. *Accord id.,* No. 22, at 138–39.

15. 5 U.S. (1 Cranch) 137 (1803). On the Marshall Court *see* George L. Haskins and Herbert A Johnson, *Foundations of Power: John Marshall, 1801–15* (New York, 1981); G. Edward White, *The Marshall Court and Cultural Change, 1815–35* (New York, 1988); Herbert A. Johnson, *The Chief Justiceship of John Marshall, 1801–1835* (Columbia, S.C., 1997).

16. Ideas about judicial review evolved in a slow and complicated manner, and the practice of judicial review changed substantially over the years. *See, e.g.,* Mary Sarah

Bilder, *The Transatlantic Constitution: Colonial Legal Culture and the Empire* (Cambridge, Mass., 2004); John Phillip Reid, *Constitutional History of the American Revolution: The Authority of Law*, 4 volumes (Madison, Wisc., 1986–93); Daniel J. Hulsebosch, *Constituting Empire: New York and the Transformation of Constitutionalism in the Atlantic World, 1664–1830* (Chapel Hill, N.C., 2005); Sylvia Snowiss, *Judicial Review and the Law of the Constitution* (New Haven, Conn., 1990); Shannon C. Stimson, *The American Revolution in the Law: Anglo-American Jurisprudence before John Marshall* (London, 1990); Christopher Wolfe, *The Rise of Modern Judicial Review: From Constitutional Interpretation to Judge-Made Law* (New York, 1986); Robert A. Burt, *The Constitution in Conflict* (Cambridge, Mass., 1992).

17. "Essays of Brutus," No. XI, in Herbert J. Storing, ed., *The Complete Anti-Federalist* (Chicago, 1981), Vol. 2, 420.

18. "Essays of Brutus," No. XI, in Storing, ed. *Complete Anti-Federalist*, Vol. 2, 420.

19. *E.g.*: Philip B. Kurland, *Politics, the Constitution, and the Warren Court* (Chicago, 1970), 57; Robert H. Bork, *The Tempting of America: The Political Seduction of the Law* (New York, 1990), 129; Robert F. Nagel, *The Implosion of American Federalism* (New York, 2001), 11.

20. Stanley Elkins and Eric McKitrick, *The Age of Federalism: The Early American Republic, 1788–1800* (New York, 1993), 703, 693. On the jurisprudence of the Federalists, *see* Stephen B. Presser, *The Original Misunderstanding: The English, the Americans and the Dialectic of Federalist Jurisprudence* (Durham, N.C., 1991), esp. 118–20, 162, 174, 178; Andrew Lenner, "A Tale of Two Constitutions: Nationalism in the Federalist Era," 40 *American Journal of Legal History* 72, 104–05 (1996). The Republicans shared many of the attitudes that marked the Federalists, including their hostility to parties and their belief that men of "virtue" should govern, though their social bases and oppositional stance led them toward relatively more flexible and tolerant views. *See, e.g.*, Sharp, *American Politics*, 135–36, 157–59, 187–88, 192–94, 216–17, 231–32, 273–74, 276; Joanne B. Freeman, "Explaining the Unexplainable: The Cultural Context of the Sedition Act," in Meg Jacobs, William J. Novak, and Julian E. Zelizer, eds., *The Democratic Experiment: New Directions in American Political History* (Princeton, N.J., 2003), 20–49.

21. Elkins and McKitrick, *Age of Federalism*, 693.

22. In 1797 and 1798 war with France threatened, and many Federalists sought to use the situation to establish a national army that could intimidate their political opponents and possibly even invade the South. Stephen G. Kurtz, *The Presidency of John Adams: The Collapse of Federalism, 1795–1800* (Philadelphia, Pa., 1957), ch. 14.

23. Charles Warren, *The Supreme Court in United States History* (Boston, 1922), Vol. 1, 158–68; Kathryn Preyer, "Jurisdiction to Punish: Federal Authority, Federalism and the Common Law of Crimes in the Early Republic," 4 *Law and History Rev.* 223, 229–31, 236–37 (1986); Sharp, *American Politics*, 169; Joyce Appleby, *Capitalism and a New Social Order: The Republican Vision of the 1790s* (New York, 1984), 5–6. *See id.* at 5–14, 58–61, 66–67, 75–77, 79–80, 93–94.

24. Because the Court was composed entirely of Federalist judges, none of those convicted sought review. Geoffrey R. Stone, *Perilous Times: Free Speech in Wartime from the Sedition Act of 1798 to the War on Terrorism* (New York, 2004), 47–48, 63, 68.

25. James F. Simon, *What Kind of Nation: Thomas Jefferson, John Marshall, and the Epic Struggle to Create a United States* (New York, 2002), 53–55; Jean Edward Smith, *John Marshall: Definer of a Nation* (New York, 1996), 284 and works cited at 610 n. 18.

26. Richard E. Ellis, *The Jeffersonian Crisis: Courts and Politics in the Young Republic* (New York, 1971); Simon, *What Kind of Nation;* Sharp, *American Politics,* chs. 8–11.

27. Hamilton, Patterson, and Washington all participated in the Philadelphia Convention; Marshall was a major advocate of the Constitution in the Virginia ratifying convention; and Adams, though a critic of the Constitution while serving as the nation's envoy to Great Britain from 1785 to 1788, returned to become Washington's vice president and a leader of the Federalist Party. While the support of Hamilton, Patterson, and Adams for the Alien and Sedition Acts was clear, the position of Washington and Marshall was less certain. The former played no active role, but he seemed to lend his support by privately conveying his views that some newspapers had long deserved punishment for their criticisms of Federalist leaders. David McCullough, *John Adams* (New York, 2001), 506. Marshall tried to avoid taking a firm stand while running for Congress in 1798. His opponent challenged the constitutionality of the Alien and Sedition Acts, but Marshall refused to do so. The evidence suggests that Marshall did not regard the statutes as unconstitutional. Simon, *What Kind of Nation,* 56; R. Kent Newmyer, *John Marshall and the Heroic Age of the Supreme Court* (Baton Rouge, La., 2001), 122–26, 172 n. 39. Smith, *John Marshall,* 239, 263, suggests that, at some later point, Marshall did develop constitutional doubts about the statutes.

28. [James Madison], "Virginia Report of 1799," in *The Virginia Report of 1799–1800, Touching the Alien and Sedition Laws* (New York, 1970 [1850]), 196 [hereafter, "*Virginia Report*"]. His criticism of judicial review in 1798 contrasted with the criticism he had expressed in 1787. Letter from James Madison to Thomas Jefferson, Oct. 24, 1787, in Robert A. Rutland *et al.,* eds., *The Papers of James Madison* (Chicago, 1977), Vol. 10, 211 [hereafter "*Papers of James Madison*"].

29. "Resolutions of Virginia," in *Virginia Report,* 22–23. The language quoted was addressed specifically to the Alien Act. The Virginia Report, often referred to as Madison's "Report of 1800," is reprinted in *Papers of James Madison,* ed. David B. Mattern *et al.* (Charlottesville, Va., 1991), Vol. 17, 303ff.

30. "Resolutions of Kentucky Legislature," in *Virginia Report,* 162, 164.

31. For a history of the idea of "states' rights" *see* Forrest McDonald, *States' Rights and the Union: Imperium in Imperio, 1776–1876* (Lawrence, Kans., 2000).

32. Farrand, *Records,* Vol. 2, 93.

33. *Federalist,* No. 39, at 249. On Madison's changing views *see* Robert A. Burt, *The Constitution in Conflict* (Cambridge, Mass., 1992), ch. 2; Jack N. Rakove, "Judicial Power in the Constitutional Theory of James Madison," 43 *William and Mary L. Rev.* 1513 (2002).

34. Letter from Thomas Jefferson to James Madison, June 20, 1787, *Papers of James Madison,* Vol. 10, 64; letter from Thomas Jefferson to James Madison, Oct. 17, 1788, *Papers of Thomas Jefferson,* ed. Julian Boyd (Princeton, N.J., 1958), Vol. 11, 659. On the evolution of Jefferson's politics, *see* R. B. Bernstein, *Thomas Jefferson* (New York, 2003), chs. 4–7.

35. Letter from Thomas Jefferson to James Madison, March 15, 1789, *Papers of James Madison,* Vol. 12, 13.

36. *Federalist,* No. 28, at 174. Hamilton made similar statements in the New York ratifying convention. *See* Elliot, *Debates,* Vol. 2, 239, 253, 304–05.

37. As late as 1798, for example, John Marshall "had not yet fully formulated his theory, set forth in *Marbury,* that constitutional questions of a legal nature were the exclusive prerogative of the Supreme Court." Newmyer, *John Marshall,* 103.

38. The states' rights views of Jefferson and Madison retained national influence through much of the antebellum period. H. Jefferson Powell, "The Principles of '98: An Essay in Historical Retrieval," 80 *Virginia L. Rev.* 689, 692–96 (1994). *See, e.g.,* Elizabeth Kelley Bauer, *Commentaries on the Constitution, 1790–1860* (New York, 1952); Theodore W. Ruger, "'A Question Which Convulses a Nation': The Early Republic's Greatest Debate about the Judicial Review Power," 117 *Harvard L. Rev.* 826 (2004).

39. *E.g., Marbury v. Madison,* 5 U.S. (1 Cranch) 137 (1803); *Martin v. Hunter's Lessee,* 14 U.S. (1 Wheat.) 304 (1816); *Osborn v. Bank of the United States,* 22 U.S. (9 Wheat.) 738 (1824).

40. Although antebellum states' rights advocates appealed to Jefferson and Madison, neither of those two founders advocated secession. *See, e.g.,* letter from Thomas Jefferson to John Taylor, June 1, 1798, *The Writings of Thomas Jefferson,* ed. Paul Leicester Ford (New York, 1896), Vol. 7, 263–66; letter from Thomas Jefferson to Elbridge Gerry, May 13, 1797, *id.,* 122–23.

41. "Hampden" [Spencer Roane], Essay No. 4, in Gerald Gunther, ed., *John Marshall's Defense of* McCulloch v. Maryland (Stanford, Calif., 1969), 147, 148 (emphasis in original).

42. John Taylor, *Tyranny Unmasked,* ed. F. Thornton Miller (Indianapolis, Ind., 1992 [1822]), 203–04, 207, 211.

43. John C. Calhoun, "The Fort Hill Address," in Ross M. Lence, ed., *Union and Liberty: The Political Philosophy of John C. Calhoun* (Indianapolis, Ind., 1992 [1831]), 380.

44. John C. Calhoun, "South Carolina Exposition and Protest," in Lence, ed., *Union and Liberty,* 348.

45. Quoted in Newmyer, *John Marshall,* 353.

46. On the Webster-Hayne debate, *see* Robert V. Remini, *Daniel Webster: The Man and His Time* (New York, 1997), ch. 18.

47. "Speech of Mr. Hayne, of South Carolina" (Jan. 27, 1830), in Herman Belz, ed., *The Webster-Hayne Debate on the Nature of the Union: Selected Documents* (Indianapolis, Ind., 2000), 169 (emphasis in original).

48. "Speech of Mr. Hayne," in Belz, ed., *Webster-Hayne Debate,* 170.

49. James Kent, "A Lecture, Introductory to a Course of Law Lectures in Columbia College" (Feb. 2, 1824), in Perry Miller, ed., *The Legal Mind in America: From Independence to the Civil War* (New York, 1962), 104, 103.

50. Joseph Story, "Address Delivered before the Members of the Suffolk Bar, at Their Anniversary on the 4th September, 1821, at Boston," in Miller, ed., *Legal Mind in America*, 63, 70, 73–74, 75. *See* R. Kent Newmyer, *Supreme Court Justice Joseph Story: Statesman of the Old Republic* (Chapel Hill, N.C., 1985), 95, 99, 109, 114, 188, 191, 193, 256.

51. Joseph Story, *Commentaries on the Constitution of the United States* (Boston, 1833), Vol. 1, 347.

52. "Speech of Mr. Webster, of Massachusetts" (Jan. 26 and 27, 1830), in Belz, ed., *Webster-Hayne Debate*, 137.

53. Herman Belz, "Foreword," in Belz, ed., *Webster-Hayne Debate*, xii. *See* James M. Banner Jr., *To the Hartford Convention: The Federalists and the Origins of Party Politics in Massachusetts, 1789–1815* (New York, 1970). Some northern states would again raise the banner of states' rights and nullification before the Civil War as part of their efforts to combat southern political power and enforcement of the federal fugitive slave laws. *See* Thomas D. Morris, *Free Men All: The Personal Liberty Laws of the North, 1780–1861* (Baltimore, Md., 1974); Stanley W. Campbell, *The Slave Catchers: Enforcement of the Fugitive Slave Law, 1850–1860* (Chapel Hill, N.C., 1970).

54. Quoted in Warren, *Supreme Court in United States History*, Vol. 2, 229.

55. On the development of theories about "levels" of scrutiny, *see* Jeffrey M. Shaman, *Constitutional Interpretation: Illusion and Reality* (Westport, Conn., 2001), 74–102; Jeffrey M. Shaman, "Cracks in the Structure: The Coming Breakdown of the Levels of Scrutiny," 45 *Ohio State L. J.* 161 (1984); G. Edward White, "Historicizing Judicial Scrutiny," 57 *South Carolina L. Rev.* 1 (2005).

56. On the increasing acceptance of judicial review at the state level during the first half of the nineteenth century, *see* William E. Nelson, "Changing Conceptions of Judicial Review: The Evolution of Constitutional Theory in the States, 1790–1860," 120 *University of Pennsylvania L. Rev.* 1166 (1972).

57. William M. Wiecek, *The Lost World of Classical Legal Thought: Law and Ideology in America, 1886–1937* (New York, 1998), chs. 2–3; Loren P. Beth, *The Development of the American Constitution, 1877–1917* (New York, 1971).

58. Quoted in Michael G. Kammen, *A Machine That Would Go of Itself: The Constitution in American Culture* (New York, 1986), 17.

59. David J. Brewer, "The Nation's Anchor," 57 *Albany L. J.* 166 (1898).

60. Thomas M. Cooley, *General Principles of Constitutional Law in the United States of America* (Boston, 1880), 143–44.

61. Woodrow Wilson, *Congressional Government: A Study in American Politics* (Boston, 1885), 33–34.

62. *See* Jack N. Rakove, "The Origins of Judicial Review: A Plea for New Contexts," 49 *Stanford L. Rev.* 1031, 1041–50 (1997); Lance Banning, *The Sacred Fire of Liberty: James Madison and the Founding of the Federal Republic* (Ithaca, N.Y., 1995), 118.

63. Letter from James Madison to George Washington, April 16, 1787, *Papers of James Madison,* Vol. 9, 383–84. *Accord* Farrand, *Records,* Vol. 1, 164.

64. Treanor, "Judicial Review," 561.

65. *Federalist,* No. 39, at 247.

66. *Federalist,* No. 62, at 402 (Madison, or possibly Hamilton). *Accord* letter from James Madison to Thomas Jefferson, Oct. 24, 1787, *Papers of James Madison,* Vol. 10, 210.

67. "A Democratic Federalist" [probably Tench Coxe], in Colleen A. Sheehan and Gary L. McDowell, eds., *Friends of the Constitution: Writings of the 'Other' Federalists, 1787–1788* (Indianapolis, Ind., 1998), 352 (emphasis in original). *Accord* "An American Citizen" [Tench Coxe], *id.* at 262; "A Freeman" [Tench Coxe], *id.* at 99; John Dickinson, "Letters of Fabius," reprinted in Farrand, *Records,* Vol. 3, 304; Elliot, *Debates,* Vol. 2, 26 (speeches of Mr. Cabot and Mr. Parsons); Elliot, *Debates,* Vol. 2, 461 (James Wilson).

68. Antebellum southerners agreed in principle with Madison's original conception of the Senate. St. George Tucker, *View of the Constitution of the United States with Selected Writings* (Indianapolis, Ind., 1999 [1803]), 98; "Hampden" [Spencer Roane], Essay No. 4, in Gunther, ed., *John Marshall's Defense,* 144–46; John C. Calhoun, "A Discourse on the Constitution and Government of the United States," in Lence, ed., *Union and Liberty,* 125.

69. *Dred Scott v. Sandford,* 60 U.S. (19 How.) 393 (1857).

70. Each of the justices wrote separately. *See* the excellent study by Don E. Fehrenbacher, *The Dred Scott Case: Its Significance in American Law & Politics* (New York, 1978).

71. *Ex parte Virginia,* 100 U.S. (10 Otto) 339, 345 (1880).

72. *Slaughter-House Cases,* 83 U.S. (16 Wall.) 36, 71 (1873). *See* Ronald M. Labbe and Jonathan Lurie, *The Slaughterhouse Cases: Regulation, Reconstruction, and the Fourteenth Amendment* (Lawrence, Kans., 2003); William E. Nelson, *The Fourteenth Amendment: From Political Principle to Judicial Doctrine* (Cambridge, Mass., 1988), chs. 3–6.

73. Edward A. Purcell Jr., "The Particularly Dubious Case of *Hans v. Louisiana:* An Essay on Law, Race, History, and 'Federal Courts,'" 81 *North Carolina L. Rev.* 1927, 1975–2039 (2003). Some historians have argued that the Court's decisions were shaped by the justices' views of federalism. *See, e.g.,* Michael Les Benedict, "Preserving the Constitution: The Conservative Basis of Radical Reconstruction," 61 *Journal of American History* 65 (1974); William E. Nelson, *The Roots of American Bureaucracy, 1830–1900* (Cambridge, Mass., 1982), 80. For contrary views, *see* Michael Kent Curtis, *No State Shall Abridge: The Fourteenth Amendment and the Bill of Rights* (Durham, N.C., 1986); Robert J. Kaczorowski, "Revolutionary Constitutionalism in the Era of the Civil War and Reconstruction," 61 *New York University L. Rev.* 863 (1986).

74. On Wilson's racist attitudes, *see* Arthur S. Link, *Woodrow Wilson and the Progressive Era, 1910–1917* (New York, 1954), 64–66; Henry Wilkinson Bragdon, *Woodrow Wilson: The Academic Years* (Cambridge, Mass., 1967), 249, 252; Arthur S. Link, *Wil-*

son: The Road to the White House (Princeton, N.J., 1947), 502; E. David Cronon, ed., *The Cabinet Diaries of Josephus Daniels, 1913–1921* (Lincoln, Neb., 1963), 32–33.

75. The "legal tender" controversy after the Civil War starkly dramatized the point. In 1870 the Court voided the Legal Tender Act of 1862, a measure passed by the Republican Congress to help finance the war. *Hepburn v. Griswold*, 75 U.S. (8 Wall.) 603 (1870). Three Republican justices dissented, and the Republican Party and much of the North were infuriated. President Ulysses S. Grant quickly filled two openings with Republican appointees, and the new justices immediately joined the three dissenters to overrule *Hepburn* and uphold the validity of the Legal Tender Act. *Legal Tender Cases,* 79 U.S. (12 Wall.) 457 (1871). *See* Charles Fairman, *Reconstruction and Reunion, 1864 – 1888* (New York, 1971), ch. 14.

76. Kramer, *The People Themselves,* 184 – 89; Rakove, "The Origins of Judicial Review," 1031, 1041 – 50 (1997); Keith E. Whittington, "'Interpose Your Friendly Hand': Political Supports for the Exercise of Judicial Review by the United States Supreme Court," 99 *American Political Science Rev.* 583 (2005).

77. *E.g., Martin v. Hunter's Lessee,* 14 U.S. (1 Wheat.) 304 (1816); *McCulloch v. Maryland,* 17 U.S. (4 Wheat.) 316 (1819).

78. *E.g.,* Edward A. Purcell Jr., *Brandeis and the Progressive Constitution:* Erie, *the Judicial Power, and the Politics of the Federal Courts in Twentieth-Century America* (New Haven, Conn., 2000), ch. 2.

79. *E.g., United States v. Curtiss-Wright Export Corp.,* 299 U.S. 304 (1936).

80. *E.g.,* Barry Cushman, *Rethinking the New Deal Court: The Structure of a Constitutional Revolution* (New York, 1998), Part IV.

81. *E.g.,* Lucas A. Powe Jr., *The Warren Court and American Politics* (Cambridge, Mass., 2000).

82. *Chicago, Milwaukee & St. Paul Railway Co. v. Minnesota,* 134 U.S. 418 (1890); *Reagan v. Farmers Loan and Trust Co.,* 154 U.S. 362 (1894); *Allgeyer v. Louisiana,* 165 U.S. 578 (1897); *Chicago, Burlington & Quincy Railroad Co. v. Chicago,* 166 U.S. 226 (1897).

83. *See generally* Wiecek, *Lost World.* On the Court's erratic efforts to distinguish state and federal regulatory "spheres," *see id.,* 148 – 49.

84. James Bradley Thayer, "The Origin and Scope of the American Doctrine of Constitutional Law," 7 *Harvard L. Rev.* 129, 144 (1893).

85. *Id.* at 150. *See* Edward A. Purcell Jr., "Learned Hand: The Jurisprudential Trajectory of an Old Progressive," 43 *Buffalo L. Rev.* 873, 884 – 96 (1995).

86. Thayer, "Origin and Scope," 144 (1893).

87. Purcell, "Learned Hand," 886 – 90 (1995). Not surprisingly, Thayer's attitude toward judicial review was shared by another Yankee whose constitutional jurisprudence was equally forged by the Civil War, Justice Oliver Wendell Holmes Jr. Oliver Wendell Holmes Jr., "Law and the Court," in *Collected Legal Papers* (New York, 1920), 295–96.

88. Purcell, "Learned Hand," 889–91 (1995).

89. *See, e.g.,* William J. Novak, "The Legal Origins of the Modern American State," in Austin Sarat, Bryant Garth, and Robert A. Kagan, eds., *Looking Back at Law's Century* (Ithaca, N.Y., 2002), 249, 264–72; Alan Dawley, *Struggles for Justice: Social Responsibility and the Liberal State* (Cambridge, Mass., 1991); Alan Brinkley, *The End of Reform: New Deal Liberalism in Recession and War* (New York, 1995); John Patrick Diggins, *The Proud Decades: America in War and Peace, 1941–1960* (New York, 1988); Steve Fraser and Gary Gerstle, *The Rise and Fall of the New Deal Order, 1930–1980* (Princeton, N.J., 1989).

90. *See, e.g.,* Barry Friedman, "The Birth of an Academic Obsession: The History of the Countermajoritarian Difficulty, Part Five," 112 *Yale L. J.* 153 (2002); Reuel E. Schiller, "Free Speech and Expertise: Administrative Censorship and the Birth of the Modern First Amendment," 86 *Virginia L. Rev.* 1 (2000); Reuel E. Schiller, "Enlarging the Administrative Polity: Administrative Law and the Changing Definition of Pluralism, 1945–1970," 53 *Vanderbilt L. Rev.* 1389 (2000); Morton J. Horwitz, *The Transformation of American Law, 1870–1960: The Crisis of Legal Orthodoxy* (New York, 1992), ch. 9; Mary L. Dudziak, *Cold War Civil Rights: Race and the Image of American Democracy* (Princeton, N.J., 2000); Mark A. Graber, *Transforming Free Speech: The Ambiguous Legacy of Civil Libertarianism* (Berkeley, Calif., 1991).

91. William M. Wiecek, *The Birth of the Modern Constitution: The United States Supreme Court, 1941–1953* (New York, 2006); Paul L. Murphy, *The Constitution in Crisis Times, 1918–1969* (New York, 1972).

92. *See, e.g.,* Noah Feldman, "From Liberty to Equality: The Transformation of the Establishment Clause," 90 *California L. Rev.* 673, 682–93 (2002); Howard Gillman, "Preferred Freedoms: The Progressive Expansion of State Power and the Rise of Modern Civil Liberties Jurisprudence," 47 *Political Research Quarterly* 623 (1994).

93. Herbert Wechsler, "The Political Safeguards of Federalism: The Role of the States in the Composition and Selection of the National Government," 54 *Columbia L. Rev.* 543 (1954).

94. Wechsler's theory, though "structural" in form, was also based on ideas of "original intent." His analysis drew on and tracked many of the arguments that the Federalists of 1787–89 had offered in defense of the Constitution.

95. Wechsler's conclusion was widely shared among post–World War II liberals. *E.g.*, Paul A. Freund, "Umpiring the Federal System," in Arthur W. McMahon, ed., *Federalism: Mature and Emergent* (New York, 1955), 163; Charles L. Black Jr., *Structure and Relationship in Constitutional Law* (Baton Rouge, La., 1969), 73.

96. 347 U.S. 483 (1954). *See* James T. Patterson, *Brown v. Board of Education: A Civil Rights Milestone and Its Troubled Legacy* (New York, 2001).

97. 163 U.S. 537 (1896) (upholding legalized racial segregation on railroads).

98. On the Warren Court *see* Morton J. Horwitz, *The Warren Court and the Pursuit of Justice* (New York, 1998); Bernard Schwartz, *The Warren Court: A Retrospective* (New York, 1996); Powe, *Warren Court.*

99. Liberal ideas subsequently received two of their most elaborate theoretical formulations in Jesse H. Choper, *Judicial Review and the National Political Process: A*

Functional Reconsideration of the Role of the Supreme Court (Chicago, 1980) and John Hart Ely, *Democracy and Distrust: A Theory of Judicial Review* (Cambridge, Mass., 1980).

100. Alexander Bickel, *The Supreme Court and the Idea of Progress* (New York, 1970); Alexander M. Bickel, *The Morality of Consent* (New Haven, Conn., 1975). *See* Edward A. Purcell Jr., "Alexander M. Bickel and the Post-Realist Constitution," 11 *Harvard Civil Rights/Civil Liberties L. Rev.* 521, 543–63 (1976).

101. Kurland, *Politics, the Constitution, and the Warren Court*, 57.

102. *E.g.*, Raoul Berger, *Federalism: The Founders' Design* (Norman, Okla., 1987), 188.

103. Lewis Kaden, "Politics, Money, and State Sovereignty: The Judicial Role," 79 *Columbia L. Rev.* 847 (1979). *Accord* Stephen G. Calabresi, "'A Government of Limited and Enumerated Powers: In Defense of *United States v. Lopez*,'" 94 *Michigan L. Rev.* 752 (1995); John C. Yoo, "The Judicial Safeguards of Federalism," 70 *Southern California L. Rev.* 1311 (1997).

104. Richard A. Epstein, *Takings: Private Property and the Power of Eminent Domain* (Cambridge, Mass., 1985); Richard A. Epstein, *Forbidden Grounds: The Case against Employment Discrimination Laws* (Cambridge, Mass., 1992); Richard A. Epstein, *Bargaining with the State* (Princeton, N. J., 1993).

105. *National League of Cities v. Usury*, 426 U.S. 833 (1976).

106. *E.g.*, *United States v. Darby*, 312 U.S. 100 (1941).

107. *Garcia v. San Antonio Metropolitan Transit Authority*, 469 U.S. 528 (1985) (overruling *National League of Cities*, 426 U.S. 833).

108. *Id.* at 577 (Powell, J., dissenting).

109. *E.g.*, *Gregory v. Ashcroft*, 501 U.S. 452 (1991); *New York v. United States*, 505 U.S. 144 (1992); *Seminole Tribe of Florida v. Florida*, 517 U.S. 44 (1996); *Printz v. United States*, 521 U.S. 898 (1997); *Florida Prepaid Postsecondary Education Expense Board v. College Savings Bank*, 527 U.S. 627 (1999); *Board of Trustees of the University of Alabama v. Garrett*, 531 U.S. 356, 365 (2001).

110. *E.g.*, *United States v. Lopez*, 514 U.S. 549 (1995); *City of Boerne v. Flores*, 512 U.S. 507 (1997); *United States v. Morrison*, 529 U.S. 598 (2000). *See* The Committee on Federal Legislation of the Association of the Bar of the City of New York, "The New Federalism," 54 *Record of the Association of the Bar of the City of New York* 712 (1999); Seth Waxman, "Defending Congress," 79 *North Carolina L. Rev.* 1073 (2001).

111. *E.g.*, Larry Kramer, "Putting the Politics Back into the Political Safeguards of Federalism," 100 *Columbia L. Rev.* 215 (2000). For a response *see* Marci A. Hamilton, "Why Federalism Must Be Enforced: A Response to Professor Kramer," 46 *Villanova L. Rev.* 1069 (2001). For a "structural" argument reinforcing the claim that the Court's primary role was to enforce national law, rather than to protect the states, *see* Akhil Reed Amar, *America's Constitution: A Biography* (New York, 2005), 212–14.

112. Mark Tushnet, *Taking the Constitution Away from the Courts* (Princeton, N.J., 1999); Larry D. Kramer, "Popular Constitutionalism, Circa 2004," 92 *California L. Rev.* 959 (2004); Jeremy Waldron, *Law and Disagreement* (New York, 1999); Keith E.

Whittington, "Extrajudicial Constitutional Interpretation: Three Objections and Responses," 80 *North Carolina L. Rev.* 773 (2002); Robert C. Post and Reva B. Siegel, "Legislative Constitutionalism and Section Five Power: Policentric Interpretation of the Family and Medical Leave Act," 112 *Yale L. J.* 1943 (2003). *See* James E. Fleming, "The Constitution Outside the Courts," 86 *Cornell L. Rev.* 215 (2000); Doni Gewirtzman, "Glory Days: Popular Constitutionalism, Nostalgia, and the True Nature of Constitutional Culture," 93 *Georgetown L. J.* 897 (2005).

113. Cass R. Sunstein, *The Partial Constitution* (Cambridge, Mass., 1993), vi.

114. Richard D. Parker, *"Here, the People Rule": A Constitutional Populist Manifesto* (Cambridge, Mass., 1994), 111.

115. *City of Boerne,* 521 U.S. at 524.

116. *Board of Trustees of the University of Alabama,* 531 U.S. at 365. *Accord Nevada Department of Human Resources v. Hibbs,* 538 U.S. 721, 728 (2003); *Dickerson v. United States,* 530 U.S. 428, 437 (2000); *City of Boerne,* 521 U.S. at 524. In 1958, during the darkest days of southern intransigence after *Brown,* it had been the liberal Warren Court that defended itself against attack by forthrightly announcing the principle of judicial supremacy. The "basic principle" of American constitutional law, it proclaimed, was "that the federal judiciary is supreme in the exposition of the law of the constitution" and that its rulings constituted "the supreme law of the land." *Cooper v. Aaron,* 358 U.S. 1, 17–18 (1958).

117. *E.g., Nevada Department of Human Resources,* 538 U.S. 721; *Tennessee v. Lane,* 541 U.S. 509 (2004); *Gonzales v. Raich,* 545 U.S. 1 (2005); *Granholm v. Heald,* 544 U.S. 460 (2005). *See* Denise C. Morgan, "Introduction: A Tale of (At Least) Two Federalisms," 50 *New York Law School L. Rev.* 615 (2006).

118. *E.g., Lopez,* 514 U.S. 549; *Printz,* 521 U.S. 898; *City of Boerne,* 521 U.S. 507; *Alden v. Maine,* 527 U.S. 706; *Morrison,* 529 U.S. 598.

Chapter 9. Evolving Understandings

1. Discussions commonly described the "values of federalism" as including protecting liberty, encouraging diversity and innovation, ensuring political accountability, promoting democratic participation, and protecting local values and interests. *See, e.g.,* Richard B. Stewart, "Federalism and Rights," 19 *Georgia L. Rev.* 917 (1985); Steven G. Calabresi, "'A Government of Limited and Enumerated Powers': In Defense of *United States v. Lopez,*" 94 *Michigan L. Rev.* 752, 787 (1995); Erwin Chemerinsky, "The Values of Federalism," 47 *Florida L. Rev.* 499 (1995); Larry Kramer, "Understanding Federalism," 47 *Vanderbilt L. Rev.* 1485 (1994).

2. Michael D. Reagan and John G. Sanzone, *The New Federalism,* 2d ed. (New York, 1981), 121. *See* Richard Briffault, "'What About the 'Ism'?' Normative and Formal Concerns in Contemporary Federalism," 47 *Vanderbilt L. Rev.* 1303 (1994); Edward L. Rubin, "The Fundamentality and Irrelevance of Federalism," 13 *Georgia State University L. Rev.* 1009 (1997); William H. Riker, *Federalism: Origin, Operation, Significance* (Boston, 1964), 139–45.

3. Gerald Gunther and Kathleen M. Sullivan, *Constitutional Law,* 13th ed. (Westbury, N.Y., 1997), 88.

4. *Garcia v. San Antonio Metropolitan Transit Authority,* 469 U.S. 528, 557, 572 (1985) (Powell, J., dissenting). The "liberty" argument was commonly advanced and, as a generality, widely accepted: *See, e.g., New York v. United States,* 505 U.S. 144, 181 (1992) (O'Connor, J.); *United States v. Lopez,* 514 U.S. 549, 552 (1995) (Rehnquist, C.J.); *Printz v. United States,* 521 U.S. 898, 921–22 (1997) (Scalia, J.); John Choon Yoo, "Federalism and Judicial Review," in Mark R. Killenbeck, ed., *The Tenth Amendment and State Sovereignty: Constitutional History and Contemporary Issues* (New York, 2002), 131, 178–79; Calabresi, "'A Government of Limited and Enumerated Powers,'" 787.

5. *See, e.g.,* James Madison, "Vices of the Political System of the United States," in Robert A. Rutland *et al.,* eds., *The Papers of James Madison* (Chicago, 1975), Vol. 9, 345–58 [hereafter, *"Papers of James Madison"*]; Jack N. Rakove, "Constitutional Problematics, circa 1787," in John Ferejohn, Jack N. Rakove, and Jonathan Riley, eds., *Constitutional Culture and Democratic Rule* (Cambridge, U.K., 2001), 57–60; Stanley Elkins and Eric McKitrick, *The Age of Federalism: The Early American Republic, 1788–1800* (New York, 1993), 702.

6. Alexander Hamilton, John Jay, and James Madison, *The Federalist,* ed. Edward Mead Earle (New York, 1937), No. 37, at 227 [hereafter, *"Federalist"*]. *Accord Federalist,* No. 44, at 291.

7. Jesse H. Choper, *Judicial Review and the National Political Process: A Functional Reconsideration of the Role of the Supreme Court* (Chicago, 1980), 252–53; Harry N. Scheiber, "Federalism and Legal Process: Historical and Contemporary Analysis of the American System," 14 *Law and Society Rev.* 663, 706 (1980).

8. Michael W. McConnell, "Federalism: Evaluating the Founders' Design," 54 *University of Chicago L. Rev.* 1484, 1501 (1987).

9. Paul E. Peterson, *The Price of Federalism* (Washington, D.C., 1995), 9.

10. Franz L. Neumann, "Federalism and Freedom: A Critique," in Arthur W. MacMahon, ed., *Federalism: Mature and Emergent* (Garden City, N.Y., 1955), 48; Ellen W. Schrecker, *No Ivory Tower: McCarthyism & the Universities* (New York, 1986), esp. 93–125. On the first "red scare," *see* William Preston Jr., *Aliens and Dissenters: Federal Suppression of Radicals, 1903–1933* (Cambridge, Mass., 1963); on the treatment of Japanese Americans after Pearl Harbor, *see* Greg Robinson, *By Order of the President: FDR and the Internment of Japanese Americans* (Cambridge, Mass., 2001); and on the McCarthy period, *see* Stanley I. Kutler, *The American Inquisition: Justice and Injustice in the Cold War* (New York, 1982). Even when state courts were free to expand individual rights, they frequently declined to do so and, instead, followed the U.S. Supreme Court's narrower interpretation of such rights. Robert M. Howard, Scott E. Graves, and Julianne Flowers, "State Courts, the U.S. Supreme Court, and the Protection of Civil Liberties," 40 *Law and Society Rev.* 845 (2006).

11. Geoffrey R. Stone, *Perilous Times: Free Speech in Wartime, from the Sedition Act of 1798 to the War on Terrorism* (New York, 2004), 181–82.

12. Stone, *Perilous Times,* 224.

13. Robinson, *By Order of the President,* 87–96.

14. G. Edward White, *Earl Warren: A Public Life* (New York, 1982), 70.

15. Stone, *Perilous Times,* 340–41, 422–23.

16. USA PATRIOT Act, Pub. L. No. 107-56, 107th Cong., 1st Sess. (2001).

17. Stephen J. Schulhofer, "At War with Liberty," *The American Prospect* (March, 2003); Stephen J. Schulhofer, *The Enemy Within: Intelligence Gathering, Law Enforcement, and Civil Liberties in the Wake of September 11* (New York, 2003); Eric Lichtblau, "Two Groups Charge Abuse of Witness Law," *New York Times,* Monday, June 27, 2005, A-10. *See Hamdi v. Rumsfeld,* 542 U.S. 507 (2004); *Hamdan v. Rumsfeld,* 126 S.Ct. 2749 (2006).

18. As of September 2005, according to a count made by the American Civil Liberties Union, resolutions criticizing all or parts of the Patriot Act were passed in seven states (Colorado, Montana, Idaho, Maine, Vermont, Alaska, and Hawaii) and 389 local communities. *See* American Civil Liberties Union website, http://www.aclu. org?SafeandFree/SafeandFree.cfm?ID=11294&c=207 (last visited Sept. 16, 2005). *See* Ernest A. Young, "Welcome to the Dark Side: Liberals Rediscover Federalism in the Wake of the War on Terror," 69 *Brooklyn L. Rev.* 1277 (2004).

19. *Truax v. Corrigan,* 257 U.S. 312, 342, 344 (1921) (Holmes, J., dissenting).

20. *Gregory v. Ashcroft,* 501 U.S. 452, 458 (1991) (O'Connor, J.); *Federal Energy Regulatory Commission v. Mississippi,* 456 U.S. 742, 787–88 (1982) (O'Connor, J., concurring in the judgment and dissenting in part); *Cruzan v. Director, Missouri Department of Health,* 497 U.S. 261, 292 (1990) (O'Connor, J., concurring); *West Lynn Creamery Inc. v. Healy,* 512 U.S. 186, 212–17 (1994) (Rehnquist, C.J., dissenting); *Lopez,* 514 U.S. at 581 (Kennedy, J., concurring). Another of the Court's late-twentieth-century conservatives, Justice Lewis Powell, invoked the laboratory metaphor in *Garcia,* 469 U.S. at 568 n. 13 (Powell, J., dissenting). Justice Scalia referenced the metaphor more cautiously. *See United States v. Virginia,* 518 U.S. 515, 566, 600 (1996) (Scalia, J., dissenting).

21. *Truax,* 257 U.S. at 338. A similar exchange occurred between Brandeis and conservative justice George Sutherland in *New State Ice Co. v. Liebman,* 285 U.S. 262 (1932). *See id.* at 279–80 (Sutherland, J., for the Court) and 306–11 (Brandeis, J., dissenting).

22. Riker, *Federalism,* 31; Martin Diamond, "What the Framers Meant by Federalism," in Robert A. Goldwin, ed., *A Nation of States: Essays on the American Federal System,* 2d ed. (Chicago, 1974), 25, 34; Jack N. Rakove, *Original Meanings: Politics and Ideas in the Making of the Constitution* (New York, 1996), 30–31.

23. *See, e.g.,* James Madison, "Vices of the Political System," *Papers of James Madison,* Vol. 9, 345–58; Gordon S. Wood, "Interests and Disinterestedness in the Making of the Constitution," in Richard Beeman, Stephen Botein, and Edward C. Carter II, eds., *Beyond Confederation: Origins of the Constitution and American National Identity* (Chapel Hill, N.C., 1987), 69–109; Rakove, "Constitutional Problematics," in Ferejohn, Rakove, and Riley, eds., *Constitutional Culture,* 57–60.

24. *Federalist,* No. 44, at 290. Max Farrand, ed., *Records of the Federal Convention of 1787,* rev ed. (New Haven, Conn., 1966 [1937]), Vol. 1, 165 [hereafter, "Farrand, *Records*"] (statement of Elbridge Gerry).

25. *Federalist,* No. 45, at 299. *Accord Federalist,* No. 62, at 402 (Madison or Hamilton).

26. Rakove, *Original Meanings,* 170. *Accord* Riker, *Federalism,* 14–15.

27. Most competition among the states before the Civil War did not involve "social experimentation" but relatively standard methods to encourage economic development. When states did adopt novel "social" policies, the characteristic ideas underlying the "laboratory" metaphor were generally absent. On the growing importance of state innovations in developing new social policies in the late nineteenth and early twentieth centuries *see, e.g.,* Susan M. Sterett, *Public Pensions: Gender & Civil Service in the States, 1850–1937* (Ithaca, N.Y., 2003).

28. On the fascination of Progressives with science and expertise *see* James T. Kloppenberg, *Uncertain Victory: Social Democracy and Progressivism in European and American Thought, 1870–1920* (New York, 1986); Dorothy Ross, *The Origins of American Social Science* (New York, 1991); Samuel P. Hays, *Conservation and the Gospel of Efficiency: The Progressive Conservation Movement, 1890–1920* (Cambridge, Mass., 1959).

29. Quoted in Richard B. Bernstein and Kym S. Rice, *Are We to Be a Nation? The Making of the Constitution* (Cambridge, Mass., 1987), 120 (referring to Hume and Adams). For Hamilton, *see Federalist,* No. 9, at 48, and No. 85, at 574. For Madison, *see Federalist,* No. 38, at 234–39.

30. *E.g., Federalist,* No. 1, at 3 (Hamilton); *Federalist,* No. 38, at 239 (Madison).

31. *E.g., Federalist,* No. 38, at 235–36 (Madison); John Jay, "An Address to the People of the State of New York," Henry P. Johnston, ed., *The Correspondence and Public Papers of John Jay, 1763–1826* (New York, 1971), Vol. 3, 318.

32. Letter from Louis D. Brandeis to Mary E. McDowell, in Melvin I. Urofsky and David W. Levy, eds., *Letters of Louis D. Brandeis, 1907–1912: People's Attorney* (Albany, N.Y., 1972), Vol. 2, 640.

33. 208 U.S. 412 (1908).

34. Louis D. Brandeis, *The Curse of Bigness: Miscellaneous Papers of Louis D. Brandeis* (New York, 1935), 73.

35. *New State Ice Co.,* 285 U.S. at 311 (Brandeis, J., dissenting).

36. *See, e.g.,* Maeva Marcus, "Louis D. Brandeis and the Laboratories of Democracy," *Federalism and the Judicial Mind: Essays on American Constitutional Law and Politics,* ed. Amy Turo *et al.* (Berkeley, Calif., 1992), 75–91.

37. *Truax,* 257 U.S. at 354–55 (Brandeis, J., dissenting).

38. Earl M. Maltz, "The Impact of the Constitutional Revolution of 1937 on the Dormant Commerce Clause—A Case Study in the Decline of State Autonomy," 19 *Harvard Journal of Law and Public Policy* 121, 127–28 (1995–96).

39. Letter from Louis D. Brandeis to Mary E. McDowell, Urofsky and Levy, eds., *Letters of Louis D. Brandeis,* Vol. 2, 639.

40. Brandeis rejected the "laboratory" metaphor, for example, when he joined the Court in its two earliest decisions that expanded substantive due process analysis to protect noneconomic fundamental rights. *Meyer v. Nebraska,* 262 U.S. 390 (1923); *Pierce v. Society of Sisters,* 268 U.S. 510 (1925). His behavior was typical. *See, e.g., Pointer v. Texas,* 380 U.S. 400, 410, 413 (1965) (Goldberg, J., concurring).

41. When the exercise of state eminent domain power endangered private property, for example, four of the "profederalism" justices of the Rehnquist Court ignored ideas about state "social experimentation" and dissented from the Court's decision refusing to limit the exercise of that power. *Kelo v. City of New London,* 545 U.S. 469 (2005) (Rehnquist, C.J., and O'Connor, Scalia, and Thomas, JJ., dissenting). Similarly, when the California legislature voted to legalize same-sex marriage in 2005, Republican state assemblyman Ray Haynes, an opponent of the measure, made the standard rejoinder: "Engaging in social experimentation with our children is not the role of the legislature." Showing rhetorical creativity, he not only rejected the "laboratory" metaphor (with its connotations of control, reason, scientific method, and orderly progress) but substituted another (suggesting uncertainty, risk, foolishness, and ultimate ruin) more suitable to his purpose. "We are throwing the dice and taking a huge gamble," he declared, "and we are gambling with the lives and future of generations not yet born." Dean E. Murphy, "Same Sex Marriage Wins Vote in California," *New York Times,* Sept. 7, 2005, A-14.

42. Quoted in Merrill D. Peterson, *The Great Triumvirate: Webster, Clay, and Calhoun* (New York, 1987), 260.

43. Charles N. Glaab, *Kansas City and the Railroads: Community Policy in the Growth of a Regional Metropolis* (Lawrence, Kans., 1993 [1962]), 95.

44. This does not implicate the further serious question of whether the states can and do, in fact, act as "laboratories." *See* Edward L. Rubin and Malcolm Feeley, "Federalism: Some Notes on a National Neurosis," 41 *U.C.L.A. L. Rev.* 903, 924–25 (1994); James A. Gardner, "The 'States-as-Laboratories' Metaphor in State Constitutional Law," 30 *Valparaiso L. Rev.* 475 (1996).

45. By the late twentieth century the idea of the states "as laboratories of democracy" appeared as a standard and unquestioned element of the rhetoric of American federalism. *See* Presidential Executive Order No. 13,132, 64 F.R. 43,255 (Aug. 4, 1999), Sec. 2 (e).

46. "Speeches of Patrick Henry," in Ralph Ketchum, ed., *The Anti-Federalist Papers and the Constitutional Convention Debates* (New York, 1986), 216.

47. Daniel J. Boorstin, *The Americans: The Colonial Experience* (New York, 1958), 362. *Accord* Joseph J. Ellis, *Founding Brothers: The Revolutionary Generation* (New York, 2000), 6, 11.

48. Walter T. K. Nugent, *Structures of American Social History* (Bloomington, Ind., 1981), 59–60, 63–64, 79, 81–82; William E. Nelson, "The American Revolution and the Emergence of Modern Doctrines of Federalism and Conflict of Laws," 62 *Publications of the Colonial Society of Massachusetts: Law in Colonial Massachusetts* 419, 437–51 (1984).

49. Thomas Bender, *Toward an Urban Vision: Ideas and Institutions in Nineteenth Century America* (Baltimore, 1975), 3.

50. R. Kent Newmyer, "John Marshall, Political Parties, and the Origins of Modern Federalism," in Harry N. Scheiber and Theodore Correl, eds., *Federalism: Studies in History, Law, and Policy,* Papers from the Second Berkeley Seminar on Federalism (Berkeley, Calif., 1988), 17. *Accord* Forrest McDonald, *Novus Ordo Seclorum: The Intellectual Origins of the Constitution* (Lawrence, Kans., 1985), 289.

51. Ralph Ketcham, "Introduction," in Ketcham, ed., *Anti-Federalist Papers,* 17.

52. "Letters from the Federal Farmer," No. 2, in Herbert J. Storing, ed., *The Complete Anti-Federalist* (Chicago, 1981), Vol. 2, 233.

53. "Essays of Brutus," No. IV, in Storing, ed., *Complete Anti-Federalist,* Vol. 2, 385.

54. *Federalist,* No. 46, at 305, 307. *Accord* Farrand, *Records,* Vol. 1, 284 (Hamilton).

55. *Federalist,* No. 29, at 180.

56. Gordon S. Wood, *The Radicalism of the American Revolution* (New York, 1991), 6.

57. Alexis de Tocqueville, *Democracy in America,* ed. Harvey C. Mansfield and Delba Winthrop (Chicago, 2000 [1835]), Vol. II, 512.

58. Robert Wiebe, *Who We Are: A History of Popular Nationalism* (Princeton, N.J., 2002), 71.

59. Theda Skocpol, *Diminished Democracy: From Membership to Management in American Civil Life* (Norman, Okla., 2003), 31, 51.

60. *See* Nugent, *Structures of American Social History;* Riker, *Federalism,* 104–110.

61. Herman Melville, *The Confidence Man: His Masquerade* (Chicago, 1984 [1857]). *See* Patricia Kelly Hall and Steven Ruggles, "'Restless in the Midst of Their Prosperity': New Evidence on the Internal Migration of Americans, 1850–2000," 91 *Journal of American History* 829 (2004).

62. William E. Nelson, *The Americanization of the Common Law: The Impact of Legal Change on Massachusetts Society, 1760–1830* (Cambridge, Mass., 1975), 165–66.

63. Lawrence M. Friedman, *Crime and Punishment in American History* (New York, 1993), 248–49. *See* Kermit L. Hall, *The Magic Mirror: Law in American History* (New York, 1989), 107–08, 120; Morton J. Horwitz, *The Transformation of American Law, 1780–1860* (Cambridge, Mass., 1977), 28–29, 84, 141–43, 155–59.

64. *See* Charles Sellers, *The Market Revolution: Jacksonian America, 1815–1846* (New York, 1991).

65. 41 U.S. (16 Pet.) 1 (1842).

66. *See* Gerald T. Dunne, *Justice Joseph Story and the Rise of the Supreme Court* (New York, 1970), 403–20; Tony A. Freyer, *Forums of Order: The Federal Courts and Business in American History* (Greenwich, Conn., 1979); Tony A. Freyer, *Harmony & Dissonance: The Swift and Erie Cases in American Federalism* (New York, 1981).

67. *See* Lawrence M. Friedman, *American Law in the 20th Century* (New Haven, Conn., 2002), 379–80; William Twining, *Karl Llewellyn and the Realist Movement* (London, 1973), 270–301.

68. *See, e.g.,* Richard White, *The Middle Ground: Indians, Empire, and Republics in the Great Lakes Region, 1650–1815* (New York, 1991); Patricia Nelson Limerick, *The Legacy of Conquest: The Unbroken Past of the American West* (New York, 1987).

69. Abraham Lincoln, "Address at Cooper Institute," Roy P. Basler, ed., *The Collected Works of Abraham Lincoln* (New Brunswick, N.J., 1953), Vol. 3, 523. Peterson, *Great Triumvirate,* 257.

70. Theda Skocpol, *Protecting Soldiers and Mothers: The Political Origins of Social Policy in the United States* (Cambridge, Mass., 1992), 65, 107, 129, 145; Anita Bernstein, "For and Against Marriage: A Revision," 102 *Michigan L. Rev.* 129 (2003); Kristin A. Collins, "Federalism's Fallacy: The Early Tradition of Federal Family Law and the Invention of States' Rights," 26 *Cardozo L. Rev.* 1761 (2005); Judith Resnik, "'Naturally' without Gender: Women, Jurisdiction, and the Federal Courts," 66 *New York University L. Rev.* 1682 (1991); Naomi R. Cahn, "Family Law, Federalism and the Federal Courts," 79 *Iowa L. Rev.* 1073 (1994).

71. Hendrik Hartog, *Man & Wife in America: A History* (Cambridge, Mass., 2000), 16; William E. Nelson, *The Fourteenth Amendment: From Political Principle to Judicial Doctrine* (Cambridge, Mass., 1988), 136–38.

72. Hartog, *Man & Wife,* 17–20, 32–39, 247–49, 258–82. *See* Norma Basch, *Framing American Divorce: From the Revolutionary Generation to the Victorians* (Berkeley, Calif., 1999); Judith Resnik, "Categorical Federalism: Jurisdiction, Gender, and the Globe," 111 *Yale L. J.* 619 (2001).

73. Sarah Barringer Gordon, *The Mormon Question: Polygamy and Constitutional Conflict in Nineteenth Century America* (Chapel Hill, N.C., 2002); *Late Corporation of the Church of Jesus Christ of Latter Day Saints v. United States,* 136 U.S. 1 (1890); Michael Grossberg, *Governing the Hearth: Law and the Family in Nineteenth-Century America* (Chapel Hill, N.C., 1985), 125–26.

74. Defense of Marriage Act, Pub. L. No. 104-99, 108th Cong., 2d Sess. (2004); "Statement [of President George W. Bush] Calling for a Constitutional Amendment Defining and Protecting Marriage," 40 *Weekly Comp. Pres. Doc.* 912 (May 17, 2004) at http://frwebgate.access.gpo.gov/cgi-bin/getdoc.cgi?dbname=2004_presidential_documents&docid=pd24MY04_TXT-11 (last visited Jan. 31, 2007).

75. Quoted in Richard Born, "Partisan Intentions and Election Day Realities in the Congressional Redistricting Process," 79 *American Political Science Rev.* 305 (1985). *See* Elmer C. Griffith, *The Rise and Development of the Gerrymander* (New York, 1907); Leroy Hardy, Alan Heslop, and Stuart Anderson, eds., *Reapportionment Politics: The History of Redistricting in the 50 States* (Beverly Hills, Calif., 1981). The Court has recognized the existence of the long-established practice. *Vieth v. Jubelirer,* 541 U.S. 267, 274–77 (2004).

76. Alexander M. Bickel, *Politics and the Warren Court* (New York, 1965), 35.

77. On the practice of gerrymandering, *see, e.g.,* Robert S. Erikson, "Malapportionment, Gerrymandering, and Party Fortunes in Congressional Elections," 66 *American Political Science Rev.* 1234 (1972); Gary King, "Representation through Legislative Redistricting: A Stochastic Model," 33 *American Journal of Political Science* 787

(1989); Vergil C. Stroud, "A Political Maneuver That Backfired," 17 *Western Political Quarterly* 125 (1964); John A. Ferejohn, "On the Decline of Competition in Congressional Elections," 71 *American Political Science Rev.* 166 (1977); Richard G. Niemi and Simon Jackman, "Bias and Responsiveness in State Legislative Districting," 16 *Legislative Studies Quarterly* 183 (1991).

78. *See, e.g.,* Thomas J. Sugrue, "All Politics Is Local: The Persistence of Localism in Twentieth-Century America," in Meg Jacobs, William J. Novak, and Julian E. Zelizer, eds., *The Democratic Experiment: New Directions in American Political History* (Princeton, N.J., 2003), 301–26; Matthew D. Lassiter, "Suburban Strategies: The Volatile Center in Postwar American Politics," in *id.,* 327–49; William A. Fischel, *The Homevoter Hypothesis: How Home Values Influence Local Government Taxation, School Finance, and Land-Use Policies* (Cambridge, Mass., 2001).

79. By the early twenty-first century, for example, a typical "local" issue was whether people in a particular geographical location could prevent Wal-Mart from opening a "supercenter" in their neighborhood. *See, e.g.,* William Burr, "Zoning Board Recommends 'No' on Planned Wal-Mart," *Tampa Tribune,* Nov. 3, 2004; David Pierson, "Wal-Mart Supercenter Gets Foot in the Door," *Los Angeles Times,* Sept. 9, 2004; Kristina Smith, "Portage Township," *News Herald* (Port Clinton, Ohio), Nov. 4, 2004; Shannon Tan, "Wal-Mart Backs Off Site at Busy Intersection," *St. Petersburg* (Fla.) *Times,* Nov. 7, 2004. Another similar "local" issue saw "hundreds of communities around the country" fighting national and international cell phone companies in efforts to prevent the erection of cellular transmission towers that residents found annoying, unattractive, and potentially dangerous to their health. Katie Hafner, "First Come Cellphone Towers, Then the Babel," *New York Times,* May 1, 2005, A-1.

80. Aaron Wildavsky, *Federalism & Political Culture,* ed. David Schleicher and Brendon Swedlow (New Brunswick, N.J., 1998), 68.

81. Letter from James Madison to Spencer Roane, Sept. 2, 1819, in Gaillard Hunt, ed., *The Writings of James Madison* (New York, 1908), Vol. 8, 448.

82. On the old distinction, *see, e.g., Kidd v. Pearson,* 128 U.S. 1, 21 (1888). On the Rehnquist Court's invocation of the same distinction, *see United States v. Morrison,* 529 U.S. 598, 617–18 (2000). For a recent example of attempts to identify the "local," *see* the four distinct opinions in *Gonzales v. Raich,* 545 U.S. 1 (2005).

83. *See, e.g.,* Jane S. Schacter, "Ely and the Idea of Democracy," 57 *Stanford L. Rev.* 737, 755–59 (2004).

84. Despite its emphasis on the importance of "accountability," for example, the Rehnquist Court repeatedly handed down decisions that denied ordinary individuals the opportunity to hold government and business accountable for their transgressions. *See, e.g.,* Vicki C. Jackson, "Seductions of Coherence, State Sovereign Immunity, and the Denationalization of Federal Law," 31 *Rutgers L. J.* 691 (2000).

85. *See, e.g.,* Herbert J. Storing, *Toward a More Perfect Union: The Writings of Herbert J. Storing,* ed. Joseph M. Bessette (Washington, D.C., 1995), 81; Rakove, *Original Meanings,* 168, 201; Daniel J. Hulsebosch, *Constituting Empire: New York and the Transformation of Constitutionalism in the Atlantic World, 1664–1830* (Chapel Hill,

N.C., 2005), 204–06, 210–13; Murray Dry, "Anti-Federalism in *The Federalist:* A Founding Dialogue on the Constitution, Republican Government, and Federalism," in Charles R. Kesler, ed., *Saving the Revolution:* The Federalist Papers *and the American Founding* (New York, 1987), 40, 55.

86. *E.g.,* R. B. Bernstein, *Thomas Jefferson* (New York, 2003), 141–43, 145–47, 166–68; Leonard W. Levy, *Jefferson and Civil Liberties: The Darker Side* (Chicago, 1989 [1963]); Joseph J. Ellis, *American Sphinx: The Character of Thomas Jefferson* (New York, 1996), 248–53.

87. Drew R. McCoy, *The Last of the Fathers: James Madison & the Republican Legacy* (New York, 1989), 80–81.

88. McDonald, *Novus Ordo Seclorum,* 224; Elkins and McKitrick, *Age of Federalism;* Gordon S. Wood, *The Creation of the American Republic, 1776–1787* (Chapel Hill, N.C., 1969); Rakove, *Original Meanings.*

89. Leonard D. White, *The Federalists: A Study in Administrative History* (New York, 1948), 389.

90. Edward S. Corwin, "The Passing of Dual Federalism," 36 *Virginia L. Rev.* 1, 4 (1950). For a judicial statement *see Tarble's Case,* 80 U.S. (13 Wall.) 397, 406 (1871).

91. "The Constitution of the United States assumed the coordination and cooperation of the general and the state governments. . . . The principle of a separate and independent administrative organization for the new government was then established. Almost from the beginning, however, the general government relied upon state agencies for help in some matters, and the idea of federal-state administrative cooperation was accepted in others." White, *Federalists,* 389.

92. Morton Grodzins, *The American System: A New View of Government in the United States,* ed. Daniel J. Elazar (Chicago, 1966). Some scholars have argued that "cooperative" federalism was "the rule in the 19th century as well as the 20th." Daniel J. Elazar, *The American Partnership: Intergovernmental Cooperation in the Nineteenth Century United States* (Chicago, 1962), 338. *Accord* Morton Grodzins, "Centralization and Decentralization," in R. Goldwin, ed., *A Nation of States* (Chicago, 1963), 210.

93. The binary division between state and federal "spheres" that marked the idea of "dual federalism" drew its strength from the development and spread in the late nineteenth century of what scholars have called "classical" legal thought. William M. Wiecek, *The Lost World of Classical Legal Thought: Law and Ideology in America, 1886–1937* (New York, 1998), 6.

94. *E.g.,* John Kincaid, "From Cooperative to Coercive Federalism," 509 *Annals of the American Academy of Political and Social Science* 139 (1990).

95. The political roots of the change were complex. *See, e.g.,* Steve Fraser and Gary Gerstle, eds., *The Rise and Fall of the New Deal Order, 1930–1980* (Princeton, N.J., 1989); Keith E. Whittington, "Taking What They Give Us: Explaining the Court's Federalism Offensive," 51 *Duke L. J.* 477 (2001); Keith E. Whittington, "Dismantling the Modern State? The Changing Structural Foundations of Federalism," 25 *Hastings*

Constitutional Law Quarterly 483 (1998); Murray Friedman, *The Neoconservative Revolution: Jewish Intellectuals and the Shaping of Public Policy* (New York, 2005); Howard Gillman, "Reconnecting the Modern Supreme Court to the Historical Evolution of American Capitalism," in Howard Gillman and Cornell Clayton, eds., *The Supreme Court in American Politics: New Institutionalist Interpretations* (Lawrence, Kans., 1999), 235–56; Michael W. Flamm, *Law and Order: Street Crime, Civil Unrest, and the Crisis of Liberalism in the 1960s* (New York, 2005).

96. The principal works drew on ideas that originated in the eighteenth century in the work of such writers as Adam Smith and the Marquis de Condorcet: Kenneth Arrow, *Social Choice and Individual Values* (New York, 1951); Charles Tiebout, "A Pure Theory of Local Expenditures," 64 *Journal of Political Economy* 416 (1956); Anthony Downs, *An Economic Theory of Democracy* (New York, 1957); Ronald Coase, "The Problem of Social Cost," 3 *Journal of Law and Economics* 1 (1960); James M. Buchanan and Gordon Tullock, *The Calculus of Consent: Logical Foundations of Constitutional Democracy* (Ann Arbor, Mich., 1962); William H. Riker, *The Theory of Political Coalitions* (New Haven, Conn., 1962); and Mancur Olsen, *The Logic of Collective Action: Public Goods and the Theory of Groups* (Cambridge, Mass., 1965).

97. *See, e.g.,* James M. Buchanan, *Explorations into Constitutional Economics* (College Station, Tex., 1989), 60–61; Barry R. Weingast, "Political Institutions: Rational Choice Perspectives," *A New Handbook of Political Science,* ed. Robert E. Goodin and Hans-Dieter Klingemann (New York, 1996), 167–90.

98. Ideas of "competitive federalism" are generally consistent, for example, with the ideas used to justify efforts to provide tax cuts for the wealthy, impose harsher terms on individual consumers (as in the Bankruptcy Abuse Prevention and Consumer Protection Act of 2005, Pub. L. No. 109-8, 109th Cong., 1st Sess. [April 20, 2005]), reduce or eliminate "class action" lawsuits (as in the Class Action Fairness Act of 2005, Pub. L. No. 109-2, 119 Stat. 4, 109th Cong., 1st Sess, [Feb. 18, 2005]), "privatize" Social Security, and adopt corporate-sponsored "tort reform" proposals designed to reduce or eliminate suits against business entities. Those ideas contrast sharply with the social insurance ideas that underlay many earlier "liberal" reforms in the twentieth century such as workman's compensation, unemployment insurance, Medicare and Medicaid, and the Social Security system.

99. James M. Buchanan, "Federalism as an Ideal Political Order and an Objective for Constitutional Reform," 25 *Publius* 19, 21–22 (1995); McConnell, "Federalism," 1491–1500 (1987); Frank H. Easterbrook, "Antitrust and the Economics of Federalism," 26 *Journal of Law & Economics* 23 (1983); Buchanan, *Explorations into Constitutional Economics;* James M. Buchanan, *Constitutional Economics* (Cambridge, Mass., 1991); Jonathan R. Macey, "Federal Deference to Local Regulators and the Economic Theory of Regulation: Towards a Public-Choice Explanation of Federalism," 76 *Virginia L. Rev.* 265 (1990); Thomas R. Dye, *American Federalism: Competition among Governments* (New York, 1990); Barry R. Weingast, "The Economic Role of Political Institutions: Market-Preserving Federalism and Economic Development," 11 *Journal*

of Law, Economics & Organization 1 (1995); John O. McGinnis and Ilya Somin, "Federalism vs. States' Rights: A Defense of Judicial Review in a Federal System," 99 *Northwestern University L. Rev.* 89 (2004).

100. The theories also drew widespread criticisms. *E.g.*, Doron Teichman, "The Market for Criminal Justice: Federalism, Crime Control, and Jurisdictional Competition," 103 *Michigan L. Rev.* 1831 (2005); David A. Super, "Rethinking Fiscal Federalism," 118 *Harvard L. Rev.* 2544 (2005); Don Herzog, "Externalities and Other Parasites," 67 *University of Chicago L. Rev.* 895 (2000); Vicki Been, "'Exit' as a Constraint on Land Use Exactions: Rethinking the Unconstitutional Conditions Doctrine," 91 *Columbia L. Rev.* 473 (1991); Jonathan Rodden and Susan Rose-Ackerman, "Does Federalism Preserve Markets?" 83 *Virginia L. Rev.* 1521 (1997); John D. Donahue, *Hazardous Crosscurrents: Confronting Inequality in an Era of Devolution* (New York, 1999); Truman F. Bewley, "A Critique of Tiebout's Theory of Local Public Expenditures," 49 *Econometrica* 713 (1981); Sheryll D. Cashin, "Federalism, Welfare Reform, and the Minority Poor: Accounting for the Tyranny of State Majorities," 99 *Columbia L. Rev.* 552 (1999); Lucian Arye Bebchuk, "Federalism and the Corporation: The Desirable Limits on State Competition in Corporate Law," 105 *Harvard L. Rev.* 1435 (1992).

101. Michael S. Greve, "Against Cooperative Federalism," 70 *Mississippi L. J.* 557, 559 (2000). *See* Michael S. Greve, *Real Federalism: Why It Matters, How It Could Happen* (Washington, D.C., 1999); Michael S. Greve, "Federalism's Frontier," 7 *Texas Rev. of Law & Politics* 93 (2003).

102. 304 U.S. 64 (1938).

103. 41 U.S. (16 Pet.) 1 (1842).

104. Michael S. Greve, "Laboratories of Democracy: Anatomy of a Metaphor," *A.E.I. Federalist Outlook*, No. 6, at 5–6 at http://www.aei.org/publications/pubID. 12743/pub_detail.asp (last visited Jan. 31, 2007).

105. Greve and many other "competitive federalism" proponents accepted limitations on states when their actions created "externalities," that is, when they imposed costs or burdens on other states or on out-of-state residents. Their definitions of "externalities" and other similar concepts, however, were often arbitrary or question-begging. Theories of "competitive federalism," for example, relied on the availability of "exit rights," a device whose very nature was to create "externalities." "Exit rights" functioned to allow states to adopt policies to induce "undesired" types of residents (however a state might conceive of such a category) to move to other states while attracting from those other states "desired" types of residents (however conceived). Movement in either direction would thereby impose "externalities" on other states and their residents. Thus, an analysis of "externalities" was, by itself, inadequate to identify situations when limitations on state actions would be proper. The wide gap between the realities of the American federal structure and the conclusions that can be drawn from an economic analysis of a generic idea of federalism is suggested, *e.g.*, in Dennis C. Mueller, *Constitutional Democracy* (New York, 1996), ch. 6.

106. *See, e.g.*, Jay E. Austin *et al.*, "Federalism as Libertarian Fantasy," in Douglas T. Kendall, ed., *Redefining Federalism: Listening to the States in Shaping "Our Federal-*

ism," (Washington, D.C., 2004), 31–49; Jules Coleman, *Markets, Morals, and the Law* (New York, 1998); Edward L. Rubin, "Rational Choice and Rat Choice: Some Thoughts on the Relationship among Rationality, Markets, and Human Beings," 80 *Chicago-Kent L. Rev.* 1091 (2005); Herbert Hovenkamp, "The First Great Law & Economics Movement," 42 *Stanford L. Rev.* 993 (1990).

107. Some progressives also tried to utilize "competitive federalism" theories or incorporate some of its ideas, such as that of "exit rights." *See* Denise C. Morgan and Rebecca E. Zietlow, "The New Parity Debate: Congress and the Rights of Belonging," 73 *University of Cincinnati L. Rev.* 1347, 1376–80 (2005).

108. Lawrence M. Friedman, *American Law: An Introduction* (New York, 1984), 126.

109. Richard Epstein, for example, acknowledged that critical elements of the economic analysis of federalism were not part of "the original constitutional plan" and "must be regarded as a modern reinterpretation." Richard Epstein, "Exit Rights under Federalism," 55 *Law and Contemporary Problems* 147, 150 (1992). *See* John Kincaid, "The Competitive Challenge to Cooperative Federalism: A Theory of Federal Democracy," in Daphne A. Kenyon and John Kincaid, eds., *Competition among States and Local Governments: Efficiency and Equity in American Federalism* (Washington, D.C., 1991), 87, 88; William H. Pryor Jr., "Madison's Double Security: In Defense of Federalism, the Separation of Powers, and the Rehnquist Court," 53 *Alabama L. Rev.* 1167, 1173 (2002); Frank H. Easterbrook, "The State of Madison's Vision of the State: A Public Choice Perspective," 107 *Harvard L. Rev.* 1328, 1333 (1994).

110. Greve, for example, identified "federalism's purpose" as "mimicking, in the government sector, the advantages of private markets—variety, consumer choice, and competition." Michael Greve, "Federalism Is More Than States' Rights," *Wall Street Journal,* July 1, 1999, A-22. "Competitive federalism" often seemed to counsel muscular judicial activism, an awkward position for a "constitutional" theory rooted in extra-constitutional premises and values. *See, e.g.,* Ilya Somin, "Closing the Pandora's Box of Federalism: The Case for Judicial Restriction of Federal Subsidies to State Governments," 90 *Georgetown L. J.* 461 (2002).

111. John Phillip Reid, *Constitutional History of the American Revolution: The Authority of Rights* (Madison, Wisc., 1986), Vol. 1, 7.

112. *See generally* Laura Kalman, *The Strange Career of Legal Liberalism* (New Haven, Conn., 1996); John Henry Schlegel, *American Legal Realism and Empirical Social Science* (Chapel Hill, N.C., 1995); Neil Duxbury, *Patterns of American Jurisprudence* (New York, 1995); Anthony Sebok, *Legal Positivism in American Jurisprudence* (New York, 1998); Gary Minda, *Postmodern Legal Movements* (New York, 1995).

113. Michael Kammen, *A Machine That Would Go of Itself: The Constitution in American Culture* (New York, 1986); Wood, *Creation of the American Republic,* 259–91; Barry Friedman, "The Cycles of Constitutional Theory," 67 *Law and Contemporary Problems* 149 (2004); Howard Gillman, "The Collapse of Constitutional Originalism and the Rise of the Notion of the 'Living Constitution' in the Course of American State-Building," 11 *Studies in American Political Development* 191 (1997).

114. Woodrow Wilson, *Congressional Government: A Study in American Politics* (Boston, 1885), 8–9. *Accord* Woodrow Wilson, *Constitutional Government in the United States* (New Brunswick, N.J., 2002 [1908]), 193.

115. Wilson, *Constitutional Government*, 194.

116. Alexander M. Bickel, *The Least Dangerous Branch: The Supreme Court at the Bar of Politics* (New York, 1962), 107; Herbert Croly, *The Promise of American Life* (Boston, 1989 [1909]), 269.

117. The idea was not limited to "liberals." *Poe v. Ullman*, 367 U.S. 497, 542 (1961) (Harlan, J., dissenting).

118. Morton J. Horwitz, "Foreword. The Constitution of Change: Legal Fundamentality without Fundamentalism," 107 *Harvard L. Rev.* 30 (1993). *E.g.*, Bruce Ackerman, *We the People: Foundations* (Cambridge, Mass., 1991), 35–37; Mark Tushnet, *Taking the Constitution Away from the Courts* (Princeton, N.J., 1999), 191.

119. *E.g.*, William H. Rehnquist, "The Notion of a Living Constitution," 54 *Texas L. Rev.* 693 (1976). *But see Dickerson v. United States,* 530 U.S. 428, 441 (2000) (Rehnquist, C.J.).

120. *See, e.g.*, William E. Leuchtenburg, *The Supreme Court Reborn: The Constitutional Revolution in the Age of Roosevelt* (New York, 1995); Barry Cushman, *Rethinking the New Deal Court: The Structure of a Constitutional Revolution* (New York, 1998).

121. 347 U.S. 483 (1954).

122. "Originalist" theories may claim foundation, inter alia, in the "intent" of those who drafted or ratified the Constitution, the collective "understanding" those parties shared about the Constitution's meaning, or the true "meaning" that the document's text conveyed to reasonable people at the time.

123. *Compare, e.g.*, Richard A. Epstein, *How Progressives Rewrote the Constitution* (Washington, D.C., 2006), 22–25, *with* Randy E. Barnett, *Restoring the Lost Constitution: The Presumption of Liberty* (Princeton, N.J., 2004), ch. 11 (Commerce Clause); and *compare* Justice Thomas concurring in *McIntyre v. Ohio Elections Commission*, 514 U.S. 334, 358 (1995) *with* Justice Scalia dissenting in *id.*, 514 U.S. at 371 (First Amendment). *See* Johnathan O'Neill, *Originalism in American Law and Politics: A Constitutional History* (Baltimore, Md., 2005), 210–11.

124. The idea of construing the Constitution in light of the "original" intent or "understanding" of the founders was a thoroughly traditional method of judicial reasoning capable of serving a variety of purposes. *E.g.*, *compare McCulloch v. Maryland*, 17 U.S. (4 Wheat.) 316 (1819) *with Dred Scott v. Sandford*, 60 U.S. (19 How.) 393 (1857). For a history of "originalist" interpretation, *see* O'Neill, *Originalism in American Law.*

125. "Originalism" has been subject to a variety of criticisms. *See, e.g.*, Henry Paul Monaghan, "Doing Originalism," 104 *Columbia L. Rev.* 32 (2004); Richard H. Fallon Jr., *The Dynamic Constitution: An Introduction to American Constitutional Law* (New York, 2004); Daniel A. Farber and Suzanna Sherry, *Desperately Seeking Certainty: The Misguided Quest for Constitutional Foundations* (Chicago, 2002), 10–54; H. Jefferson Powell, *A Community Built on Words: The Constitution in History and Politics* (Chi-

cago, 2002); Dennis J. Goldford, *The American Constitution and the Debate over Originalism* (New York, 2005); Michael C. Dorf, "Recipe for Trouble: Some Thoughts on Meaning, Translation, and Normative Theory," 85 *Georgetown L. Rev.* 1857 (1997); Cass R. Sunstein, "Five Theses on Originalism," 19 *Harvard Journal of Law and Public Policy* 311 (1996); Laurence H. Tribe and Michael C. Dorf, "Levels of Generality in the Definition of Rights," 57 *University of Chicago L. Rev.* 1057 (1990); Paul Brest, "The Misconceived Quest for the Original Understanding," 60 *Boston University L. Rev.* 204 (1980); Bret Boyce, "Originalism and the Fourteenth Amendment," 33 *Wake Forest L. Rev.* 909 (1998).

126. Justice Scalia's defense of originalism illustrated the point. The original meaning of a constitutional provision "usually" is "easy to discern and simple to apply," and "not very often" would there be "disagreement regarding the original meaning," he declared sweepingly. At the same time, however, he felt compelled immediately to qualify his assertions. There is "plenty of room for disagreement as to what original meaning was, and even more as to how that original meaning applies to the situation before the Court." Moreover, in "new fields" of law dealing with post-eighteenth-century developments, "the Court must follow the trajectory" of developing law, which "is not entirely cut-and-dried but requires the exercise of judgment." Antonin Scalia, *A Matter of Interpretation: Federal Courts and the Law* (Princeton, N.J., 1997), 45. Indeed, the justice acknowledged, "almost every originalist would adulterate [original understandings] with the doctrine of *stare decisis*." Antonin Scalia, "Originalism: The Lesser Evil," 57 *University of Cincinnati L. Rev.* 849, 861 (1989). Ultimately, Justice Scalia's defense of originalism came down to the assertion that "the originalist at least knows what he is looking for: The original meaning of the text." Scalia, *Matter of Interpretation,* 45. With respect to the true and proper "balance" of American federalism, this inquiry suggests that such a quest seeks an imaginary goal. Knowing that one is looking for the Holy Grail does not mean that the Holy Grail exists.

127. On the use of "originalism" as a method of justifying constitutional change and innovation, *see* Alfred H. Kelly, "Clio and the Court: An Illicit Love Affair," 1965 *Supreme Court Rev.* 119.

128. There is nothing intrinsically or substantively "conservative" about "originalism." It is simply a method, useful in some cases and for some purposes. *See, e.g.,* Barry Friedman and Scott B. Smith, "The Sedimentary Constitution," 147 *University of Pennsylvania L. Rev.* 1 (1998); Akhil Reed Amar, "Foreword: The Document and the Doctrine," 114 *Harvard L. Rev.* 26 (2000).

129. If considered as one potential source of guidance and inspiration, of course, originalism may make useful contributions to many constitutional issues. For a recent and sophisticated effort to develop an originalist interpretation of the Constitution, *see* Randy E. Barnett, *Restoring the Lost Constitution: The Presumption of Liberty* (Princeton, N.J., 2004).

130. The loss would include the guiding force of precedent and the disruption of established assumptions and patterns of behavior. *See, e.g.,* Henry P. Monaghan, "Stare Decisis and Constitutional Adjudication," 88 *Columbia L. Rev.* 723 (1988). *See* "Can

Originalism Be Reconciled with Precedent? A Symposium on *Stare Decisis,*" 22 *Constitutional Commentary* 257 (2005).

131. For examples of the plastic nature of "originalist" analyses, *see* Robert H. Bork, *The Tempting of America: The Political Seduction of the Law* (New York, 1990), chs. 7–8; Barnett, *Restoring the Lost Constitution;* and John Yoo, *The Powers of War and Peace: The Constitution and Foreign Affairs after 9/11* (Chicago, 2005). For critiques of these three books *see* Ronald Dworkin, *Freedom's Law: The Moral Reading of the American Constitution* (Boston, 1996), ch. 14, and "Bork's Jurisprudence," 57 *University of Chicago L. Rev.* 657 (1990); Steven G. Calabresi, "The Originalist and Normative Case against Judicial Activism: A Reply to Professor Randy Barnett," 103 *Michigan L. Rev.* 1081 (2005); and David Cole, "What Bush Wants to Hear," 52 *New York Rev. of Books* 8 (Nov. 18, 2005) (Yoo).

132. Originalism was frequently defended on the ground that it limited judicial discretion. *See, e.g.,* Keith E. Whittington, *Constitutional Interpretation: Textual Meaning, Original Intent, and Judicial Review* (Lawrence, Kans., 1999), 47–61; Scalia, "Originalism," 849, 863–64. As a general matter the assertion seems dubious and is surely unproved. Applied to federalism, it seems clearly mistaken. *See* Robert M. Howard and Jeffrey A. Segal, "An Original Look at Originalism," 36 *Law and Society Rev.* 113 (2002); Farber and Sherry, *Desperately Seeking Certainty,* 44–54; Mark A. Graber, "Clarence Thomas and the Perils of Amateur History," in Earl M. Maltz, ed., *Rehnquist Justice: Understanding the Court Dynamic* (Lawrence, Kans., 2003), 87–90; Erwin Chemerinsky, "The Constitutional Jurisprudence of the Rehnquist Court," in Martin H. Belsky, ed., *The Rehnquist Court: A Retrospective* (New York, 2002), 207–12.

133. The majority justices on the Rehnquist Court sometimes acknowledged the inadequacies of originalism. *Federal Maritime Commission v. South Carolina State Ports Authority,* 535 U.S. 743, 755 (2002) (Thomas, J.); *City of Boerne v. Flores,* 521 U.S. 507, 519–20 (1997) (Kennedy, J.); *Morrison v. Olson,* 487 U.S. 654, 671 (1988) (Rehnquist, C.J.); *James B. Beam Distilling Co. v. Georgia,* 501 U.S. 529, 548, 549 (1991) (Scalia, J., concurring in the judgment). For an early assessment of the inconsistencies in the Rehnquist Court's use of "originalist" theories, *see* Erwin Chemerinsky, "Foreword: The Vanishing Constitution," 103 *Harvard L. Rev.* 43 (1989). For a recent version of "originalism" that moves actual history even more deeply into the background in favor of constitutional interpretation based on an explicitly "hypothetical mind existing in the late eighteenth century," *see* Gary Lawson and Guy Seidman, "Originalism as a Legal Enterprise," 23 *Constitutional Commentary* 47, 71 (2006).

134. David P. Currie, *The Constitution in Congress: The Federalist Period, 1789–1801* (Chicago, 1997), 117. *See, e.g.,* Bernard Bailyn, *Faces of Revolution: Personalities and Themes in the Struggle for American Independence* (New York, 1990) (highlighting the varieties and complexities of late eighteenth-century American political and legal thought), and Saul Cornell, *The Other Founders: Anti-Federalism & the Dissenting Tradition in America, 1788–1828* (Chapel Hill, N.C., 1999) (exploring the variations and changes that occurred in Anti-Federalist thought).

135. 2 U.S. (2 Dall.) 419 (1793). The issue was whether the national courts could hear suits for money due against states brought by citizens of other states.

136. The justices were, in order of reference, John Jay (New York), William Cushing (Massachusetts), John Blair (Virginia), and James Wilson (Pennsylvania). John V. Orth, *The Judicial Power of the United States: The Eleventh Amendment in American History* (New York, 1987), 12, 22.

137. The dissenting justice was James Iredell (North Carolina). Orth, *Judicial Power*, 12, 22.

138. U.S. Const. Amend. XI (1798).

139. Orth, *Judicial Power*, 28.

140. Currie, *Constitution in Congress: The Federalist Period*, 296; Maeva Marcus and Natalie Wexler, "The Judiciary Act of 1789: Political Compromise or Constitutional Interpretation?" in Maeva Marcus, ed., *Origins of the Federal Judiciary: Essays on the Judiciary Act of 1789* (New York, 1992), 13; Elkins and McKitrick, *Age of Federalism*, 263–70

141. "A Friend of the Constitution" [John Marshall], Essay No. 1, in Gerald Gunther, ed., *John Marshall's Defense of McCulloch v. Maryland* (Stanford, Calif., 1969), 155.

142. "Hampden" [Spencer Roane], Essay No. 1, in Gunther, ed., *John Marshall's Defense*, 110.

Chapter 10. The "Arduous Enterprise"

1. The claim is not, of course, that the original nature of the federal structure made *any conceivable* change possible or that it made *any particular* change inevitable.

2. For the most part, "meanings" attributed to the Constitution are the result of highly complex processes that involve not just the text of the document and the historical materials that surround it but also the standards of the legal profession, the precedents and practices of the judiciary, the changing conditions and values of American society, and the diverse individual attitudes (legal and other) of the individuals who articulate those "meanings." On the interplay between "facts" and "values," *see, e.g.,* Hilary Putnam, *The Collapse of the Fact/Value Dichotomy* (Cambridge, Mass., 2002); Amartya Sen, *Rationality and Freedom* (Cambridge, Mass., 2002); Amartya Sen, "Elements of a Theory of Human Rights," 32 *Philosophy & Public Affairs* 315 (2004).

3. At different times in American history, in other words, trained constitutional lawyers would have been able to agree on many basic propositions about the operations of the federal structure. The Court, after all, is involved in the constant effort to articulate sets of coherent, consistent, and generalized rules that seem compatible with the Constitution, dominant cultural values, the demands of practicality, and the inclinations of its members. At most given times, therefore, large areas of contemporaneously relevant constitutional law seemed relatively clearly settled.

4. The three Civil War amendments, by themselves, prevent—indeed, prohibit—any proposed "return" to some hypothesized "original" Constitution.

5. For contrary suggestions, *see* Douglas H. Ginsburg, "Delegation Running Riot," 18 *Regulation* 83 (1995); Randy E. Barnett, *Restoring the Lost Constitution: The Presumption of Liberty* (Princeton, N.J., 2004); Andrew P. Napolitano, *The Constitution in Exile: How the Federal Government Has Seized Power by Rewriting the Supreme Law of the Land* (Nashville, Tenn., 2006); Mark R. Graber, "Rethinking Equal Protection in Dark Times," 4 *University of Pennsylvania Journal of Constitutional Law* 314 (2002).

6. The persistence of change, whether the result of specific formal actions or general historical evolution, meant that efforts to maintain any desired "balance" in the structure sometimes required additional compensatory or offsetting changes in the levels and branches, changes that altered the structure and its operations even more and removed them ever farther from the "original" system that existed in 1789. *See, e.g.,* Adrian Vermeule, "Hume's Second-Best Constitutionalism," 70 *University of Chicago L. Rev.* 421 (2003).

7. 426 U.S. 833 (1976).

8. 426 U.S. at 852.

9. The Court attempted to apply its approach in, *e.g., Hodel v. Virginia Surface Mining and Reclamation Association, Inc.,* 452 U.S. 264 (1981), and *Federal Energy Regulatory Commission v. Mississippi,* 456 U.S. 742 (1982). It overruled *National League of Cities v. Usury,* 426 U.S. 833 (1976), in *Garcia v. San Antonio Metropolitan Transit Authority,* 469 U.S. 528 (1985).

10. "[S]uch commands are fundamentally incompatible with our constitutional system of dual sovereignty." *Printz v. United* States, 521 U.S. 898, 935 (1997) (Scalia, J.). *Accord New York v. United States,* 505 U.S. 144 (1992). *See* Martin H. Redish, "Constitutionalizing Federalism: A Foundational Analysis," 23 *Ohio Northern University L. Rev.* 1237, 1240 (1997). It is important to note that the "anti-commandeering" principle may serve the goals and values of federalism well only at times. *See, e.g., AT&T Corp. v. Iowa Utilities Board,* 525 U.S. 366, 402, 411–12 (1999) (Thomas, J., concurring in part and dissenting in part); *Printz,* 521 U.S. at 959 (Stevens, J., dissenting). *See generally* Neil S. Siegel, "Commandeering and Its Alternatives: A Federalism Perspective," 59 *Vanderbilt L. Rev.* 1629 (2006).

11. *Compare United States v. Lopez,* 514 U.S. 549 (1995) and *United States v. Morrison,* 529 U.S. 598 (2000) *with Granholm v. Heald,* 125 S. Ct. 1885 (2005) and *Gonzales v. Raich,* 125 S. Ct. 2195 (2005).

12. *Compare Morrison,* 529 U.S. 598; *Kimel v. Florida Board of Regents,* 528 U.S. 62 (2000); *Board of Trustees of the University of Alabama v. Garrett,* 531 U.S. 356 (2001); and *Federal Maritime Commission v. South Carolina State Ports Authority,* 535 U.S. 743 (2002) *with Nevada Department of Human Resources v. Hibbs,* 538 U.S. 721 (2003) and *Tennessee v. Lane,* 541 U.S. 509 (2004).

13. The varying views that individuals held about federalism naturally reflected complex personal and social factors, including diverse understandings of the Constitution, American history, and the requirements of constitutional government. Thus, when judges decided cases, they were seldom acting "simply" in a "political" way; that is,

they were not simply or usually trying to enforce their own personal policy preferences without regard for other considerations and limitations. The judicial process and the judicial role, even with its personal component taken fully into account, is far more complex and constrained than that. *See, e.g.,* Karl N. Llewellyn, *The Common Law Tradition: Deciding Appeals* (Boston, 1960), 19–61; Keith E. Whittington, "Taking What They Give Us: Explaining the Court's Federalism Offensive," 51 *Duke L. J.* 477 (2001); Barry Friedman, "The Politics of Judicial Review," 84 *Texas L. Rev.* 257 (2005); Ronald Kahn and Ken I. Kersch, "Introduction," in Kahn and Kersch, eds., *The Supreme Court and American Political Development* (Lawrence, Kans., 2006), 13–21.

14. One marker of the process is the inconsistent and erratic use of such diverse constitutional "sources" as text, structure, history, precedent, convenience, efficiency, philosophy, institutional competence, foreign legal materials, and propositions claimed to be based on "original" meanings or understandings. *E.g.,* Vicki C. Jackson, "Narratives of Federalism: Of Continuities and Comparative Constitutional Experience," 51 *Duke L. J.* 223, 252–54 (2001).

15. Thus, to evaluate the Rehnquist Court in terms of "federalism" is to misunderstand the nature of both American federalism and the Rehnquist Court. *See, e.g.,* Richard H. Fallon Jr., "The 'Conservative' Paths of the Rehnquist Court's Federalism Decisions," 69 *University of Chicago L. Rev.* 429 (2002); Andrew M. Siegel, "The Court Against the Courts: Hostility to Litigation as an Organizing Theme in the Rehnquist Court's Jurisprudence," 84 *Texas L. Rev.* 1097 (2006).

16. Judge Richard Posner, in a sharp exchange with Professor Richard Epstein, recently made a similar point about formal theories and arguments. Posner noted that Epstein has "changed his legal philosophy over the years, [but] he has not changed his policy views; and it is apparent that they well out of temperamental and other personal factors, and political convictions, rather than being generated by jurisprudential theory." Richard A. Posner, "Legal Pragmatism Defended," 71 *University of Chicago L. Rev.* 683, 684–85 (2004).

17. "My motives must remain in the depository of my own breast. My arguments will be open to all, and may be judged of by all." Alexander Hamilton, John Jay, and James Madison, *The Federalist,* ed. Edward Mead Earle (New York, 1937), No. 1, at 6 (Hamilton) [hereafter, "*Federalist*"].

18. To stress the point once again: the claim is not that "federalism" has no normative significance but that its significance must be sought in the thick context of normative considerations that constitute the American constitutional enterprise. As Stephen Griffin explained, American constitutionalism is "a text-based institutional practice" that "should be appreciated as a dynamic political and historical process rather than as a static body of thought laid down in the eighteenth century." Stephen M. Griffin, *American Constitutionalism: From Theory to Politics* (Princeton, N.J., 1996), 56, 5. For a similar view *see* Richard H. Fallon Jr., *The Dynamic Constitution: An Introduction to American Constitutional Law* (New York, 2004).

19. *See, e.g.,* Joseph F. Zimmerman, *Contemporary American Federalism: The Growth of National Power* (New York, 1992); Andrzej Rapaczynski, "From Sovereignty

to Process: The Jurisprudence of Federalism after *Garcia*," 1985 *Supreme Court Rev.* 341; V. F. Nourse, "Toward a New Constitutional Anatomy," 56 *Stanford L. Rev.* 835 (2004); Deborah Jones Merritt, "The Guarantee Clause and State Autonomy: Federalism for a Third Century," 88 *Columbia L. Rev.* 1 (1988).

20. *Federalist*, No. 85, at 574. Madison chose the identical word to characterize the specific problem of resolving questions of federalism. *Federalist*, No. 37, at 228.

21. *Federalist*, No. 10, at 62. Similarly, when defending the Constitution against charges that it lacked a bill of rights, Hamilton began by noting that the first protection of the people's rights lay in "the structure of the government." *Federalist*, No. 84, at 556.

22. *Federalist*, No. 85, at 573.

23. *Federalist*, No. 84, at 555–61.

24. The Eighteenth Amendment is the commonly recognized exception.

25. U.S. Const. Art. VI, para. 2.

26. It is critical to recognize that the Constitution underwrites *a* rule of law, not *the* rule of law. Beyond the realms of cliché and philosophy, there is no single and "true" rule of law; there are only varieties of cultural and institutional forms for conducting, in widely varying contexts and under diverse value systems, what Lon Fuller termed "the enterprise of subjecting human conduct to the governance of rules." Lon L. Fuller, *The Morality of Law*, rev. ed. (New Haven, Conn., 1969), 106. The Constitution establishes the governing structure and normative foundation for a complex and highly contextualized rule of law that is flexible, value-based, aspirational, institutionally defined, and deeply embedded in the nation's culture and history.

27. The adoption of the three Civil War amendments caused a fundamental transformation in the constitutional structure. *See, e.g.*, Akhil Reed Amar, *The Bill of Rights: Creation and Reconstruction* (New Haven, Conn., 1998); Michael Kent Curtis, *No State Shall Abridge: The Fourteenth Amendment and the Bill of Rights* (Durham, N.C., 1986).

28. Carl L. Becker, "Some Generalities That Still Glitter," 29 *Yale Rev.* 649 (1940).

29. The founders studied the past assiduously, *e.g., Federalist*, Nos. 17–19, but sifted with care. "But a nation of philosophers is as little to be expected as the philosophical race of kings wished for by Plato." *Federalist*, No. 49, at 329. More important, the founders exercised what proved to be remarkably astute judgment. Their final compromise product was hardly perfect, Hamilton explained, but it was "the best which our political situation, habits, and opinions will admit" and "the best that the present views and circumstances of the country will permit." *Federalist*, No. 85, at 570.

30. The last paragraph of Article VI requires that all state and federal officials "shall be bound by Oath or Affirmation, to support this Constitution." U.S. Const. Art. VI, para. 3.

31. U.S. Const. Art. VI, para. 3.

32. Perhaps the "greatest achievement" of the founders was "the creation of a shared political and legal language that made reasoned debate possible." H. Jefferson Powell, "The Political Grammar of Early Constitutional Law," 71 *North Carolina L. Rev.* 949,

950 (1993); Daniel J. Hulsebosch, *Constituting Empire: New York and the Transformation of Constitutionalism in the Atlantic World, 1664–1830* (Chapel Hill, N.C., 2005), 204–06, 210–13.

33. Even the tenth *Federalist,* a sacred text of political "realism," was not without its optimistic and aspirational component. *Federalist,* No. 10, at 59–60. *See* Bernard Bailyn, *Faces of Revolution: Personalities and Themes in the Struggle for American Independence* (New York, 1990), 259–65.

34. Max Farrand, ed., *The Records of the Federal Convention of 1787* (New Haven, Conn., 1960 [1937]), Vol. 2, 643.

35. This conclusion points toward a *truly* "conservative" jurisprudence. *E.g., Griswold v. Connecticut,* 381 U.S. 479, 499, 501 (1965) (Harlan, J., concurring); Albert W. Alschuler, *Law without Values: The Life, Work, and Legacy of Justice Holmes* (Chicago, 2000), 190–94.

36. Charles L. Black Jr., "On Worrying about the Constitution," 55 *University of Colorado L. Rev.* 469 (1984). Wisely, Black distinguished the nature and function of the Constitution's "federalism" provisions from its provisions guaranteeing individual rights. *Id.* at 485–86. In an earlier work he urged the use of "structural" and "relational" principles in constitutional interpretation, stressed the primacy of "judgment" over both "text" and "logic," and declared that "the creation and protection of individual rights is the highest function of any government" (at 25). Charles L. Black Jr., *Structure and Relationship in Constitutional Law* (Baton Rouge, La., 1969) (quotations at 94 and 25).

37. For an example of the power of both historical change and personal values in shaping constitutional theories, contrast Black's "structural" interpretations with the "structural" views of another distinguished commentator, Judge J. Harvie Wilkinson III. *Compare* Black, *Structure and Relationship with* J. Harvie Wilkinson III, "Our Structural Constitution," 104 *Columbia L. Rev.* 1687 (2004). *See* Barry Friedman and Scott B. Smith, "The Sedimentary Constitution," 147 *University of Pennsylvania L. Rev.* 1 (1998).

38. Samuel H. Beer, *To Make a Nation: The Rediscovery of American Federalism* (Cambridge, Mass., 1993), 379.

39. "The recent federalism decisions are best understood as assertions that the Constitution does embody a conception of the relation between state and national power, [and] that that conception can find expression in constitutional doctrine. . . . The energy behind these decisions is the rule of law." The Rehnquist Court's "project" is "to reverse *not* the course of history but the course of constitutional doctrine's abdication to politics." Charles Fried, *Saying What the Law Is: The Constitution in the Supreme Court* (Cambridge, Mass., 2004), 46–47.

40. *Compare, e.g., Exxon Mobile Corp. v. Allapattah Services, Inc.,* 545 U.S. 546 (2005) *with* the Class Action Fairness Act of 2005, Pub. L. No. 109-2, 119 Stat. 4 (2005). For the effect of the Rehnquist Court's federalism decisions in the area of civil rights, *see, e.g.,* Denise C. Morgan, Rachel D. Godsil, and Joy Moses, *Awakening from the Dream: Civil Rights under Siege and the New Struggle for Racial Justice* (Durham, N.C., 2006).

41. Herbert Wechsler, "The Political Safeguards of Federalism: The Role of the States in the Composition and Selection of the National Government," 54 *Columbia L. Rev.* 543 (1954).

42. This is the basic conclusion suggested in Larry D. Kramer, "Putting the Politics Back into the Political Safeguards of Federalism," 100 *Columbia L. Rev.* 215 (2000).

43. In part, the "original" structure was changed, and its operations evolved over time. The Sixteenth Amendment, authorizing a federal income tax, expanded the power of the federal government drastically, while the Seventeenth Amendment, providing for the popular election of senators, diminished state power and placed new demands on the Court. Similarly, the internal evolution of the three national branches altered the structure's dynamics and steadily magnified the power of the central government. *See generally, e.g.,* Lewis Kaden, "Politics, Money, and State Sovereignty: The Judicial Role," 79 *Columbia L. Rev.* 847 (1979).

44. *New York v. United States,* 505 U.S. 144, 157 (1992).

45. To support its position, *New York* quoted from *United States v. Butler,* 297 U.S. 1 (1936), the notorious opinion in which the Court set forth its most extreme affirmation of the clarity of the Constitution and the objectivity of judicial review. "The question is not what power the Federal Government ought to have," *New York* declared, quoting *Butler,* "but what powers in fact have been given by the people." *New York,* 505 U.S. at 157, *quoting Butler,* 297 U.S. at 63. Intriguingly, *New York* did not quote the oft-scorned language in *Butler* that provided, in the paragraph immediately preceding the sentence that *New York* did quote, the earlier opinion's fundamental jurisprudential premise: "When an act of Congress is appropriately challenged in the courts as not conforming to the constitutional mandate the judicial branch of the Government has only one duty; to lay the article of the Constitution which is invoked beside the statute which is challenged and to decide whether the latter squares with the former." 297 U.S. at 62 (1936). Given the fact of *Butler*'s notoriety on the point, and the further fact that the quote *New York* used was entirely unnecessary to its decision, it seems that the Court was purposely using *Butler* to suggest that its decision was wholly "objective" but that it remained unwilling to make that claim explicitly. It seems doubtful that Justice O'Connor, who wrote for the majority, actually accepted the *Butler* view that *New York* echoed. *Compare* Sandra Day O'Connor, "Testing Government Action: The Promise of Federalism," in Stephen E. Gottlieb, ed., *Public Values in Constitutional Law* (Ann Arbor, Mich., 1993), 35–43.

46. To say the Court's decision is "discretionary" is not to say that the justices are subject to no limits of any kind. *See, e.g.,* Ronald Dworkin, *Taking Rights Seriously* (Cambridge, Mass., 1978), 31–39, 69–71. It is to say that the Constitution does not dictate the result, that the relevant legal materials could justify a range of diverse decisions, and consequently that individual justices must exercise their personal judgments on the variety of legal and practical factors that they consider properly relevant to the issue at hand. Indeed, when the Court turned to analyze the specific issue presented in *New York,* it seemed to contradict its claim of a "mechanical" judicial process and a specifically directive Constitution. To reach its decision, the Court examined conse-

quences, stressing in particular the ways in which the challenged statute would weaken political accountability in the federal structure, 505 U.S. at 168–69, 181–83. The Court explicitly acknowledged, moreover, that "[s]tate sovereignty is not just an end in itself" and declared that its decision "follows from an understanding of the fundamental purpose served by our Government's federal structure." 505 U.S. at 181. As the Court itself noted, in other words, its reasoning was not simply "formalistic," 505 U.S. at 187, but also purposive and pragmatic.

47. *Garcia,* 469 U.S. at 550.

48. Constitutional limits on the Court's "license" have long been implied, for example, from the provisions of Article III. For a general review of the issue, *see* Henry P. Monaghan, "Constitutional Adjudication: The Who and When," 82 *Yale L. J.* 1363 (1973). In addition, the Court's "license" is further limited by a variety of social, political, cultural, institutional, and professional constraints on the justices. *See, e.g.,* Rogers Smith, "Political Jurisprudence, the 'New Institutionalism,' and the Future of Public Law," 82 *American Political Science Rev.* 89 (1988); Llewellyn, *Common Law Tradition,* 19–61. Finally, the Court's license is limited by the scope of its institutional competence, which is unsuited for making certain kinds of complex practical judgments. Larry Kramer, "Understanding Federalism," 47 *Vanderbilt L. Rev.* 1485, 1500 (1994).

49. *Compare, e.g.,* Kramer, "Putting the Politics Back," *with* Lynn A. Baker, "Putting the Safeguards Back into the Political Safeguards of Federalism," 46 *Villanova L. Rev.* 951 (2001) and Marci A. Hamilton, "Why Federalism Must Be Enforced: A Response to Professor Kramer," 46 *Villanova L. Rev.* 1069 (2001) (same). For a more general discussion supporting judicial enforcement, *see* Ernest A. Young, "Making Federalism Doctrine: Fidelity, Institutional Competence, and Compensating Adjustments," 46 *William and Mary L. Rev.* 1733 (2005).

50. For a broad examination of the Court's role as an essentially "political" institution construing a largely indeterminate Constitution, *see* Terri Jennings Peretti, *In Defense of a Political Court* (Princeton, N. J., 1999).

51. *See, e.g.,* Timothy R. Johnson, James F. Spriggs II, and Paul J. Wahlbeck, "Passing and Strategic Voting on the U.S. Supreme Court," 39 *Law and Society Rev.* 349 (2005); Jay S. Bybee and Tuan N. Samahon, "William Rehnquist, the Separation of Powers, and the Riddle of the Sphinx," 58 *Stanford L. Rev.* 1735, 1759–61 (2006).

52. *E.g., City of Boerne v. Flores,* 521 U.S. 507, 519 (1997); *Federal Maritime Commission,* 535 U.S. at 755.

53. *Morrison,* 529 U.S. at 617–18; *Lopez,* 514 U.S. at 567–68.

54. The Court frequently invokes truisms and suggests that they have some directive bearing on its decisions when, in fact, they have none. *E.g.:* "Dual sovereignty is a defining feature of our Nation's constitutional blueprint." *Federal Maritime Commission,* 535 U.S. at 751.

55. In both its recent Commerce Clause and Fourteenth Amendment cases the Court has imposed heavy evidentiary burdens on Congress to demonstrate that its legislation was appropriate. *See, e.g., Lopez,* 514 U.S. at 562–64; *Florida Prepaid Postsecondary Education Expense Board v. College Savings Bank,* 527 U.S. 627, 637–41

(1999); *Morrison*, 529 U.S. at 614–16, 626–27; *Board of Trustees of the University of Alabama*, 531 U.S. at 368–72. *See* Adrian Vermeule, *Judging under Uncertainty: An Institutional Theory of Legal Interpretation* (Cambridge, Mass., 2006), esp. chs. 6 and 8.

56. *Morrison*, 529 U.S. at 615.

57. *Federalist*, No. 55, at 365 (Madison [or Hamilton]). Indeed, as Amartya Sen pointed out, Adam Smith, the reputed author of the concept of the "economic man," did not, in fact, believe that "self-love" was "adequate for a good society." Amartya Sen, *On Ethics and Economics* (Oxford, U.K., 1987), 24.

INDEX